Intuitive Cognition

This book is an exhaustive and evidence-based introduction to the concepts of intuitive cognition. It will provide an intriguing insight into intuition focusing on the foundation of intuitive cognition and its applications in shaping collective beliefs, values, and attitudes, as well as its significance in diverse fields of teaching, education, art, psychotherapy, business, and marketing. The book examines the co-existence of intuition with deliberate information processing and intuitive cognition's applicability from a multidisciplinary approach. Most interestingly, this edited volume is an attempt to plunge deep inside information processing to explore the intuitive exquisite of the human mind. Different perspectives from multiple fields come together in one frame to build the understanding of how intuitive cognition enhances innovative decision-making in business, brings diversity in creative art and social cognition, develops insight into psychotherapeutic practices, and naturalizes education by aligning it to experiential knowledge among learners, finally, it addresses intuition-artificial intelligence interface.

This volume will be useful for a wide range of audiences with an interest in intuitive cognition, including scholars, researchers, and academicians from the fields of psychology, neuroscience, cognitive psychology, cognitive sciences, education, organizational behavior, management studies, cultural studies, philosophy, and literature.

Pritha Mukhopadhyay is a Professor, Department of Psychology and Dean of Science, University of Calcutta (CU), India.

Sharmistha Banerjee is Professor of Business Management at the University of Calcutta, India.

Ishita U. Bharadwaj is an Associate Professor at the University of Delhi, India.

Intuitive Cognition

Multifaceted Paradigms and Applications

Edited by Pritha Mukhopadhyay, Sharmistha Banerjee and Ishita U. Bharadwaj

Routledge
Taylor & Francis Group
LONDON AND NEW YORK

First published 2026
by Routledge
4 Park Square, Milton Park, Abingdon, Oxon OX14 4RN

and by Routledge
605 Third Avenue, New York, NY 10158

Routledge is an imprint of the Taylor & Francis Group, an informa business

British Library Cataloguing-in-Publication Data
A catalogue record for this book is available from the British Library

ISBN: 978-1-032-44519-9 (hbk)
ISBN: 978-1-032-45598-3 (pbk)
ISBN: 978-1-003-37775-7 (ebk)

DOI: 10.4324/9781003377757

Typeset in Sabon
by SPi Technologies India Pvt Ltd (Straive)

This book is dedicated to intuition; a natural intellectual endowment.

Contents

Figures

Tables

Contributors

Nandita Babu is a Senior Professor and Department of Psychology, University of Delhi, India. She has done phenomenal work in the area of applied cognitive psychology and developmental psychology with a specific focus on cognitive development, theory of mind, multilingual systems in Indian schools, early childhood development and education, and developmental psychopathology.

Samadrita Bhattacharya is a Clinical Psychologist and is currently serving at The Pavlov and the Center of Excellence at Calcutta National Medical College and Hospital, Kolkata, under the Department of Health and Family Welfare, Government of West Bengal, India. Holding a Ph.D. in Applied Psychology, her areas of expertise and interest include various psychotherapeutic practices, particularly Creative Therapy, Child and Adolescent Counseling, clinical training, and life coaching. She is also a member of the WHO Global Clinical Practice Network.

Swati Bhattacharya, former Associate Professor at Government College of Art and Craft, Kolkata, India, is a senior educator, researcher, writer, and translator, based in Kolkata. She has been lecturing on various aspects of Indian Art and Aesthetics at Ramakrishna Mission Institute of Culture, Birla Academy of Art & Culture, and Rajya Charukala Parshad, India. She has also worked as a Guest Faculty in the University of Calcutta, West Bengal State University, Rabindra Bharati University, and Aliah University, India. She is a prolific writer on literature, visual art, and aesthetics.

Shrestha Chakrabarty currently pursuing a Ph.D. from St. Xavier's University, Kolkata, India, in the area of human resource management. She has 20 years of experience in the education industry with a deep understanding of student counseling and enrolment. Shrestha balances her professional career as a Senior Manager in an esteemed private college in Kolkata where she is involved in preparing and executing business development strategies and overseeing the entire student acquisition life cycle. She has a keen in the field of human behavior and business development.

Tanusree Dutta is an Associate Professor and Dean of Academics at the Indian Institute of Management, Ranchi, India. She has also served in the Rekhi Centre of Excellence for the Science of Happiness, IIT Kharagpur, India, for a year on lien from IIM Ranchi. She obtained her Postgraduate and Doctorate degrees from Banaras Hindu University and the Indian Institute of Technology, Kharagpur, India. She has various research publications in peer-reviewed national and international journals. She also has to her credit an Edited book titled "Bias in Human Behavior."

Sujay Ghosh is an Associate Professor of Genetics in the Department of Zoology, University of Calcutta, India. He was the only Asian scientist to participate in a global study on COVID-19 infection in individuals with Down syndrome, organized by the Trisomy 21 Research Society and World Health Organization (WHO). He serves as the nodal officer for the Indian wing of the International Human Trisome Project Network, organized by the National Institutes of Health, USA, and Colorado University, USA. He has published over seventy research papers and five book chapters.

Sanjay Sen Gupta is a practicing artist, researcher, writer, and educator based in Kolkata, India. He has an M.V.A. in Painting and a Ph.D. in Fine Arts (Visual Arts) from the University of Calcutta, India. He has been teaching various aspects of Drawing, Painting, Design, and Composition in several institutes in West Bengal, India. He is presently working as an Associate Professor and Head, Department of Fine Arts and Design, Sister Nivedita University, India. He is a Member of the Editorial Board of The Chitrolekha Journal on Art and Design and an Advisory Board Member of Ahanā.

Santoshi Halder, Ph.D., is a Professor at the Department of Education, University of Calcutta, India. She is a Board-Certified Behaviour Analyst (BACB, USA) and has a Special Educator license (Rehabilitation Council of India, RCI). She is awarded the prestigious "*Extraordinary Professorship*" by the University of Pretoria, South Africa (2023). She has been the recipient of various competitive prestigious International awards; Fulbright Scholar in Residence (S-I-R), 2024, USA. She has edited and or authored six international books on Inclusion and Technology. Her research interests include the inclusion of marginalized communities and people.

Shazia Hasnain is an Assistant Professor at Aliah University in the Department of Education, Kolkata, India. She has completed a Ph.D. in Education from the University of Calcutta. Her areas of research interest are Pedagogy of English, Educational Psychology, and Teacher Education. She has co-authored articles in reputed journals related to the "Task-based language teaching" approach. She has also co-authored a research paper on inclusive education in an edited book.

Poonam Joshi is an Assistant Professor at Amity University, Jaipur, Rajasthan, India. She has completed her M.Phil. degree in Clinical Psychology from the Gujarat Forensic Sciences University, Gandhinagar, Gujarat, India, and pursuing a Ph.D. degree from Amity University, Jaipur, Rajasthan, India. She has authored and co-authored several research papers in peer-reviewed indexed journals.

Meharmeet Kaur is a Ph.D. scholar at the Department of Psychology, University of Delhi, India. She is working in the area of postpartum depression. She has published and presented papers, that mainly center around themes of death anxiety, premenstrual syndrome, and psychological challenges of trans-genders in the Indian context.

Radhika Khurana is a Ph.D. candidate and currently working as Guest Lecturer in Daulat Ram College, University of Delhi, India in the Department of Psychology, University of Delhi, India. She is interested in the field of developmental psychology. Particularly, she works in the area of children and lying, theory of mind, cognitive development, and socio-cultural factors influencing child development.

Manas Kumar Mandal is a Distinguished Visiting Professor at the Indian Institute of Technology (IIT), Kharagpur, an Adjunct Professor at the National Institute of Advanced Studies, and at Allahabad University, and an Emeritus Resource Professor at Rashtriya Raksha University, India. He was formerly a Distinguished Scientist and Director-General (LS–DRDO) and a Professor of Psychology at IIT-Kharagpur. He was awarded the "Technology Leadership Award" by the Defense Minister of India and has received numerous prestigious awards. He has to his credit 14 books and over 100 research papers in international journals.

Kaustav Manna is a faculty member of the Department of Psychology at Maharani Kasiswari College, University of Calcutta (CU), India. He was a former Research Scholar in the UGC-funded project, Centre with Potential for Excellence in a Particular Area (CPEPA), University of Calcutta, India. He is pursuing his Ph.D. in Psychology from CU. He has completed his post-graduation degree in Psychology with a specialization in Experimental Psychology from CU. He has four publications in peer-reviewed national and international journals.

Ritu Mudgal is a research scholar at the University of Delhi, India, focusing on reflective practices among therapists. She is a clinically trained psychologist from Indian Institute of Human Behaviour and Allied Sciences (IHBAS) and is licensed by the Rehabilitation Council of India (RCI). She primarily works with adults with various mental health issues, conducting psychological assessments, and providing psychotherapy. Her approach is eclectic, tailored to each individual's needs while being mindful of the sociocultural context. She is interested in exploring the role of the therapist's self and its impact on clinical practice.

Aritra Mukherjee is a research scholar at the University of Delhi, India, studying the effects of collective victimhood among disenfranchised groups. He has published papers in national journals in the area of Organizational Behavior and Social Psychology. He has delivered lectures in universities from the UK, the US, and also in some Indian Universities. He has presented at both international and national conferences. He has interned with DRDO and worked with Sthapaak as a research associate previously. His interests are in the area of political psychology, social, and attitudinal psychology.

Mouma Nag is a Ph.D. research Scholar in the Department of Psychology, University of Calcutta, India, and currently working as Guest Faculty in Maharani Kasiswari College, University of Calcutta, India. She is working in the area of experimental psychology and cognitive psychology. She has published papers in international and national journals in the areas of cognitive neuropsychology, mindfulness, and social psychology. She has presented at both international and national conferences. She has interned with the Indian Statistical Institute on R programming software.

Priyadarshi Patnaik is a Professor and former Head, Department of Humanities & Social Sciences, and former founder Chairman, Rekhi Centre of Excellence for the Science of Happiness, Indian Institute of Technology (IIT), Kharagpur, India. His current projects include Indio-Canadian Collaborative Projects (with the University of Waterloo) on different aspects of community well-being. He has more than 90 academic papers in national and international peer-reviewed journals and proceedings, 17 volumes of academic and creative writing/edited volumes, and he has published poetry, fiction, and photographs in international journals.

Ipsita C. Patranabis is an Associate Professor, Department of Management Science, Techno International New Town, Kolkata, India. She is a passionate academician and researcher in the field of Organizational Behavior and Human Resource Management. She has completed her MBA from Jadavpur University, India. Following her M.Phil. in Management, she gained her Ph.D. degree from the Department of Business Management, University of Calcutta, India. She has significant contributions to research paper presentations and publications across various national and international conferences and journals.

Raghubir Singh Pirta joined the Department of Psychology, Himachal Pradesh University, Shimla, India, in 1985, and retired in 2010. His theoretical insights were refined in brief sojourns to the Center for Ecological Sciences, Indian Institute of Science (IISc), Bangalore, India. His research on the cooperative life of primates coalesces into the Cognitive Science of Religion, mainly how people face adversities in life.

Swarup Poria is currently working as a Professor at the Department of Applied Mathematics, University of Calcutta, India. He is one of the principal investigators of the UGC project, Centre with Potential for Excellence in a Particular Area (CPEPA) at the University of Calcutta, India. His areas of research interest are nonlinear dynamics and its applications in physics and biology. He has published 62 research papers in internationally reputed SCI journals and supervised 12 students for their Ph.D. degrees.

Piya Saha is a faculty in the Department of Psychology at Nabagram Hiralal Paul College, University of Calcutta (CU), India. She was a former Research Scholar in the UGC-funded project, Centre with Potential for Excellence in a Particular Area (CPEPA),University of Calcutta, India. She has completed her Ph.D. degree from CU and post-graduation in Counseling Psychology from West Bengal State University, India. She has five publications in national and international journals. One book chapter was published by a reputed publishing house. She has received two Best Paper awards at national and international conferences.

Deepak Kumar Salvi is a Professor and Head of Department of the Clinical Psychology at Pacific Medical College & Hospital, Udaipur, India. He has completed his M.Phil. from the National Institute of Mental Health and Neurosciences, Bengaluru, India, and his Ph.D. degree from Rajasthan University, Jaipur. He has also worked as a head examiner for the standardization of the Wechsler Intelligence Scale for Children (WISC–IV) in Rajasthan, India, conducted by Pearson Clinical Talent & Assessment Corporation, Bengaluru. He has authored several research papers in peer-reviewed indexed journals.

Ananya Sengupta is a Ph.D. research Scholar in the Department of Psychology, University of Calcutta, India. She has three published papers in international and national journals. She has presented at both international and national conferences. She is currently working as a Research Assistant in a DHR-GIA project on cognitive retraining in patients with neurological complaints having cognitive deficits at All India Institute of Medical Sciences, Kalyani, India.

Ravikesh Tripathi is an Assistant Professor of Clinical Psychology at the National Institute of Mental Health and Neurosciences (NIMHANS), Bengaluru, India. He has completed his M.Phil. and Ph.D. also from NIMHANS. His research interests are in the areas of Neuropsychological Assessment, Memory and Related Disorders, Behavioral Addiction, and Positive Psychology. He has published papers in various peer-reviewed indexed international and national journals.

Foreword

The invitation to write a foreword for this book on *Intuition* has triggered my curiosity about this fascinating but insufficiently explored phenomenon. Here is a volume that is devoted to a topic that is not commonly discussed. The phenomenon of Intuition has been inquired into by many experts and has been referred to as "gut feeling," "hunch," "snap judgment," or "premonition," implying that it is a form of non-reasoned cognition. For the newly initiated, intuition is something that comes up inadvertently, without conscious effort. As such, there are bound to be many questions about intuition. Experts have come to the rescue of the curious, and have inquired into the dynamics of this phenomenon. This book attempts to answer many of these questions. A strong reason for reading it is that the reader will find new facets of intuition, explored and interpreted by researchers belonging to varying disciplines and specializations—cognitive, social, clinical, developmental and neuro-psychology, education, business management, entrepreneurship, neuromarketing, literature and art, zoology, molecular biology, mathematics, and computer science. Demonstrating a remarkable level of scholarship, Professor Pritha Mukhopadhyay and her team have brought to light the multiple hues of an inadequately understood process or phenomenon.

The idea for this edited book emerged out of a seminar on the topic, held at the Partha Ghosh Academy of Leadership, IIT Kharagpur, in which scholars from different disciplines presented various approaches to Intuition. It is one thing to experience, as many of us do, a "gut feeling," suddenly getting ideas, or solutions to problems without actively thinking about them. But it is quite another to be exposed to the amazing diversity of expression of this phenomenon. In any domain requiring and exhibiting creativity, the role of intuition cannot go unnoticed, whether it is that of a path-breaking scientific endeavor, or a beautiful piece of art, music, dance, or literature. For example, intuition may be seen in Leonardo da Vinci's inventions, and also in Kekulé's discovery of the benzene ring following his dream of "a snake eating its own tail." Literature is a storehouse of writings that reveal not only human sensitivity but also intuitive ideas, intertwined with keen observation. The magic found in the works of innumerable *littérateur* such as Kalidas, Shakespeare, Munshi Premchand, Rabindranath Tagore, Garcia Marquez, and J.K. Rowling of Harry Potter fame, to cite a few instances, and in the creations by artists, sculptors, dancers, musicians, and playwrights that make our heads turn, never fail to arouse the question: *How did they get such ideas?* This book provides some well-analyzed answers to this question.

Philosophers have argued for, as well as against the reliability of intuitive thinking, considering that it ostensibly lacks a logical or rational base. Psychologists have approached intuition mainly as a cognitive process, but clearly, it involves many sub-processes beyond those that are conventionally studied. This makes the term "*intuitive* cognition" an appropriate platform for multi-disciplinary elaboration. It has also been suggested by some experts that so-called intuition is not truly without reasoning; such reasoning may take place at the unconscious level of thinking. Attention has been drawn to the need for distinguishing between the intuitive process and intuitive judgment, in order to avoid misconceptions about intuition. Counter-*intuitive* or paradoxical as it may seem, intuition is said to be a robust foundation for effective decision-making, a process that is usually considered to be the result of conscious planning and mindful thinking.

Since the experience of intuitive cognition occurs naturally, in a non-learned way, neuropsychologists, zoologists and biologists have looked into the role of the neural system in activating intuition. At the same time, the social and cultural milieu in which intuition may be experienced and expressed cannot be ignored. The very possibility that intuitive ideas may be reflected in folklore and folk songs, or concepts of motherhood is intriguing. This phenomenon is seen from childhood onward if one studies the developmental trends of intuition. For those who wish to know more about how intuitive cognition can be assessed or "measured," there are lessons one can learn from both quantitative and qualitative techniques. For others who may be interested in how intuitive cognition can be developed through training, or prompted through "nudging," there is thought-provoking information.

The list of possible arenas of intuitive expressions does not end there. Many more avenues of exploration are opened up by the essays in this volume, containing all the nuances of intuitive thinking. Readers may take the cue from suggestions from experts. Marquez suggested that writers should follow their intuition rather than intellect. Joel Pearson cites a quotation, said to be Einstein's view: "*The intuitive mind is a sacred gift and the rational mind is a faithful servant. We have created a society that honours the servant and has forgotten the gift.*"

I thank the editors for giving me this opportunity to peek into their book and congratulate all the authors for producing a "must-read" book that reminds us about this valuable gift.

Lilavati Krishnan
Former Professor of Psychology
Department of Humanities and Social Sciences
Indian Institute of Technology, Kanpur, India

Preface

The core objective of this book is to explore the path of experiential learning to understand its long-term trace to build up an associative network unique to a person. Cognition becomes apparent through deliberate and intuitive pathways in the process of new knowledge acquisition. Since the manifestation of our unconscious in our conscious responses has individual differences, the question arises whether it is data-based and is a scientific process of learning. Unlike deliberate thinking, intuitive thinking is unconscious and unintentional. However, alike deliberate thinking, intuition is reliable and authentic, being endorsed by a positive feeling emerging from the solution when based on a large amount of "experiential learning." Hence, creativity, discovery, innovation, and invention are not possible without being mediated by rich intuitive thinking. It is a subconscious process of "knowing something without knowing how one knows it." It is possible because of the automatic activation of the memory network that is interlinked through the associative chains by integrating the entire stream of prior experiences, which are critically related to the event. The integrative approach of experiential learning is applied in a myriad of different fields. Our authors from multiple disciplines contribute unique chapters that finally provide a holistic view of our thought processes, highlighting how intuition enriches deliberate thinking.

Historical evidence of some great scientific discoveries substantiates the importance of experiential knowledge in the innovative footsteps of the human mind. Mathematical genius Srinivasa Ramanujan interweaved the deliberately acquired knowledge subconsciously in the dream that led to his creative masterpiece in the conscious plane. This assimilation of knowledge highlights the significance of experiential learning in effective decision-making. In the educational set-up, teachers can take the initiative to activate the intuitive process that demands a spontaneous cognitive and affective absorption of the students in the learning task.

Therefore, an attempt is made through this volume to offer a detailed discussion on how intuitive cognition aids in the process of integration of new information with existing knowledge. The book aims to explore the efficacy of this intuitive process across multiple domains, such as creative art, education, entrepreneurship, neuro-marketing, and artificial intelligence.

Acknowledgments

Writing this book was no less than an inner journey for the editors. It was our intuitive conviction that finally made the work see the light of the day!

Working on this book has been both captivating and extremely rewarding. Its completion involved immense hard work and dedication not only from the editorial team but also to those many hands that chiseled and shaped the hard labor of our efforts. We owe heartfelt gratitude to everyone who advised, guided, and supported us, making this unsteady journey a stable one.

First and foremost, we extend thanks to the Partha Ghosh Academy of Leadership at IIT Kharagpur for an invited talk on "intuition" that broadened the spectrum of interest in the intuitive processes and motivated Prof. Pritha Mukhopadhyay, Prof. Manas Kumar Mandal, and Prof. Priyadarshi Patnaik to explore it from new perspectives. The inspiration has culminated in the form of a book, addressing the intuitive processes from different angles rather than limiting it to a single journal article.

We are thankful to the eminent academician, Prof. Girishwar Misra, for inspiring us in this endeavor. We express our regard to Dr. Leena Nair Sengupta for sharing her insightful suggestions in this domain.

We extend our deepest gratitude to our revered Prof. Lilavati Krishnan, Retired Professor of the Humanities and Social Science Department at IIT Kanpur, for kindly agreeing to write the foreword for the book.

We are indebted to all our esteemed authors for contributing chapters to this book, exploring the idea of the intuitive process from their unique perspectives. They also joined us in meetings to become acquainted with each other's chapters, ensuring that the book is not just a collection of discrete chapters but a cohesive work with a comprehensive understanding of the intuitive process. We wish to extend cordial thanks to all our authors for their forthcoming approach toward feedback.

We are also thankful to those participants who have given their consent to participate in our study making the volume more pragmatic.

We are thankful to the Secretary of the Faculty of Science, University of Calcutta, for providing us with space for holding a book-related workshop.

We are also thankful to our colleagues in the Department of Psychology at our respective universities for their inspiration and support. We are indebted to the librarians of our universities for their tireless assistance with plagiarism checking. We wish to extend our regards to Ms. Madhuparna Banerjee, copy editor for being on board with us. A word of special thanks to the Commissioned editors from Routledge for helping us in binding this work.

We highly appreciate the diligence, patience, and tireless effort of our editorial team. Without their ardent efforts and dedication, this book would not have become a reality. Their skill in incorporating ideas to enhance the writing of the chapters by various esteemed authors is truly admirable. The constant support of our beloved family members inspires us to persevere in this endeavor.

Finally, we appreciate the open communication and teamwork that defined this project, enabling us to overcome challenges and deliver results we can all be proud of.

Chapter 1

Introduction

Pritha Mukhopadhyay, Sharmistha Banerjee and Ishita U. Bharadwaj

Introductory note

Intuition as a concept has gathered keen interest in the last two decades in varied academic fields and also found a place on the shelf of motivational reading. Intuition is the ability to gain knowledge without conscious reasoning or explanation, more like a gut feeling or inner insight, and is often based on implicit knowledge. Intuition can be used to recognise patterns and cues in the environment to improve problem-solving. Intuition is not based on a collection of random facts but in an intuitive process, the latent knowledge stored in the neural nodes spontaneously forms an organised pattern of thinking, keeping relevance to the purpose.

Cognition is a term for a deterministic mental process, including attention, perception, learning, memory thinking, and language. Intuitive cognition is a type of cognition that involves making decisions and judgements based on implicit pattern recognition of a situation. It is a rapid, automatic, and holistic process that is independent of conscious control.

The shift of focus from cognition to beyond, the merger of cognition with intuition is a fascinating construct and worth examining. The cognitive revolution beyond the process of judgement and decision-making is what initiates a deeper psychological inquiry into the concept of intuition.

From the very outset of this book writing project, we came across terms, like instinct, intuition, and insight, that have been used almost interchangeably or very close to each other. Presumably, they are the constituents of intuition. The term intuition originates from the Latin word "intueor" meaning "to see" or "inteuri" meaning to look at, originally used in the theological context to indicate insight, direct or immediate cognition, and spiritual perception. Thus, intuition refers to the ability to acquire direct access to unconscious knowledge or unconscious cognition. Since its earliest conception, it has been understood as trusting one's gut, or sixth sense, which is commonly denoted as an "immediate apprehension" about a potential upcoming danger or threat. This apprehension entails peculiar sensations in the context of its temporalities and inception. The etymological origin of intuition dates back

DOI: 10.4324/9781003377757-1

to the fifteenth century in a writing (details unknown) through seventeenth-century scholars positing it as, "the spiritual perception or immediate knowledge, ascribed to angelic and spiritual beings, with whom vision and knowledge are identical" ("Intuition" The Oxford English Dictionary, 2000). Later writings of thinkers such as Jung (1921) define intuition as a psychological function where an individual senses the possibility of the unknown, which is often implicit, and instinctively apprehends the immediate future. Over the years, researchers have delved deep into this terrain generating insights about the concept and coming up with different notions, perspectives, and sometimes overlapping ideas to unravel the truth. Western science for long, reserved the term "intuition" as a prerogative for Parapsychology. Intuition being a quick recognition of patterns (Aqil & Mujib, 2022), in 2011, Jean E. Pretz (2008) suggested intuition as a holistic kind emerging from an automated analytical process.

In the study of the mind, in the past in Eastern cultures, importance was put on intuition while in Western culture more emphasis is placed on conscious cognition. According to Desiraju (2006), intuition emerges as a certainty of knowledge and subsequently, cognition consciously compares that certainty with other probabilities that finally generate the decision. Darshan in oriental perspective, is generally translated as "philosophy" but actually it means "intuitive vision". The wisdom gained from this intuitive vision is the basis for philosophical inquiry into metaphysical doctrines, ethical codes, logical truths, and religious practices.

Since the Freudian era, instincts have been considered as the innate source of energy, a frontier between biology and psyche. Freud posited "instinct to be the psychical representation of the stimuli originating from within and reaching the mind" (Hall & Lindzey, 1968) Though both instinct and intuition are rapid, spontaneous, and have a few physiological associates, they have different origins. Intuition is not instinctive; instincts hold a strong biological disposition, while intuition has a strong disposition in the experiential acquisition of knowledge and wisdom (Dörfler & Ackermann, 2012; Ussher, 2019). It is a cognitive process that transcends logical thinking, and it can help people make better decisions with a deeper understanding.

Since the source of knowledge is not identifiable in the case of intuition and is integrated into wisdom-based knowledge, it becomes transcendent knowledge and not merely a part of information-based knowledge. Intuitive knowledge is part of the self. Being merged with one's "being", knowledge is cathected with and absorbed in the true affect associated with that knowledge in the flow state of mind (Csikszentmihalyi (2002).

Though intuition may be considered a gift of nature and does not follow the process of deliberate thinking, it has a unique process of its own. Unlike the analytic process of deliberate thinking that needs formal training, intuition is automatic and fast. Because of its fast processing, it is not considered to be grounded in logic and its error-proneness is highlighted. It is an integration of the entire stream of prior experiences critically related to the triggering event through the associative chains that has a strong scientific foundation (Adinolfi & Loia, 2022). Perception of coherence through associative process yields a pattern. Parallel sets of information operate simultaneously in an implicit plane to form the pattern of thinking that culminates in decision, which is no way less in its cognitive richness when compared to deliberate thinking. Intuition comes in the synthesised form that resembles the construct of wisdom. Thus, it is definitely superior to instinct and never is an equivalent term. Intuition is no way less than deliberate thinking and there is no contradiction between the two, rather they are complementary to each other. Deliberate thinking is more analytic; intuition is holistic in nature.

Intuition is the essential constituent of the creative process, it has been seen that the creative process follows a sequence that starts from preparation and is followed by incubation, illumination, evaluation, and verification. But creativity is not a term restricted to specific areas for exceptional only. Creativity is normally distributed. It is involved in any novel decision-making. In this process, the post-incubation phase characterised by illumination has two constituent parts—intuition and insight. Though both are non-analytical mental functioning, intuition is spontaneous, where new connections are formed by integrating relevant nodes, where acquired knowledge is stored. This experience-based perception of coherence gets its affirmation or negation from the gut feeling.

In the case of intuitive decision-making, the more it is expertise-based, the greater is its predictability. Like the erroneous process leads to invalid decisions in deliberate thinking, in intuition too loosely formed patterns cause ineffectual decisions. Any urgent decision-making, if required in everyday life, may utilise the intuitive process associating itself with a huge database residing in an unconscious plane in an implicit knowledge system. Such a huge amount of data cannot be accommodated in a conscious plane. The gut feeling associated with intuition is not exclusive to this process. Even in deliberate processing, when some problem is solved or work is completed, the gut feeling assents it, but it is often attributed to the cognitive part of decision-making undermining the associated affective component.

Intuitive processes work in a flow state of mind. Flow is generally associated with heightened focus, concentration, and absorption while engaging in a challenging situation. Individuals who readily experience intense flow are regarded as possessing an autotelic personality trait. This trait that inclines to embrace challenges by intrinsic motivation can link cognitive and affective processes in intuitive thinking.

Since the intuitive thinking process is a natural endowment, it is inherited by an organism. Ready adoption of safety measures for self-protection and apprehending danger, even with an incomplete database, is the function of an intuitive process. A child learns a lot through this intuitive process. Training in learning through an associative process and then relating it with the deliberate mode of training could open up a new mode of knowledge acquisition and its effective utilisation makes learning more effortless, and retrievable, slowing down the process of decay.

In this book, a humble attempt has been taken to discuss intuition as it is understood by researchers from different perspectives, including how cognition has evolved, how the construct of intuition has been conceptualised, and how the intuitive process can be facilitated and applied in different domains of knowledge.

With this conceptual background, we have arranged the book in 17 chapters from heterogenous perspectives. Following this introduction (Chapter 1), Chapter 2 focuses on the two most prominent modes of thinking—deliberate and intuitive cognition. Fundamentally, a distinction has been made between the two modes of thinking in terms of their underlying processes. The chapter gives a comprehensive view of intuitive cognition. Unlike logical sequential processing of deliberate thinking, the intuitive process utilises the knowledge stored in the neural nodes through the parallel distributed processing system, where different concepts, and their relations, reside in intermediate or hidden layers with the potential to be manifested in an output layer and sparks with an immediacy to bring all the related concepts in a single coherent frame. Chapter 3 focuses on the anatomical foundation of cognition and intuition in humans with special reference to functional interaction among its various components that deal with the mind–body dichotomy. Life science and Psychology interface continues in Chapter 4, which focuses on the genetic underpinning of intuition and its contribution to intuitive cognition. The chapter unravels that parallel to the evolution of complex brain anatomy in humans, natural selection also screens more efficient genetic systems that reinforce molecular interplay and impact the successive higher level of cognition. Chapter 5 highlights understanding social cognition from the perspective of neuropsychology. Social cognition and neuropsychology interface depicts that the role of intuitive process in understanding the social norms and rules, which are written nowhere, but utilised as social cues in social behaviour and communication. A shift in perspective to culture and intuition is reflected in the next chapter. Chapter 6 looks into the interface between folk mind and intuitive cognition that depicts that the meaning of intuition lies in converting the inner power of pain to a creative end for the sake of the survival and growth of human race, regardless of culture, language, and national boundary. An issue of contemporary relevance, gender occupies the focus in the next chapter. Chapter 7 discusses gender shades of intuition in the context of motherhood. The chapter discusses how motherhood is bound by prescribed norms to possess motherly instinct and how a mother can easily understand the social cues, emotional cues, and the manifestation of this motherly instinct in every sphere of life. Moving wider in scope, and covering human behaviour in totality, Chapter 8 presents how intuition blooms out of heuristics in decision-making. The chapter discusses that people are born with an intuitive skill, by which they understand the behaviour of other people and also account for their own behaviour. This knowingness can be developed through language, culture, and historical situations. A variant topic, Arts is not left behind, Chapter 9 portrays the process of unmaking visual arts and details how intuitive excellence is achieved by an artist through lifelong practices with accumulation of knowledge through repeated practice and multiple degrees of craftsmanship. In Chapter 10, the implicit cognitive process with affective absorption has been addressed as a necessary underlying state of mind in the intuitive process of thinking in creative art. The chapter resorts to the painting of Rabindranath Tagore to explain this phenomenon. Addressing issues of diversity, Chapter 11 addresses how people with mental illness excel in their art-making process expressing their inner self through artwork, utilising the implicit intuitive process. Chapter 12 looks into the rich process of intuition, which is often neglected in the teaching-learning situation. It has been noted in this chapter how the experiential learning of language when nurtured, children get the agency to make decisions about their own learning and the role of metacognitive strategies in skill acquisition. Chapter 13 explores the metacognitive and intuitive strategies in children's learning. Children are born with intuitive capacity, but if it is not nurtured, it does not bloom. It highlights the importance of training through intuitive mode providing them with a sense of discovery. Chapter 14 depicts how the novelty of experience, nurturance of autonomy, and exposure to diversified experience convert immature epistemic beliefs into mature intuition, where the intervention with experiential learning in a positive ambience has been found to facilitate the intuitive process. It is evident in Chapter 15 that intuition plays a pivotal role in psychotherapy for the experienced clinical practitioners. Therapists accumulate a database in their implicit plane of mind through years of experiences in clinical practices that create a moment of meaning in therapeutic sessions. In Chapter 16, the book takes a different turn. The empirical evidence revealed how intuition plays a major role in taking risks and new efforts in business. Most importantly, the data of successful women entrepreneurs indicate their greater reliance on intuition than only on logical thinking. The effectiveness of intuition for entrepreneurs has been discussed as the function of interaction between experience and expertise. In Chapter 17, the intuitive process has been addressed in the field of neuromarketing focusing on the concept of system-1, that is, blinking and intuitive, and system-2, that is, slow and deliberate. The chapter discusses how consumer happiness greatly relies upon the understanding of their sensory experiences, nudges, subliminal cues, and choice architecture. The latest focus of the world, artificial intelligence, cannot be ignored in any contemporary collection of articles. Chapter 18 discusses intuition in relation to artificial intelligence. In this era of globalisation, artificial intelligence starts to replicate not only intelligence but human intuition too. The chapter delineates how developing different algorithms of intuition and artificial intelligence try to overpower the human mind. The chapter emphasises developing an artificial intuition model of decision-making. Finally, the concluding chapter (Chapter 19) delves into the continuity of the intuitive process within the context of divergence.

References

"Intuition" The Oxford English Dictionary. 2nd ed. 1989. OED Online. Oxford University Press. 4 April 2000. https://dictionary.oed.com/cgi/entry/00181778

Adinolfi, P., & Loia, F. (2022). Intuition as emergence: Bridging psychology, philosophy and organizational science. *Frontiers in Psychology*, 12. https://doi.org/10.3389/fpsyg.2021.787428

Aqil, R. S., & Mujib, A. (2022). Intuition in Islamic and contemporary psychology. *Jurnal Indo-Islamika*, 12(1), 12–34. https://doi.org/10.15408/jii.v12i1.24693

Csikszentmihalyi, M. (2002). *Flow: The classic work on how to achieve happiness.* London: Rider. (Original work published in 1990).

Desiraju, G. R. (2006). Intellect and intuition. *Nature*, 443(7110), 398–398. https://doi.org/10.1038/443398a

Dörfler, V., & Ackermann, F. (2012). Understanding intuition: The case for two forms of Intuition. *Management Learning*, 43(5), 545–564. https://doi.org/10.1177/1350507611434686

Hall, C. S., & Lindzey, G. (1968). The relevance of Freudian psychology and related viewpoints for the social sciences. In G. Lindzey, & E. Aronson (Eds.), *The handbook of social psychology* (Vol. 1). California: Addison-Wesley Publishing Company.

Jung, C. C. (1921). Psychological types. In H. Read, M. Fordham, & G. Adler (Eds.), *Collected works of C. G. Jung* (Vol. 6). Princeton, NJ: Princeton University.

Pretz, J. E. (2008). Intuition versus analysis: Strategy and Experience in complex everyday problem solving. *Memory and Cognition*, 36(3), 554–566.

Ussher, C. J. (2019). Intuitive wisdom in leadership: Exploring the exercise of intuitive wisdom among aministry leaders in New Zealand (dissertation). Intuitive wisdom in leadership: exploring the exercise of intuitive wisdom among ministry leaders in New Zealand.

Part I

Intuition and Cognition

Cognitive and Biological Base

Chapter 2

Intuitive cognition

A construct beyond cognition

Pritha Mukhopadhyay, Manas Kumar Mandal and Priyadarshi Patnaik

Introduction

The field of intuition is diverse. Intuition is seen either as mysterious and unexplainable or as something inaccurate, hokey, or epiphenomenal (Lieberman, 2000). Understanding intuition, therefore, is a challenge for science today and is subject to intense scientific inquiry. Many scientific researchers (Czerniak & Berkner, 2016; Okoli et al., 2014) consider intuition as a complex process and a valuable component in decision-making. Klein (2003) in his attempt to demystify intuition described it as the process of translating our experiences into action, as every individual is embedded in a continuous flow of experience, is it conscious or unconscious (2002).

The process of intuition is mostly unknown to us since it is not subject to direct examination like rational or deliberate cognitive processes. Therefore, the controversy arises in terms of its scientific status. However, from the perspective of cognitive science, many researchers have proposed the idea that two different systems of thought co-exist—one is automatic and the other is deliberate (Epstein & Pacini, 1999; Evans, 2006; Kahneman & Frederick, 2005; Lieberman, 2003; Sloman, 1996, 2014; Stanovich, 2004). In contrast to the deliberate process, which is slow, analytic, linear, controlled, and rule-based, intuition is automatic, effortless, fast, implicit, and unconscious (Sloman, 1996). Intuition is an efficient mechanism of decision-making but is sometimes subject to errors. It is also described as the self-evident solution that unexpectedly pops into the mind of the decision-maker without an available, tangible explanation for it. This raises the question about its reliability, as the database on which it is grounded is not conscious appreciation.

Hence, systematic attempts have been made to explore whether intuitive decisions are opposites or complementary to rational decisions, based on reasoning or affective process, derivatives of conscious or unconscious process, a gift of nature or the product of implicitly nurtured database, or intuition is a mix of these opposites or a bridge in-between. The construct has raised more questions than answers. In the following section, we will discuss some of these issues.

DOI: 10.4324/9781003377757-3

In the path of exploring the nature of intuitive decisions, the first question that comes to our mind is whether intuition is an outcome of logical thinking or random blinking. It is evident that intuition is fast and reflexive in sharp contrast to logical thinking or reasoning, which is generally a slow and reflective thought process. Evans (2010) viewed intuition as the "immediate apprehension in the absence of reasoning" and is based on a large amount of "experiential learning". The vast pre-existing knowledge is the foundation for rapid intuitive decisions or solutions. Intuitive decisions can reach an apex of accuracy when it is based on unconscious assimilation of huge datasets absorbed in the implicit plane, which were once acquired by the conscious mind experientially or purposefully. It is a "low effort" mechanism and does not require elaborate involvement of the central processing mechanism. Intuition can utilise a large amount of data in a short span of time, which exceeds the capacity of working memory. Accordingly, intuition does not require access to working memory or executive memory.

With this theoretical position, supported by experimental evidence, a dual-process theory has been proposed (Evans, 2008). Dual-process models come in many flavours (Evans, 2008), but they all suggest a clear distinction between cognitive operations that are quick and associative in nature, and those which are slow and rule-governed. The theory suggests that there may be two different modes of thought holistic and analytic. Type I is slow, reflective, conscious and Type II is fast, parallel, subconscious. Although it was stated that intuition and deliberation are not completely distinct categories of cognitive process, others are of the opinion that these two are discrete and are fundamentally different to each other (Stanovich, 2010; Stanovich & West, 2000). It is believed that Type I, based on working memory principles would process information in normal circumstances but individuals may switch on Type II or intuition that is based on parallel or rapid processing in case of time constraint due to emergency or the urgency of creative solutions. The dual-process theory with its typologies (Types I and II) has a nearly similar parallel in the behaviour economics literature. Daniel Kahneman (2011) proposed two processing systems: one that operates automatically, holistically, intuitively, and unconsciously ("System-I") and the other that operates slowly, analytically, logically, and consciously ("System-II"). He believed these two systems are discrete and fundamentally different from each other.

Sometimes, the solution to an intricate problem may suddenly arise in the mind and the decision-maker or problem-solver may immediately recognise the complex connectivity amongst the array of relevant knowledge that is spread over the cognitive field. Finally, the solution is reached by restructuring the existing information in a new way (Duncker, 1935; Ohlsson, 1992; Wertheimer, 1959) based on the Type I or System-I process of decision-making, which is at the core of problem-solving, scientific discovery or invention, artwork, and any other sort of creativity. Zander (2016) explained this process with the example of the former smoke jumper Wagner Dodge, who handled an accidental huge fire outbreak when everyone else was petrified as their acquired skills for fire-fighting failed. After a while, the solution popped up in the mind of Wagner Dodge, all of a sudden. Presumably, when all the fragments of implicit knowledge are unconsciously combined in a new way (by creating an additional fire by igniting an area of vegetation to resist the blaze of the fire, etc.), the fire is brought under control. The intuitive decision-making assisted Dodge in the emergency. Much of the out-of-the-box thinking falls into this intuitive category (Gilhooly, 2016), which does not work in void, but depends on the pre-existing knowledge or the enriched database relevant to the task in hand (Klein, 2011). Epstein (2010) opined that experiential knowledge will more likely provide actors with the ability to integrate complex sets of cues concurrently, it is the exact requirement of complex problem-solving (Salas et al., 2009).

Another interesting phenomenon related to intuitive thinking is that the actor fails to give a clear rationale for his decision-making instantaneously. The incident of Getty Kouros (Zander et al., 2016), is worth mentioning where J. Paul Getty Museum questioned the authenticity of a Greek statue. A group of experts used scientific tools, analytical reasoning, and deliberate process to reach a logical decision, and became sure of the genuineness of the statue. However, when the senior experienced experts were consulted, they at a glance felt that the statue was not genuine, failing to provide the reason for their decision at the moment. Previous studies also reported how despite experts' competence, they remained quite passive in providing a useful explanation for making intuitive decisions. But it does not happen by fluke. In line with Buddhism, Sinclair (2011) also advocated that intuitive expertise is based on quick pattern matching that is too fast for humans to register and acknowledge consciously (Klein, 1989, 2003, 2011).

It may be explicable in terms of the associative process of cognition. Presumably, the senior experts had such a vast knowledge base that automatically activated their memory network, with the activation of spreading of the "associative chains" (Quillian, 1968) in the brain that integrate the entire stream of prior experiences critically related to the task given to them. It created a coherent pattern of impressions towards the kouros artwork through an associative process and not by sequential logical deductive reasoning. The appreciation of this decision got its strength endorsed by the interoceptive microclimate of the experts as the decision was integrally related to the experts' gut feeling, affirming the genuineness of the decision. This intuitive processing was based on adequate utilisation of the knowledge base yes of those experts. The importance of the perception of coherence in divergent data sets has been found with the RAT test and CDM model (Zhang & Guo, 2018).

For clarification, a hypothetical representation has been done in Figure 2.1. For example, each specimen of artwork representing a certain era in art history possesses specific characteristics, which contribute to the formation of a distinct pattern in the cognitive plane of the artwork of each era. The

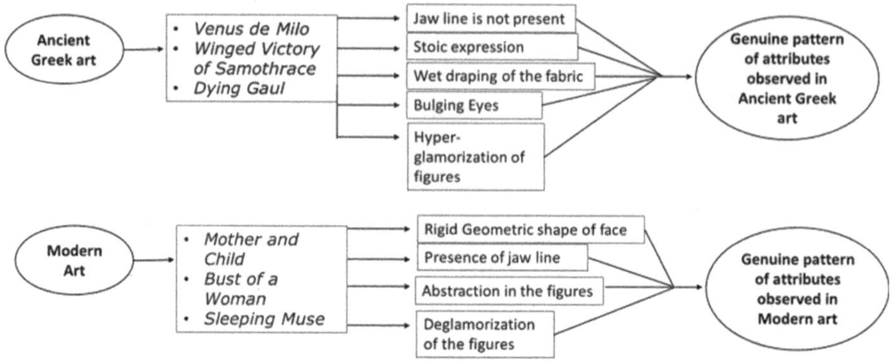

Figure 2.1 The distinct pattern of attributes observed in Ancient Greek Art and Modern Art affirming the genuineness of the artworks.

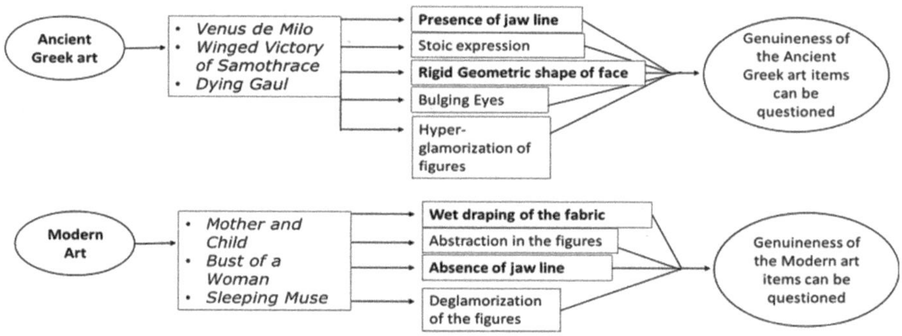

Figure 2.2 The mixed pattern of attributes observed in Ancient Greek Art and Modern Art.

knowledge developed from the understanding of the pattern becomes so inherent to the experts' practising work in the respective fields that minimal alteration in the attributes was easily sensed by them (Figure 2.2).

A pattern mismatch between the distinct ancient art form (Figure 2.1) and the one presented for evaluation (Figure 2.2) with a mix of both the forms together could be readily sensed by the expert eye through the process of intuition independent of immediate conscious cognition of the attribute differences.

Earlier research assumed that the experiential and semantic information resides as associative chains in the stored category representation, linked together in a taxonomically organised processing hierarchy (Collins & Loftus, 1975; Collins & Quillian, 1969), which can provide an efficient mechanism for storing and retrieving that information (Quillian, 1968). Later, Rumelhart et al. (1986) advocated that in our mnemonic system, all the impressions are spread over the brain with its intricacies in a well-organised manner through the parallel processing system. The quick processing of intuition is possible as it processes vast amounts of information through parallel processing (Betsch, 2008) through holistic associations by associatively recognizing features and patterns, owing to its link to tacit knowledge. The association could be formed based on knowledge or skill once acquired through explicit, deliberate, logical, and sequential processing.

Thereby, intuition though looks to follow simple cognitive heuristics, it is the reflection of a very efficient cognitive management process to deal with huge databases automatically. All the information spread over in our brain in a patterned form, lies dormant. Presumably, with the presence of the stimulus situation, only the relevant correlated nodes develop the potential to flow to form the pattern incorporating non-consciously held knowledge (Quillian, 1968). The actor recognises the pattern with certainty. This cognitive certainty is endorsed by the gut feeling of the actor. The strength of this unconscious cognition is evident from the fMRI study that finds the activation of the areas of the brain, which is related to unconscious processing during intuitive decision-making. It shows that intuitive learning is not the impulsive overt response; it has a deep internal representation in different layers in a parallel distributed processing system (Ilg et al., 2007).

Taking this incident into account, in the presented sculpture of the "Goddess Venus" (see Figures 2.1 and 2.2) that was presently stored as a new input in the internal hidden layer of PDP, gets connected with different propositions related to the function of the original Goddess Venus, like what she possesses (nodes of HAS) or the characteristics (nodes of IS). The nodes with original preexisting knowledge with greater weightage flowed towards the central domain of cognition and the mismatch with non-original nodes of information about Goddess Venus flashed in the mind of the experts with cognitive and gut assurance. The attributes of this automaticity depend on the strength of the parallel processing pathway (Cohen et al., 1990). This is how intuitive or implicit and deliberate process works in association with the PDP model.

The next question that arises to understand intuition, relates to the origin or locus of intuitive process in our biological system. Neuroscientists differ in their opinions. While some neuroscientists believe that intuition has its origin in the right hemisphere, others believe in its origin in the gut. The cerebral hemisphere is anatomically divided into two halves, left and right. Studies have found that these two halves functionally complement each other. The left hemisphere is considered analytical, sequential, logical, rational, and objective. The right hemisphere is holistic, parallel, creative, reflexive, and intuitive (Bryden, 1982; Mandal et al., 2000). The role of the right hemisphere in intuition, therefore, is more an extension of an existing school of thought. The right hemisphere can think in symbols and patterns, handles imagination, and the big picture. The right hemisphere is also considered to be the seat of emotions and has an indirect link with the gut. A previous study indicates that the caudate and putamen, in the basal ganglia, are the central components of both intuition and implicit learning (Lieberman, 2000). Scientific viewpoint and experiential learning tell us that people can make accurate decisions when they rely on their gut feeling, which is basically an interoceptive feeling that guides our behaviour. These sensations carry inputs that originate from different visceral organs like the heart, lung, skin, bladder, etc., affirming the rightness of the decision why? People who are supposed to make complex decisions from a very large set of data or complex set of information rely on gut feeling. Many people depend on their gut feeling or intuition, as it is difficult to process all such inputs in a logical and analytical manner. Mayer (2016) proposed the gut as "the second brain" and showed evidence that the gut has the capability to make decisions efficiently bypassing our logical cognitive system involving executive memory. The gut and the brain are also connected via a thick neural structure, referred to as the gut-brain axis that serves as an internal intercom system wherein messages are delivered back and forth from these two organs. The importance of this microbial brain (the gut) lies in the mode of responding. While the brain takes some time to respond, the gut responds to warning signals almost instantaneously. These signals act as intuition for the brain. Jung-Beeman et al. (2004) and Ilg et al. (2007) reported with fMRI studies that both intuition and insight are associated with the activation of the brain region of the right superior temporal cortex (intuition and insight paper) that plays a role in response to the unconsciously activated information (Ilg et al., 2007). Bilateral parietal activation, which is associated with decision-making under the situation of uncertainty, also gets activated during intuitive decision-making. This feeling of uncertainty or pressure of time constraint is not related only to the emergency problem-solving situation, but any sort of inventive or creative endeavour creates an inner urge that also has a demand on the immediacy of the response to the need for moving from uncertainty to certainty, indecision to decision, unresolved to resolution, validated by the second-brain.

Another question revolves around the issue of conscious–subconscious dilemma in intuition. It is not clearly known whether intuition is a derivative of the conscious (a robust voice) or of the subconscious (a nudge within) mind. The subconscious or unconscious mind influences our thought process automatically and the dynamics are not amenable to introspection. Therefore, we cannot directly link our subconscious mental processes (like dreams, automatic thoughts, and verbal slips) to our conscious mind. There are several barriers between the conscious and unconscious mind, for example, limitations of our sense organs in absorbing all inputs in and around our world. Such barriers are overcome in case of emergency or environmental constraints or in the inner urgency of creation, when the subconscious plays a role in mutating the incoming inputs, which are then processed via a fast channel. This phenomenon is referred to as rapid cognition (Gladwell, 2007), a gross equivalent to the concept of intuition.

Gladwell did not call it intuition since he believed that intuition, as a term, is linked to emotional, irrational or mystical concepts. However, by "blink", he did mean unconscious picking up of cues in the environment that are beyond our conscious radar or cognitive framework. Some authors call this unconscious process "deliberation without attention" (Dijksterhuis, 2004). Dijksterhuis et al. (2006) put forward two reasons in support of their theory: first, the unconscious has a much larger capacity to process information as compared to the conscious, and second, the unconscious thought works "bottom-up" and prioritises different attributes of objects in a much simpler way.

Besides, another issue that surrounds the concept of intuition is in terms of its outcome whether intuition is an efficient trustworthy or a deficient, error-prone process. Putting it in other words, can we rely on intuition? To answer this question, we need to borrow inputs from the research of behavioural economists like Daniel Kahneman (2011). Kahneman observed that System I (fast, intuitive) is more error-prone but its advantage lies in anticipating threats or envisaging opportunities. System II (slow, deliberate) has a lesser chance of making errors since it applies logic, and makes a person critical about the outcome but entails a slow process. Gigerenzer (2008) gives an alternative viewpoint. He considers intuition as the "unconscious intelligence" and believes in its merit that is largely ignored in the scientific domain. With the controversies of this gradually revealing field, it is necessary to uncover its applicability in the field of education, particularly in teaching-learning set-up. It is imperative to understand how the intuitive process can be maximally utilised for the benefit of the students, at different levels of curricular study and even beyond, for trainees in different fields, like management, engineering, and so on. Hence, the following section will discuss its role in decision-making.

Application of intuition in decision-making

Intuition is a process based on natural, deep-seated knowledge, and never be explained explicitly. It assists proficient decision-makers in making fast and high-quality decisions, and its accuracy depends upon the experiences that are processed in the unconscious framework of the mind (Nalliah, 2016). Therefore, intuitive decision-making can be defined as an implicit comparison of previously stored information with presently encountered experiences, which is reflected in our decisions.

There are many controversies about its impact on decision-making. Since in intuitive thinking, one cannot delineate the tangible route to reach the decision, the precision of the judgement is questioned. Although deliberate process is also subject to error, with inaccurate application of data or flawed logical derivation; in the case of intuition, the doubt prevails around its grounding in the authentic data and knowledge base, resulting in doubting the reliability of the intuitive decision. Since one is unaware of the underlying process through which a decision is reached, its reliability is questioned and its acceptance as a scientific process of learning faces dispute. Its applicability is not universally acceptable due to the perceived possibility of greater error components in intuitive decisions. The effectiveness of intuitive decision lies in (1) its role in the situational meaning-making process at the ground level (2) its immunity to distractions and interruptions, causing its accuracy to persist even after extended intervals and (3) its significant contribution in handling environmental complexities of everyday living (Patterson et al., 2017). Its application is beyond question in successful decision-making.

Intuitive learning in decision-making

Learning and *retrieval* are also highly relevant to influence intuitive decisions. In declarative learning, one is aware of his knowledge and can declare it to others upon demand; it finds expression via intentional thinking (System-II) usually following a logical pathway. However, a lot of everyday decisions and scientific persuasion are based on intuitive learning, which does not mean that it is independent of any data or knowledge base. The study of Sahm and von Weizsäcker (2015) can be mentioned, where they wanted to incorporate some of their own real-life experiences as avid chess players in determining the extent of the impact of their background knowledge in effective deliberate vs. intuitive processing. In their childhood, the observation and imitation of the moves of their opponent acted as a source of information in developing intuition. Later, they enriched their knowledge with more information gathered from chess books. All those resources collected over the years were stored in a parallel distribution in the brain. The huge reservoir of this information along with regular practice for a prolonged period assured accuracy in the moves making the entire game an intuitive and procedural activity for them. Instead of a conscious approach towards every move, they implicitly executed their huge database of knowledge with proper speed and precision and over time they turned out to be successful chess players, winning international prizes (Kutsch, 2019). In this way, an intuitive process strengthens itself by combining previously stored distributed information acquired through consistent practice, which also contributes to effective decision-making.

Affective aspects of intuition in decision-making

It is perhaps in intuition that the total being of a person is involved in the decision-making process. Perception, the first step of the implicit decision-making process, involves neural activity, which results from the interaction between the ongoing integrated sensory information and interoceptive information from the body (Barrett and Bar, 2009). This interoceptive process is thought to regulate our emotions and help in experiencing them (Zamariola et al., 2019).

It also helps to provide an affective colour to our perceptions and influence our decisions (Soosalu et al., 2019). Every part of the stored sensory information is fused with the affective valence that consequently helps to integrate information while generating intuitive decisions that get validated by real-life scenarios. For example, a mother, whose daughter was abused, was interrogated to identify the perpetrator committing such a heinous act. She closed her eyes for some time and uttered the correct name. As it was a significant negative event in her daughter's life, she became attentive to and engrossed in the emotional flow centring the event. For this reason, when she was asked, all possible faces in her knowledge came into her visuospatial template organised through parallel processing. The identification of the person who had the maximum possibility (maximum weightage) to commit the act was done by matching the existing pattern of the person with that of the present requirement. However, when one is in a uni-dimensional flow of emotions carried by the particular situation, like in case of this mother, all the relevant information in the processing system gets an automatic entry, by automatic exclusion of the irrelevant (Gladwell, 2007). The association work starts among the relevant information at the implicit plane and quick integration of the associated information leads to the flashing of the decision, through identification of the signal overcoming the noise of the huge parallely placed information.

The importance of emotional flow in intuitive decision-making is not only true for negative emotions but also for positive ones. When the child meets her grandpa at different intervals, the enjoyable experience shared by both induces positive emotions. The interoceptive process recognises this positive emotion associated with the meeting experience. Therefore, mental averaging sets a modal value for the interval of the meeting being computed in the mind of the child as well as the grandpa and the interoceptive need state develops based on the computed modal value. A discomfort is generated centring the modal value that creates an automatic need, predicting the possibility of the next meeting. Hence, the child tells her mother that "her grandpa will come" and on the other hand the grandpa also wants to meet the child again. This expectancy is intuitive in nature, where the emotion entangled with the present situation acts as a vital conjecture for intuitive decision-making.

Intuition in education

Intuition is also relevant in teaching-learning set-up, be it at an early or late stage of formal education. It was noted earlier that the intuitive process for the acquisition of knowledge is based on the implicit process of learning, which is non-declarative and utilises parallel sets of information that operate simultaneously, readily associate discrete data, resulting in automatic, fast processing. This activation of the implicit process that automatically generates and reveals integrated information comes as an illumination or discovery, when receiving an impetus. It was also illustrated in the early discussion that this intuitive process cannot be initiated unless the total being of the person is involved in the issue. Therefore, the teachers in the academic set-up can take the initiatives in inducing curiosity among the students that results in the involvement of their entire being to develop intuition in the path of effective learning. For example, the teacher intends to develop the concept of "force" in her students. She initiates the discourse with them as "what happens in a tug of war when two people are on one side and four on the other side?"—They may not be able to give the formula (Force = Mass × Acceleration) accurately, but, in their own way, can say which side will lose and can relate it to the greater magnitude of the mass without any assistance of the teacher. In the present scenario, the teacher is the representative of deliberate knowledge. Later on, when a student, not yet exposed to Newton's law of universal gravitation (1687) with the formula $F = G \times (m_1m_2/R^2)$, is asked, "Why do apples fall down from the tree and does not go up and vanish into the sky?", a sense of knowing arises at once in the student's mind and he begins to relate it explicitly with the situation of "tug of war". In this context, the sense of knowing is the intuitive knowledge that facilitates the deliberate process creating an analogical connection between the already learnt situation (tug of war) and the present one (gravitational force). Therefore, intuition acts as an interplay between deliberate and implicit processes of thinking and plays a crucial role in education.

A strong assumption regarding the interplay of intuitive and deliberate processes is made by Sloman (1996, 2002). He postulates that intuition and deliberation are completely distinct and separable processes. He suggests, that "two systems, two algorithms are designed to achieve different computational goals" (Sloman, 1996, p. 6). Both systems can be activated simultaneously and may result in distinct responses. On the other hand, some theories do not postulate such a clear distinction between intuitive and deliberate processes. An example of the integrative model of automatic and deliberate decision-making was proposed by Glöckner and Betsch (2008). The model assumes that every decision is based on an automatic process. If a person perceives a decision-making situation, a mental representation of the decision task is automatically constructed, which can be modelled by parallel constraint satisfaction (PCS) networks. A core assumption of the network is that people can integrate a multitude of information in a weighted compensatory manner within a short timeframe due to automatic intuitive processes. However, these automatic intuitive processes can be supervised and modified by the deliberate system and this intuitive process plays a crucial role in decision-making.

Intuition in creative arts

Intuition and innovation have an integral relationship with each other. Innovation or creativity has an association with the creation of new knowledge. Intuition, being the implicit mode of information processing provides consistent assistance in the process of innovative creation. In this creative process, intuition is referred to as an experiential phenomenon, where lexical articulation does not occur and it also holds some basic characteristics of dissolution of identity, state of disinterestedness and ecstatic awareness about the creative knowledge (Vaidya & Bilimoria, 2018). In elaboration, a state of complete immersion occurs on the creator's part when he is involved in the creative process, which is facilitated by the co-creators or the audience. This complete absorption with one's own creation acts as a fuel to develop intuition. This absorption is so gross that it dissolves the person's identity and that absorption in the creation leads to a state of disinterestedness about the external world. Finally, the detachment from the extraneous environment gives enormous pleasure and paves the way for ecstatic awareness about the creation. Therefore, the implicit or intuitive process including these three characteristics involves the entire being of the creator and helps them to identify and associate more with their creation. For example, when a dancer is immersed in dance, the audience also becomes engrossed in it, which compels a detachment from both the creators' and appreciators' part from the surroundings, associating their mental state with a gratifying experience. This implicit association in the form of intuitive knowledge also helps the dancers enrich their art form. Hence, it proves the role of intuitive knowledge in creative expression.

The principal aim of the present review is to explore the potential link between intuition and creative expressions in a process-centric framework to consider how intuition would be implicated in different phases of creative problem-solving. Creative art implicates all the traditional characterisation of intuition (Dörfler & Ackermann, 2012; Hogarth, 2001; Sadler-Smith, 2008), which treats the process as one which is rapid (instantaneous), spontaneous (less effortful and voluntarily controlled), and alogical (not following logical rules). Further, the outcomes, yielded in artwork, also follow the intuitive mode characterized by the intuitive process. Such results are generally holistic or gestalt in nature as it is mainly concerned with the whole situation instead of its parts. The process of artwork cannot be verbalised or articulated with sufficient details but can be made with high confidence that resembles the tacit intuitive process. More so, for a creative problem, an original solution is often unthinkable in advance; thus, creative ideas and solutions occur in the absence of objective criteria against which a creative product can be measured. Moreover, problems that require creative solutions are ill-defined, primarily because there are multiple hypothetical solutions that would satisfy the goals (Reitman, 1965). Thus, it becomes extremely difficult to find the solutions to the problem as there is a lack of objective criteria based on which the solution can be traced.

It reminds the concept of Adaptive Regression in Service of Ego (ARISE) postulated by Ernst Kris (1952) which refers to a momentary and moderately controlled use of primitive, non-logical, and drive-dominated modes of thinking in the primary stages of the creative process (Holt, 1978). Like the dancer, any creative worker, for example, a novelist, regresses and identifies with the characters he aims to depict by utilising the primary process and comes back to reality to write it down.

The two essential operations of the creative problem-solving process are (1) the generation of ideas and (2) the evaluation and selection of appropriate outcome(s) (e.g., Finke et al., 1992; Lubart, 2001; Reiter-Palmon & Illies, 2004). Both steps are complementary to each other and since the creative problem-solving process is dynamic, idea generation and evaluation involve several iterations before reaching the final solution (Kozbelt & Durmysheva, 2007; Lonergan et al., 2004; Runco, 2003). Bowers et al.'s (1990) classical model describes the role of intuition in the quest for an intuitive solution to a creative problem in two stages. In the first stage, clues (such as words, shapes, voices, odours, etc.) from the environment are accumulated together and synthesised to form an ambiguous pattern of coherence. In the second stage, when the vague patterns of coherence of these clues gradually integrate and exceed a threshold, they enter into awareness. This results in the perception of the hunch or judgment treated as a solution (Pétervári et al., 2016). This entire integration often occurs in the resting state of the brain, when the subconscious mind continues the pursuit of the solution to the problem.

This notion is substantiated from real-life reports. There is historical evidence of some great scientific or mathematical solutions in dreams during sleep. Self-organisation theory advocates how the self-organising mechanism of our brain assists in forming a coherent pattern of fragmented long-term memories to construct a dream image in the form of a narrative (Kahn & Hobson, 1993). When the conscious mind absorbs plenty of data in a wakeful state, the subconscious mind assimilates them and makes sense of data while asleep. This assimilated data can be referred to as intuitive knowledge. Creative minds absorb enormous amounts of data from the periphery of their creative interests and that information assimilation in sleep with their manifestation in dreams leads to many creative marvels. The lexical explanation of the creative mechanism cannot be clearly provided, but the default mode network (DMN) which is the neurological underpinnings of the mental activities during lower attentional demands (Gronchi & Giovannelli, 2018) may be the basis of the spontaneous cognition (Buckner et al., 2008) that results in the intuitive creative process. It acts as the "autopilot" of the brain (Gronchi & Giovannelli, 2018), and possesses an integrative property (Guldenmund et al., 2012; Vatansever et al., 2015), which helps to assimilate the information to generate intuitive knowledge.

Conclusion

Traditionally, intuition was considered as belonging to the realm of the unknown, of mystery or madness, of God-realisation or sorcery. With the advance of science, it was relegated to the background as chance, accident, fluke, something not worth exploring. In recent times, with the advance of cognitive sciences, significant strides have been taken to understand intuition. However, the tendency to favour rationality is so deeply embedded in our lives that education and training using intuitive processes in most areas is not counted. Centuries of emphasis on left-brain-oriented, linear, sequential, and logic-oriented learning and decision-making need to be interrogated and alternative methodologies to be addressed. Left and right need to go hand in hand, though intuition and deliberation are "two systems, two algorithms designed to achieve different computational goals" (Sloman, 1996, p. 6), they coexist and despite processing differences, work together for a final response generation. It is the need of the hour for academicians, educators, and teachers to explore methods of teaching and learning that allow students to use their intuitive powers.

References

Barrett, L., & Bar, M. (2009). See it with feeling: Affective predictions during object perception. *Philosophical Transactions of the Royal Society of London, Series B: Biological Sciences*, 364, 1325–1334.

Betsch, T. (2008). The nature of intuition and its neglect in research on judgment and decision making. In H. Plessner, C. Betsch, & T. Betsch (Eds.), *Intuition in judgment and decision making* (pp. 3–22). Lawrence Erlbaum Associates Publishers.

Bowers, K. S., Regehr, G., Balthazard, C., & Parker, K. (1990). Intuition in the context of discovery. *Cognitive Psychology*, 22, 72–110. https://doi.org/10.1016/0010 0285(90)90004-N

Bryden, M. P. (1982). *Laterality: Functional Asymmetry in the Intact Brain*. New York: Academic Press.

Buckner, R. L., Andrews-Hanna, J. R., & Schacter, D. L. (2008). The brain's default network: Anatomy, function, and relevance to disease. *Annals of the New York Academy of Sciences*, 1124, 1–38. https://doi.org/10.1196/annals.1440.011

Cohen, J. D., Dunbar, K., & McClelland, J. L. (1990 July). On the control of automatic processes: A parallel distributed processing account of the Stroop effect. *Psychological Review*, 97(3), 332–361. https://doi.org/10.1037/0033-295x.97.3.332. PMID: 2200075.

Collins, A. M., & Loftus, E. F. (1975). A spreading-activation theory of semantic processing. *Psychological Review*, 82, 407–428.

Collins, A. M., & Quillian, M. R. (1969). Retrieval time from semantic memory. *Journal of Verbal Learning and Verbal Behavior*, 8, 240–247.

Czerniak, C., & Berkner, J. (2016). Exploring the relationship between developing intuition and intuitive decision-making: A quasi-experimental research design. [Master's theses, St. Catherine University]. St. Catherine University, Sophia. https://sophia.stkate.edu/cgi/viewcontent.cgi?article=1006&context=ma_hhs

Dijksterhuis, A. (2004). Think different: The merits of unconscious thought in preference development and decision making. *Journal of Personality & Social Psychology*, 87, 586–598.

Dijksterhuis, A., Bos, M. W., Nordgren, L. F., & Van Baaren, R. B. (2006). On making the right choice: The deliberation-without-attention effect. *Science*, 311, 1005–1007.

Dörfler, V., & Ackermann, F. (2012). Understanding intuition: The case for two forms of intuition. *Management Learning*, 43, 545–564. https://doi.org/10.1177/1350507611434686

Duncker, K. (1935). *Zur Psychologie des Produktiven Denkens* [*On the Psychology of Productive Thinking*]. Berlin: Springer.

Epstein, S. (2010). Demystifying intuition: What it is, what it does, and how it does it. *Psychological Inquiry*, 21(4), 295–312.

Epstein, S., & Pacini, R. (1999). Some basic issues regarding dual-process theories from the perspective of cognitive-experiential theory. In S. Chaiken, & Y. Trope (Eds.), *Dual-Process Theories in Social Psychology* (pp. 462–482). New York: Guilford Press.

Evans, J. B. T. (2010). Intuition and reasoning: A dual process perspective. *Psychological Inquiry*, 21, 313–326.

Evans, J. S. B. (2006). The heuristic-analytic theory of reasoning: Extension and evaluation. *Psychonomic Bulletin and Review* 13, 378–395. https://doi.org/10.3758/BF03193858

Evans, J. S. B. (2008). Dual-processing accounts of reasoning, judgment, and social cognition. *Annual Review of Psychology*, 59, 255–278. https://doi.org/10.1146/annurev.psych.59.103006.093629

Finke, R. A., Ward, T. B., & Smith, S. M. (1992). *Creative Cognition: Theory, Research, and Applications*. Cambridge, MA: MIT Press

Gigerenzer, G. (2008). *Gut Feelings: The Intelligence of the Unconscious*. New York, NY: Viking.

Gilhooly, J. K. (2016). Incubation and intuition in creative problem solving. *Frontiers in Psychology*, 7, 1076. https://doi.org/10.3389/fpsyg.2016.01076

Gladwell, M. (2007). *Blink:The Power of Thinking Without Thinking*. New York: Little, Brown & Co.

Glöckner, A., & Betsch, T. (2008). Modeling option and strategy choices with connectionist networks: Towards an integrative model of automatic and deliberate decision-making. *Judgment and Decision Making*, 3, 215–228.

Gronchi, G., & Giovannelli, F. (2018). Dual process theory of thought and default mode network: A possible neural foundation of fast thinking. *Frontiers in Psychology*, 9. https://doi.org/10.3389/fpsyg.2018.01237

Guldenmund, P., Vanhaudenhuyse, A., Boly, M., Laureys, S., & Soddu, A. (2012). A default mode of brain function in altered states of consciousness. *The Archives Italiennes de Biologie*, 150, 107–121.

Hogarth, R. M. (2001). *Educating Intuition*. Chicago, IL: University of Chicago Press.

Holt, R. R. (1978). *Methods in Clinical Psychology* (Vol. I). Projective assessment. New York: Plenum.

Ilg, R., Vogeley, K., Goschke, T., Bolte, A., Shah, J. N., Pöppel, E., & Fink, G. R. (2007). Neural processes underlying intuitive coherence judgments as revealed by fMRI on a semantic judgment task. *NeuroImage*, 38(1), 228–238. https://doi.org/10.1016/j.neuroimage.2007.07.014

Jung-Beeman, M., Bowden, E. M., Haberman, J., Frymiare, J. L., Arambel-Liu, S., Greenblatt, R., Reber, P. J., & Kounios, J. (2004). Neural activity when people solve verbal problems with insight. *PLoS Biology*, 2(4), E97. https://doi.org/10.1371/journal.pbio.0020097

Kahn, D., & Hobson, J. A. (1993). Self-organization theory of dreaming. *Dreaming*, 3, 151–178. https://doi.org/10.1037/h0094378

Kahneman, D. (2011). *Thinking, Fast and Slow*. London: Penguin Books.

Kahneman, D., & Frederick, S. (2005). A model of heuristic judgment. In K. J. Holyoak, & R. G. Morrison (Eds.), *The Cambridge Handbook of Thinking and Reasoning* (pp. 267–293). Cambridge, England: Cambridge University Press.

Klein, G. A. (2003). *Intuition at Work: Why Developing Your Gut Instincts will Make You Better at What You Do*. New York, NY: Currency/Doubleday.

Klein, G. A. (2011). Expert intuition and naturalistic decision making. In *Handbook of Intuition Research*. Cheltenham, England: Edward Elgar.

Klein, J. (1989). *A Commentary on Plato's Meno*. Chicago: University of Chicago Press.

Kozbelt, A., & Durmysheva, Y. (2007). Understanding creativity judgments of invented alien creatures: The roles of invariants and other predictors. *The Journal of Creative Behavior*, 41, 223–248. https://doi.org/10.1002/j.2162-6057.2007.tb01072.x

Kris, E. (1952). *Psychoanalytic Explorations in Art*. New York, NY: International University Press.

Kutsch, L. (2019, August 15). Can we rely on our intuition? *Scientific American*. https://www.scientificamerican.com/article/can-we-rely-on-our-intuition/

Lieberman, M. D. (2000). Intuition: A social Cognitive neuroscience approach. *Psychological Bulletin*, 126(1), 109–137. https://doi.org/10.1037//0033-2909.126.1.109

Lieberman, M. D. (2003). Reflective and reflexive judgment processes: A social cognitive neuroscience approach. In J. P. Forgas, K. R. Williams, & W. von Hippel (Eds.), *Social Judgments: Implicit and Explicit Processes* (pp. 44–67). New York, NY: Cambridge University Press.

Lonergan, D. C., Scott, G. M., & Mumford, M. D. (2004). Evaluative aspects of creative thought: Effects of appraisal and revision standards. *Creativity Research Journal*, 16, 231–246. https://doi.org/10.1080/10400419.2004.9651455

Lubart, T. I. (2001). Models of the creative process: Past, present and future. *Creativity Research Journal*, 13, 295–308. https://doi.org/10.1207/S15326934CRJ1334_07

Mandal, M. K., Bulman Fleming, M. B., & Tiwari, G. (2000). *Side Bias: A Neuropsychological Perspective*. North Holland: Kluwer Academic Publishers.

Mayer, E. (2016). *The Mind – Gut Connection: How the Hidden Conversation within Our Bodies Impacts Our Mood, Our Choices, and Our Overall Health*. New York: HarperCollins.

Nalliah, R. P. (2016). Clinical decision making – Choosing between intuition, experience, and scientific evidence. *British Dental Journal*, 221(12), 752–754.

Ohlsson, S. (1992). Information-processing explanations of insight and related phenomena. In M. Keane, & K. Gilhooly (Eds.), *Advances in the Psychology of Thinking* (pp. 1–44). London: Harvester-Wheatsheaf.

Okoli, J. O., Weller, G., & Watt, J. (2014). Information processing and intuitive decision-making on the fireground: Towards a model of expert intuition. *Springer-Verlag London*, 3(2), 118–130.

Patterson, R. E., & Eggleston, R. G., & Patterson, W. (2017). Intuitive cognition. *Journal of Cognitive Engineering and Decision Making*, 11(1), 5–22.

Pétervári, J., Osman, M., & Bhattacharya, J. (2016). The role of intuition in the generation and evaluation stages of creativity. *Frontiers in Psychology*, 7. https://doi.org/10.3389/fpsyg.2016.01420

Quillian, M. R. (1968). Semantic memory. In M. Minsky (Ed.), *Semantic Information Processing* (pp. 227–270). Cambridge, MA: MIT Press.

Reiter-Palmon, R., & Illies, J. J. (2004). Leadership and creativity: Understanding leadership from a creative problem-solving perspective. *The Leadership Quarterly*, 15, 55–77. https://doi.org/10.1016/j.leaqua.2003.12.005

Reitman, W. R. (1965). *Cognition and Thought*. New York, NY: Wiley.

Rumelhart, D. E., Smolensky, P., McClelland, J. L., & Hinton, G. E. (1986). Schemata and sequential thought processes in PDP models. In J. L. McClelland, D. E. Stanovich, G. E. Hinton, & R. F. West (Eds.), (2000). *Advancing the Rationality Debate* (Vol. 23, pp. 701–726) Behavioral & Brain Sciences. Cambridge University Press.

Runco, M. A. (2003). *Critical Creative Processes*. Cresskill, NJ: Hampton Press.

Sadler-Smith, E. (2008). *Inside Intuition*. Abingdon: Routledge.

Sahm, M., & von Weizsäcker, R. K. (2015). Reason, intuition, and time. *Managerial and Decision Economics*, 37(3), 195–207. https://doi.org/10.1002/mde.2711

Salas, E., Rosen, M. A., & DiazGranados, D. (2009). Expertise-based intuition and decision making in organizations. *Journal of Management*, *36*(4), 941–973. https://doi.org/10.1177/0149206309350084

Sinclair, M. (Ed.). (2011). *Handbook of Intuition Research*. Cheltenham, England: Edward Elgar.

Sloman, S. A. (1996). The empirical case for two systems of reasoning. *Psychological Bulletin*, 119, 3–22.

Sloman, S. A. (2002). Two systems of reasoning. In T. Gilovich, D. Griffin, & D. Kahneman (Eds.), *Heuristics and Biases: The Psychology of Intuitive Judgment* (pp. 379–398). Cambridge, UK: Cambridge University Press.

Sloman, S. A. (2014). Two systems of reasoning, an update. In J. Sherman, B. Gawronski, & Y. Trope (Eds.), *Dual Process Theories of the Social Mind* (pp. 69–79). New York, NY: Guilford Press.

Soosalu, G., Henwood, S., & Deo, A. (2019). Head, heart, and gut in decision making: Development of a multiple brain preference questionnaire. *SAGE Open*, 9(1), 215824401983743. https://doi.org/10.1177/2158244019837439

Stanovich, K. E. (2004). *The Robot's Rebellion: Finding Meaning in the Age of DARWIN*. Chicago, IL: University of Chicago Press.

Stanovich, K. E. (2010). *Rationality and the Reflective Mind*. New York, NY: Oxford University Press.

Stanovich, K. E., & West, R. F. (2000). Advancing the rationality debate. *Behavioral & Brain Sciences*, 23, 701–726.

Vaidya, A. J., & Bilimoria, P. (2018). *Intuition* in classical Indian philosophy: Laying the foundation for a cross-cultural study. In S. Wuppuluri, & F. Doria (Eds.), *The Map and the Territory. The Frontiers Collection*. Cham: Springer. https://doi.org/10.1007/978-3-319-72478-2_3

Vatansever, D., Menon, D. K., Manktelow, A. E., Sahakian, B. J., & Stamatakis, E. A. (2015). Default mode dynamics for global functional integration. *Journal of Neuroscience*, 35(46), 15254–15262.

Wertheimer, M. (1959). *Productive Thinking*. New York, NY: Harper.

Zamariola, G., Frost, N., Van Oost, A., Corneille, O., & Luminet, O. (2019). Relationship between interoception and emotion regulation: New evidence from mixed methods. *Journal of Affective Disorders*, 246, 480–485. https://doi.org/10.1016/j.jad.2018.12.101

Zander, P., Ollinger, M., Volz, G. K. (2016). *Intuition and Insight: Two Processes That Build on Each Other or Fundamentally Differ?* (Vol. 7). https://doi.org/10.3389/fpsyg.2016.01395

Zhang, W., & Guo, B. (2018). Freud's dream interpretation: A different perspective based on the self-organization theory of dreaming. *Frontiers in Psychology*, 9. https://doi.org/10.3389/fpsyg.2018.01553

Chapter 3

Cognition and intuition

Exploring anatomical foundation and origin

Sujay Ghosh

Introduction

Survival and reproduction are the ubiquitous basic instincts of the living world that include simple organisation like bacteria on one hand and complex organisation like humans on the other. In his "The Origin of Species" (1859), Darwin wrote "It is not the strongest of the species that survives, not the most intelligent that survives. It is the one that is the most adaptable to change". This "change" is dynamic and ever-occurring alteration in the environment that obviously poses challenges to the survival of the living world and the members of this world struggle in their own ways to make them fit to these changes. The words "own way" is pivotal and rely on the organisational complexity of a given creature. If we consider different living forms as "random designs" as considered by Richard Dawkins[1] (The Blind Watchmaker, 1986) created by nature, then all the designs, despite their organisational differences, share an important commonness that has enabled them to survive in an ever-changing environment. This common attribute is their ability to perceive nature and the environment and to respond accordingly. This ability is known as the "ability of cognition". In the biological framework, the cognitive system includes the anatomical structures and physiological processes concerned with the acquisition, retention, and use of information (Dukas, 2004). This framework extends to analyse information for anticipating the incoming stimulus and then responding in the correct manner, which is "intuition". The cognitive system in animals can be divided into a few inter-connected action-domains such as perception, information capture, learning, memory keeping, decision-making, and functional execution. The first stage of cognitive process is perception, which is an information capture process from the external environment and subsequent translation into a physiologically defined process within the animal's body supported by a complicated tract of neurons. At the terminal end, the information collection process is mediated by receptors specialised to capture distinct cues. These receptors are visual, auditory, olfactory, flavour or physical

DOI: 10.4324/9781003377757-4

contact and are keeping constant surveillance over the incidence in the surrounding environment.

Newly collected information may either wane away rapidly, remain for a short duration needed to perform a given action or consolidate into long-lasting internal impression. The process of adding new information to the internal storage system of the animal body is termed "learning". Learning always involves changes in behavioural attributes in performing specific action toward an environmental signal following experience. Animals take prompt decisions to respond to the environment based on their perception and previously collected information and then they execute the sequence of behaviours that resulted in a given action (Anderson, 2015; Dukas, 2004; Rolls, 2014). This entire course of sequential events evolves gradually in different animals, starting from simple organisation as in protozoa to more complex form like that of the human body with random interactions among environment, genetic architecture, and information reception-processing system. Among humans a great variation in all cognitive discourses is observed and these variations are presented in the form of variations in intuitive thinking capacity ultimately manifesting a human quality which we often called "intelligence". Natural selection acts as a "filter" and has been working on different forms of this attribute to pick the most suitable one, someone more fit to this changing environment from the others. Thus "Intelligence is the ability to attain goals in the face of obstacles by means of decisions based on rational rules.[2] (How the Mind Works, Pinker, 1997). As rational rules are being generated in minds through the power of perception and recognition, intuition is sometimes regarded as "nothing more and nothing less than recognition" by some authority.[3] (Thinking, Fast and Slow, Kahneman, 2011).

This chapter focuses on the biological basis of the cognition-building process, particularly in the human body. Understanding the biological foundation of cognition and intuition is a challenging approach that involves incisive, brainstorming studies on both the clinical subjects and model organisms. Though not fully understood, the genetic system probably provides a blueprint, that is, "command" of the cognitive display of a person, whereas anatomical organisation acts as "hardware" and physiological processes execute as "running program" to give it a final shape at the performance level. Thus "The mind is a neural computer, fitted by natural selection with combinatorial algorithms for causal and probabilistic reasoning about plants, animals, objects, and people"[4] (How the Mind Works, Pinker, 1997). But the human mind differs from a high-throughput computer by its ability to achieve gradual perfection in interaction with environmental cues that build up "experience" and experience then synthesises the ability of intuition. So, intuition is a by-product of cognition and the scientific foundation of the cognitive system supports the intuitive ability of humans. Intuition is a judgement-based anticipatory decision-making and execution of function that strongly depends on cognitive physiology and regulation. We often describe intuition as "gut feeling" and sometimes we believe it as a special and supernatural power or capacity. But "gut feelings are not God-given instincts but learned rules of thumb that help us navigate the world's complexities.[5] (Gut Feelings: The Intelligence of the Unconscious, Gigerenzer, 2007). Surprisingly, this unconscious intelligence is a quality that has been underrated, and a resource that can be tapped into to make better decisions.[6] (Gut Feelings: The Intelligence of the Unconscious, Gigerenzer, 2007). Here we tried to explore the biological foundation of cognition from which we can extrapolate the scientific understanding regarding intuitive decision-making systems in humans. Both the conscious and unconscious minds have their roots in the brain and different and overlapping biological foundations of brain anatomy house the controlling centres of conscious rational thoughts and unconscious intuitive anticipation. We can say "The brain is essentially a pattern recognition machine. We respond not just to the conscious processing of stimuli, but to a multitude of unconscious signals that our brain has learned to interpret through experience".[7] (The Brain: The Story of You, Eagleman, 2015).

Cerebellum: The cognition regulator

The first breakthrough in the understanding of cerebellum's work beyond the motor function came from the ground-breaking study by Petersons and his colleagues (Petersen et al., 1988, 1989) who used neuro-imaging methods like PET scan and fMRI to measure brain function while people viewed words and involved in more elaborate performance of action. Their aim was to characterise the functional anatomy of the human brain in single word processing. At the basic level, the volunteer participants viewed some noun words (cake, dog, tree) passively. At the second level, the participants were asked to read the words aloud and that action needs activation of the motor control section of the brain. At the most advanced level participants were asked to write the "action verbs" related to the presented noun words. This action demanded the cognitive ability of individuals. During the time of this action PET scan recorded a strong response from the right lateral cerebellum and this response was distinct from the expected signal of motor action from the anterior part of the cerebellum. A number of different studies were conducted following the foot-steps of Petersen to get insight into the functional anatomy of the human brain related to the execution of cognition-related works. Through a beautifully designed experiment, Raichle et al. (1994) demonstrated that the cognitive cerebellar response can be impoverished keeping the motor response constant. The author demonstrated that the regions of the brain that elicit strong signals during naïve performance exhibit poor signal in practice performance. When new words were presented to the volunteers, their anterior cingulate, left prefrontal and left posterior temporal cortices, and the right cerebellar hemisphere were found more active than their performance in repeating the same noun words over the time. These results suggest that two distinct neural circuits are used for verbal response selection and normal subjects can change the brain circuits used during task performance following practice. One critical factor in determining the circuitry used appears to be the degree to which a task is learned or automatic. Further fMRI imaging study by Desmond et al. (1998) suggested that frontal and cerebellar regions contribute differentially in cognitive performance. The left-frontal (and striatal) activations control response selection, when many appropriate responses are available. On the other hand, right-cerebellar activation controls the selection of responses, when a single appropriate response is difficult to retrieve. Kim et al. (1994) conducted a study on seven people who were offered to solve a puzzle. The fMRI revealed three to four times more activation of bilateral dentate nucleus in the cerebellar region than its involvement in motor activity and the authors inferred cerebellum as the controlling centre of cognitive activity. Recent meta-analyses (Keren-Happuch et al., 2012; Stoodley et al., 2010) summarised the outcome of neuroimaging studies and concluded that cerebellum is the part of cognitive networks with the prefrontal and parietal association cortices. Cerebellar activation is needed in performance of higher cognitive activities, involving emotions, executive function, learning, language, music, timing, and working memory.

Anatomy of "cognition" processing system

The cognitive functions rely upon connections between the cerebellum and regions of the brain that support higher functions. Trans-synaptic viral tract-tracing studies have revealed—in addition to connections with motor cortices—the cerebellum forms reciprocal links with prefrontal and parietal cortices via cerebello-thalamo-cortical and cortico-ponto-cerebellar loops (Kelly & Strick, 2003, Leiner et al., 1986; Middleton & Strick, 2000; Schmahmann & Pandya, 1997). The spinocerebellar tracts, parts of the inferior olivary complex that receive inputs from the spinal cord, and pontine nuclei receiving information from sensorimotor regions of the cerebral cortex, project to the cerebellar anterior lobe (lobules I–V) and lobule VI, along with lobule VIII. The regions of the inferior olive and pontine nuclei that do not receive sensorimotor afferents fibre projects into cerebellar lobules VI and VII (Figure 3.1 shows the cerebellum with the lobules labelled). The cerebro-cerebellar circuits that connect the cerebellum and prefrontal cortex are more developed in humans than non-human primates, like ape (Ramnani et al., 2006; Whiting & Barton, 2003) and suggest engagement of the cerebellum in human cognitive functions, besides it motor-control attributes.

Table 3.1 shows the connectivity between the cerebral cortex and cerebellum involved in information processing. According to functional connectivity patterns, the cerebellum can be divided into two control regions, namely "sensorimotor" and "associative" regions (Heath et al., 1979). These

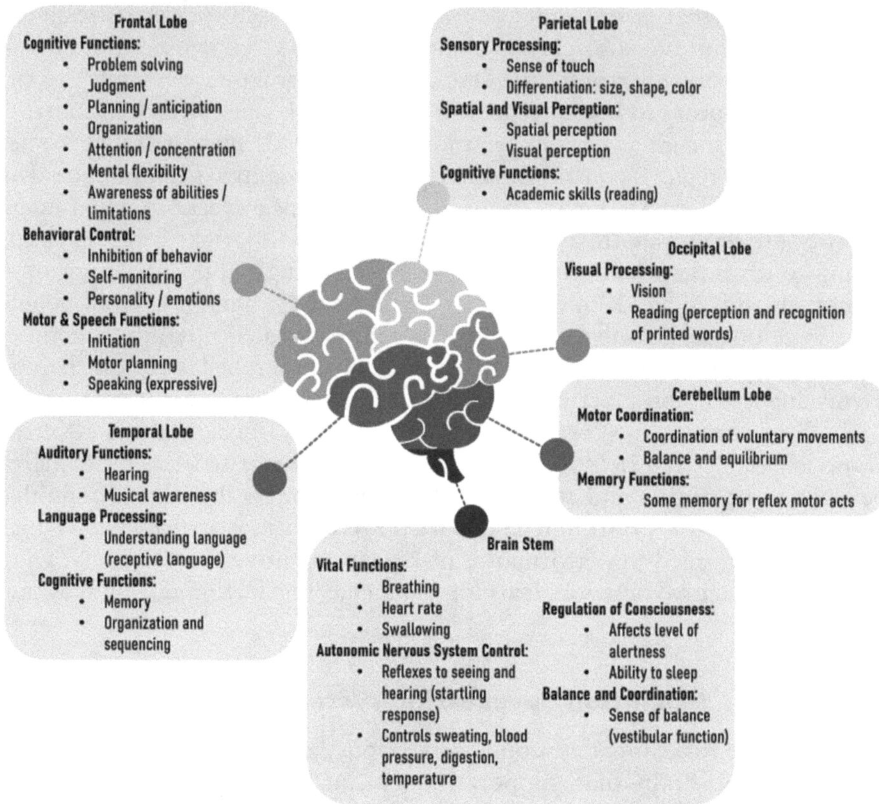

Figure 3.1 Functional components of human brain.

Table 3.1 Functional connections of limbic system with other parts of human brain that regulate signal of cognition and intuitions

Structures	*Connections*
Dentate gyrus	From entorhinal cortex (via perforant pathway and alvear pathway) To hippocampus (via mossy fibers)
Hippocampus	From dentate gyrus (via mossy fibers), septum (via fornix), limbic lobe (via cingulum) To mamillary bodies, anterior thalamus, septal area, and tuber cinereum (via fornix); subcallosal area (via longitudinal striae)
Septal area	From olfactory bulb, amygdala, fornix To medial forebrain bundle, hypothalamus, habenula
Amygdala	From primitive temporal cortex and sensory association cortex, opposite amygdala (via anterior commissure) To hypothalamus (direct amygdalofugal pathway), septal area, and hypothalamus (via stria terminalis)

findings provide strong support to the concept that the cerebellum participates in distributed neural-networks involved in both sensorimotor and higher-level functions, and suggest different regions of the cerebellum involved in various networks. So, it can be inferred that there is a functional topography within the cerebellum that reflects underlying cerebro-cerebellar circuits.

Cerebellum activation during cognitive tasks

Different parts of cerebellum exhibit activation in execution of different cognitive tasks like language and reading performance, spatial processing, working memory, and social interactions (Figure 3.2).

Other brain components involved in cognition-intuition processing

a **Limbic System (Emotional Processing)**
The limbic system is a complex set of brain structures located deep within the brain, primarily responsible for regulating emotions, memory, motivation, and certain aspects of behaviour. It plays a crucial role in how we process emotions, form memories, and respond to environmental stimuli, particularly those related to survival (e.g., fear, pleasure, anger). The limbic system is located in the forebrain, specifically within the medial temporal lobe and portions of the subcortical structures. It sits between the cerebrum and the brainstem, wrapping around the top of the brainstem in a ring-like fashion. The major components of the limbic system are found in areas like the temporal lobe (where the hippocampus is located),

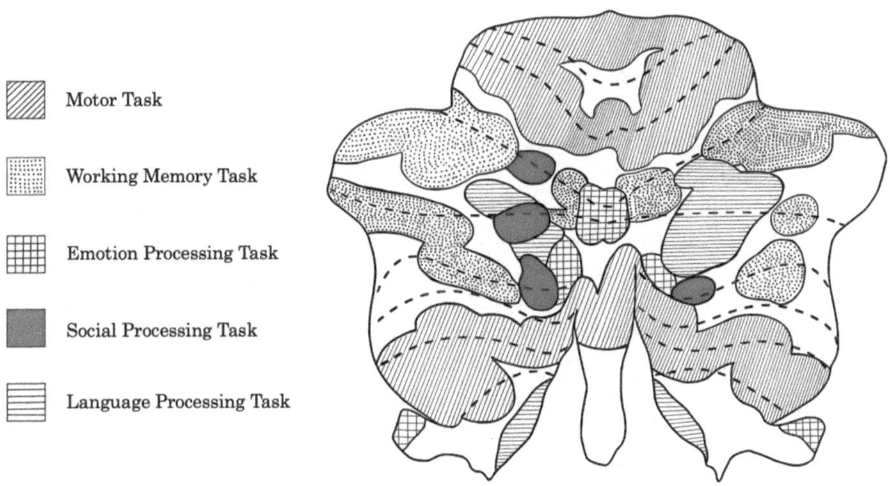

Figure 3.2 Human cerebellum and its components.

the medial and frontal lobes (for structures like the cingulate gyrus), and deeper in the brain, near the thalamus and hypothalamus. It's sometimes referred to as the "emotional brain" due to its strong role in emotion and memory processing. The components of the limbic system that are actively involved in cognition and intuition are amygdala, hippocampus, and anterior cingulate cortex.

Amygdala: Plays a critical role in emotional processing and fear responses. It helps assess emotional significance and threat levels in situations, which often informs rapid, intuitive decisions.

Hippocampus: Involved in memory formation and retrieval. The hippocampus helps access past experiences that might unconsciously inform current decisions, even if we aren't explicitly recalling those experiences.

Anterior Cingulate Cortex (ACC): Involved in error detection and emotional evaluation. The ACC helps monitor potential outcomes based on past experiences, influencing intuitive judgements.

Thalamus: Acts as a relay station, transmitting sensory and motor signals to the cerebral cortex. It also plays a role in consciousness and alertness.

Cingulate Gyrus: Involved in processing emotions and behaviour regulation. It helps regulate autonomic motor function and is linked to emotional responses to pain.

Septal Nuclei: Involved in reward and pleasure pathways, influencing feelings of pleasure and emotional responses.

Mammillary Bodies: Important for memory formation and recollection, particularly in relation to episodic memory.

Fornix: A bundle of nerve fibres that connects the hippocampus to other parts of the limbic system, facilitating communication between different regions.

Parahippocampal Gyrus: Involved in memory encoding and retrieval, particularly with respect to spatial memory (Figures 3.3 and 3.4).

b **Basal Ganglia (Pattern Recognition and Habit Formation)**
The basal ganglia are a group of nuclei located deep within the cerebral hemispheres, beneath the cerebral cortex, primarily within the telencephalon, near the thalamus and lateral ventricles. The basal ganglia are involved in motor control, as well as in functions related to learning, habit formation, and emotion. The basal ganglia play a key role in pattern recognition, learning from past behaviours, and habitual actions. It allows individuals to respond to familiar situations quickly without conscious deliberation by recognising patterns and making automatic responses.

c **Ventral Striatum (Reward System)**
The ventral striatum is located in the basal forebrain, specifically within the basal ganglia. It lies at the junction of the caudate nucleus and

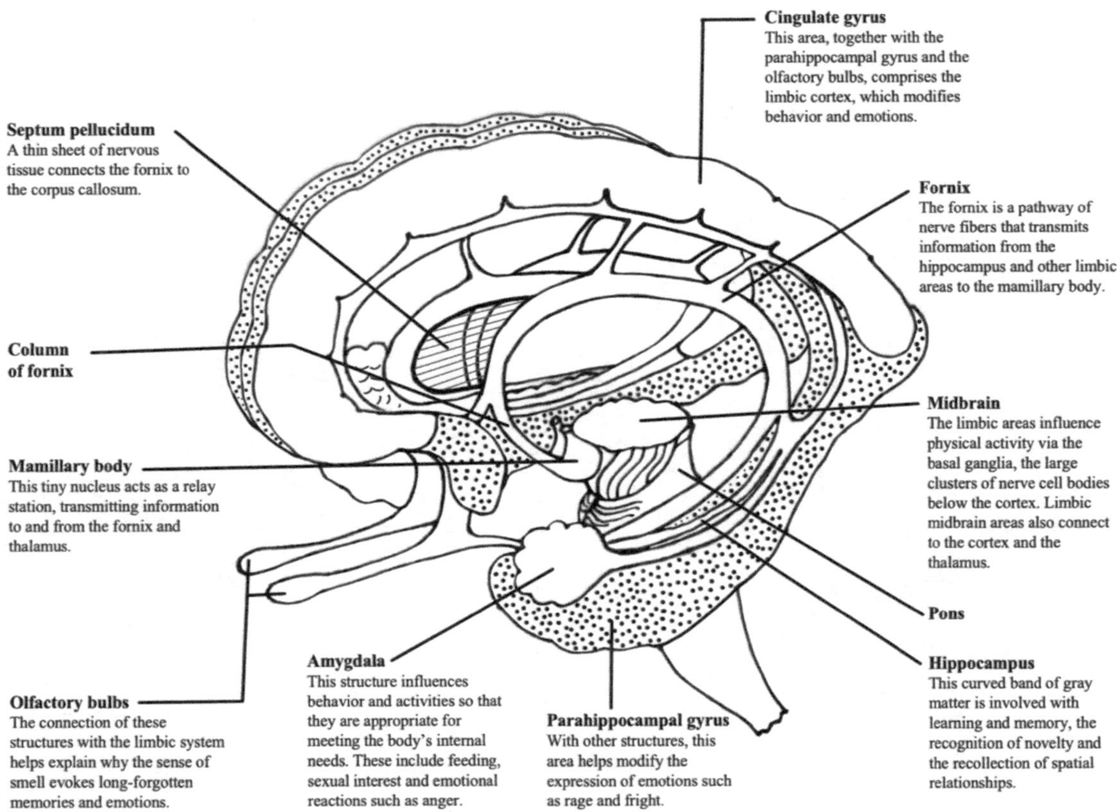

Figure 3.3 Anatomical components of limbic system.

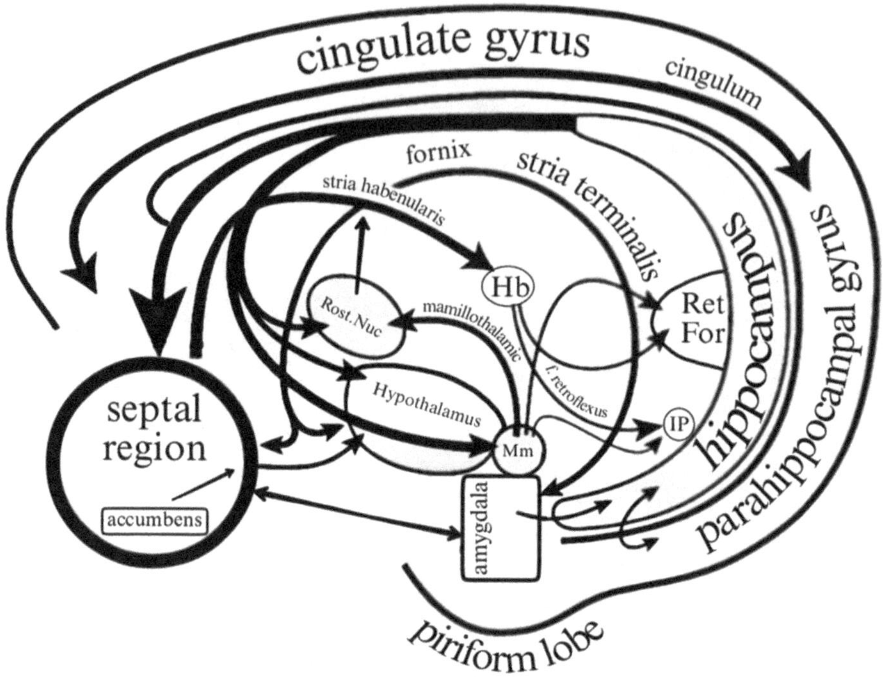

Figure 3.4 Functional interactions among different components of limbic system.

putamen, and it includes key structures such as the nucleus accumbens and the olfactory tubercle. This area is involved in the brain's reward system. The ventral striatum, especially the nucleus accumbens, helps process positive outcomes associated with previous decisions, leading to a reinforcement of intuitive choices that previously worked well, forming a "gut feeling" about what might work in the future.

d **Prefrontal Cortex (Executive Function and Decision-Making)**
The prefrontal cortex (PFC) is located at the front of the frontal lobe of the brain, which is part of the cerebral cortex. It is situated just behind the forehead and encompasses the anterior portion of the frontal lobes. The prefrontal cortex is associated with deliberate, analytical thought. The dorsolateral prefrontal cortex, though mainly involved in logical thinking, can modulate how much influence intuitive processes have over decisions. Ventromedial Prefrontal Cortex (VMPFC): Plays a role in emotion regulation, decision-making, and social cognition, it integrates information from the limbic system and emotional responses to guide intuitive decision-making. It helps balance rational thinking with emotional and instinctive judgements. Orbitofrontal Cortex (OFC): Involved in evaluating rewards and punishments, emotional regulation, and impulse control.

e **Default Mode Network (DMN)**
The default mode network (DMN) is a network of interacting brain regions that are active when the brain is at rest or focused on internal thoughts, such as daydreaming, introspection, or recalling memories. The DMN is spread across multiple brain regions in both hemispheres, and its components are located primarily in the medial prefrontal cortex, posterior cingulate cortex, precuneus, and parts of the parietal lobes. This network remains active when we are not focused on a specific task. This network supports "daydreaming" and mind-wandering, during which unconscious problem-solving or intuitive thinking often occurs. The DMN facilitates the brain's ability to make connections between disparate ideas or memories, contributing to intuitive insights. The key components of DMN and their functions are appended below.

f **Medial Prefrontal Cortex (mPFC)**
Located in the front of the brain, within the prefrontal cortex. This area is involved in self-referential thinking, decision-making, and processing emotions.

g **Posterior Cingulate Cortex (PCC)**
Situated near the centre of the brain, it plays a role in memory retrieval, visualising the future, and consciousness. It is considered a core hub of the DMN.

h **Precuneus**
Located in the superior part of the parietal lobe, just behind the PCC. The precuneus is involved in visuospatial imagery, self-consciousness, and episodic memory.

i **Inferior Parietal Lobule (IPL)**
Found in the lateral parietal lobe, the IPL contributes to attention, social cognition, and integrating sensory information with memory.

j **Hippocampus (Medial Temporal Lobe)**
Involved in memory formation and retrieval, the hippocampus is connected to the DMN, particularly in its role in episodic memory and envisioning future scenarios.

Major limbic system connections that organise heuristic pathways for cognition and intuitions are given in Table 3.1.

Biological evolution of human brain for supporting complex behaviour

The evolution of cognition and intuition in humans are enigmatic. Human, the Homo sapiens have created, developed some practices and performed some unique actions to aid their survival that suggest its supremacy over its nearest relatives from primate groups. Cognition evolved as a "middle man" of an evolving brain and evolving behaviour. According to the "new-thinking", cognition in humans has evolved like hands, that can perform various unprecedented functions as and when required. Like the human hand, cognitive efficiency is so flexible that it could accommodate every unknown signal and then respond accordingly in the best suitable way guided by genetically determined instinct. The cognitive efficacy of a human is so intense that he can perform a wide variety of technical and social functions on one hand, and also respond perfectly to the smallest change in emotional cues. The understanding of origin and evolution of cognition and intuition in humans probably rooted back to the Pleistocene epoch, the period of origin of Homo sapiens and crucial time for evolving cognitive ability. Phylogenetic comparative analysis of the neocortex and cerebellum among mammals has been accomplished by Barton (2012) and he inferred that the neocortex and the cerebellum have co-evolved together among all the mammals, though the relationship is not straight forward all the ways, rather very mysterious. In general, it is thought that the neocortex is associated with higher cognition, such as planning and executive control, while the cerebellum is connected with sensorimotor processing. But non-corollary between the anatomical parts associated with these two functions in many species, that is, variations in relation between neocortex and cerebellum suggest different selection pressures acted on different neural systems in different species through the evolutionary trajectory in different ways. For example, visual pathway expansion in primates, and cerebellar expansion in apes. So, brain size and composite brain ratios therefore combine different neural adaptations (Barton, 2012).

The anatomical evolution of the human brain from our ape ancestors is a critical factor in the development of cognition and intuition. Several key changes in brain structure have played a role in supporting these functions, and numerous scientific studies have documented these evolutionary developments.

1 **Expansion of the Neocortex**
The most notable change in the human brain compared to non-human primates is the significant expansion of the neocortex, particularly in the frontal and parietal lobes. Studies have shown that humans have a much larger neocortex relative to brain size than apes, with the expansion particularly prominent in areas responsible for executive functions (e.g., planning, decision-making, and social behaviour) (Herculano-Houzel, 2009). This enlargement has provided the neural infrastructure necessary for both cognitive processing and intuitive judgements.
2 **Development of the Prefrontal Cortex**
The PFC is involved in higher cognitive functions such as decision-making, planning, reasoning, and social behaviour. In humans, the PFC is much more developed than in other primates, which is a key aspect of our ability to perform complex cognitive tasks. Research has shown that the PFC integrates information from multiple brain regions, which helps balance both rational thought and intuitive processing (Fuster, 2002).

3 **Mirror Neuron System and Social Cognition**
The mirror neuron system, which is active both when performing an action and when observing others, has been proposed as a key feature that supports social cognition and intuitive understanding of others' emotions and intentions. This system is thought to allow humans to quickly and automatically understand the emotional states and intentions of others, a critical aspect of social interaction and intuitive behaviour. Research has shown that the mirror neuron system is more complex in humans compared to other primates, supporting the idea that the evolution of this system has enhanced both intuitive social cognition and the ability to make judgements based on empathy (Rizzolatti & Sinigaglia, 2010).

Limbic system and emotional processing

The human limbic system, responsible for processing emotions, has also evolved to support both cognition and intuition. In humans, the amygdala tends to be more intricately connected with the prefrontal cortex, enabling a higher degree of emotional regulation and the ability to integrate emotions with higher cognitive functions such as reasoning and decision-making. In contrast, in apes, the amygdala may have more direct connections with the brainstem, allowing for more instinctual, less regulated responses (LeDoux, 2007). Similarly, the hippocampus gradually attends larger size in humans compared to its ancestor, and it has more direct involvement in emotional processing. This larger hippocampus in humans helps with more sophisticated memory formation and emotional memory processing.

Brain connectivity and integration

As the human brain evolved, there was an increase in neural connectivity, particularly in the corpus callosum, which links the left and right hemispheres of the brain. This greater connectivity allows for better integration of cognitive and intuitive processes. For instance, humans have the capacity to use both logical reasoning (typically associated with the left hemisphere) and intuitive processing (associated with the right hemisphere) in a complementary manner. The integration of these two types of thinking is key to making informed decisions, particularly in complex or uncertain situations (Gazzaniga, 2005).

Conclusion

The entire discussion of this chapter is focused on the anatomical foundation of cognition, which by virtue of its existence in anatomy and physiology, by its refinement through evolutionary processes enjoyed the recognition of the scientific community. Cognition is a weapon by which we explore environmental resources and combat adverse situations. Intuition is a subconscious analytical power that is being generated out of experience using cognitive processes; so, intuition is a combination of "simple heuristics that are like a pair of scissors: the two blades of the environment and our cognitive processes work together to cut through the complexity of the world"[8] (Gut Feelings: The Intelligence of the Unconscious, Gigerenzer, 2007). Keeping all these facts in mind we cannot deny the science of intuition. Intuition is not merely an outcome of learning and experience. Learning and experience only can sharpen the power of intuition. Even if we consider learning as the foundation of intuition and environmental factors that ultimately shape intuitive power, we should not derecognise the genetic variations that underpin the variations in learning and analysing human ability. In a classroom of kids who received almost similar ambience of grooming exhibits variable learning outcome of the same lesion due to variation in intelligence and keenness to the subjects. Usually, a good learner shows good power of intuition. So, intelligence, memory, and analytical capacity provide necessary back-up to intuition. As the capacity of recognition is not all abstract and underpinned by defined biological processes, all these attributes that are linked with generation of intuition have a strong biological foundation, and intuitive ability is operated by complicated biological functions. As intuitive capacity is a prompt decision-making process it should have the shortest neuronal signalling route that eliminates unnecessary informational chaos and picks the most important one. So, "the art of intuition is based on knowing what to ignore".[9] (Gut Feelings: The Intelligence of the Unconscious, Gigerenzer, 2007). Intuition is like "a resonance and pleasure that persists in mind even after a musician stops playing through strings of his instrument". We cannot disagree regarding the existence of this eternal feeling for music. With the advancement of technology and sophisticated scientific approaches to characterise the most complicated part of the brain, scientists now have identified the probable "intuition" origin centre in the human brain. This intuitive signal processing centre is embodied into *Von Economo neurons* (VENs), a recently evolved cell type and this bunch of neurons may be involved in the fast intuitive assessment of complex situations. Allman et al. (2005) hypothesised that the VENs relay an output of fronto-insular and anterior cingulate cortex to the parts of frontal and temporal cortex associated with theory-of-mind, where fast intuitions are melded with slower, deliberative judgements. The VENs emerge mainly after birth and increase in number until age 4 yrs. In neurodegenerative diseases and intellectual disability, this set of neurons does not work properly and results in poor cognition and impaired intuition. The VENs are also found in ape (Allman et al., 2010) and cetaceans (Butti & Hof, 2010) and its occurrence justify strong cognitive functions and intuitive judgement ability of these animals. Woodward and Allman (2007) suggested, following their incisive analyses that moral intuition centre includes neural substances as discussed in this chapter. Unfortunately, we did not pay sufficient attention to explore the biological existence of the subconscious intuitive thinking process. "We need to rediscover the rationality of the unconscious".[10] (Gut Feelings: The Intelligence of the Unconscious, Gigerenzer, 2007). Because we have now realised that "the emotional brain responds to an event more quickly than the thinking brain".[11] (Emotional Intelligence: Why It Can Matter More Than IQ, Goleman, 1995). We have reached a point of time when unravelling the biological foundation of cognition and intuition from its deep core through its complexity will provide many answers for the human mind and its various forms of imperilment. This is because "Intuition is the highest form of intelligence, transcending all individual abilities and skills".[12] (The Courage to Create, May, 1975). To get more insight into the biological foundation we will discuss the genetic and molecular basis of intuition and cognition in next chapter.

Notes

1 Richard Dawkins describes the concept of "random design" in his book *The Blind Watchmaker*. In this work, Dawkins argues against the idea of a designer or creator by explaining how the process of natural selection, while not directed by any conscious agent, can give rise to complex biological systems that appear to be designed. He uses the term "random design" to illustrate that the complexity and functionality we see in biological organisms are not the result of deliberate design but rather the cumulative outcome of random genetic mutations that are filtered through natural selection. This process, over vast periods of time, results in organisms that seem purposefully designed but are actually the product of "blind" evolutionary processes.

2 Steven Pinker is a Canadian-American psychologist and professor at Harvard University. He made this comment in his book *How the Mind Works*. Pinker offers a concise definition of intelligence as a flexible, adaptive process rooted in rational decision-making.

3 Daniel Kahneman is an Israeli-American psychologist best known for his work on the psychology of judgement and decision-making as well as behavioural economics, for which he was awarded the 2002 Nobel Memorial Prize in Economic Sciences together with Vernon L. In the book *Thinking, Fast and Slow*, Daniel Kahneman explores the dual systems of thought that shape our decision-making processes. Kahneman identifies two modes of thinking, fast-automatic-intuitive and slow-deliberate-analytical. He made this statement in explaining the role of explicit recognition in intuition. This emphasises that what we often perceive as intuition is fundamentally rooted in our ability to recognise patterns and draw on past experiences.

4 This quote reflects Pinker's view of the mind as a computational system shaped by evolution to handle complex problems related to survival and interaction with the environment in *How Mind Works*.

5 Gerd Gigerenzer is a German psychologist and a leading researcher in the field of decision-making and behavioural economics. He is known for his work on heuristics—simple, efficient rules that people use to make decisions and solve problems. He is the director of the Harding Center for Risk Literacy at the Max Planck Institute for Human Development in Berlin. He argues that intuition, or "gut feelings", is not some mystical force but the result of the brain's learned heuristics, based on experience in his book *Gut Feeling: The Intelligence of the Unconscious*.

6 Gigerenzer argues that our gut feelings, often dismissed as irrational, can actually serve as powerful tools for making effective decisions.
7 David Eagleman is a neuroscientist, author, and science communicator known for his work on brain function, perception, and the nature of consciousness. He is an associate professor at Stanford University. In *The Brain: The Story of You*, David Eagleman explores the intricacies of how the brain functions and the processes that shape our perceptions and behaviours. The quote highlights the brain's role as a "pattern recognition machine", emphasising that much of our response to the world occurs below the level of conscious awareness. Eagleman argues that our brains continuously analyse and interpret a vast array of stimuli, drawing on past experiences to make quick judgements and decisions. This unconscious processing enables us to navigate complex environments and respond to social cues effectively.
8 In this context, Gigerenzer argues in *Gut Feeling: Intelligence of the Unconscious*, that just as scissors have two blades that work together to cut effectively, our cognitive processes and the external environment collaborate to simplify decision-making. By using heuristics, we can efficiently process information and make choices without getting overwhelmed by every detail, allowing us to respond effectively in various situations. The quote highlights the interplay between our innate cognitive abilities and the real-world context we operate in.
9 In this context, Gigerenzer emphasises that skilled decision-makers can focus on the most significant cues in a given situation, allowing them to make quick and effective judgements. This selective attention is crucial, as it helps individuals navigate complex environments without becoming overwhelmed. Overall, the quote underscores the idea that intuition is a refined skill that involves discernment and simplification, enhancing our ability to act wisely with limited information. So, effective decision-making often relies on focusing on the most relevant information while ignoring unnecessary data, rather than overanalysing every detail.
10 Here, Gigerenzer, in *Gut Feeling: Intelligence of Unconscious*, emphasised the idea that unconscious judgements can be surprisingly effective and rational, challenging traditional views that prioritise conscious reasoning. Gigerenzer advocates for recognising the strengths of intuitive thinking, especially in complex situations where quick decisions are necessary. By understanding the rational basis of these unconscious processes, we can improve our decision-making strategies in both personal and professional contexts.
11 Daniel Goleman is an American *psychologist*, author, and *science journalist* in the New York Times. In his book *Emotional Intelligence: Why It Can Matter More Than IQ*, Goleman explored the role of emotions in decision-making and behaviour, highlighting how the emotional brain (primarily the amygdala) can trigger responses faster than the rational, thinking brain (primarily the neocortex).
12 Rollo Reece May was an American existential psychologist and author of many influential books on human psychology. The quote about intuition being the highest form of intelligence in *The Courage to Create* reflects May's belief that intuition transcends mere cognitive skills and individual capabilities. He views intuition as a fundamental aspect of human creativity, suggesting that it allows individuals to access deeper insights and understand complex truths that may elude rational analysis. May argues that embracing intuition can lead to more authentic expressions of creativity and self-understanding. In this context, intuition is seen not just as a spontaneous feeling but as a vital source of knowledge that informs our actions and decisions, urging individuals to trust their inner wisdom.

References

Allman, J. M., Tetreault, N. A., Hakeem, A. Y., Manaye, K. F., Semendeferi, K., Erwin, J. M., Park, S., Goubert, V., & Hof, P. R. (2010). The Von Economo neurons in frontoinsular and anterior cingulate cortex in great apes and humans. *Brain Structure & Function*, *214*(5–6), 495–517. https://doi.org/10.1007/s00429-010-0254-0

Allman, J. M., Watson, K. K., Tetreault, N. A., & Hakeem, A. Y. (2005). Intuition and autism: A possible role for Von Economo neurons. *Trends in Cognitive Sciences*, *9*(8), 367–373. https://doi.org/10.1016/j.tics.2005.06.008

Anderson, J. R. (2015). *Cognitive psychology and its implications* (8th ed.). MacMillan.

Barton, R. A. (2012). Embodied cognitive evolution and the cerebellum. *Philosophical Transactions of the Royal Society: Biological Sciences*, *367*(1599), 2097–2107.

Butti, C., & Hof, P. R. (2010). The insular cortex: A comparative perspective. *Brain structure & function*, *214*(5–6), 477–493. https://doi.org/10.1007/s00429-010-0264-y

Darwin, C. R. (1859). *The origin of species*. John Murray.

Dawkins, R. (1986). *The blind watchmaker*. W.W. Norton & Company, Inc.

Desmond, J. E., Gabrieli, J. D. E., & Glover, G. H. (1998). Dissociation of frontal and cerebellar activity in a cognitive task: Evidence for a distinction between selection and search. *Neuroimage*, *7*, 368–376

Dukas, R. (2004). Evolutionary biology of animal cognition. *Annual Review of Ecology, Evolution, and Systematics*, *35*, 347–374.

Eagleman, D. (2015). *The brain: The story of you*. Pantheon Books.

Fuster, J. M. (2002). Prefrontal cortex and the physiology of cognition. In *Handbook of neuropsychology* (Vol. 6, pp. 61–76). Elsevier. https://doi.org/10.1016/S0922-3936(02)80263-2

Gazzaniga, M. S. (2005). *The ethical brain*. Dana Press.

Gigerenzer, G. (2007). *Gut feelings: The intelligence of the unconscious*. Penguin Press.

Goleman, D. (1995). *Emotional intelligence: Why it can matter more than IQ*. Bantam Books.

Heath, R. G., Franklin, D. E., & Shraberg, D. (1979). Gross pathology of the cerebellum in patients diagnosed and treated as functional psychiatric disorders. *The Journal of Nervous and Mental Disease*, *167*(10), 585–592. https://doi.org/10.1097/00005053-197910000-00001

Herculano-Houzel, S. (2009). The human brain in numbers: A linearly scaled-up primate brain. *Frontiers in Human Neuroscience*, *3*, 31. https://doi.org/10.3389/neuro.09.031.2009

Kahneman, D. (2011). *Thinking, fast and slow*. Macmillan.

Kelly, R. M., & Strick, P. L. (2003). Cerebellar loops with motor cortex and prefrontal cortex of a nonhuman primate. *The Journal of Neuroscience*, *23*, 8432–8444.

Keren-Happuch, E., Chen, S. H. A., Ho, M. H. R., & Desmond, J. E. (2012). A meta-analysis of cerebellar contributions to higher cognition from PET and fMRI studies. *Human Brain Mapping*, *35*(2), 593–615. https://doi.org/10.1002/hbm.22194

Kim, S., Ugurbil, K., & Strick, P. (1994). Activation of a cerebellar output nucleus during cognitive processing. *Science*, *265*(5174), 949–951. https://doi.org/10.1126/science.8052851

LeDoux, J. E. (2007). The amygdala and emotional memory. *Neurobiology of Learning and Memory*, *87*(3), 273–285. https://doi.org/10.1016/j.nlm.2006.09.002

Leiner, H. C., Leiner, A. L., & Dow, R. S. (1986). Does the cerebellum contribute to mental skills? *Behavioral Neuroscience*, *100*, 443–454.

May, R. (1975). *The courage to create*. W. W. Norton & Company.

Middleton, F. A., & Strick, P. L. (2000). Basal ganglia and cerebellar loops: Motor and cognitive circuits. *Brain Research Reviews*, *31*(2–3), 236–250.

Petersen, S. E., Fox, P. T., Posner, M. I., Mintun, M., & Raichle, M. E. (1988). Positron emission tomographic studies of the cortical anatomy of single word processing. *Nature*, *331*, 585–589.

Petersen, S. E., Fox, P. T., Posner, M. I., Mintun, M., & Raichle, M. E. (1989). Positron emission tomographic studies of the processing of singe words. *Journal of Cognitive Neuroscience*, *1*, 153–170.

Pinker, S. (1997). *How the mind works*. W.W. Norton & Company.

Raichle, M. E., Fiez, J. A., Videen, T. O., MacLeod, A. M., Pardo, J. V., Fox, P. T., & Petersen, S. E. (1994). Practice-related changes in human brain functional anatomy during nonmotor learning. *Cerebral Cortex*, *4*(1), 8–26. https://doi.org/10.1093/cercor/4.1.8

Ramnani, N., Behrens, T. E. J., Johansen-Berg, H., Richter, M. C., Pinsk, M. A., Andersson, J. L. R., Rudebeck, P., Ciccarelli, O., Richter, W., Thompson, A. J., Gross, C. G., Robson, M. D., Kastner, S., & Matthews, P. M. (2006). The evolution of prefrontal inputs to the cortico-pontine system: Diffusion imaging evidence from macaque monkeys and humans. *Cerebral Cortex*, *16*(6), 811–818. https://doi.org/10.1093/cercor/bhj024

Rizzolatti, G., & Sinigaglia, C. (2010). The functional role of the parieto-frontal mirror circuit: Interpretations and misinterpretations. *Nature Reviews Neuroscience*, *11*(4), 264–274. https://doi.org/10.1038/nrn2805

Rolls, E. T. (2014). *Emotion and decision-making explained*. Oxford University Press.

Schmahmann, J. D., & Pandya, D. N. (1997). The cerebrocerebellar system. *International Review of Neurobiology*, *41*, 31–60.

Stoodley, C. J., Valera, E. M., & Schmahmann, J. D. (2010). An fMRI study of intra-individual functional topography in the human cerebellum. *Behavioural Neurology*, *23*(1–2), 65–79. https://doi.org/10.3233/BEN-2010-0268

Whiting, B. A., & Barton, R. A. (2003). The evolution of the cortico-cerebellar complex in primates: Anatomical connections predict patterns of correlated evolution. *Journal of Human Evolution*, *44*(1), 3–10. https://doi.org/10.1016/s0047-2484(02)00162-8

Woodward, J., & Allman, J. (2007). Moral intuition: Its neural substrates and normative significance. *Journal of Physiology, Paris*, *101*(46), 179–202. https://doi.org/10.1016/j.jphysparis.2007.12.003

Chapter 4

Cognition and intuition

Exploring genetic and molecular foundation

Sujay Ghosh

Introduction

The anatomical foundation of cognition and intuition process in humans co-evolved with the molecular ancillaries that cause necessary changes at the cellular level for executing emotional outcomes. These two evolving systems must have filtered through the process of natural selection and therefore have a third co-evolving component that underpinned anatomy and chemistry, the genetic structures. We can imagine the complexity of the genetic system that supports the architecture of the super-complex human brain and its untra-complex chemistry and function. In recent decades, however, advancements in genetic and molecular biology have begun to unravel how cognition is deeply intertwined with the genetic code and the molecular machinery that governs cellular activity. In his book *The Gene: An Intimate History*, Siddhartha Mukherjee (2016) reminds us that "the gene is the blueprint of life, and yet, it is not a static code. It evolves, adapts, and expresses itself in ways that can shape our most fundamental traits, including our thoughts, behaviors, and abilities." At the heart of cognition lies an intricate network of genes, proteins, and signaling pathways that work together to create the neural circuits responsible for thought, memory, and decision-making. This chapter explores how these molecular and genetic processes shape the brain's function, from the formation of synapses to the plasticity of neural networks that allow us to learn and adapt to new information. The first significant step toward understanding the molecular basis of cognition begins at the synapse—the connection point between two neurons. Here, chemical signals like neurotransmitters and neurotrophins, guided by genetic instructions, mediate the transmission of information that leads to thought and action. As Nobel Prize-winning neuroscientist Eric Kandel (2006) notes in *In Search of Memory*, "Memory is not stored in the brain as a static recording but is instead a dynamic process of biochemical change that involves genes and proteins... cognition itself is a dynamic, ever-changing process driven by our molecular machinery." From the perspective of genetics, researchers have increasingly recognized that cognition is not solely the product of

DOI: 10.4324/9781003377757-5

environmental experiences, but is deeply embedded in our genetic code. Specific genes regulate the development and function of neural networks, and alterations in these genes can lead to significant cognitive outcomes. For example, variations in the *BDNF* gene (brain-derived neurotrophic factor) have been linked to memory failure and learning incapability. As the renowned molecular biologist Bruce McEwen (2002) states in his book *The End of Stress as We Know It*, "genes determine the architecture of the brain, but experience shapes how that architecture is put to work. The interface between nature and nurture occurs at the molecular level."

At the molecular level, the brain's neurons communicate through complex signaling pathways involving neurotransmitters such as dopamine, serotonin, and glutamate. These molecules influence not only mood and emotion but also higher cognitive functions like attention, reasoning, and creativity. For instance, dopamine, often referred to as the "feel-good" neurotransmitter, plays a crucial role in reward-based learning, memory consolidation, and decision-making (Grace, 2000). Similarly, research has shown that *NMDA* receptors, which mediate synaptic plasticity, are essential for long-term memory formation and the ability to learn from experience (Malenka & Bear, 2004). In *How to Create a Mind*, Ray Kurzweil (2012) writes, "The mind is a pattern-recognition machine, and the brain's molecular machinery is the substrate upon which this pattern recognition unfolds."

As we delve into the genetic and molecular mechanisms of cognition in this chapter, we will explore how the brain's inherent biological architecture gives rise to complex behaviors and mental processes.

Evolution of genetic system that supports cognition in humans

The co-evolution of the genetic system that supports evolving brain structure and its functioning at the molecular level is complex and intriguing. The cerebellum carries a great number of neurons that evolved as anatomical and physiological adaptations in the form of cortico-cerebral networks that enable control, organization, and comprehension of complex sequences needed for technical and social intelligence and language development (Hauser et al., 2002). This notion draws its support from the work of Sterelny (2012). Sterelny narrated that hominids evolved as social foragers starting their journey from late australopithecines through some intermediate forms with large brains. Gradually, they developed the skill to cooperate, communicate, and plan (Sterelny, 2007, 2011, 2012). Natural selection supports genetic variations that increase the efficacy of these qualities and underpin neural designs. This leads to the eventual development of language (Barton, 2012). So, language evolution is one of the major leaps toward the development of cognition and intuition in humans, which is co-evolved with the cortico-cerebellar connectivity that provides the foundation for the development of gestural communication, gradually syntax, and language (Sterelny, 2012). According to Fitch (2009) the motor control of physical action and hierarchical action planning system in the human mind adapted secondarily to the already developed syntax and communicative system (Sterelny, 2011). Genetic basis of the evolving cognitive system in humans is not very clear. Comparative genomic study including chimpanzees and humans revealed nearly ~35 million nucleotide substitutions that had occurred to mark the genomic difference between these two species. Some of them have occurred in the human lineage and some in chimpanzee line. Out of these changes a small proportion, 31389 substitutions have occurred in the human genome after it was departed from Neanderthal. About 60000 amino acid replacements have been recorded that occurred in 20000 protein coding genes through the journey from Neanderthal to *Homo sapiens*. Rest of the changes probably occurred in conserved non-coding regions and regulatory regions that are targeted by epigenetic marks. These changes either may have had impact in changing gene function that characterizes the transition from anthropoid ape to human or they were neutral to any transitional changes.

Evolution of cognition is not unique in humans; rather non-human primates also show different degrees of cognitive ability. The evolutionary development in cognition that is unique to humans is the development of social cognition that includes cooperation and cumulative cultural practices. Recent comparative behavioral studies have revealed that the emergence of cooperation among humans is one of the important factors for human brain evolution. The evolution of language is one iconic event in human cognitive development. We can discuss the most studied gene that is involved in language development, one of the major cognition-intuition demanding features in human. Sets of genes for laryngeal function and motor control have evolved by positive selection. The candidate gene FOXP2 is such an example. Humans that are heterozygous for FOXP2 null-allele suffer from impairment in speech and language development (Graham & Fisher, 2015; Lai et al., 2001; Vargha-Khadem et al., 2005; Watkins, 2011). Analyses of molecular structure of FOXP2 revealed two amino acid substitutions, which became fixed in the human lineage after it was diverged from the chimpanzee line. It was suggested that these two substitutions enjoyed positive selection due to their beneficial effect on speech and language (Enard et al., 2002; Zhang et al., 2002). To confirm the functional consequences of these two substitutions on cognitive systems, a mouse model carrying these substitutions in the endogenous FOXP2 gene was created (Enard et al., 2009). These mice exhibited alterations in the cortico-basal ganglia circuit, including changes in dopamine levels, striatal synaptic plasticity, dendrite morphology, and gene expression profile (Enard, 2011; Enard et al., 2009; Reimers-Kipping et al., 2011, Schreiweis et al., 2014). On the other hand, the transgenic mice carrying the humanized FOXP2 allele exhibited faster learning of stimulus-response associations. This observation revealed that the two amino acid changes influence the striatum-dependent evolution of the human vocal system

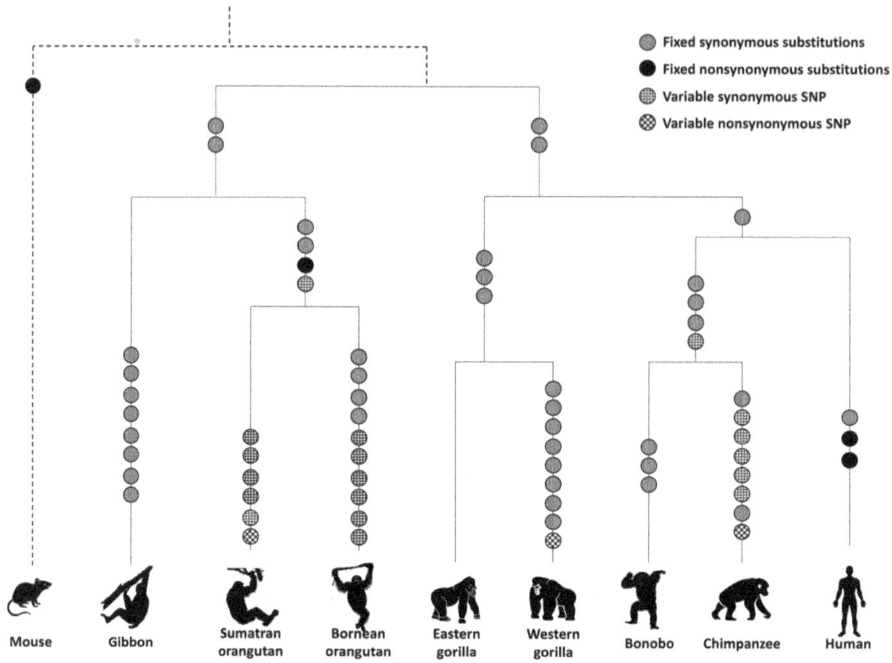

Figure 4.1 Evolution of FOXP2 gene among primates.

(Schreiweis et al., 2014). Probably FOXP2 affects dopamine-dependent learning processes in specific regions of the striatum (Schreiweis et al., 2014) and support to this prediction came from the findings that dopaminergic innervation changed specifically in the human lineage and specifically in one striatal region (Raghanti et al., 2016). A schematic summary of FOXP2 evolution among different primate groups is given below (Figure 4.1).

In addition to this, some clinical phenotypes in humans provide opportunities to study the evolution of the genes that build the foundation of cognitive ability in humans and other primates. Autism spectrum disorders and other psychiatric manifestations in humans that exhibit cognitive impairments are of particular interest. Genome-wide association studies have identified some genetic loci significantly associated with schizophrenia and autism that are found conserved in 11 primate species and 34 non-primate species (Ogawa & Vallender, 2014). This observation makes the understanding of the evolution of sets of genes associated with cognitive processes more complicated. This result further suggests that change in the nucleotide sequence in the conserved genes associated with psychiatric disorders may not be sufficient to explain the higher-order cognitive and intuitive ability in humans. Additionally, studies conducted on psychiatric disorders may remain insufficient to identify the loci that are exclusive for controlling the human cognitive ability.

So, it is hypothetical that several sets of genes have evolved in human lineage owing to their adaptive advantage in cognitive process in conjunction with the genes that support higher neural connectivity needed for finer cognitive efficiency. Genes that are responsible for higher performance of cognitive ability in human not only differ structurally, but possibly underwent change in expression pattern upon exposure to social activities and have evolved rapidly.

Molecular genetic regulation of cognition and intuition

Genes involved in cognition and intuition

The best-studied aspect of human cognition is linguistic ability. Sets of information derived from neuropsychological studies on brain-injured patients and use of high throughput neuro-imaging suggested that human prefrontal cortex is critical for executive functioning of various cognitive activities (Benton, 1994). The genes that are expressed in the prefrontal cortex have been identified as possible candidates involved in the regulation of cognitive function. Among them, dopamine has been identified as a regulator of six predominantly left-hemisphere cognitive skills—the 'executive functions' that are critical to human language and thought processes (Previc, 1999). The functional relation between prefrontal cortex and dopamine has been recognized through different studies.

The very first evidence in favor of the involvement of Dopamine (DA) in cognitive ability has come from the study on the patients of Perkinson's disease whose working memory deficit could be improved by the administration of L-DOPA (Mattay et al., 2002). Support for this observation has been provided by the study on primate model rhesus monkeys who exhibited impaired memory owing to the depletion of DA in the prefrontal cortex (Brozoski et al., 1979). Similar rescue of the working memory is evident following the application of DA agonist in the primates' model (Goldman-Rakic, 1995). Application of DA agonist bromocriptine has revealed (Luciana & Nelson, 1998) improvement in the working memory performance of individuals. A recent neuroimaging study demonstrated a correlation between the density of dopaminergic neurons in the caudate nucleus and the performance of individuals in memory tests (Remy & Samson, 2003). All these studies unambiguously suggest a possible involvement of DA in cognitive function.

However, the function of DA in cognition is intriguing. Dopamine can retard cognitive function in contrast to its enhancing effect. Administration of a DA D2 receptor agonist Bromocriptine, was shown to improve cognitive function that needs low-baseline memory capacity, but impair function that needs higher memory capacity (Kimberg et al., 1997). Experimentation conducted by Mattay et al. (2000) showed that the application of dextroamphetamine, a drug that increases dopaminergic activity causes improvement of cognitive performance in the subjects with low-titre of DA, but once DA receptor stimulation reached a certain threshold, the working memory function showed deterioration. Thus, the relationship between DA level and cognitive performance generates an inverted 'U' shaped curve that suggests both suboptimal and supra-optimal DA activity impairing prefrontal function (Cools & Robbins, 2004).

This interesting relationship may arise from the differential effects of D1 and D2 receptor binding at the prefrontal cortex. Theoretically, D2 receptor binding by DA generates a signal in the presence of reward-based information and allows the PFC network to respond by immediate modulation of its working memory (Weinberger et al. 2001). On the other hand, D1 receptor stimulation following DA binding plays an assembly role in controlling the response before sending it to PFC. Thus, D1 receptor activation stabilizes activity within the PFC neural circuit and protects the network from distraction by other stimuli until the appropriate behavioral response is generated (Weinberger et al., 2001).

Catechol O methyltransferase (COMT) enzyme is pivotal in regulating the function of the fronto-striatal network in cognition. The enzyme COMT is concentrated in the extrasynaptic spaces (Deutch and Roth, 1999). Genetic analysis by Egan et al. (2001) revealed the presence of a single nucleotide polymorphism (SNP) of this gene that affects cognition function. The gene is located on chromosome 22q11 and the said polymorphisms (GenBank accession no. Z26491) result in the substitution of valine (val) with methionine (met) at codon 158 of the protein sequence. The methionine-carrying isoform of the enzyme is less stable and less active in comparison to valine-containing isoform.

The D1/D2 binding ratio to their receptor is critical for optimum cognitive function. If this D1/D2-binding ratio gets disturbed, cognitive performance becomes impaired (theoretically) either in a hypodopaminergic state or a hyperdopaminergic state. In the hyperdopaminergic state inadequate D1-mediated signaling in the PFC causes decay in neural inputs, resulting in poor differentiation of target from background (Winterer & Weinberger, 2004). This may be manifested in the form of impulsive and distractible behaviors and poor working memory and planning, the actions that are mediated by the PFC. In extreme cases, this may result in delusions, paranoia, and neurocognitive dysfunction which are characteristics of schizophrenia (Winterer & Weinberger, 2004). On the other hand, a hyperdopaminergic state caused by excessive D1 stimulation resulted in a lack of modulation in response from PFC that leads to the manifestation of perseverative or stereotypic behavior (Weinberger et al., 2001) and impaired performance on tasks requiring cognitive flexibility (Cools & Robbins, 2004). Besides DA and D1/D2 receptors, two enzymes play a pivotal role in determining individual variations in cognitive and intuitive performance. These are catechol-O-methyltransferase

(COMT), and dopamine transporter (DAT). Followings are some potential candidates that have a role in the execution of cognition.

CATECHOL-O-METHYLTRANSFERASE (COMT)

The COMT is found concentrated in the extrasynaptic spaces of dopaminergic neurons in PFC (Deutch and Roth, 1999) and it appears to play an important role in the modulation of fronto-striatal networks. A SNP of the COMT gene (val158met) located on chromosome 22q11 has been identified recently that results in the substitution of valine (val) with methionine (met) at 158th codon (GenBank accession no. Z26491). The met allele produces an enzyme that is unstable at body temperature and has only 25% of the activity of the val-containing polypeptide (Egan et al., 2001). The valine-containing high-activity isoform results in reduced stability of PFC neural networks which may in turn cause decreased ability to maintain information in working memory (Bilder et al. 2004; Winterer & Weinberger, 2004); additionally, it enhances the ability to update the contents of working memory with new information (Cools & Robbins, 2004). Alternatively, the low activity methionine containing isoform is associated with an elevated PFC DA level and increased D1 receptor binding; this probably enhances the stability of PFC networks and decreases cognitive flexibility (Bilder et al., 2004; Winterer & Weinberger, 2004).

Egan et al. (2001), tested the allelic variations of COMT and reported that the high-activity valine allele was associated with poorer performance in the Wisconsin Card Sorting Test (WCST), a reliable test for 'executive' function, lower efficiency in physiological response in the dorsolateral PFC during a working memory task. Moreover, this valine-containing isoform was found more frequent among schizophrenia patients. Egan et al. (2001) hypothesized that the COMT genotype accounted for 4% of the variance in performing WCST test, and this was supported by Joober (2002), Bilder et al. (2002) and Goldberg et al. (2003).

SLC6A3 (DAT)

Dopamine transporter SLC6A3 is a member of the sodium- and chloride-dependent neurotransmitter transporter family. The 3' UTR of this gene contains a 40 bp that is, a VNTR, which can be varied among individuals from 3 to 11 copies. Variation in the number of repeats is associated with idiopathic epilepsy, attention-deficit hyperactivity disorder, dependence on alcohol and cocaine, susceptibility to Parkinson disease and protection against nicotine dependence. In context to cognitive ability the intronic polymorphisms of this gene, namely, rs40184C > T has been studied (Karalija et al., 2021; PMID: 34742942). The author found that T-carriers (heterozygous "CT") of the DAT exhibited higher performance in cognitive function than the homozygous "CC" individuals and this association remained consistent in follow-up study too.

DRD1 AND DRD2

The important influence of COMT variants on the DRD1/DRD2 (D1/D2) receptor-activation ratio intuitively suggests that functional polymorphisms of these two receptor genes may contribute to variable expression of cognitive performance. The D1 receptor is expressed in the glutamatergic pyramidal cells of the PFC (Lidow et al., 1991). Arnsten et al. (1994) demonstrated that a D1 receptor antagonist causes a decline in the working memory of monkeys, while a D1 agonist improves memory performance. Similarly, D1 receptor knockout mice display spatial learning impairment (El-Ghundi et al., 1999).

The gene D2 subtype of the dopamine receptor is located on chromosome 11 (cytogenetic locus: 11q23.2; Gene ID: 1813). This G-protein coupled receptor inhibits adenylyl cyclase activity. Alternative splicing of this gene results in two transcript variants encoding different isoforms. The D2 receptors are most commonly found on the GABAergic interneurons of the PFC and appear to play a role in depressing N-Methyl-D-Aspartate (NMDA) receptor-mediated excitatory neurotransmission (Kotecha et al., 2002). Mehta et al. (1999) experimentally administered sulpiride, a D2 receptor antagonist, to healthy volunteers and demonstrated that the drug impaired spatial working memory. In a follow-up study, the authors found a shifting of cognitive set that is particularly sensitive to D2 receptor antagonism (Mehta et al., 2004). Kimberg et al. (1997) proved experimentally that a D2 receptor agonist improved cognition in individuals with a low-baseline memory capacity. Additionally, it has been hypothesized that a decrease in D2 receptors with advancing age is responsible for cognitive decline in the elderly.

The lack of studies on D1 receptor polymorphisms does not allow us to get more insight into the contribution of D1 receptors in cognitive variations in man. On the other hand, the TaqIA polymorphism of D2 receptors is a well-studied subject. The DRD2 gene is about 270 kb long and contains nine exons, with the TaqIA site located in the untranslated region (UTR) of the gene (Noble, 2000). Preliminary evidence suggested that the A1 allele of the D2 receptor was associated with reduced density of DRD2 receptors in the striatum and hence less signaling (Pohjalainen et al., 1998). A study by Duan et al. (2003) has revealed a synonymous SNP (C957T) that affects mRNA stability and receptor expression. This finding was confirmed by Hirvonen et al. (2004), through in vivo experimentation. The C957T variant was found to be in linkage disequilibrium with the TaqI A variant in a Caucasian but not an African-American sample (Duan et al., 2003).

DRD4

The receptor DRD4 has a role in modulating the GABAergic signaling and pre-frontal modulation. The DRD4 belongs to the same class of receptors as DRD2, exerting an inhibitory effect on the adenylyl cyclase-mediated secondary messenger system and is found primarily in the limbic regions and on PFC pyramidal neurons (Wang et al., 2002). The DRD4 gene is located on the short arm of chromosome 11 (cytogenetic location:11p15.5, Gene ID: 1815) and contains a 48 bp VNTR polymorphism in the third exon of the gene. This VNTR polymorphism has been studied widely in genetic association studies (Ding et al., 2002). Wang et al. (2002) The authors demonstrated experimentally that activation of DRD4 receptors, located in close vicinity of GABAA receptors on dendrites, reduces GABAA receptor-mediated signal in the PFC (Wang et al., 2002). Thus, both DRD4 and genes coding for components of the GABAergic system are also candidates for influencing individual variation in cognition.

The association between an exonic DRD4 variable number tandem repeat (VNTR) variant and attention deficit hyperactivity disorder (ADHD) is one of the well-established findings in psychiatric genetics (DiMaio et al., 2003). Both case-control and family-based association studies have revealed that the longer or 7R allele is a risk factor for ADHD (DiMaio et al., 2003). The polymorphic repeated segment codes for amino acids in the third intracellular loop of the receptor, a domain that binds G proteins and therefore mediates intracellular signaling (Asghari et al., 1995). A study by Asghari et al. (1995) found differences in cyclic adenosine monophosphate inhibition between the 4R and 7R alleles, as well as between a 2R and 4R combined heterozygous group, and the 7R allele. Among them, the 4R allele has been reported to be more sensitive to pharmacological DA agonists (Fossella et al., 2002).

Four different studies have reported an association between DRD4 48 bp VNTR polymorphism and cognitive performance (see Table 4.1). Three out of these four studies were conducted on individuals with ADHD. While Swanson et al. (2000), Fossella et al. (2002), and Manor et al. (2002) reported that children with a 4R allele or other shorter (2–5R) alleles performed more poorly on tests of attention and executive functioning, Langley et al. (2004) report increased impulsivity and poor performance on a test of behavioral inhibition among the carriers of the 7R allele. In addition to VNTR polymorphisms, an SNPs that involves C > T transition at 521 bp upstream from the transcription-initiation site has been identified for its possible functional effect. According to Okuyama et al. (1999), the "T" variant is transcribed with 40% less efficiency than the "C" allele. More recent study by D'Souza et al. (2004) has identified that the longer allele of a 120-bp tandem repeat in the 50-flanking region of the DRD4 gene, has lower levels of transcriptional activity than the shorter allele. These variants have also been identified in ADHD (Kustanovich et al., 2004) and may have emerged as pivotal candidates in the genetics of cognition.

BRAIN-DERIVED NEUROTROPHIC FACTOR (BDNF)

The BDNF gene is located on chromosome 11p13 and is composed of eight exons that exhibit alternative mRNA splicing (Jiang et al., 2005) and generate different isoforms. Egan et al. (2003) identified an SNP in the gene (rs6265)

Table 4.1 Summary of genes and their functions involved in cognition and intuition

Genes (alternative names)	*NCBI ID*	*OMIM ID*	*Chr. location*	*Functions*
COMT	1312	116790	22q11.21	It transfers a methyl group from S-adenosylmethionine to catecholamines, including the neurotransmitters dopamine, epinephrine, and norepinephrine. This O-methylation results in one of the major degradative pathways of the catecholamine transmitters. Polymorphisms/mutations were found associated with OCD, schizophrenia, and anorexia nervosa.
SLC6A3 (DAT)	6531	126455	5p15.33	Dopamine transporter which is a member of the sodium- and chloride-dependent neurotransmitter transporter family; mediates the active reuptake of dopamine from the synapse and is a principal regulator of dopaminergic neurotransmission; mutations/ polymorphisms were found associated with Attention-Deficit Hyperactivity Disorder, Tourette Syndrome, Bipolar Disorder, Infantile Parkinsonism-Dystonia 1.
DRD1	1812	126449	5q35.2	D1 subtype of the dopamine receptor is most abundant in the central nervous system. This G-protein coupled receptor stimulates adenylyl cyclase and activates cyclic AMP-dependent protein kinases and regulates neuronal, development, mediates some behavioral responses, and regulates working memory. Polymorphisms and mutations of these genes were found among patients with schizophrenia.
DRD2	1813		11q23.2	D2 subtype of the dopamine receptor. This G-protein coupled receptor inhibits adenylyl cyclase activity.

DRD4	1815	11p15.5	The D4 subtype is a G-protein coupled receptor which inhibits adenylyl cyclase. It is a target for drugs which treat schizophrenia and Parkinson's disease.
BDNF (ANON2)	627	11p14.1	It encodes a member of the nerve growth factor; neuronal survival in the adult brain. It regulates the stress response and emotions; reduced expression is reported in Alzheimer's, Parkinson's, and Huntington's disease.
APOE	348	19q13.32	It binds to a specific liver and peripheral cell receptor and is essential for the normal catabolism of triglyceride-rich lipoprotein constituents.
FOXP2	93986	7q31.1	Encodes a member of the forkhead/winged-helix (FOX) family of transcription factors, expressed in brain, required for proper development of speech and language regions of the brain during embryogenesis.
CREB1/ CREB	1385	2q33.3	Encodes a transcription factor of the leucine zipper family of DNA binding proteins that binds to the cAMP-responsive element.
MTOR (FRAP)	2475	1p36.22	The family of phosphatidylinositol kinase mediates cellular responses to stresses such as DNA damage and nutrient deprivation and promotes cell survival and cell cycle progression, regulates neurogenesis, particularly in the hippocampus, and controls memory function.
SYNI (EPILX)	6853	Xp11.3-p11.23	Encode neuronal phosphoproteins which are associated with the cytoplasmic surface of synaptic vesicles, regulation of neurogenesis, and synaptogenesis. Mutations in this gene may be associated with X-linked disorders with primary neuronal degeneration such as Rett syndrome.

(*Continued*)

Table 4.1 (Continued)

Genes (alternative names)	*NCBI ID*	*OMIM ID*	*Chr. location*	*Functions*
SYNII	6854		3p25.2	This member of the synapsin family encodes a neuron-specific phosphoprotein that selectively binds to small synaptic vesicles in the presynaptic nerve terminal. Polymorphisms in this gene are associated with abnormal presynaptic function and related neuronal disorders, including autism, epilepsy, bipolar disorder, and schizophrenia.
SYNIII	8224		22q12.3	Synaptogenesis and the modulation of neurotransmitter release, suggesting a potential role in several neuropsychiatric diseases.
PSD	5662		10q24.32	A Pleckstrin homology and SEC7 domain-containing protein that functions as a guanine nucleotide exchange factor. The encoded protein regulates signal transduction by activating ADP-ribosylation factor 6.

Abbreviations: NCBI: National Center for Biotechnology Information; OMIM: Online Mendelian Inheritance of Man; COMT: Catechol-O-methyltransferase; SLC6A3: Solute carrier family 6 (neurotransmitter transporter, dopamine), member 3; DRD1: Dopamine receptor D1; DRD2: Dopamine receptor D2: Dopamine receptor D2; DRD4: Dopamine receptor D4; BDNF: Brain-derived neurotrophic factor; APOE: Apolipoprotein E; FOXP2:Forkhead box protein P2; CREB: cAMP responsive element binding protein 1; MTOR: mechanistic target of rapamycin kinase; SYNI: Synapsin 1; SYNII: Synapsis II; SYNIII: Synapsin III; PSD: Pleckstrin and Sec7 domain-containing.

that causes amino-acid substitution val to met amino acid at codon 66 (val-66met); this polymorphism has been identified to affect the activity-dependent secretion of BDNF. Depolarization-linked secretion of BDNF is impaired by the mutant 'met' containing isoform. The met-BDNF isoform is not delivered correctly into the secretory vesicle from the Golgi apparatus; but the polymorphism does not affect the protein functions (Egan et al., 2003). Egan et al. (2003) and Hariri et al. (2003) hypothesized that the rs6265val > met variant may affect human hippocampal function and memory. In analyzing the association of these polymorphisms with schizophrenic individuals in a case-control study, the met allele was shown to be associated with poorer episodic memory, a disruption of the normal hippocampal fMRI disengagement pattern during a working memory task, and lower hippocampal n-acetyl aspartate which is an intracellular marker of neuronal function (Egan et al., 2003). Additionally, studies by Hariri et al. (2003) demonstrated that met-BDNF isoform carriers exhibited reduced hippocampal involvement during both the encoding and retrieval of a spatial task and made significantly more recognition errors on this task than val/val homozygous individuals. However, this finding is controversial as it received support from the study by Dempster et al. (2005), but contradicted the study by Strauss et al. (2004).

The outcome of the study by Rybakowski et al. (2003) suggested that the performance of "met" containing isoform is poor than val/val homozygotes in PFC functions. This finding was supported by the recent study of Pezawas et al. (2004). The authors demonstrated that met-BDNF carriers exhibited age and gender-independent dorsolateral PFC gray matter regression and volume reductions. Pezawas et al. (2004) proposed that this variation in PFC morphology is at least partly the result of long-term BDNF-mediated effects on the developmental process and is not simply a reflection of transient val-66met moderated neurotransmitter fluctuations during memory formation. Tsai et al. (2004) showed that val/val homozygotes performed significantly better than carriers of the "met"-allele and the result contradicted the outcome of the study by Egan et al. (2003). Study on patients of Parkinson's disease by Foltynie et al. (2005) suggested that the met allele was associated with better performance by the patients, particularly in planning ability. The effect of the BDNF val66met polymorphism in Perkinson's disease may be due to complex interactions between BDNF secretion and degeneration of the nigro-striatal dopaminergic neurons which may result in a prefrontal-striatal dopamine imbalance (Foltynie et al., 2005).

In summary, studies on preclinical animal models suggest that BDNF protects neurons from damage incurred by any agent, plays a role in modulating synaptic connections, and modulates hippocampal long-term potential. Studies on human subjects have demonstrated that the "met"-allele is associated with lower hippocampal volume or functional output. Genetic analyses revealed the "val66met" polymorphic variant is associated with compromised performance in memory and "executive" function.

APOE (APOLIPOPROTEIN E)

The APOE gene (Apolipoprotein E) plays a critical role in lipid metabolism and is most widely studied for its involvement in neurodegenerative diseases, particularly Alzheimer's disease (AD). APOE protein is a major candidate for apoprotein of the chylomicron. It binds to a specific liver and peripheral cell receptor and is essential for the normal catabolism of triglyceride-rich lipoprotein constituents that are pivotal for neuronal functioning. APOE has been shown to modulate cognitive performance even in individuals It is increasingly recognized as a genetic modulator of cognitive function, including learning, memory, and potentially intuition. APOE plays a direct role in synaptic plasticity, which is essential for memory formation and retention. APOE influences brain regions such as the prefrontal cortex, hippocampus, and amygdala, which are involved in both cognitive and emotional processing. The APOE gene has three main alleles: ε2, ε3, and ε4, with the APOE ε4 variant being associated with an increased risk of cognitive decline and Alzheimer's disease. A meta-analysis by Small et al. (2004) analyzed multiple studies and found that APOE ε4 carriers exhibited greater cognitive decline with aging, particularly in episodic memory and learning. This suggests that APOE influences the cognitive systems underlying intuition, as intuitive judgments often rely on rapid memory recall and learning from past experiences.

Reiman et al. (2009) used functional MRI (fMRI) to examine how APOE ε4 influences brain activity in young adults before any symptoms of cognitive decline appear. They found that APOE ε4 carriers showed differences in brain activity in regions critical for cognition, including the hippocampus and posterior cingulate cortex, which are involved in intuitive and reflective thinking. Honea et al. (2009) found that APOE ε4 carriers showed reduced hippocampal volume and altered brain activation during memory tasks compared to non-carriers, even in healthy older adults. Filbey et al. (2006) demonstrated that APOE ε4 carriers showed altered brain activity in the prefrontal cortex during decision-making tasks, indicating impaired flexibility. In a longitudinal study by Corder et al. (1993), it was demonstrated that APOE ε4 carriers have a significantly higher risk of developing Alzheimer's disease, with earlier onset and more severe cognitive decline. The study followed patients over time and showed that ε4 carriers displayed earlier cognitive deficits related to memory, attention, and decision-making, all of which are important for intuitive processes.

APOE ε4 is less efficient in clearing amyloid-β, a protein that accumulates in Alzheimer's disease, leading to neurotoxicity and synaptic dysfunction. This negatively impacts regions like the hippocampus and prefrontal cortex, impairing memory and decision-making. APOE is involved in cholesterol transport, which is critical for maintaining neuronal membranes and supporting synaptic function. The ε4 variant is less efficient in these processes, leading to reduced synaptic plasticity, which underlies learning and intuition.

APOE ε4 is associated with increased neuroinflammation, which can accelerate cognitive decline. Chronic inflammation in brain areas like the hippocampus can impair the encoding and retrieval of memories, thus affecting both reflective and intuitive cognition.

FOXP2 (FORKHEAD BOX P2)

FOXP2 is most famous for its role in the development of speech and language. It regulates gene networks involved in neural pathways essential for controlling the fine motor skills required for speech, including coordination between the brain's motor cortex and the muscles used in vocalization. The gene is involved in the formation and regulation of neural circuits that allow for the precise coordination of movements, an ability crucial for both verbal and non-verbal communication. Beyond speech and motor control, FOXP2 is implicated in broader cognitive functions. It has been found to influence neural plasticity, allowing the brain to adapt and form new connections during learning. This suggests its involvement in other cognitive domains, such as learning, memory, and even decision-making processes. The gene is also involved in intuition and creative problem-solving. However, concrete experimental evidence directly linking FOXP2 to intuition or abstract thinking remains limited. Its influence on neural plasticity and cognitive adaptability hints at possible roles in these higher cognitive functions, but these areas are still being explored.

One of the most well-known pieces of evidence comes from studies of the KE family, where a mutation in the FOXP2 gene led to a specific language impairment. Affected family members showed difficulties in speech articulation and grammar use, confirming the gene's role in speech and language development (Lai et al., 2001). Individuals with FOXP2 mutations display developmental verbal dyspraxia, which is characterized by impaired coordination of speech muscles, alongside broader language deficits such as grammatical processing problems (Watkins et al., 2002). Knockout mice (with one or both copies of the FOXP2 gene removed) exhibit motor abnormalities, such as difficulties with learning new motor tasks. Transgenic mice carrying the human version of FOXP2 show increased ability in learning motor sequences, providing evidence for its role in motor learning (Konopka & Roberts, 2016). Genetic variants of FOXP2 result in altered activation of brain regions associated with language impairment as revealed by an MRI study (Pinel et al., 2012).

Neurotransmitters and signaling pathways

i **Dopamine:** Dopamine plays a crucial role in cognitive functions such as attention, working memory, and decision-making. The dopaminergic system (involving pathways like the mesocortical and mesolimbic pathways) is central to regulating reward, motivation, and intuitive judgments.

ii **Serotonin:** The **serotonergic system** is important for mood regulation, emotional processing, and cognition. Serotonin influences decision-making, especially in uncertain or ambiguous situations, which can affect intuition.

iii **Glutamate:** As the primary excitatory neurotransmitter, glutamate is involved in synaptic plasticity, learning, and memory formation. NMDA receptors (a type of glutamate receptor) are essential for long-term potentiation (LTP), a mechanism underlying learning and the formation of intuitive insights.

iv **Acetylcholine:** The cholinergic system, particularly involving nicotinic and muscarinic receptors, regulates attention, learning, and memory. Acetylcholine enhances cognitive flexibility, helping individuals make intuitive leaps based on incomplete information.

Transcription factors and signaling molecules

i **CREB (cAMP response element-binding protein):** CREB is a transcription factor that regulates the expression of genes involved in synaptic plasticity and memory consolidation. It plays a key role in cognitive functions, particularly in learning and the long-term storage of information, which is important for developing intuition. CREB is essential for long-term memory consolidation. When CREB is activated, it promotes the expression of genes that strengthen synapses, a process necessary for converting short-term memories into long-term ones. Studies in mice have shown that overexpression of CREB enhances memory, while its inhibition impairs memory formation. CREB plays a key role in synaptic plasticity, which is the ability of synapses (connections between neurons) to strengthen or weaken over time. This plasticity is the foundation of learning and adaptation. By regulating genes involved in neural growth and connectivity, CREB ensures that neurons can adapt and form new circuits in response to learning stimuli. Intuition often arises from unconscious learning and pattern recognition. CREB-mediated plasticity could enhance the brain's ability to process and recognize patterns based on previous experiences, making intuitive judgments more efficient. CREB is involved in regions such as the amygdala, which plays a critical role in emotional memory and responses. Emotional intuitions, like "gut feelings," may be facilitated by CREB-mediated synaptic changes in these regions.

ii **mTOR (mechanistic target of rapamycin):** mTOR is a central regulator of cell growth, proliferation, and synaptic plasticity. It has been implicated in learning and memory, particularly through its role in protein synthesis at synapses during memory formation. mTOR is pivotal in the formation of long-term memory by controlling protein synthesis at the synapse. It contributes to long-term potentiation (LTP), a process where synaptic connections are strengthened in response to learning. This is essential for memory consolidation, and studies have shown that impairments in mTOR signaling lead to deficits in both spatial and associative memory. The mTOR pathway regulates neurogenesis, particularly in the hippocampus, which is central to learning and memory. By modulating the growth and differentiation of neurons, mTOR supports the development of the neural circuits required for cognition. While intuition is less studied at a molecular level, mTOR's role in synaptic plasticity and neuronal connectivity could contribute to the brain's ability to form quick, unconscious decisions based on previous experiences. Intuition relies on the ability to rapidly process and integrate information, which may be enhanced by efficient mTOR-mediated synaptic modifications. The mTOR pathway is also involved in regions like the amygdala and prefrontal cortex, which are critical for emotional regulation and decision-making. Enhanced mTOR activity in these areas could support rapid emotional assessments and judgments often attributed to intuitive processes.

iii **Synaptic proteins (e.g., PSD-95, synapsin)**: Proteins involved in maintaining and modifying synaptic connections are crucial for cognitive processes. Synaptic plasticity, the ability to strengthen or weaken connections, is fundamental for learning and intuitive problem-solving. Synapsins are involved in synaptic vesicle trafficking, helping regulate the release of neurotransmitters at synapses, which is essential for synaptic plasticity. Plasticity is the ability of synapses to strengthen or weaken over time, a key mechanism underlying learning and memory. Studies have shown that the absence of synapsins leads to reduced synaptic plasticity, negatively impacting memory formation (Kao et al., 1999). Experimental models, particularly in synapsin knockout mice, demonstrate deficits in spatial learning and contextual fear memory. These mice exhibit impairments in long-term potentiation (LTP), a synaptic process crucial for memory encoding (Cesca et al., 2010). For instance, synapsin I and II are specifically linked to cognitive functions by controlling vesicle mobilization at presynaptic terminals, facilitating neurotransmitter release during heightened neuronal activity. Disruptions in synapsin expression are associated with cognitive disorders such as epilepsy, schizophrenia, and autism spectrum disorder (ASD).

Epigenetic modifications

i **DNA methylation:** DNA methylation, a process that involves adding a methyl group to DNA, can influence gene expression without altering the underlying genetic sequence. Changes in DNA methylation patterns can influence the expression of genes involved in cognition, memory, and emotion. Epigenetic changes regulate how environmental factors (like stress, education, and nutrition) shape cognitive abilities and intuitive decision-making. Su and Tsai (2012) discussed how DNA methylation changes can affect cognitive aging. The authors suggest that alterations in DNA methylation patterns can impact brain function and cognition over time, linking epigenetic modifications to cognitive processes like memory and learning.

ii **Histone modification:** Acetylation or methylation of histones can impact gene expression related to synaptic plasticity and neural connectivity, which affects learning and the development of intuition. Acetylation of histones has been associated with enhanced cognitive functions. A study by Ding et al. (2023) found that increased histone acetylation in the hippocampus (a critical region for memory) was linked to improved memory formation and deacetylation is associated with age-related memory loss. The methylation of histones also impacts cognition. A study by Mohd Murshid et al. (2022) demonstrated that specific histone methylation marks can influence synaptic plasticity, which is essential for learning and memory.

Neurotrophic factors

i **Neurotrophins (e.g., BDNF, NGF):** These are growth factors that promote the survival, development, and function of neurons. BDNF, in particular, is essential for synaptic plasticity, learning, and memory, which are all critical to cognitive function and the ability to make intuitive leaps based on prior experiences.

ii **IGF-1 (Insulin-like growth factor 1):** IGF-1 supports neural development and synaptic plasticity and has been shown to enhance cognitive functions such as memory retention and intuitive problem-solving.

Cognitive-related pathways

i **Wnt/β-catenin pathway:** Involved in neurogenesis and synaptic plasticity, the Wnt/β-catenin pathway is crucial for learning and memory. Disruptions in this pathway can impair cognitive flexibility and intuition. Support for this notion can be obtained from the studies focused on pharmacological intervention of neuropsychiatric and neurodegenerative disorders that involves correction of candidates from Wnt/β-catenin signaling system (Kang et al. 2023; Vallée, 2022; Wang et al. 2022)

ii **PI3K/AKT pathway:** This signaling pathway is essential for cell growth and survival, and it is involved in synaptic plasticity. It plays a role in memory formation, cognitive processing, and potentially in intuitive thinking. This signaling pathway is involved in Alzheimer's pathology (Abubakar et al., 2022). Several therapeutic studies on Alzheimer's disease and neuroinflammation showed upregulation of PI3K/AKT pathways that suggest the involvement of this signaling system in cognitive information processing at the molecular level (de Paiva et al. 2023).

Stress-related molecules

i **Cortisol (via the HPA axis)**: Chronic stress and elevated levels of cortisol can impair cognitive function, particularly working memory and decision-making, which are important for intuition. The hypothalamic-pituitary-adrenal (HPA) axis regulates cortisol release, influencing emotional and cognitive responses.

ii **CRH (corticotropin-releasing hormone)**: CRH plays a role in the body's response to stress, and its dysregulation can affect memory and cognition, potentially impacting the ability to rely on intuition in stressful situations.

Conclusion

Ultimately, the molecular and genetic foundations of cognition present a compelling narrative of how, at the molecular level, the very essence of what makes us human—the ability to think, reason, and remember—emerges from a dynamic interplay of genes, proteins, and neurons. Understanding this intricate biological orchestration is essential for unlocking the mysteries of the mind. In this chapter, we have explored the molecular underpinnings of cognition and intuition, shedding light on how biochemical processes shape our thoughts, behaviors, and decision-making abilities. Cognition, encompassing memory, learning, problem-solving, and perception, is heavily influenced by complex interactions at the molecular level, involving neurotransmitters, receptors, and signaling pathways. Similarly, intuition—often described as the ability to make judgments without conscious reasoning—also has a molecular basis that taps into the brain's extensive neural networks and the integration of sensory information.

When it comes to intuition, it is believed that the brain draws upon vast, implicit knowledge stored in neural circuits, including those within the basal ganglia and anterior insula, to make rapid, unconscious judgments. These neural networks facilitate pattern recognition and decision-making, often without the person being aware of the cognitive process at work. Recent studies suggest that intuition may be linked to the brain's ability to process and filter a wide range of information in parallel, thereby allowing for quick, seemingly instinctive conclusions (Dane & Pratt, 2007). Additionally, the role of emotion in cognition and intuition cannot be overlooked. Emotional responses, mediated by neuropeptides such as oxytocin and cortisol, can shape the way we process information and make decisions. For example, emotional signals may enhance intuition, guiding decision-making based on past experiences and learned associations (Bechara, 2004). As research progresses, we are likely to uncover more molecular details of how neural circuits integrate cognitive and intuitive processes. The advent of advanced technologies, such as optogenetics and advanced imaging techniques, will further illuminate the complex interplay between molecules and brain function, deepening our understanding of the molecular foundation of human cognition and intuition.

References

Abubakar, M. B., Sanusi, K. O., Ugusman, A., Mohamed, W., Kamal, H., Ibrahim, N. H., Khoo, C. S., & Kumar, J. (2022). Alzheimer's disease: An update and insights into pathophysiology. *Frontiers in Aging Neuroscience*, *14*(1), 742408. https://doi.org/10.3389/fnagi.2022.742408

Arnsten, A. F. T., Cai, J. X., Murphy, B. L., & Goldman-Rakic, P. S. (1994). Dopamine D1 receptor mechanisms in the cognitive performance of young adult and aged monkeys. *Psychopharmacology*, *116*(2), 143–151. https://doi.org/10.1007/bf02245056

Asghari, V., Sanyal, S., Buchwaldt, S., Paterson, A., Jovanovic, V., & Van Tol, H. H. (1995). Modulation of intracellular cyclic AMP levels by different human dopamine D4 receptor variants. *Journal of Neurochemistry*, *65*(3), 1157–1165. https://doi.org/10.1046/j.1471-4159.1995.65031157.x

Barton, R. A. (2012). Embodied cognitive evolution and the cerebellum. *Philosophical Transactions of the Royal Society B: Biological Sciences*, *367*(1599), 2097–2107.

Bechara, A. (2004). The role of emotion in decision-making: Evidence from neurological patients with orbitofrontal damage. *Brain and Cognition*, *55*(1), 30–40.

Benton, A. (1994). Neuropsychology: Past, present and future. In F. Boller, & J. Grafman (Eds.), *Handbook of Neuropsychology* (pp. 3–27). Elseiver Science.

Bilder, R. M., Goldman, R. S., Volavka, J., Czobor, P., Hoptman, M., Sheitman, B., Lindenmayer, J. P., Citrome, L., McEvoy, J., Kunz, M., Chakos, M., Cooper, T. B., Horowitz, T. L., & Lieberman, J. A. (2002). Neurocognitive effects of clozapine, olanzapine, risperidone, and haloperidol in patients with chronic schizophrenia or schizoaffective disorder. *The American Journal of Psychiatry*, *159*(6), 1018–1028. https://doi.org/10.1176/appi.ajp.159.6.1018

Bilder, R. M., Volavka, J., Lachman, H. M., & Grace, A. A. (2004). The catechol-O-methyltransferase polymorphism: Relations to the tonic-phasic dopamine hypothesis and neuropsychiatric phenotypes. *Neuropsychopharmacology: Official Publication of the American College of Neuropsychopharmacology*, *29*(11), 1943–1961. https://doi.org/10.1038/sj.npp.1300542

Brozoski, T. J., Brown, R. M., Rosvold, H. E., & Goldman, P. S. (1979). Cognitive deficit caused by regional depletion of dopamine in prefrontal cortex of rhesus monkey. *Science (New York, N.Y.)*, *205*(4409), 929–932. https://doi.org/10.1126/science.112679

Cesca, F., Baldelli, P., Valtorta, F., & Benfenati, F. (2010). The synapsins: Key actors of synapse function and plasticity. *Progress in Neurobiology*, *91*(4), 313–348. https://doi.org/10.1016/j.pneurobio.2010.04.006

Cools, R., & Robbins, T. W. (2004). Chemistry of the adaptive mind. *Philosophical Transactions. Series A, Mathematical, Physical, and Engineering Sciences*, *362*(1825), 2871–2888. https://doi.org/10.1098/rsta.2004.1468

Corder, E., Saunders, A., Strittmatter, W., Schmechel, D., Gaskell, P., Small, G., Roses, A., Haines, J., & Pericak-Vance, M. (1993). Gene dose of apolipoprotein E type 4 allele and the risk of Alzheimer's disease in late onset families. *Science*, *261*(5123), 921–923. https://doi.org/10.1126/science.8346443

D'Souza, U. M., Russ, C., Tahir, E., Mill, J., McGuffin, P., Asherson, P. J., & Craig, I. W. (2004). Functional effects of a tandem duplication polymorphism in the 5′flanking region of the DRD4 gene. *Biological Psychiatry*, *56*(9), 691–697. https://doi.org/10.1016/j.biopsych.2004.08.008

Dane, E., & Pratt, M. G. (2007). Exploring intuition and its role in managerial decision making. *Academy of Management Review*, *32*(1), 33–54.

de Paiva, I. H. R., da Silva, R. S., Mendonça, I. P., Duarte-Silva, E., Botelho de Souza, J. R., & Peixoto, C. A. (2023). Fructooligosaccharide (FOS) and Galactooligosaccharide (GOS) Improve neuroinflammation and cognition by up-regulating IRS/PI3K/AKT signaling pathway in diet-induced obese mice. *Journal of Neuroimmune Pharmacology*, *18*(3), 427–447. https://doi.org/10.1007/s11481-023-10069-8

Dempster, E., Toulopoulou, T., McDonald, C., Bramon, E., Walshe, M., Filbey, F., Wickham, H., Sham, P. C., Murray, R. M., & Collier, D. A. (2005). Association between BDNF val66 met genotype and episodic memory. *American Journal of Medical Genetics: Part B, Neuropsychiatric Genetics: The Official Publication of the International Society of Psychiatric Genetics*, *134B*(1), 73–75. https://doi.org/10.1002/ajmg.b.30150

Deutch, A. Y., & Roth, R. H. (1999). Neurochemical systems in the central nervous system. In D. S. Charney, E. J. Nestler, & B. S. Bunney. (Eds.), *Neurobiology of Mental Illness*. Oxford University Press. https://doi.org/10.1093/med/9780199798261.003.0002

DiMaio, S., Grizenko, N., & Joober, R. (2003). Dopamine genes and attention-deficit hyperactivity disorder: A review. *Journal of Psychiatry & Neuroscience: JPN*, *28*(1), 27–38.

Ding, Y., Liu, C., & Zhang, Y. (2023). Aging-related histone modification changes in brain function. *Ibrain*, *9*(2), 205–213. https://doi.org/10.1002/ibra.12106

Ding, Y. C., Chi, H. C., Grady, D. L., Morishima, A., Kidd, J. R., Kidd, K. K., Flodman, P., Spence, M. A., Schuck, S., Swanson, J. M., Zhang, Y. P., & Moyzis, R. K. (2002). Evidence of positive selection acting at the human dopamine receptor D4 gene locus. *Proceedings of the National Academy of Sciences of the United States of America*, *99*(1), 309–314. https://doi.org/10.1073/pnas.012464099

Duan, W., Guo, Z., Jiang, H., Ware, M., & Mattson, M. P. (2003). Reversal of behavioral and metabolic abnormalities, and insulin resistance syndrome, by dietary restriction in mice deficient in brain-derived neurotrophic factor. *Endocrinology*, *144*(6), 2446–2453. https://doi.org/10.1210/en.2002-0113

Egan, M. F., Goldberg, T. E., Kolachana, B. S., Callicott, J. H., Mazzanti, C. M., Straub, R. E., Goldman, D., & Weinberger, D. R. (2001). Effect of COMT Val108/158 Met genotype on frontal lobe function and risk for schizophrenia. *Proceedings of the National Academy of Sciences of the United States of America*, *98*(12), 6917–6922. https://doi.org/10.1073/pnas.111134598

Egan, M. F., Kojima, M., Callicott, J. H., Goldberg, T. E., Kolachana, B. S., Bertolino, A., Zaitsev, E., Gold, B., Goldman, D., Dean, M., Lu, B., & Weinberger, D. R. (2003). The BDNF val66met polymorphism affects activity-dependent secretion of BDNF and human memory and hippocampal function. *Cell*, *112*(2), 257–269. https://doi.org/10.1016/s0092-8674(03)00035-7

El-Ghundi, M., Fletcher, P. J., Drago, J., Sibley, D. R., O'Dowd, B. F., & George, S. R. (1999). Spatial learning deficit in dopamine D (1) receptor knockout mice. *European Journal of Pharmacology*, *383*(2), 95–106. https://doi.org/10.1016/s0014-2999(99)00573-7

Enard, W. (2011). FOXP2 and the role of cortico-basal ganglia circuits in speech and language evolution. *Current Opinion in Neurobiology*, *21*(3), 415–424. https://doi.org/10.1016/j.conb.2011.04.008

Enard, W., Gehre, S., Hammerschmidt, K., Hölter, S. M., Blass, T., Somel, M., Brückner, M. K., Schreiweis, C., Winter, C., Sohr, R., Becker, L., Wiebe, V., Nickel, B., Giger, T., Müller, U., Groszer, M., Adler, T., Aguilar, A., Bolle, I., & Calzada-Wack, J. (2009). A humanized version of foxp2 affects cortico-basal ganglia circuits in mice. *Cell*, *137*(5), 961–971. https://doi.org/10.1016/j.cell.2009.03.041

Enard, W., Przeworski, M., Fisher, S. E., Lai, C. S. L., Wiebe, V., Kitano, T., Monaco, A. P., & Pääbo, S. (2002). Molecular evolution of FOXP2, a gene involved in speech and language. *Nature*, *418*(6900), 869–872. https://doi.org/10.1038/nature01025

Filbey, F. M., Slack, K. J., Sunderland, T. P., & Cohen, R. M. (2006). Functional magnetic resonance imaging and magnetoencephalography differences associated with APOEepsilon4 in young healthy adults. *Neuroreport*, *17*(15), 1585–1590. https://doi.org/10.1097/01.wnr.0000234745.27571.d1

Fitch, W. T. (2009). The biology & evolution of language: "Deep homology" and the evolution of innovation. In M. S. Gazzaniga (Ed.), *The Cognitive Neurosciences* (Vol. IV, pp. 873–885). MIT Press.

Foltynie, T., Lewis, S. J., Goldberg, T. E., Blackwell, A. D., Kolachana, B. S., Weinberger, D. R., Robbins, T. W., & Barker, R. A. (2005). The BDNF Val66Met polymorphism has a gender specific influence on planning ability in Parkinson's disease. *Journal of Neurology*, *252*, 833–838.

Fossella, J., Sommer, T., Fan, J., Wu, Y., Swanson, J. M., Pfaff, D. W., & Posner, M. I. (2002). Assessing the molecular genetics of attention networks. *BMC Neuroscience*, *3*, 14. https://doi.org/10.1186/1471-2202-3-14

Goldberg, M. E., Gorn, G. J., Peracchio, L. A., & Bamossy, G. (2003). Understanding materialism among youth. *Journal of Consumer Psychology*, *13*(3), 278–288. https://doi.org/10.1207/s15327663jcp1303_09

Goldman-Rakic, P. S. (1995). Cellular basis of working memory. *Neuron*, *14*(3), 477–485. https://doi.org/10.1016/0896-6273(95)90304-6

Grace, A. A. (2000). The dopamine system and its role in cognitive function. *Neuropsychopharmacology*, *23*(1), 1–6.

Graham, S. A., & Fisher, S. E. (2015). Understanding language from a genomic perspective. *Annual Review of Genetics*, *49*(1), 131–160. https://doi.org/10.1146/annurev-genet-120213-092236

Hariri, A. R., Goldberg, T. E., Mattay, V. S., Kolachana, B. S., Callicott, J. H., Egan, M. F., & Weinberger, D. R. (2003). Brain-derived neurotrophic factor val66met polymorphism affects human memory-related hippocampal activity and predicts memory performance. *The Journal of Neuroscience: The Official Journal of the Society for Neuroscience*, *23*(17), 6690–6694. https://doi.org/10.1523/JNEUROSCI.23-17-06690.2003

Hauser M. D., Chomsky N., & Fitch W. T. (2002). The faculty of language: What is it, who has it, and how did it evolve? *Science*, *298*, 1569–1579. https://doi.org/10.1126/science.298.5598.1569

Hirvonen, M., Laakso, A., Någren, K., Rinne, J. O., Pohjalainen, T., & Hietala, J. (2004). C957T polymorphism of the dopamine D2 receptor (DRD2) gene affects striatal DRD2 availability in vivo. *Molecular Psychiatry*, *9*(12), 1060–1061. https://doi.org/10.1038/sj.mp.4001561

Honea, R. A., Vidoni, E., Harsha, A., & Burns, J. M. (2009). Impact of APOE on the healthy aging brain: A voxel-based MRI and DTI study. *Journal of Alzheimer's Disease: JAD*, *18*(3), 553–564. https://doi.org/10.3233/JAD-2009-1163, http://mitpress.mit.edu/catalog/item/default.asp?ttype=2&tid=11998

Jiang, X., Xu, K., Hoberman, J., Tian, F., Marko, A. J., Waheed, J. F., Harris, C. R., Marini, A. M., Enoch, M. A., & Lipsky, R. H. (2005). BDNF variation and mood disorders: A novel functional promoter polymorphism and Val66Met are associated with anxiety but have opposing effects. *Neuropsychopharmacology: Official Publication of the American College of Neuropsychopharmacology*, *30*(7), 1353–1361. https://doi.org/10.1038/sj.npp.1300703

Joober, R. (2002). Catechol-O-methyltransferase val-108/158-met gene variants associated with performance on the Wisconsin Card Sorting Test. *Archives of General Psychiatry*, *59*(7), 662–663. https://doi.org/10.1001/archpsyc.59.7.662

Kandel, E. R. (2006). *In Search of Memory: The Emergence of a New Science of Mind*. W.W. Norton & Company.

Kang, X., Wang, D., Zhang, L., Huang, T., Liu, S., Feng, X., Guo, Y., Zhang, Z., Wang, Z., Ren, H., & Yuan, G. (2023). Exendin-4 ameliorates tau hyperphosphorylation and cognitive impairment in type 2 diabetes through acting on Wnt/β-catenin/NeuroD1 pathway. *Molecular Medicine*, *29*(1). https://doi.org/10.1186/s10020-023-00718-2

Kao, H. T., et al. 1999. Synapsin facilitates GABA transmission in the hippocampus. *Journal of Neuroscience*, *19*(13), 4918–4927.

Karalija, N., Papenberg, G., Wåhlin, A., Johansson, J., Andersson, M., Axelsson, J., Riklund, K., Lindenberger, U., Nyberg, L., & Bäckman, L. (2021). Sex differences in dopamine integrity and brain structure among healthy older adults: Relationships to episodic memory. *Neurobiology of Aging*, *105*, 272–279. https://doi.org/10.1016/j.neurobiolaging.2021.04.022

Kimberg, D. Y., D'Esposito, M., & Farah, M. J. (1997). Effects of bromocriptine on human subjects depend on working memory capacity. *Neuroreport*, *8*(16), 3581–3585. https://doi.org/10.1097/00001756-199711100-00032

Konopka, G., & Roberts, T. F. (2016). Insights into the neural and genetic basis of vocal communication. *Cell*, *164*(6), 1269–1276. https://doi.org/10.1016/j.cell.2016.02.039

Kotecha, S. A., Oak, J. N., Jackson, M. F., Perez, Y., Orser, B. A., Van Tol, H. H. M., & MacDonald, J. F. (2002). A D2 class dopamine receptor transactivates a receptor tyrosine kinase to inhibit NMDA receptor transmission. *Neuron*, *35*(6), 1111–1122. https://doi.org/10.1016/s0896-6273(02)00859-0

Kurzweil, R. (2012). *How to Create a Mind: The Secret of Human Thought Revealed*. Viking.

Kustanovich, V., Ishii, J., Crawford, L., Yang, M., McGough, J. J., McCracken, J. T., Smalley, S. L., & Nelson, S. F. (2004). Transmission disequilibrium testing of dopamine-related candidate gene polymorphisms in ADHD: Confirmation of association of ADHD with DRD4 and DRD5. *Molecular Psychiatry*, *9*(7), 711–717. https://doi.org/10.1038/sj.mp.4001466

Lai, C. S., Fisher, S. E., Hurst, J. A., Vargha-Khadem, F., & Monaco, A. P. (2001). A forkhead-domain gene is mutated in a severe speech and language disorder. *Nature*, *413*(6855), 519–523. https://doi.org/10.1038/35097076

Langley, A. K., Bergman, R. L., McCracken, J., & Piacentini, J. C. (2004). Impairment in childhood anxiety disorders: Preliminary examination of the child anxiety impact scale-parent version. *Journal of Child and Adolescent Psychopharmacology*, *14*(1), 105–114. https://doi.org/10.1089/104454604773840544

Lidow, M. S., Goldman-Rakic, P. S., Gallager, D. W., & Rakic, P. (1991). Distribution of dopaminergic receptors in the primate cerebral cortex: Quantitative autoradiographic analysis using [3H]raclopride, [3H]spiperone and [3H]SCH23390. *Neuroscience*, *40*(3), 657–671. https://doi.org/10.1016/0306-4522(91)90003-7

Luciana, M., & Nelson, C. A. (1998). The functional emergence of prefrontally-guided working memory systems in four- to eight-year-old children. *Neuropsychologia*, *36*(3), 273–293. https://doi.org/10.1016/s0028-3932(97)00109-7

Malenka, R. C., & Bear, M. F. (2004). LTP and LTD: An embarrassment of riches. *Neuron*, *44*(1), 5–21.

Manor, I., Tyano, S., Mel, E., Eisenberg, J., Bachner-Melman, R., Kotler, M., & Ebstein, R. P. (2002). Family-based and association studies of monoamine oxidase A and attention deficit hyperactivity disorder (ADHD): Preferential transmission of the long promoter-region repeat and its association with impaired performance on a continuous performance test (TOVA). *Molecular Psychiatry*, *7*(6), 626–632. https://doi.org/10.1038/sj.mp.4001037

Mattay, V. S., Callicott, J. H., Bertolino, A., Heaton, I., Frank, J. A., Coppola, R., Berman, K. F., Goldberg, T. E., & Weinberger, D. R. (2000). Effects of dextroamphetamine on cognitive performance and cortical activation. *NeuroImage*, *12*(3), 268–275. https://doi.org/10.1006/nimg.2000.0610

Mattay, V. S., Fera, F., Tessitore, A., Hariri, A. R., Das, S., Callicott, J. H., & Weinberger, D. R. (2002). Neurophysiological correlates of age-related changes in human motor function. *Neurology*, *58*(4), 630–635. https://doi.org/10.1212/wnl.58.4.630

McEwen, B. S. (2002). *The End of Stress As We Know It*. Joseph Henry Press.

Mehta, A. D., Rock, R. S., Rief, M., Spudich, J. A., Mooseker, M. S., & Cheney, R. E. (1999). Myosin-V is a processive actin-based motor. *Nature*, *400*(6744), 590–593. https://doi.org/10.1038/23072

Mehta, M. A., Manes, F. F., Magnolfi, G., Sahakian, B. J., & Robbins, T. W. (2004). Impaired set-shifting and dissociable effects on tests of spatial working memory following the dopamine D2 receptor antagonist sulpiride in human volunteers. *Psychopharmacology*, *176*(3–4), 331–342. https://doi.org/10.1007/s00213-004-1899-2

Mohd Murshid, N., Aminullah Lubis, F., & Makpol, S. (2022). Epigenetic changes and its intervention in age-related neurodegenerative diseases. *Cellular and Molecular Neurobiology*, *42*(3), 577–595. https://doi.org/10.1007/s10571-020-00979-z

Mukherjee, S. (2016). *The Gene: An Intimate History*. Scribner.

Noble, E. P. (2000). The DRD2 gene in psychiatric and neurological disorders and its phenotypes. *Pharmacogenomics*, *1*(3), 309–333. https://doi.org/10.1517/14622416.1.3.309

Ogawa, L. M., & Vallender, E. J. (2014). Evolutionary conservation in genes underlying human psychiatric disorders. *Frontiers in human neuroscience*, *8*, 283. https://doi.org/10.3389/fnhum.2014.00283

Okuyama, Y., Ishiguro, H., Toru, M., & Arinami, T. (1999). A genetic polymorphism in the promoter region of DRD4 associated with expression and schizophrenia. *Biochemical and Biophysical Research Communications*, *258*(2), 292–295. https://doi.org/10.1006/bbrc.1999.0630

Pezawas, L., Verchinski, B. A., Mattay, V. S., Callicott, J. H., Kolachana, B. S., Straub, R. E., Egan, M. F., Meyer-Lindenberg, A., & Weinberger, D. R. (2004). The brain-derived neurotrophic factor val66met polymorphism and variation in human cortical morphology. *The Journal of Neuroscience: The Official Journal of the Society for Neuroscience*, *24*(45), 10099–10102. https://doi.org/10.1523/JNEUROSCI.2680-04.2004

Pinel, P., Fauchereau, F., Moreno, A., Barbot, A., Lathrop, M., Zelenika, D., Le Bihan, D., Poline, J. B., Bourgeron, T., & Dehaene, S. (2012). Genetic variants of FOXP2 and KIAA0319/TTRAP/THEM2 locus are associated with altered brain activation in distinct language-related regions. *The Journal of Neuroscience: The Official Journal of the Society for Neuroscience*, *32*(3), 817–825. https://doi.org/10.1523/JNEUROSCI.5996-10.2012

Pohjalainen, T., Rinne, J. O., Någren, K., Lehikoinen, P., Anttila, K., Syvälahti, E. K., & Hietala, J. (1998). The A1 allele of the human D2 dopamine receptor gene predicts low D2 receptor availability in healthy volunteers. *Molecular Psychiatry*, *3*(3), 256–260. https://doi.org/10.1038/sj.mp.4000350

Previc, F. H. (1999). Dopamine and the origins of human intelligence. *Brain and Cognition*, *41*(3), 299–350. https://doi.org/10.1006/brcg.1999.1129

Raghanti, M. A., Edler, M. K., Stephenson, A. R., Wilson, L. J., Hopkins, W. D., Ely, J. J., Erwin, J. M., Jacobs, B., Hof, P. R., & Sherwood, C. C. (2016). Human-specific increase of dopaminergic innervation in a striatal region associated with speech and language: A comparative analysis of the primate basal ganglia. *The Journal of Comparative Neurology*, *524*(10), 2117–2129. https://doi.org/10.1002/cne.23937

Reiman, E. M., Chen, K., Liu, X., Bandy, D., Yu, M., Lee, W., Ayutyanont, N., Keppler, J., Reeder, S. A., Langbaum, J. B. S., Alexander, G. E., Klunk, W. E., Mathis, C. A., Price, J. C., Aizenstein, H. J., DeKosky, S. T., & Caselli, R. J. (2009). Fibrillar amyloid-burden in cognitively normal people at 3 levels of genetic risk for Alzheimer's disease. *Proceedings of the National Academy of Sciences*, *106*(16), 6820–6825. https://doi.org/10.1073/pnas.0900345106

Reimers-Kipping, S., Hevers, W., Pääbo, S., & Enard, W. (2011). Humanized Foxp2 specifically affects cortico-basal ganglia circuits. *Neuroscience*, *175*, 75–84. https://doi.org/10.1016/j.neuroscience.2010.11.042

Remy, P., & Samson, Y. (2003). The role of dopamine in cognition. *Current Opinion in Neurology*, *16*. https://doi.org/10.1097/00019052-200312002-00007

Rybakowski, J. K., Borkowska, A., Czerski, P. M., Skibińska, M., & Hauser, J. (2003). Polymorphism of the brain-derived neurotrophic factor gene and performance on a cognitive prefrontal test in bipolar patients. *Bipolar Disorders*, *5*(6), 468–472.

Schreiweis, C., Bornschein, U., Burguière, E., Kerimoglu, C., Schreiter, S., Dannemann, M., Goyal, S., Rea, E., French, C. A., Puliyadi, R., Groszer, M., Fisher, S. E., Mundry, R., Winter, C., Hevers, W., Pääbo, S., Enard, W., & Graybiel, A. M. (2014). Humanized Foxp2 accelerates learning by enhancing transitions from declarative to procedural performance. *Proceedings of the National Academy of Sciences of the United States of America*, *111*(39), 14253–14258. https://doi.org/10.1073/pnas.1414542111

Small, B. J., Rosnick, C. B., Fratiglioni, L., & Bäckman, L. (2004). Apolipoprotein E and cognitive performance: A meta-analysis. *Psychology and Aging*, *19*(4), 592–600. https://doi.org/10.1037/0882-7974.19.4.592

Sterelny, K. (2007). Social intelligence, human intelligence and niche construction. *Philosophical Transactions of the Royal Society of London. Series B, Biological Sciences*, *362*(1480), 719–730. https://doi.org/10.1098/rstb.2006.2006

Sterelny, K. (2011). From hominins to humans: How sapiens became behaviourally modern. *Philosophical Transactions of the Royal Society of London. Series B, Biological Sciences*, *366*(1566), 809–822. https://doi.org/10.1098/rstb.2010.0301

Sterelny, K. (2012). Language, gesture, skill: The coevolutionary foundations of language. *Philosophical Transactions of the Royal Society of London. Series B, Biological Sciences*, *367*, 2141–2151 https://doi.org/10.1098/rstb.2012.0116

Strauss, J., Barr, C. L., George, C. J., Ryan, C. M., King, N., Shaikh, S., Kovacs, M., & Kennedy, J. L. (2004). BDNF and COMT polymorphisms: Relation to memory phenotypes in young adults with childhood-onset mood disorder. *NeuroMolecular Medicine*, *5*(3), 181–192. https://doi.org/10.1385/nmm:5:3:181

Su, S. C., & Tsai, L.-H. (2012). DNA methylation in cognition comes of age. *Nature Neuroscience*, *15*(8), 1061–1062. https://doi.org/10.1038/nn.3169

Swanson, J. M., Flodman, P., Kennedy, J., Spence, M. A., Moyzis, R., Schuck, S., Murias, M., Moriarity, J., Barr, C., Smith, M., & Posner, M. (2000). Dopamine genes and ADHD. *Neuroscience and Biobehavioral Reviews*, *24*(1), 21–25. https://doi.org/10.1016/s0149-7634(99)00062-7

Tsai, G., Lane, H. Y., Yang, P., Chong, M. Y., & Lange, N. (2004). Glycine transporter I inhibitor, N-methylglycine (sarcosine), added to antipsychotics for the treatment of schizophrenia. *Biological Psychiatry*, *55*(5), 452–456. https://doi.org/10.1016/j.biopsych.2003.09.012

Vallée, A. (2022). Neuroinflammation in schizophrenia: The key role of the WNT/β-Catenin Pathway. *International Journal of Molecular Sciences*, *23*(5), 2810. https://doi.org/10.3390/ijms23052810

Vargha-Khadem, F., Gadian, D. G., Copp, A., & Mishkin, M. (2005). FOXP2 and the neuroanatomy of speech and language. *Nature Reviews. Neuroscience*, *6*(2), 131–138. https://doi.org/10.1038/nrn1605

Wang, Q., Huang, X., Su, Y., Yin, G., Wang, S., Yu, B., Li, H., Qi, J., Chen, H., Zeng, W., Zhang, K., Verkhratsky, A., Niu, J., & Yi, C. (2022). Activation of Wnt/β-catenin pathway mitigates blood–brain barrier dysfunction in Alzheimer's disease. *Brain*, *145*(12), 4474–4488. https://doi.org/10.1093/brain/awac236

Wang, X., Zhong, P., & Yan, Z. (2002). Dopamine D4 receptors modulate GABAergic signaling in pyramidal neurons of prefrontal cortex. *The Journal of Neuroscience: The Official Journal of the Society for Neuroscience*, *22*(21), 9185–9193. https://doi.org/10.1523/JNEUROSCI.22-21-09185.2002

Watkins, C. E., Jr. (2011). Does psychotherapy supervision contribute to patient outcomes? Considering thirty years of research. *The Clinical Supervisor*, *30*(2), 235–256. https://doi.org/10.1080/07325223.2011.619417

Watkins, K. E., Dronkers, N. F., & Vargha-Khadem, F. (2002). Behavioural analysis of an inherited speech and language disorder: Comparison with acquired aphasia. *Brain*, *125*,452–464.

Weinberger, D. R., Egan, M. F., Bertolino, A., Callicott, J. H., Mattay, V. S., Lipska, B. K., Berman, K. F., & Goldberg, T. E. (2001). Prefrontal neurons and the genetics of schizophrenia. *Biological Psychiatry*, *50*(11), 825–844. https://doi.org/10.1016/s0006-3223(01)01252-5

Winterer, G., & Weinberger, D. R. (2004). Genes, dopamine and cortical signal-to-noise ratio in schizophrenia. *Trends in Neurosciences*, *27*(11), 683–690. https://doi.org/10.1016/j.tins.2004.08.002

Zhang, J., Webb, D. M., & Podlaha, O. (2002). Accelerated protein evolution and origins of human-specific features: FOXP2 as an example. *Genetics*, *162*(4), 1825–1835. https://doi.org/10.1093/genetics/162.4.1825

Part II

Intuitive Cognition, Aesthetics and Culture

Chapter 5

Understanding the social brain

Social cognition and neuropsychology interface

Deepak Kumar Salvi, Ravikesh Tripathi and Poonam Joshi

Introduction

The social world forms an integral part of our life. Our social communication often involves processing multiple informations, which could be subtle, complex, or contradictory in nature. Effective processing of social information depends on the integrity of several basic and complex socio-cognitive abilities, such as face processing, making inferences about others' intentions, imputing beliefs and emotions, understanding social context (norms, rules, and roles), and synthesizing multiple information to guide our behaviors and decision-making. These social cognitive and intuitive processes are collectively termed social intuition which helps us to understand the world around us (Lieberman, 2000).

In today's world, the increasing complexity of the social environment not only provides more exposure to diverse social interactions but creates increased complexity in the immediate decision-making process as well. Surprisingly, nowadays humans are increasingly experiencing a state of confusion in some of these situations while implying established conscious rational tactics for making decisions. Social intuition in any social situation generally involves the immediate processing and decision-making about the underlying intentions, beliefs, and emotions of people (Lieberman, 2000). As compared to the intuition concept, social cognition has been widely studied in social psychology research (Heider & Simmel, 1994) and recently received growing interest in the fields of clinical psychology, psychiatry, and neuroscience. During the last two decades, social cognition has been a dominant theme in clinical neuropsychological practice and research. The literature was gathered from PubMed using the term social cognition between the period 2000 and 2021. This initial search identified a total of 36,790 articles and the year 2021 witnessed the highest number of publications on social cognition. Our review of the literature found various components of social cognition in which four domains have been identified as the most researched domains and their descriptions are as follows;

DOI: 10.4324/9781003377757-7

Theory of mind (ToM)

ToM also known as perspective taking, mind reading and mentalization is conceptualized as an ability to understand the mental state of an individual and make predictions and explanations of his or her social behavior on the basis of these mental states (Astington, 1991). Premack and Woodruff (1978) first used the term ToM, mentioning the ability to ascribe mental states to self and others, including intentions, knowledge and desires, and beliefs facilitating the prediction of behaviors.

A division made by Dennis et al. (2013) suggests three divisions of ToM: (i) Cognitive ToM—Concerns with Cognitive mental states like false belief and perspective taking about other person's belief and motivation, (ii) Affective ToM—Concerns with affective mental states like the inference related to feelings, facial emotion expression, and emotive communication (how we want others to perceive one's emotions), and (iii) Conative ToM—Concerns with social communication where one person exerts influence on other's behavior, like, giving ironic criticism or empathic praise. This ToM plays an essential and fundamental role in many social and communicative interactions, allowing successful and mutual exchanges of information between individuals, and is considered critical for quality social relationships (Carpandale & Lewis, 2004; Hamilton, 2009; Ahmed & Miller, 2011).

Emotional processing

Emotional processing, also called emotion perception and emotion recognition is the ability of an individual to perceive, recognize, and manage emotional information (Green et al., 2008). Emotional processing has long been a topic of discourse in psychological literature. Emotion has several components such as behavioral, expressive, subjective/experiential, physiological, and cognitive, and these components of emotion work in relative synchrony (Kring & Bachorowski, 1999). Emotions are crucial for our survival and subserve a number of adaptive organizational and motivational functions in our lives (Izard, 2009). They attach a valence to our daily experiences and influence our overall perception and behavior. It is argued that effective emotional processing enables a person to perceive and regulate emotions in order to achieve a range of adaptive and successful outcomes.

Attributional style/bias

Attributional style is believed to represent a style also known as explanatory style in which naturally occurring events are attributed and can be classified into three fundamental causal inferences along the dimensions of Internal vs external, stable vs unstable, and global vs specific causes (Kelley & Michela, 1980; Abramson et al., 1978). Hence, an attribution style can be defined as a tendency of a person to infer a specific type of causal explanation to uncontrollable/controllable life events.

Social perception

Making an accurate sense of the social environment is the key process of social cognition in which social perception plays a vital role in the process of understanding social cues. Social perception is considered to be the initial stage of the social cognitive process, including the evaluation of the intentions of others through their actions (Allison et al., 2000). It is an ability to recognize human actions in complex patterns of social interactions and make appropriate inferences about people's verbal and non-verbal behavior, including social rules, roles, and goals. Hence, in order to identify the complex social situation, it also includes social understanding or knowledge of social norms, roles, and context across social interactions and situations. Social perception may be divided into two main subdomains, that is face perception and voice perception (Green et al., 2015). The first category as the name suggests is the ability of a person to figure out affective information about people's facial expressions. On the other hand, the latter involves the ability to recognize and discriminate between the various underlying acoustic properties or meanings of speech and the corresponding affective content. However, both classification commonly involves a person's ability to figure out others' emotional cues either through facial or vocal tones.

The query emerges as to how the implicit process affects social cognition, which is a conscious interaction between two social agents. Considering the TOM, all three components of TOM as stated above, are the bases of taking others' perspectives and maintaining meaningful interaction. Thus, any social interaction needs immediate dynamic reciprocation keeping pace with the dynamic demand of the environment. Appropriate or inappropriate response to a given social situation determines one's adaptivity to that situation which usually ends there. This characteristic of a social situation demands an immediate response with all its cognitive, affective, and conative aspects. Here comes the importance of intuition, an underlying implicit process.

Considering emotional processing, in a study by Bolte et al. (2003), it was found that positive emotions produce better intuitive judgement and negative emotion creates a detrimental effect on intuitive coherence. Person in positive mood connects the close associates or cues in guessing an event in a better way due the better spreading of activation. According to this theory (Anderson, 1983), we can think of some ideas more easily than others in a certain situation because our environment on the basis of emotional relevance triggers ideas closer in our existing "network" map in our brain. As a result, the ideas that are more available to us will be thought of faster. Sensing and intuiting is an attributional style, where people try to find out the causal relationship between events on the basis of current information or matching the possibilities with the current data (Jung, 1961; Manley, 2016). Intuitive being prefers looking into a situation with all its future possibilities gives a direction toward diagnostic research. In this study, the intuitive made more causal attributions in identifying a system malfunction indicating the role of intuition in attribution (Boreham, 1987). It may help in identifying the intention of a behavior which is the prerequisite of intuitive process.

People have a popular notion about intuition which is an irrational automatic response as it arises in the mind of a person. However, the primary pre-condition of intuition is pre-existing knowledge and experience. Intuitive knowledge matures in the prepared mind. In intuition, relevant aspects of implicit knowledge are combined together to reach a decision. Inferences when not knowledge-based, cannot be claimed as intuition. In intuition, underlying cognitive processing is based on widespread implicit knowledge though it is not acquired on purpose.

Thus it is obvious when an individual takes others' perceptions, feeling the emotional cues from any interaction, it can be understood, felt, and responded, to based on the matching of the present pattern of interaction with a given person in the context of an existing pattern. As we respond based on our existing sets of related schema, we construct our reality. This schemata is widespread in our brains and has been explained by different models of parallel distributed processing(Rumelhart, 1984). According to this theory, people process information in a parallel fashion, matching the present experience with a previously laid down pattern of related experience, and adding new information to it enriching the existing node or creating a new node of the network. For instance, when we are meeting a new person, our brain starts processing all the cues and assimilates the cues with existing information from that point in time. This unconscious processing is assumed to take place to weave all the emotional, nonverbal, and verbal expressions coming from another person in one trajectory. Thereafter, the concerned individual at the end senses some holistic idea about the other person and predicts some of the personality traits and emotional state of the other. Therefore, the theory in any interaction comes to mind with this unconscious intuitive processing.

Social cognition and intuition

Both explicit and implicit processes are believed to coordinate various types of social learning and related intuition. Social cognition represents how we make sense of others and ourselves (Fiske & Taylor, 2013). According to Brothers (1990), social cognition is the processing of any information, which facilitates the accurate perception of the dispositions and intentions of other individuals. Social cognition is defined as "the ability to construct representations of the relations between oneself and others and to use those representations flexibly to guide social behavior" (Adolphs, 2001, p. 231). The content of representation is always social in nature; this is why social cognition is described as "people thinking about peoples" (Green et al., 2005). In a recent review, Happé et al. (2017) defined social cognition "as the processing of stimuli relevant to understanding agents and their interactions."

With respect to information processing in the social world, intuition has increasingly emerged as a higher socio-cognitive function (McCrea, 2010). It has long been observed that beyond the fundamental skills for being aware of our social environment, there seem to be some additional cognitive abilities, which are assumed to be connected to our perception of the social world. In this regard, intuition can be understood as a subjective experience of mostly non-conscious information process and hence becoming an interesting topic in the area of social cognitive neuroscience (Hodgkinson et al., 2008; Lieberman, 2000). Intuition is considered to be an intrinsic aspect of our social concepts and collective mind (McCrea, 2010). Furthermore, intuition tends to occur promptly, which is assumed to precede conscious social reasoning and insight. However, there seems to be a difference between intuition and social cognitive processes in which intuition is considered a part of implicit memory, whereas social cognition is related to explicit memory. Additionally, social cognition involves a conscious thinking process whereas intuition reflects unconscious processing and hence the blend of these two processes of the collective mind is thought to emerge as a higher process of social cognition. Keeping in view the intriguing nature of the cognitive process, implicit learning and memory processes are considered the socio-cognitive element of intuition (Lieberman, 2000), which involves encoding and decoding in everyday interactions and is termed social intuition. For example, when people sometimes accurately promptly evaluate the emotions, personality, intentions, and attitudes of another person without utilizing any social logic, this may be explained in terms of the complex interplay of the social perception process without having full conscious awareness (Lewicki et al., 1992). According to Lieberman (2000), in our social surroundings various forms of nonverbal cues, including body postures, gestures, and even subtle facial expressions can ignite social intuitive processes and can form the basis of our intuitions. He further referred to this process as the "learning of nonverbal decoding." Intuitive thinking has a link with the emotional process, which is generally manifested via nonverbal communication, and thus, gestures are considered to be the main expressway of intuition and social cognition (Lieberman, 2000). There is growing evidence about the existence of a core network of social cognition and intuition. It should be highlighted that variability in conceptualizing social cognition including methodological differences between the study might produce a lot of noise (Schurz et al., 2014).

Though being a part of the non-declarative memory system, intuition is assumed to be the process of the continuous process of insight development throughout the life span as an acquired ability, it has the tendency to activate automatically and has an influence on overall social cognitive process and subsequent judgment. Hence, it can also be referred as an instinctual insight.

Putative domains of social cognition and intuition

Intuition has long been observed as the ability of effective problem-solving through which people predict and explain various life events where our judgment and decision-making abilities generally follow the dual system of information processing. In the judgment of events and optimal understanding of the world, human beings are thought to have two widely accepted systems of information processing that is considered to have two parallel functioning systems viz. analytic and intuitive processing systems (Harteis & Billett, 2013). To date, a very little empirical evidence exists regarding the putative domains of the intuitive ability in social environment. With respect to the specific domains of intuition, in a study conducted by Pretz and Totz (2007) identified three types of domains in intuition that is, holistic, inferential, and affective domains. In another study, Sobkow and his colleagues (2018) described intuition as a multifaceted concept involving three types of major intuitive abilities that is, subjective ability, implicit process, and coherence and insight. Furthermore, there are assumed to be several individual factors such as, creativity, expertise, decision-making, and coherence and insight abilities, which may influence intuitive process of a person (Sobkow et al., 2018; Dörfler & Ackermann, 2012). A few researches have also demonstrated the individual differences in intuitive abilities (Pretz et al., 2014). Existing body of literature indicates to the importance of intuitive processes in the domain of social cognition, especially in the hidden and complex correlated variations in the environment (Greenwald & Lai, 2020; Seger, 1994).

Research in the field of intuition has stemmed from different approaches. Intuitive theories generally describe how we get intuitions of the world and our surroundings, social interaction, and the world without following any existing scientific explanation (Mahr & Csibra, 2022). It is assumed to be related to two major fields of broad intuitive comprehension of Physics and Psychology, which help various cognitive functions drive prediction and subsequently generate alternatives to all life events and their possible explanation (Gerstenberg & Tenenbaum, 2017).

One of the widely used approaches is dual system or process theory explaining that overall information processing of human beings can be divided into two different types viz. "Type 1" processes that are automatic and rapid and "Type 2" which are analytical, time-consuming, and slower in process (Newton, Feeney & Pennycook, 2023; Evans & Stanovich, 2013; Kahneman, 2011). The theory further states that intuition plays an important role in the "Type 1" process whereas reflective thinking is an executive function of the "Type 2" process.

With respect to social cognition, it includes a neural network and a wide range of socio-cognitive processing such as face expression recognition, mentalization, social perception, and emotional processing which organize social information to make accurate decisions. Kennedy and Adolphs (2012) suggested four major social processing networks, namely, amygdala, mentalizing, empathy, and mirror networks. In order to evaluate the social stimuli, the role of the amygdala in social cognition has been explored most extensively in facial emotional recognition. According to him, damage to the amygdala may lead to an impaired ability to recognize emotional facial expressions. Additionally, the amygdala and orbitofrontal regions are involved in threat detection and emotional processing. The second network known as a mentalizing network is implicated in perspective-taking or thinking about the mental states of others. The empathy network is the third network that is activated during the expression of empathy and related behavior. The last network known as mirror network is activated during observation of the actions of others, including their emotional expressions. All four networks can be said to have three fundamental mechanisms of social processing viz. mentalizing, emotional processing, and mirror mechanism. Figure 5.1 exemplifies the basic mechanisms of social processing.

Generally, the figure depicts a child interacting with his teacher for the first time going through three basic social processes: mentalizing, emotional processing, and mirror mechanism. Mentalizing helps the child to sense the emotional expressions and verbal and non-verbal messages coming from the teacher. They also perceive whether the teacher is giving a pleasant or unpleasant vibe. Accordingly, the individual will perceive it as threatening or non-threatening. Through the aforementioned three mechanisms, the child in his first meeting with the teacher gets an implicit understanding of the emotion (here in the figure positive emotion) of the teacher. All these three social processing synergistically get strengthened with frequent experiences, ultimately enhancing the weightage of this particular experience. This strong schematic appraisal of the teacher as a positive agent becomes so lucid that it emerges as an intuitive flow within the child's mind, when it interacts with any teacher in later years of life also.

Neural correlates of social cognition and intuition

Understanding social cues is essential for any human being. This understanding requires an adaptive human brain that has the potential to execute various explicit and implicit processes of information gathering in order to gain social insight. Multiple information processes contribute when an individual attempts to adapt to ever-changing social scenarios. The social brain hypothesis states that primates require a large brain to deal with socially complex systems (Dunbar, 2009). The hypothesis further states that our social world imposes greater challenges of sociality ranging from deception to cooperation and this could have led to the evolution of notably extended brain size or system in primates. Non-verbal cues are very important in the development and shaping of social behavior (Mega et al., 2015; Critchley et al., 2000). Evolutionarily, perceiving non-verbal communication, such as,

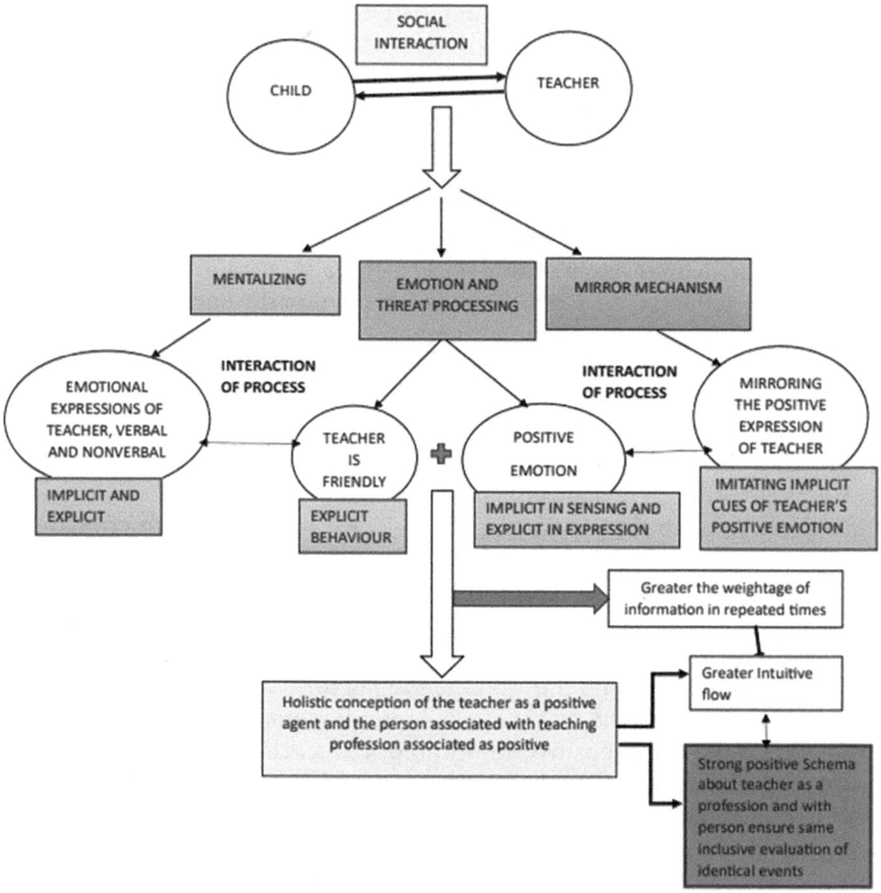

Figure 5.1 Social processing of a child while interacting with the teacher moves through mentalizing in terms of an implicit and explicit understanding of the expressions, simultaneously emotion and threat processing by sensing the teacher as positive figure occurs and that reflects in mirroring the positive cues in own behavior. Finally, greater weightage of similar experiences creates an intuitive flow and strong positive schema about the teacher.

people's facial expressions are considered to be the hallmark cues for making any social judgement, which isconsidered to have an underlying intuitive process (Mega et al., 2015). These judgments are known to be involved in mentalizing and intuitive processes involving the brain structures of Orbito Frontal Cortex (OFC) and anterior Insula (Sloman, 2014). A very few studies have shown the involvement of the lateral portion of the amygdale, median OFC, anterior insula, and ventral occipito-temporal areas of brain in intuition (Volz & Von Cramon, 2006). However, the distinct brain structure and potential neural correlates of intuition are still an inquiry of research. As compared to intuition, several putative brain regions are implicated for social cognition.These brain regions are also believed to activate intuitive process, which seems to be partly driven by adaptation in social situations. Hence, intuition can be regarded as the precursor of all processes of social cognition, which are evident in the functioning of various social brain regions. One of the oldest reviews summarizing the structures of the social brain had proposed a set of three brain regions, that is, the amygdala, the orbitofrontal cortex, and the temporal poles, which were thought to be involved in social behavior (Brothers, 1990). Subsequently, more recent reviews have highlighted the importance of these brain areas in addition to other brain regions and networks highlighted the such as temporoparietal junction, dorsomedial prefrontal cortex, superior temporal sulcus/gyrus, fusiform face area, ventromedial prefrontal cortex/orbitofrontal cortex and mirror neuron mechanism in social cognition and related intuition (Jellema et al., 2024; Kennedy & Adolphs, 2012).

Future direction

Attempts have been made to measure the domains of intuition and a large number of scales have been constructed to measure the dual process of human cognition, that is, implicit and explicit processes (Newton et al., 2023). However, almost all of these test measures both intuitive and analytic thinking styles suggesting a lack of scientific evidence regarding the nature of human judgment. Considering intuition as a multifaceted construct, Types of Intuition Scale (TIntS) developed by Pretz et al. (2014) deserves a special mention here. This scale measures three types of intuition, that is, holistic, inferential, and affective intuitive abilities that were identified in a literature review by Pretz and Totz (2007). In a recent study done by Dennin et al. (2022), the study concluded several kinds of relationship of different cognitions with intuition types. In this study, holistic intuition was found to be related with different types of thinking styles of a person. Affective intuitive abilities were related to a person's religious and political beliefs without having a proper scientific explanation. However, the inferential intuition was not found to be associated with any of the study variables. Research exploring the role of intuitive and analytic processes to social understanding are still in its infancy period. Overall, the role of intuition in the further processing of social cognitive domains such as insight, judgment and decision-making warrant more standardized measures and systematic nature of scientific studies in future.

Social cognition is often considered distinct and independent or partially independent from neurocognition. However, the relationship between neurocognition and social cognition is quite complex and not adequately addressed, thus requires systematic exploration in the future. Neurocognition could account for 20–40% of variance in functional outcome and a larger proportion of variance is still unaccounted for (Green et al., 2000; Lim et al., 2019). Given the role of social cognition in social and occupational functioning and quality of life, social cognition is regarded as an important construct that may have a greater impact than cognition on social outcomes in schizophrenia research. There is growing evidence suggesting that social cognition mediates the relationship between neurocognition and functional outcomes. Managing social cognitive impairments results in an improvement in real-world social outcomes (Pinkham et al., 2014). Therefore, improving overall social cognitive processes have become an important treatment target for several psychiatric and neurological conditions.

References

Abramson, L. Y., Seligman, M. E. P., & Teasdale, J. D. (1978). Learned helplessness in humans: Critique and reformulation. *Journal of Abnormal Psychology*, *87*, 49–74.

Adolphs, R. (2001). The neurobiology of social cognition. *Current Opinion in Neurobiology*, *11*, 231–239.

Ahmed, F. S., & Miller, L. S. (2011). Executive function mechanisms of theory of mind. *Journal of Autism and Developmental Disorders*, *41*, 667–678.

Allison, T., Puce, A., & McCarthy, G. (2000). Social perception from visual cues: Role of the STS region. *Trends in Cognitive Sciences*, *4*(7), 267–278.

Anderson, J. R. (1983). *The Architecture of Cognition*. Harvard University Press.

Astington, J. W. (1991). Intention in the child's theory of mind. *British Journal of Developmental Psychology*, *9*, 7–31.

Bolte, A., Goschke, T., & Kuhl, J. (2003). Emotion and intuition: Effects of positive and negative mood on implicit judgments of semantic coherence. *Psychological Science*, *14*(5), 416–421.

Boreham, N. C. (1987). Causal attribution by sensing and intuitive types during diagnostic problem solving. *Instructional Science*, *16*(2), 123–136.

Brothers, L. (1990). The social brain: A project for integrating primate behaviour and neurophysiology in a new domain. *Concepts in Neuroscience*, *1*, 27–51.

Carpandale, J., & Lewis, C. (2004). Constructing an understanding of mind: The development of children's social understanding within social interaction. *Behavioral and Brain Sciences*, *27*, 79–151.

Critchley, H. D., Daly, E. M., Bullmore, E. T., Williams, S. C., Van Amelsvoort, T., Robertson, D. M., ... & Murphy, D. G. (2000). The functional neuroanatomy of social behaviour: Changes in cerebral blood flow when people with autistic disorder process facial expressions. *Brain*, *123*(11), 2203–2212.

Dennin, A., Furman, K., Pretz, J. E., & Roy, M. M. (2022). The relationship of types of intuition to thinking styles, beliefs, and cognitions. *Journal of Behavioral Decision Making*, *35*(5), e2283.

Dennis, M., Simic, N., Bigler, E., Abildskov, T., Agostino, A., Taylor, G. H., Rubin, K., Vannatta, K., Gerhardt, C. A., Stancin, T., & Yeates, K. (2013). Cognitive, affective, and conative theory of mind (ToM) in children with traumatic brain injury. *Developmental Cognitive Neuroscience*, *5*, 25–39.

Dörfler, V., & Ackermann, F. (2012). Understanding intuition: The case for two forms of intuition. *Management Learning*, *43*(5), 545–564.
Dunbar R. I. (2009).The social brain hypothesis and its implications for social evolution. *Annals of Human Biology*, *36*(5), 562–572.
Evans, J. S. B., & Stanovich, K. E. (2013). Dual-process theories of higher cognition: Advancing the debate. *Perspectives on Psychological Science*, *8*(3), 223–241.
Fiske, S. T., & Taylor, S. E. (2013).*Social Cognition: From Brains to Culture*. SAGE.
Gerstenberg, T., & Tenenbaum, J. B. (2017). Intuitive theories. In M. R. Waldmann (Ed.), *The Oxford Handbook of Causal Reasoning* (pp. 515–547). Oxford University Press.
Green, M. F., Horan, W. P., & Lee, J. (2015). Social cognition in schizophrenia. *Nature Reviews. Neuroscience*, *16*(10), 620–631. https://doi.org/10.1038/nrn4005
Green, M. F., Kern, R. S., Braff, D. L., & Mintz, J. (2000). Neurocognitive deficits and functional outcome in schizophrenia: Are we measuring the "right stuff"? *Schizophrenia Bulletin*, *26*(1), 119–136. https://doi.org/10.1093/oxfordjournals.schbul.a033430
Green, M. F., Olivier, B., Crawley, J. N., Penn, D. L., & Silverstein, S. (2005). Social cognition in schizophrenia: Recommendations from the MATRICS New Approaches Conference. *Schizophrenia Bulletin*, *31*(4), 882–887.
Green, M. F., Penn, D. L., Bentall, R., Carpenter, W. T., Gaebel, W., Gur, R. C., & Heinssen, R. (2008). Social cognition in schizophrenia: An NIMH workshop on definitions, assessment, and research opportunities. *Schizophrenia Bulletin*, *34*(6), 1211–1220.
Greenwald, A. G., & Lai, C. K. (2020). Implicit social cognition. *Annual Review of Psychology*, *71*, 419–445.
Hamilton, A. F. (2009). Goals, intentions and mental states: Challenges for theories of autism. *Journal of Child Psychology and Psychiatry*, *50*, 881–892.
Happé, F., Cook, J. L., & Bird, G. (2017). The structure of social cognition: In(ter)dependence of sociocognitive processes. *Annual Review of Psychology*, *68*, 243–267.
Harteis, C., & Billett, S. (2013). Intuitive expertise: Theories and empirical evidence. *Educational Research Review*, *9*, 145–157.
Heider, F., & Simmel, M. (1994). An experimental study of apparent behavior. *The American Journal of Psychology*, *57*(2), 243–259.
Hodgkinson, G. P., Langan-Fox, J., & Sadler-Smith, E. (2008). Intuition: A fundamental bridging construct in the behavioural sciences. *British Journal of Psychology*, *99*(1), 1–27.
Izard, C. E. (2009). Emotion theory and research: Highlights, unanswered questions, and emerging issues. *Annual Review of Psychology*, *60*, 1–25.
Jellema, T., Macinska, S. T., O'Connor, R. J., & Skodova, T. (2024). Social intuition: Behavioral and neurobiological considerations. *Frontiers in Psychology*, *15*, 1336363.
Jung, C. G. (1961). *Memories, Dreams & Reflections*. Pantheon.
Kahneman, D. (2011). *Thinking, Fast and Slow*. Macmillan.
Kelley, H. H., & Michela, J. L. (1980). Attribution theory and research. *Annual Review of Psychology*, *31*(1), 457–501.
Kennedy, D. P., & Adolphs, R. (2012). The social brain in psychiatric and neurological disorders. *Trends in Cognitive Sciences*, *16*(11), 559–572.

Kring, A. M., & Bachorowski, J. A. (1999). Emotions and psychopathology. *Cognition & Emotion*, *13*(5), 575–599.

Lewicki, P., Hill, T., & Czyzewska, M. (1992). Nonconscious acquisition of information. *American Psychologist*, *47*(6), 796.

Lieberman, M. D. (2000). Intuition: A social cognitive neuroscience approach. *Psychological Bulletin*, *126*(1), 109.

Lim, K., Lee, S. A., Pinkham, A. E., Lam, M., & Lee, J. (2019).Evaluation of social cognitive measures in an Asian schizophrenia sample. *Schizophrenia Research. Cognition*, *20*, 100169.

Mahr, J. B., & Csibra, G. (2022). A short history of theories of intuitive theories. In *A Life in Cognition: Studies in Cognitive Science in Honor of Csaba Pléh* (pp. 219–232). Springer Nature. https://doi.org/10.1007/978-3-030-66175-5_16

Manley, D. P. (2016). Personality and positive psychology in social media and post-secondary education. *Journal of Professional Communication*, *4*(2), 77–92.

McCrea, S. M. (2010). Intuition, insight, and the right hemisphere: Emergence of higher sociocognitive functions. *Psychology Research and Behavior Management*, *3*, 1–39.

Mega, L. F., Gigerenzer, G., & Volz, K. G. (2015). Do intuitive and deliberate judgments rely on two distinct neural systems? A case study in face processing. *Frontiers in Human Neuroscience*, *9*, 456.

Newton, C., Feeney, J., & Pennycook, G. (2023). On the disposition to think analytically: Four distinct intuitive-analytic thinking styles. *Personality and Social Psychology Bulletin*, *50*(6), 906–923.

Pinkham, A. E., Penn, D. L., Green, M. F., Buck, B., Healey, K., & Harvey, P. D. (2014). The social cognition psychometric evaluation study: Results of the expert survey and RAND panel. *Schizophrenia Bulletin*, *40*(4), 813–823.

Premack, D., & Woodruff, G. (1978). Does the chimpanzee have a theory of mind? *Journal of Behaviour & Brain Sciences*, *4*, 515–526.

Pretz, J. E., Brookings, J. B., Carlson, L. A., Humbert, T. K., Roy, M., Jones, M., & Memmert, D. (2014). Development and validation of a new measure of intuition: The types of intuition scale. *Journal of Behavioral Decision Making*, *27*(5), 454–467.

Pretz, J. E., & Totz, K. S. (2007). Measuring individual differences in affective, heuristic, and holistic intuition. *Personality and Individual Differences*, *43*(5), 1247–1257.

Rumelhart, D. E. (1984). Schemata and the cognitive system. In R. S. Wyer, Jr., & T. K. Srull (Eds.), *Handbook of Social Cognition*, (Vol. 1, pp. 161–188). Lawrence Erlbaum Associates Publishers.

Schurz, M., Radua, J., Aichhorn, M., Richlan, F., & Perner, J. (2014). Fractionating theory of mind: A meta-analysis of functional brain imaging studies. *Neuroscience and Biobehavioral Reviews*, *42*, 9–34.

Seger, C. A. (1994). Implicit learning. *Psychological Bulletin*, *115*(2), 163–196.

Sloman, S. (2014). Two systems of reasoning: An update. In J. W. Sherman, B. Gawronski, & Y. Trope (Eds.), *Dual-Process Theories of the Social Mind* (pp. 69–79). The Guilford Press.

Sobkow, A., Traczyk, J., Kaufman, S. B., & Nosal, C. (2018). The structure of intuitive abilities and their relationships with intelligence and Openness to Experience. *Intelligence*, *67*, 1–10.

Volz, K. G., & Von Cramon, D. Y. (2006). What neuroscience can tell about intuitive processes in the context of perceptual discovery. *Journal of Cognitive Neuroscience*, *18*(12), 2077–2087.

Chapter 6

Interface between folk mind and intuitive cognition

Raghubir Singh Pirta

This chapter explores the interface between the folk mind and intuitive cognition primarily by way of visions in the narratives on loss and ensuing suffering. Loss implies separation from a loved object, and it stirs pain in a person with a blend of anger, sadness, and yearning. The central premise of this chapter is that the pain of separation (*biraha*), in some people, grows into a kind of inner source for transformation, in the sense that these people engage in activities that are good for them as well as for others. These activities may include creative works in arts and sciences as well. Metaphorically, the pain of separation is depicted as a fire burning inside which drives a person to engage in prosocial activities despite bearing the loss. Colloquially it is *biraha ki aag* or the *fire of biraha*. These cases though rare become examples for others facing inevitable loss.

An allusion to the following selective cases may serve the purpose here. A collection of poems (Kumar, 2000) by a Punjabi poet Shiv Batalvi, introduced me to the spirit behind '*biraha agn*' or fire of *biraha*. He suffered forcible separation at a tender age from his 'half mother' the present-day Pakistan. In a faraway place, Korean writer Han Kang portrays a city demolished by Nazis. The forms who resisted the power come alive in this snowy cold from the mist. Elsewhere, blooming 'flowers of fire' stirs memories of lost loved ones. In another scene, a mother in extreme poverty bearing the delivery pain, stitches a white newborn gown (Kang, 2016/2024). The spirit behind this portrayal is to 'live' in spite of all. As a Sufi in Shiv Batalvi sings, the body without *biraha* is, but a dead body (Kumar, 2000). No less remarkable is the triumph of a manic-depressive, Kay Redfield Jamison, who inherited this illness. She not only becomes a notable healer of suffering minds but also delves into the relationship of manic-depressive illness and artistic temperament. Jamison (1994, p. 240) infers manic-depressive illness gives a touch of fire, is a creative force, but it may take life as well.

Moore and Desmond (2004) bring us closer to the preceding context, they write 'humanitarian fire' fueled Charles Darwin's lonely quest for mankind's origins. The humanitarian fire refers to Darwin's crusade against slavery in the abolitionist mind and views of Quakers. Darwin puts together scientific

DOI: 10.4324/9781003377757-8

evidence that humans share the family of apes and monkeys. Since the civilized and the savage stood now on the same ground, Darwin intuitively imagined the end of slavery. His biographers, Moore and Desmond (2004), narrate that while writing *The Descent of Man*, Charles Darwin endured immense loss: his close companions left him alone, his health deteriorated, and some loved ones also departed.

Last, I refer to the travails of two persons, who were later to become eminent psychologists. They endured the extreme callousness in the concentration and extermination camp at Auschwitz and then strived to make common man's life more meaningful. Viktor Frankl elaborates the key phrase 'tragic optimism' (Frankl, 1959/2008) in various ways, which I think also resonates in the fire of *biraha*. The other Auschwitz survivor, Edith Eger, narrates her experiences in her book *The Gift* (Eger, 2021) at the age of 92. The human mind is so sturdy that it provides intuitive choices even in the darkest moments. Eger reminisces about Auschwitz's experiences, when she was dying of hunger, a choice sprang up, eat flesh from a carcass, or eat blades of grass.

These are wise counsels, intuitively drawn under harsh social conditions. After facing adversities in life, individuals learn to achieve goals without getting sidetracked by hindrances, it becomes a habit. This effortless attention to information, outer and inner, gives them experience of flow (Csikszentmihalyi, 1990/2002, p. 192). The effortless attending is Csikszentmihalyi's important contribution to psychology in view of Kahneman (2012, p. 40), that is attention not only involves effort, it is 'psychic energy' energy for effort. In the above examples from literature, psychiatry, science, and psychology, the persons effectively facing tragedies are narrated as experiencing fire. Presumably, a metaphor for mental energy. So, it is not wrong to propose psychic energy as a factor in the fire of *biraha*.

This overview of facing inevitable events in life is apparently universal, the present chapter aims to present this phenomenon from a culture-specific point of view. Such an exploration derives information from legends, memories, and myths, in the repository of the community, on individuals who say yes to life while enduring suffering. This allows us to explore the uniqueness of a phenomenon, for example, the *fire of biraha*. One may perceive this uniqueness in a genre of folk songs sung in the Bhojpuri-speaking belt of North India. As far back as 1886, the legendary linguist George Grierson refers to '*biraha*' among the folk singers of this region (see Manuel, 2012). A study on folk songs on *biraha* associates the Hindi word *biraha* with longing and mental pain arising in separation, deprivation, loss, and loneliness. *Biraha* is a song of cowherder pastoralists of Uttar Pradesh and Bihar in North India. These people, taken as slaves to distant regions of the world, naturally sang *biraha* where ever they were, for example, working in the plantations of Caribbean islands in the middle of the Americas (Manuel, 2012). Lately, in Uttar Pradesh and Bihar, the *biraha* genre assimilates every streak of loss in the folk mind (Siaram, 2012).

My intuitions about the mental processes inspiring genres of *biraha* had a context in the episodes of pain after the loss of a loved one (Pirta, 2023). In this reference, I have explored its origins in the narratives on *boir*, in the ethnographic and anthropological work (Moran, 2011; Sax, 2006; Sutherland, 2003–2004; Vidal, 2006; Zoller, 1997), a primitive warfare, the *boir*, which is now obsolete, among the Khoshias of the western Himalaya (Pirta, 2024a). These are tales of the struggle for survival between adjacent villages involving love and hate. These episodes of *boir* are followed by reconciliation processes between the rival villages. My hypothesis is that during this reconciliation phase minds of people are charged with the *fire of biraha*, ensuing from loss in warfare. In the plains of Punjab, people have been cultivating the *fire of biraha*, the Sikh gurus (Chauhan, 2014), and the Sufi saints (Safvi, 2022), for spiritual transformations.

The intuitive cognitions of people embedded in traditions (e.g., Ohri, 2020), religious and moral values (White, 2021), and their history (Valentine, 2024), I suggest, are vital to figuring out the workings of the human mind. This is a society and science dialogue to lay the foundation of a cognitive science of human well-being. I see this approach as a search for a novel hypothesis about a phenomenon, which serves as feedback to a culturally universal look at how people endure loss in their lives.

Biraha, unconscious, and creativity

The chapter proposes a relation between the pain of separation and ensuing emotional and cognitive changes in a person when he or she engages in activities that are not only good for the survival of the individual but also beneficial for the society. In addition, it is argued that this transformation in an individual primarily involves the intuitive process of cognition.

The argument assumes the following processes. Some events, such as the loss of a loved one, intensely affect the emotional memory system of a person. He or she feels love and hate toward the lost loved object, which creates a state of ambivalence in the mind. It is further proposed that, in these transitions of emotions, everything that is in flesh and blood seeps deeper into the mind of the griever. Unconscious of it, the person goes into a state of gloom. But some persons are able to bear the pain of separation, and also engage in creative works. It is this transformation that requires explanation. It is termed a positive change for two reasons. First, the person suffering from the pain of separation from the loved object endures it. Not only that, this person engages in activities that are essential for living. Second, this person goes beyond this, he masters activities, which are beneficial for the good of others. In this process, a person has to make decisions that are not ordinary, in the sense that, in spite of all suffering, he or she makes morally loaded decisions, which seems largely intuitive.

The processes of decision-making in the context of emotional arousal have a long history which goes back to William James, who suggested that the information essential for the survival of an organism travels unconsciously from brain to body for immediate behavioral action. The feedback loops from the body to the brain and then produces a conscious experience. Damasio (1994/2005), and LeDoux (1994) have made pioneer discoveries in discerning these conscious and unconscious pathways that underlie the flow of information between body and brain. The area is now known as Interoception (Damasio, 2023).

This integration is astonishingly popular in literary work. The literary work of Gitanjali Shree may be referred. Whether Shree drew her inspiration from the sources in cognitive science and psychiatry, or not, should not concern us. Her *Ret Samadhi* (Shree, 2018; English translation: *Tomb of Sand*, 2022) is rich in subtle meanings. Consider a revelation, *ilham*, that might have arisen in the mind of bandit Ratnakar, who became sage Valmiki the writer of the Hindu epic *Ramayana* in Sanskrit. Her hypothesis is that the matter perceived semiconsciously sometimes reveals true reality. The elegy of partition of India in 1947 sung by Shree through a literary feat acquaints with nostalgia after loss. If separation is reality, and ruinous, its passion lights a flame inside.

Much of the transformations after loss are not unlike changes that occur in trances or semiconscious states. Though Kakar (2015) refers to these states as 'cognitive unconscious,' it is important to see if this concept is in consonance with the psychoanalytic view of Sigmund Freud on the unconscious. The cognitive unconscious has a basis in experimental work in cognitive science (Kandel, 2012), where the investigators independently acknowledge the unconscious processing of information in decision-making. Perhaps analogous mental processes underlie the integration of *biraha*, unconscious, and creativity. Kakar (2015) also introduced the concept of 'spiritual unconscious.' He views linguistic creativity and visions of Rabindranath Tagore through the spiritual unconscious and assumes it as distinct from Western notions of the unconscious. But in view of Biswas (2003), Tagore has leaned on the Freudian view of the unconscious. The Gitanjali (Tagore, 1920) is a creation of this great poet, where he pours suffering into songs.

Modes of mind and psychic energy

The fire of *biraha* captures the intense longing and emotional anguish, the interplay of love and hate that comes with separation from a loved one. This ambivalence, a state of chaos, I believe is fertile soil for the origin of the *fire of biraha*. Presumably, there is an effort to conserve the psychic energy, soothe the distress, and engage in self and other survival functions. If one is unable to conserve this energy, he or she is likely to succumb to the traumatic event. The notable reflection from Kakar (2015) further underlines this premise that the pain of loss serves to open a channel for the flow of creative processes.

This allusion to the concept of energy in mental processes spans a long period, from James (1907/1987) to Duckworth (2016/2019). Equating mental energy to physical energy may be questionable, simply because we have no measure for mental energy in behavioral sciences (Bateson, 1972/1987). But it is so convincing when a person attends to information, especially when facing challenging situations. The attending thus implies 'psychic energy' (Csikszentmihalyi, 1990/2002, p. 33). In addition, he suggests the term 'negentropy' which has significance for a positive transformation suggested in the fire of *biraha*, as opposed to 'psychic entropy.' The latter is a disorder in the consciousness of a person after experiencing of tragic event. Individuals achieving mastery in skills in facing adversity are likely to use the fast mode of cognition. This unconscious process resembles the *System I* of Kahneman (2012), which is unconscious, fast, automatic, and intuitive. This intuitive mode thus uses less psychic energy (i.e., effortlessly), and operates largely without the awareness of an individual.

It is natural for a biologist like E. O. Wilson that the primary human values are written in genetic codes of fitness, but this staunch materialist is not oblivious to the secondary values enabling survival. These secondary values include enthusiasm, exploration, triumph, altruism, affection, and national pride (Wilson, 1978, p. 199). He further observes that perhaps 'a kind of principle of conservation of energy' operates behind these secondary mental processes. This energy is not unlike psychic energy, but Csikszentmihalyi (1990/2002, p. 192) looks at the processes in an entirely opposite way. He underlines that experiences like exploration, loving and helping others, and coming out of trauma are in fact primary for psychology, and make us uniquely human.

Along with this, I refer to the 'ego depletion model' behind the concept of willpower (Baumeister & Tierney, 2011), which also implies 'energy' of experiential nature. The term 'ego' is in honor of Sigmund Freud who first proposed mental energy. The ego depletion model suggests that willpower sustains an individual in harsh times, a salient feature of the fire of *biraha* hypothesis (Pirta, 2023). It becomes possible through self-control in conserving energy.

My hunch is that the very psychic energy, the *fire of biraha*, stemming from one's negative experiences in life essentially finds a creative expression if one can transcend beyond the emotional ambivalence. People, in this view, transcend conflicts with innate intuitive skills for survival, which manifests through rituals, deception, or other religious practices.

Somewhere in the late sixth century, an Assyrian army led by Captain Holofernes put siege to the city of Bethulia in Israel (Pirta, 2024b). A pious widow Judith went into contemplation in front of her God. After her lamentations before God for the safety of the people of Bethulia, she silently embarks upon a secret mission wearing the look of a charming woman. She confronts Captain Holofernes; ensnared as he felt from Judith's seductive looks, he invites her for a feast in his tent, where at some opportune time at midnight Judith beheads Holofernes. She carries his head to Bethulia. The head of a fierce enemy elicits a rallying response among the Bethulians, and they rout the Assyrian army in no time. Our concern in the legend of Judith evolves from the analysis of a painting (Kandel, 2012, p. 120) on her by the pioneer of expressionism in art Gustav Klimt in 1901 in Vienna. Kandel analyses the painting of Judith layer by layer but in the language of chemicals and brain parts. Both Klimt in the painting of Judith and Kandel in its neurological analysis, confine to woman's amorous aspects. I see, however, a strategy of deceit in Judith's secret plan, initiated intuitively, following a common evolutionary way. It is self-sacrificial hive instinct even at the stake of her honor.

One might ask why I am exploring folk narratives of loss; the answer is to understand human cognition and motivation by assigning meaning to the intuitions of people. But my inquiry does not end here, it moves on to explore recovery from loss toward positive change. It is not a dissenting note to knowledge in psychology on these issues, rather this is an effort to validate it, and seek its generalization outside the workroom.

Loss and suffering

Everything that occurs around us does not end up in the physical domain. It makes impressions in the mind, more specifically in the systems of memory (Kandel, 2007, 2012). One such system, the episodic memory keeps intact the temporal sequences of events. The mental processes in this memory system begin quite early when the child weaves stories around the objects she encounters. These narratives animate the world of the child, and slowly the real episodes of life form its part. The emotional memory system begins working even earlier than the episodic memory and coolly stores tragic events. They are likely to stir up later. Enrichment and protection of the memory system from trauma, in the early years of life, is therefore meaningful for society.

In the context of *dukkha* or suffering, it is important to understand that some tragedies leave behind deep scars in the emotional memory system of a person. In Suttie's view (1935) hate has its origins in the threat or withdrawal of love by the mother or companions resulting in separation anxiety. The separation from the loved object can be a source of immense psychic energy. This mobilized energy even goes against the opponent to protect the loving bond. These events, we believe, involve ambivalence of emotions, love, and hate toward the lost loved object. There occur radical transitions in emotions in this process. However, instead of direct expression in action, those who can bear the social pain, engage in creative works. These positive experiences take various forms. Even though the group life is an evolutionary achievement to cope with threats, dangers, and other adversities (Bowlby, 1969/1997), many of these tragedies may arise in group life, for example, from an attack by an adjacent group member, or from the loss of loved one within the group. The transitions of emotions in this process are of ambivalent nature (Bowlby, 1980/1998b). The ambivalence of emotional and motivational systems has traditionally been common in psychoanalysis, but ambivalence has also been an important concept in the studies of ethologists (Eibl-Eibesfeldt, 1970). In fact, experimental psychologists also have used novel paradigms to study ambivalence of love and hate (McCauley, 2020).

This chapter also underlines such ambivalent interactions in the emotional context among the members of communities, which follow the inward movement of consciousness where self and other interact.

Preamble to the cultural context

It is important to note, first, that Kakar (2015) conceptualizes the spiritual unconscious to explore creativity in the Indian context as he thinks that Indian perspectives diverge substantially from contemporary Western findings on creativity. And second, his insight that the pain assists to open creative channel is provides important context, as this chapter underlines. However, the focus here is on folk institutions, rather than unknown spiritual. Here is a maxim, an involuntary expression of the spokesperson of deity in trance: '*Tuai, tobai ahaon!*' which translates as '*You are, therefore I am.*' In other words, it is an expression of unity of the people with their deity. Or, as if the deity emanating from the beliefs of its devotees. In a note (Pirta, 2014), I simply put it as an intuition expressing knowledge that lay scattered in society, to which we seldom pay attention.

The interactions among the members of communities follow the inward movement of consciousness where self and other interact. These interactions involve ambivalence of emotions. As early as 1900 we find a long discourse by Das (1908) on ambivalence of emotions and self-other interactions. The author underlines compound emotions of love and hate, which not only attract attention but impress memory exceptionally. The jealousy, for example, is love toward one object, and at the same time, hate toward the person who prevents acquisition of that object. The amorous relationships described by poets are full of such social relationships. But the focus of essay is a special case of compound emotions: the love and hate directed toward one and the same object. That is a loved one, after its loss, becomes an object of hate.

That such ambivalence has significance for the development of courage as a quality of character Shand (1914), is important here. Such qualities make one face challenges in life, as is assumed in the *fire of biraha*. The most significant hypothesis about ambivalence is well illustrated in Freud's

(1920/2001b) great opposition between the life and death instincts, and between polarities of love (or affection) and hate (or aggressiveness). Later Suttie (1935) gave an alternative thesis on love and hate, which is more relevant to the ambivalence of emotions explored in this chapter. In this view love, as observed during infant's interaction with mother, replaces the postulate of sex common in psychoanalysis of that time. The need for a companion being primary. In Suttie's view, and we also believe, hate has its origins in the threat or withdrawal of love by the mother or companions, which results in separation-anxiety.

This brings us to the systems theory and information theory approaches that form the basis of studies on attachment relations by Bowlby (1969/1997) and Harlow (see Blum, 2002/2011). In loving relationships many communications take place beyond the conscious process of learning, which gives us sense of security with the emergence of comfort of automatic compatible adaptive behavior. Attachment with loved ones, with homeland, mother tongue, deity-devotee relationship is grounded in affectionate bond between mother and infant.

The moral intuitions precede moral reasoning in cementing these pro-social relationships (Haidt, 2013, 2006/2021). They are automatic and instantaneous. Neurological studies report that a person with damage in the prefrontal and ventromedial regions of brain suffers from a syndrome where one is fully aware of moral reasoning, but lacks in intuitive feelings arising from emotional centers (Damasio, 1994/2005). Humans in general do not engage in abstract forms of reasoning and symbolic behavior, rather they use intuitive ways in various spheres of life. For them morality is not based on notions of justice and fairness, but it is an intuitive blending of purity, authority, loyalty, conformity, and reciprocity (Haidt's 2013). The sociogenic origin of these intuitions was first suggested by Richard Shweder in his studies on common folks of Orissa, India, and followed by Haidt (2013, 2006/2021). When this bond is broken (see Blum, 2002/2011; Bowlby,1973/1998a, 1980/1998b), the shared comfort blows apart and the pain of separation takes over the affected individual or group.

Western Himalayan cultural context

My limited studies on healing (Pirta, 2018, 2019) have a basis in the community approach by looking deity-devotee relationship as an attachment system (Kirkpatrick, 1992). Also, group cohesiveness, as studies on nonhuman primates suggest (see Pirta & Ramalingam, 2021, 2022), has a basis in innate patterns of non-zero-sum (cooperative) interactions. Thus, it is possible to explore folk healing rituals as intuitive learning strategies. Bateson (1972/1987) has implied the importance of such an exploration in contexts of Pavlovian conditioning, instrumental reward and escape, and instrumental avoidance. The movement of the sufferer into wider social space within the community, and then from mortals to realms of transcendent spirits. This becomes possible by the manipulation of belief, faith, and respect that the devotee imposes on the deity. Where the medium uses rewarding and punishing regimes to modify the behavior of a devotee, common in learning paradigms of psychology.

Some tragedies, as argued in this chapter, leave behind deep scars in the emotional memory system of a person. These events, as suggested above, involve ambivalence of emotions, love, and hate toward the lost loved object. There occur radical transitions in emotions in this process, and everything that is in flesh and blood seeps deeper in the mind of the griever. Unconscious of it, the person goes into a state of gloom. But the rare ones, who are able to bear the social pain, engage in creative works, which is the focus of our inquiry. These positive experiences take various forms. It has been reflected in the Himalayan culture. I began my search into the *fire of biraha* from such feuds between groups, the *boir*, in a western Himalayan region (Pirta, 2020). In further observations of a narrative of *boir*, the feud between two villages, a woman at a crucial point came out with an intuitive way to communicate a grave danger to a man from her maternal clan (Pirta, 2024b). This man Jhongia has been invited from the rival village for a treaty. But in fact, there was a plan to behead Jhongia by the villagers where the woman was married. When this woman came to know this secret, she was extremely worried. There was no way that she could approach the meeting place, the Zaaga of Dhar village, where the villagers had encircled Jhongia. From the balcony of her house, facing the Zaaga, she loudly greeted her kin Jhongia, in a customary way. Momentarily, when Jhongia caught her attention to reciprocate, right away the woman conveyed the imminent danger to his life through the hand-chop gesture. Taking the cue, Jhongia jumped from the wall and saved his life. Likewise, there are different accounts (see Pirta, 2023) where through the application of intuitive strategies many fatal consequences have been avoided and community got empowered.

A narrative preserved in folklore indicates the fatal transition of emotions with reference to attachment objects. The leader of a group worried about the fate of the members of his community being tormented by the king's functionaries who went on the warpath. The leader Hoku Rawat, having strong attachment to his deity, went to seek her blessing for a victory in war (see Moran, 2011). However, the failure of the ritual appeasement of the beloved deity further aggravated the fear of loss in the battle. In an outburst of anger Hoku Rawat hurled his shoe toward the beloved goddess, and advanced on war front, where he was killed.

Another narrative from the terrain recreates an imagery of warriors or *khoonds* of the Bangan (Zoller, 1997). The focus is on a woman Jotari, who lost her two beloved persons, her husband Dalu, and her son Jitu in a warfare or *boir* with the other *khoond*. Burning in the pain of *biraha* of the unexpected loss of loved ones, Jotari pleaded with her maternal kin, the other related *khoonds*, and, the deity Mahasu to restore the honor of her family. But her wishes remained unfulfilled. For over 300 years, estimates Zoller, the heroic ballads and the village folk narrate the tale of Jotari's pain and fire of revenge in various forms in social life. These forms deeply entrenched in religious beliefs include unmet wishes and taboos.

Intuition and adaptivity

A broader concept 'cognitive niche' (Pinker, 2010), can supplement the narrow 'adaptive unconscious' mentioned above. Humans occupy a role in an ecosystem. Members of a group evolve ways to increase their chances of survival by the better use of resources. They do this not by abstract intelligence, but by intuitive conceptions analogous to physics, biology, economics, psychology, and so on. Intuitive psychology is to infer another person's goals (Pinker, 2002/2019). Within the group, it enhances cooperation, and between groups it helps to assess danger, to evolve more efficient strategies for survival. The idea finds beautiful illustrations in the literary composition of Ghosh (2022).

The story of Judith of the Biblical times cited above is still alive in religion and art. The two prominent aspects of the story are the intuitions that guide much of our strategic behavior, and its emphasis on affectionate relations among the members of a community. When this bonding is broken, this intuitively shared comfort is shattered and pain of separation emerges automatically. Ethology can help us understand some finer aspects of Judith's behavior which are innate as well as intuitive. Eibl-Eibesfeldt (1975) was perhaps first to photograph the eye movements and instant changes in face while women engage in enticing males across cultures. These gestures were perhaps crucial during interactions between Judith and Holofernes. They are part of the Machiavellian tactics in evolution. These tactics are common in our primate lineage (Byrne, 1996). Judith intuitively weaves these fine patterns of deception to assault an enemy. Her maternal instinct in guise of amorous armor was pivotal in eliciting teamwork among the Bethulians to route Assyrians. This is the anticipation of separation or *biraha* from the loved ones unless the safety measure is not taken that intuitively arises in individuals as it has survival value for the group. In these social interactions, various strategies, innate and learned, conscious and unconscious, are intuitively recruited to achieve the goal, to promote others' safety and protection of self from the pain of *biraha*.

The pain of *biraha* may find transformation through psychological processes acting first on experiences. I noted narratives of women mourning the sudden death of their dear son indicate embedding in the past through symbolism. It is the warfare between villages, the *boir*. They were addressing the deceased boy as a *boire* or enemy. It was strange, why these women were addressing the lost son as an enemy. I thought the memories of the dear son were tormenting them. So, they were indirectly referring to the lost dear son as *boire* or enemy. This was indicative of ensuing depressive rumination. In my view, the concept of the enemy in the *boir* or feud between the villages has taken a new meaning in the cognition of these women. In the new form, a loved object becomes the enemy or the *boire*. When the unbearable pain is caused by the person being deceased, the pain is identified as the hurt caused by any enemy. This fire of *biraha* generated from the separation of the child due to death created such turmoil in the mother that the intuitively uttered word '*boire hoa*' for the deceased child enabled her to emotionally survive by reducing the excitation within a tolerable range. This intuitive utterance created an emotional distance from the child by reducing the cognitive dissonance, attributing enmity to the child for whom infliction of pain is normal. The above intuitive word *boire hoa* (in the context of the narratives on warfare) of the Pahari dialect has greater universality than the author has imagined.

It is not entirely wrong to assume that, as suggested above, these transitions in the emotional states involve the release of psychic energy. If this psychic energy is not sublimated through mourning processes, which is normal, it affects the person negatively; a veil of gloom envelopes the person. But a few transform this psychic energy into positive work, this mental state is colloquially known as the *fire of biraha*. It is a change in cognition, emotion, and behavior after a loss where a person not only faces the trauma but works for the sake of others. This positive transformation is not uniform, it varies according to contexts, underlying processes, and various other aspects. Therefore, it is not wrong to talk of various kinds of positive transformations, namely, antithetical, metaphorical, artifactual, dissipative, and, simulative (Pirta, 2023). These categories are provisional.

Such positive transformations, for long, have been noticed and valued in literature and religion. These changes in facing adversity also find importance in psychology (Csikszentmihalyi, 1990/2002; Seligman, 2011/2013; Staub, 2018). However, the conceptualization of intense fire burning inside is intuitive and specific to a person who has lost a loved one. The person moves away from the pain of loss and seeks proximity to the lost loved one through creative works, prayers, and service to society.

Turning suffering into creative activities is like using the waste energy, the pain of separation, for positive change. And thus, it is a pedagogic problem of immense significance and requires continuous dialogue between science and society.

Society and science dialogue

In this concluding section of the essay, our aim is to arrive at some consensus of the phenomenon of the *fire of biraha* through a science and society dialogue. The intuitive experience is very much observed in different spheres of society. Long ago, James (1902/1987) underlined that psychology must face the challenge of bringing intuitions, visions, and related experiential phenomena to the realms of science. In the local communities of the western Himalayan region where ambivalence is part of narratives, myths and legends, tales, and lyrics of folk tradition, the analyses in this essay suggest transitions toward positive change. Studies also report that hardships in life are not only present in a bifurcation in life but they also make us stronger to take up the challenge that bifurcation imposes, and one is motivated toward working hard, even for the sake of others. Society evaluates such actions of individuals and groups. The loss of a loved one is one such event of bifurcation.

There is a chasm between the East and the West about the embeddedness of consciousness in the spiritual realms. In the East, the spiritual consciousness becomes an integral part of the concept of separation, where it denotes the separation of the individual (soul) from the God (universal Soul). But at the same time, there is no denial of the pain of separation or *biraha* that one experiences in real life. In the exploration of the *biraha* or separation in the latter sense, Freud's (1917/2001a) classic paper on mourning and melancholia is an essential reading. He thought that breaking of bonds causes pain. Freud's influence in this regard reached in literary circles quite far. As is reported in Rabindranath Tagore's orientation to Freud's work in his prose and verses in the last years (1939–1940) of life (Biswas, 2003). This finds expression, Biswas says, for example, in a poem 'Aspashta.'

The attachment theory of Bowlby (1969/1997; 1973/1998a, 1980/1998b) offered a new paradigm, in the psychoanalytic tradition, where the origin of *biraha*, the pain of separation, has its origins in the primitive infant-mother bond. He borrowed ideas from systems theory, cognitive science, and ethology. Curiously, western researches in the area of attachment are also exploring bonding with God under the primary attachment of the infant to her mother (Kirkpatrick, 1992). The primary bond between infant and mother, from cradle to grave, has four sub-stems: proximity maintenance, secure base, safe haven, and separation anxiety (Pirta, 2018). The *biraha*, we are talking here, is the separation anxiety felt as social pain. Thus, we find similarity between the East and the West as far as the *biraha* symbolizes separation anxiety.

An epidemiological study of more than 30,000 Americans shows that the loss of a loved one was significantly associated with major depressive episodes and other psychiatric disorders in nearly 14,000 persons (Keyes et al., 2014).

More than a century ago, Freud's (1917/2001a) intuition on these fatal transitions of emotions from attachment to anger and enmity toward the loved one is remarkable. Could it be that this anger and enmity toward the loved one, who is no more, is turned toward the self? The grieving person ruminating on the attachment relationships with the loved one feels acute mental pain, and unable to bear this psychache, the person takes the fatal step that is suicide.

The visions and intuitions in narratives on the *boir*, the warfare between villages the author explored in this chapter and in earlier works (Pirta, 2023, 2024a), support the preceding thesis.

The analysis of the Biblical legend of Judith in this essay also supports similar conclusions. Therefore, it is important to understand the modulation of anger toward the lost loved one. Though this essay narrates the arousal of anger during separation from a culture-specific view, it appears universal feature. Psychiatrists have recorded anger as a component of grief due to the loss of a loved one, as we find in the exhaustive analysis of attachment relationships. Generally, these transformations of emotions related to lost loved ones have fatal consequences for the well-being of a person. These mental upheavals surface in the form of curtailment of self-other interaction, self-brooding or rumination, and suicidal tendencies. But it is not to deny the fact that they also manifest in the literary genre, where the pain of separation is a source of enormous psychic energy. Culture shows enrichment in various other forms in the context of separation anxiety, and one such dimension is the intuitive cultivation of separation by the individual from God.

Last, we refer to an example of vision from the Bronze Age, the myth of Gilgamesh from ancient Sumerian culture (Valentine, 2024). The vision narrates the land of the dead. These events fill the heart of Gilgamesh with sorrow, and the fear of death overpowers him. The Gilgamesh myth is a mirror of the Sumerian psyche involving two sides of brain, the left-brain functions in language, and the right-brain in emotions. King Gilgamesh also suffers from the loss of his dear friend (Ge & Yang, 2023), a theme explored in this essay. From the perspective of the history of evolution, visions form a significant part of every religion, and are interpreted by respective shamans and priests to maintain tribal unity (Wilson, 2012; White, 2021). Essentially it is a group selection argument, where at a certain period of human evolution religion began as a factor of sociality.

To conclude, the inevitable upsets and fissures in social bonding, which are the beginning of conflicts in human life, have origins in individual and group-level selection pressures. This most important aspect of human nature is inextricably linked with culture and religion in the community. The essay explores the ambivalence of emotions due to loss which culminates in the *fire of biraha*. The hypothesis is that people with the *fire of biraha* learn to transform the energy of the pain of separation for creative purposes through sublimation. Some communities inculcate such transformations in the religious domain for transcendence. The complexity that evolves within a community in the forms of cultural and religious elements not only ensures cohesiveness within a group, these cognitive strategies may have given the human species an edge over the other social species.

References

Bateson, G. (1987). *Steps to an ecology of mind. Collected essays in anthropology, psychiatry, evolution and epistemology*. Jason Aronson Inc. (Original work published in 1972).

Baumeister, R. F., & Tierney, J. (2011). *Willpower: Rediscovering the greatest human strength*. Penguin Press.

Biswas, S. (2003). Rabindranath Tagore and Freudian thought. *International Journal of Psychoanalysis*, *84*, 717–732.

Blum, D. (2011). *Love at Goon Park: Harry Harlow and the science of affection*. Basic Books. (Original work published in 2002).

Bowlby, J. (1997). *Attachment and loss Vol. 1. Attachment*. Pimlico. (Original work published in 1969).

Bowlby, J. (1998a). *Attachment and loss: Vol. 2. Separation, anxiety and anger*. Pimlico. (Original work published in 1973).

Bowlby, J. (1998b). *Attachment and loss: Vol. 3. Loss, sadness and depression*. Pimlico. (Original work published in 1980).

Byrne, R. W. (1996) Machiavellian intelligence. *Evolutionary Anthropology*, *5*(5), 172–180. (Original work published in 2006).

Chauhan. (2014). *Bani of Bhagats. Complete bani of bhagats as enshrined in Shri Guru Granth Sahib Part II All saints except Swami Rama Nand and Sant Kabir ji*. All India Pingalwara Charitable Society (Regd.).

Csikszentmihalyi, M. (2002). *Flow: The classic work on how to achieve happiness*. Rider. (Original work published in 1990).

Damasio, A. (2005). *Descartes' error. Emotion, reason, and the human brain*. Penguin Books. (Original work published in 1994).

Damasio, A. (2023). *Feeling and knowing. Making minds conscious*. Robinson.

Das, B. (1908). *The science of the emotions*. Theosophical Publishing Society.

Duckworth, A. (2016/2019). *Grit*. Vermilion Life Essentials.

Eger, E. (2021). *The gift*. Rider.

Eibl-Eibesfeldt, I. (1970). *Ethology. The biology of behavior*. Holt, Rinehart and Winston.

Eibl-Eibesfeldt, I. (1975). Aggression in the !Ko-Bushmen. In T. Williams (Ed.), *Psychological anthropology* (pp. 317–328). De Gruyter Mouton. https://doi.org/10.1515/9783110802818.317

Frankl, V. E. (1959/2008). *Man's search for meaning*. Rider.

Freud, S. (2001a). Mourning and melancholia. In J. Strachey (Ed.), *The Standard Edition of the complete psychological works of Sigmund Freud* (Vol. XIV, pp. 243–258). Vintage. (Original work published in 1971).

Freud, S. (2001b). Beyond the pleasure principle. In J. Strachey (Ed.), *The standard edition of the complete psychological works of Sigmund Freud* (Vol. XVIII, pp. 7–64). Vintage. (Original work published in 1920).

Ge, B. H., & Yang, F. (2023). Transcending the self to transcend suffering. *Frontiers in Psychology*, *14*, 1113965. https://doi.org/10.3389/fpsyg.2023.1113965

Ghosh, A. (2022). *The living mountain. A fable for our times*. Fourth Estate.

Haidt, J. (2013). *The righteous mind. Why good people are divided by politics and religion*. Penguin Books.

Haidt, J. (2021). *The happiness hypothesis. Putting ancient wisdom to the test of modern science*. Penguin Books. (Original work published in 2006).

James, W. (1902). The varieties of religious experience: A study in human experience. In B. Kuklick (Ed.), *William James. Writings 1902–1910* (pp.1–478). The Library of America. (Original work published in 1987).

James, W. (1907). The energies of men. In B. Kuklick (Ed.), *William James. Writings 1902–1910.* (pp. 1223–1241). The Library of America. (Original work published in 1987).

Jamison, K. R. (1994). *Touched with fire. Manic-depressive illness and the artistic temperament.* Free Press Paperback.

Kahneman, D. (2012). *Thinking fast and slow.* Penguin Books.

Kakar, S. (2015). The artistic genius: Western and Indian perspectives. In S. Kakar, & G. Blamberger (Eds.), *On creativity* (pp. 1–21). Penguin.

Kandel, E. R. (2007). *In search of memory. The emergence of a new science of mind.* W. W. Norton & Company.

Kandel, E. R. (2012). *The age of insight: The quest to understand the unconscious in art, mind and brain from Vienna 1900 to the present.* Random House.

Kang, H. (2016/2024). *The White book.* (Translated by Deborah Smith). Granta.

Keyes, K. M., Pratt, C., Galea, S., McLaughlin, K. A., Koenen, K. C., & Shear, M. K. (2014). The burden of loss: Unexpected death of a loved one and psychiatric disorders across the life course in a national study. *American Journal of Psychiatry, 171*(8), 864–871.

Kirkpatrick, L. A. (1992). An attachment-theory approach to the psychology of religion. *The International Journal for the Psychology of Religion*, 2(1), 3–28.

Kumar, S. (2000). *Poora kavi sangreh.* Aarsi Publishers. (Transliteration in Hindi)

LeDoux, J. E. (1994). Emotion, memory and the brain. *Scientific American*, June, 32–39.

Manuel, P. (2012). The trajectories of transplants: Singing Alha, Birha, and the Ramayan in the Indic Caribbean. This work is made publicly available by the City University of New York (CUNY). Contact: AcademicWorks@cuny.edu Accessed on 21 January, 2022.

McCauley, C. (2020). The essence of love and hate. In R. J. Sternberg (Ed.), *Perspectives on hate: How it originates, develops, manifests, and spreads* (pp. 43–64). APA Books.

Moore, J., & Desmond, A. (2004). Introduction. In Charles Darwin (Ed.), *The descent of man, and selection in relation to sex* (pp. xi–lviii). Penguin Books.

Moran, A. (2011). On the evolution of genealogical narratives in the western Himalayas. *Religions of South Asia, 56*(1/2), 443–470.

Ohri, L. (2020). Journeying sovereignties: Ritual traveling and networks of power in West Himalayan kingdom. In C. Bergmann, & J. Schaflechner (Eds.), *Ritual journeys in South Asia: Constellations and contestations of mobility and space* (pp. 29–62). Routledge.

Pinker, S. (2010). The cognitive niche: Coevolution of intelligence, sociality, and language. *Proceedings of the National Academy of Sciences, 107*(2), 8993–8999.

Pinker, S. (2019). *The blank slate. The modern denial of human nature.* Penguin Books. (Original work published in 2002).

Pirta, R. S. (2014). Knowledge in society as an empirical base for Indian psychology. *Psychological Studies, 59*(2), 105–106.

Pirta, R. S. (2018). Cognitive foundations of community mental healthcare: The role of local institutions and practices. In G. Misra (Ed.), *Psychosocial interventions for health and well-being* (pp. 253–273). Springer.

Pirta, R. S. (2019). Self in the supernatural belief context: A conceptual analysis. *Psychological Studies*, *64*(3), 283–294.

Pirta, R. S. (2020). Reflections on changing narratives of identity, empathic understanding and creative transformation. *International Journal of the Asia Pacific School Psychology*, *1*(2), 126–138.

Pirta, R. S. (2023). Positive transformation in cognition, emotion, and behavior after loss. *International Journal of the Asia Pacific School Psychology*, *4*(1), 9–31.

Pirta, R. S. (2024a). Knowledge, emotions, and well-being: A vision into psychic conflicts from the Khoshias of western Himalaya. In G. Misra & I. Misra (Eds.), *Emotions in cultural context: International and cultural psychology*. Springer Nature. https://doi.org/10.1007/978-3-031-46349-5_19

Pirta, R. S. (2024b). Turning loss into creative change: Exploring *the fire of biraha*. *Journal of the Indian Academy of Applied Psychology*, *50*(1), 9–23.

Pirta, R. S., & Ramalingam, P. (2021). Movement toward effortless states of mind where creativity emerges. *International Journal of the Asia Pacific School Psychology*, *2*(1), 9–25.

Pirta, R. S., & Ramalingam, P. (2022). Gain and pain of self-other interactions. *International Journal of the Asia Pacific School Psychology*, *3*(1), 9–32.

Safvi, R. (2022). *In search of the divine. Living histories of Sufism in India*. Hachette India.

Sax, W. S. (2006). Rituals of the warrior khund. *European Bulletin of Himalayan Research*, *29–30*, 120–133.

Seligman, M. E. P. (2013). *Flourish. A visionary new understanding of happiness and well-being*. Atria Paperback. (Original work published in 2011).

Shand, A. F. (1914). *The foundations of character. Being a study of tendencies of the emotions and sentiments*. Macmillan.

Shree, G. (2018). *Ret-Samadhi*. Rajkamal Paperbacks. (in Hindi).

Shree, G. (2022). *Tomb of Sand* (Translation of RET-SAMADHI by Daisy Rockwell). Penguin Books.

Siaram. (2012). *Awadhi biraha lokgeeton ka Adhyayan*. (Study of Awadhi biraha folk songs). Omega Publications. (in Hindi).

Staub, E. (2018). Preventing violence and promoting active bystandership and peace: My life in research and applications. *Peace and Conflict: Journal of Peace Psychology*, *24* (1), 95–111.

Sutherland, P. (2004). Local representations of history and the history of local representation: Timescapes of theistic agency in the western Himalaya. *European Bulletin of Himalayan Research*, *25–26*, 80–118.

Suttie, I. D. (1935). *The origins of love and hate*. Kegan Paul, Trench and Trubner & Co.

Tagore, R. (1920). *Gitanjali (song offerings)*. Macmillan Company.

Valentine, R. (2024). *The global origins of psychology. Neurology, language and culture in the ancient world*. Routledge.

Vidal, D. (2006). The test of traditions: An history of feuds in Himachal Pradesh. *European Bulletin of Himalayan Research*, *29–30*, 135–159.

White, C. (2021). *An introduction to the cognitive science of religion. Connecting evolution, brain, cognition, and culture*. Routledge.
Wilson, E. O. (1978). *On human nature*. Harvard University Press.
Wilson, E. O. (2012). *The social conquest of earth*. Liveright Publishing Corporation.
Zoller, C. P. (1997). Heroic ballads and the biography of a woman: On coping with conflicts in the western Garhwal Himalaya. In I. Stellrecht, & M. Winiger (Eds.), *Perspectives on history and change in the Karakoram, Hindukush, and Himalaya* (pp. 473–497). Rudiger Koppe.

Chapter 7

Culture, gender, and intuitive cognition

Relational dialectic

Ishita U. Bharadwaj, Meharmeet Kaur, Ritu Mudgal and Aritra Mukherjee

Introduction

In the advent of growth and development, human life is seen through the lens of meaning and purpose weaved around success, accomplishment, good adjustment, better management, and access to resources. To achieve the said path, successful strategic thinking, prioritising one's needs and goals, and further learning the ways to negotiate with the given to make the best of it is something on which socialisation across cultures has thrived. This stands in need of constant cognitive efforts in making various day-to-day decisions to act appropriately to the situation, further aiding the growth process. These day-to-day acts involve a series of decision-making processes that can be seen at two levels.

First, it can be said as cognition or *cognoscere* in Latin, which focuses on 'getting to know' and refers to all mental processes leading to thought, awareness, and knowledge. These processes are mediated relatively in the conscious realm of the knower, facilitating an individual's decision-making ability. The second level can be seen as a subconscious process—intuitiveness, which refers to implicit beliefs and assumptions regarding causal explanatory relationships. It shapes the way we organise experiences, influencing behaviour, social interactions, and inferences (Gelman & Legare, 2011, p. 380). The interaction within these two layers makes the decision-making process more dynamic and complex, enriching the experience of knowing.

In this chapter, we delve into understanding this process through a gender perspective, offering insights into women's intuition—its nature, significance, and potential applications to the current context.

To begin with, to understand how we situate women's intuition, it is pertinent to discuss how the authors have operationalised the understanding of intuitive cognition. Intuition is a type of knowing that comes from our gut feeling or sixth sense rather than conscious thought. It can help us to make quick decisions, solve problems, and understand complex situations, even when we do not have all the information. The discussion surrounding intuitive cognition is multifaceted and intricate, with experts from various fields, such as cognitive psychology, neuroscience, and philosophy, contributing their perspectives.

DOI: 10.4324/9781003377757-9

One of the key issues in the debate is the nature of intuitive cognition itself. Some scholars argue that intuitive cognition is a distinct form of cognition. In contrast, others argue that it simply manifests other cognitive processes, such as heuristics or implicit biases, which occur through years of training and socialisation. Another key issue in the debate is the accuracy and reliability of intuition in decision-making. Some scholars argue that intuitive cognition can be a valuable tool for making quick and efficient decisions, while others argue that it can lead to errors and biases. The debate around intuitive cognition, often characterised as 'expert knowledge', has important implications for various fields, including education, business, and healthcare. For example, if intuition is a distinct form of cognition, it may be essential to develop educational programmes that teach students how to develop and use intuition effectively. Similarly, if intuition can be a valuable tool for decision-making, then it may be essential to develop business and healthcare practices that encourage leaders and practitioners to listen to their gut feelings. One of the important areas where it becomes crucial is psychotherapy, where intuitive cognition helps therapists connect with clients on a deeper level and make more informed clinical decisions.

While much work on intuitive cognition has focused on the cognitive implications of such a mode of thinking, it has less focused on or addressed different factors that may contribute to variations in aspects of intuitive decision-making and behaviour, especially demographic factors like gender (Epstein et al., 1996; Evans, 2008; Kruglanski & Gigerenzer, 2011).

In general also, when it comes to thinking, there seems to be a gender difference in terms of perception around these processes. Rationality has been pivotal for personifying human development across cultures since their inception, a crucial marker to highlight the journey of mankind. Historically, rationality has been associated with the male gender, often owing to certain and sometimes religious-spiritual beliefs, such as the use of the term *purusha* (translated 'man' in English) in Indian Psychology, wherein the former is considered to be stable and permanent. Unlike rationality, intuition is seen as a female thought.

One of the first accounts of differences between men and women was highlighted by G. Stanley Hall (1904), who posited that women work with intuition and fear, making them prone to living their emotions in greater range and intensity. Stanley's perspective was also an extension of Kant's belief of men as experts on abstract principles and women on concrete details.

It is not surprising that the idea of gut feeling as a 'woman thing' is a dominant association in most cultures. For instance, Gigerenzer et al. (2014) found that people in many different countries, especially Germany, tend to stereotype women as being more intuitive than men. This stereotype is based on the Essentialist notion that there is a fundamental difference in the way men and women think.

Women's ways of knowing: Gendering knowledge

The gendered understanding of knowledge primarily stems from the Cartesian school of thought, which believes men have been competent 'holders of knowledge' since the methods for knowing 'truths and realities' are rational in nature and only men are capable of such abilities (Goldberger, 1996). While the quest for knowledge is perennial, a key difference exists in the mechanism of what constitutes knowledge and the legitimacy of the method of gaining knowledge. A four-part study by Ward and King (2020) reveals that women rely on intuition, highlighting that they tend to value intuitive knowledge, and believe in non-rational ways of gaining knowledge, especially magical beliefs. While, in contrast, men tend to brush off magical causes with actions. Similar observations were noticed in other studies emphasising women tend to engage in more intuitive processing than men (Kersey et al., 2018; Sadler-Smith, 2011). A series of studies by Buckwalter and Stich (2014) found that women have different philosophical intuitions than men regarding reasoning. Ward and King (2020) also highlighted that women tend to believe more in spiritual realms of knowledge and endorse *Karma* as a legitimate causal proposition compared to men. However, there were few arguments mentioned regarding the reason for such a difference in their work.

Some scholars believe this is due to innate biological differences between men and women, while others attribute it to social and cultural factors. There is some evidence to suggest that biological differences between men and women could explain the intricacies of the genderedness of intuitive cognition. For example, studies (McRae et al., 2008) have shown that women have more grey matter in the brain, which is associated with processing emotions and social cues. Additionally, women have higher levels of oxytocin, which is thought to play a role in empathy and bonding. Often, it has been speculated that these differences are a consequence of sex/gender-specific evolutionary processes that ultimately determine sex/gender-specific roles in societies (Jäncke, 2018).

A study by Bao (2022) demonstrated women have less reaction time and more intuitive tools than men. It also emphasised the significance of social and cultural factors, beyond biological factors, that can play a significant role in gender differences regarding intuition. The concept of the social heuristics hypothesis can help us understand how 'social strategies' used in our daily realities often transmute to intuitive responses. According to this hypothesis, it can be understood that women are more likely to use their intuition in social situations owing to their socialisation processes, which endow them with more sensitivity towards social cues and value interpersonal relationships. Various studies have also demonstrated that girls are more likely to be encouraged to develop their emotional intelligence and social skills through role-play games in childhood than boys (Rhodes & Chalik, 2014). Women engaging in social role plays facilitate attentional and perceptual processes around social reality, further aiding intuitive judgements about how they are expected to behave.

Interestingly, the early studies (Epstein et al., 1996) have found non-significant difference between men's and women's scores in faith and intuition. However, the difference became more significant over a period, wherein Sadler-Smith, in 2011, found slight differences among the genders and recommended that women need not be socially stereotyped as intuitive or rely on intuition. Furthermore, women's subscription to intuitive ways of knowing could be due to the stereotypes attributed to them, which can lead to women being more likely to embrace their intuition and to trust their gut feeling and could act in a self-fulfilling prophecy.

On one hand, it is surprising to see how women's intuitive reservoir has been regarded as one of the essentials of womanliness. It has been seen as an important asset in care's social roles and responsibility. At the same time, ironically, on the other hand, having faith in intuition is also associated with the stigma of being naive and holding more unrealistic beliefs than others (gender) in social situations. This dilemma sparks a socio-political debate around the validity of women's thought, rendering women's intuitive knowledge less valid or reliable than men's rational knowledge. Moreover, it might also be possible that men value their intuition in different avenues, such as supporting their favourite football team or placing a bet that might be considered legitimate or socially sanctioned.

This often places women in a difficult position regarding their own knowledge. On one hand, they may perceive themselves as better at understanding situations through emotions and social cues. On the other hand, they may devalue their rational thinking and doubt their abilities. This gendering of knowledge silences women's voices and perspectives in knowledge production. In India, it is common to see women struggle to express their thoughts in personal or professional settings.

The silence of women in most decision-making processes is a common experience in media portrayals, workplace decision-making, education, and so on. Belenky et al. (1986) argue that women do not feel competent to construct their knowledge; rather, they believe they are mere receivers of knowledge from (male) authority. Women perceive themselves as 'voiceless and mindless' with regard to external authority. One of the central themes of the interviews in Belenky et al.'s (1986) study of women's ways of knowing was discovering their own voice. Metaphors such as 'speaking up' and 'being silenced' explored women's confidence and how they connected with others. Belenky et al. (1986) posits that the notion of discovering their voice epitomised their experience of what can be termed 'knower', thereby retrieving their agency and autonomy.

Feminists felt that the (re)construction and reconciliation of 'multiple knowledge' were needed to generate a greater understanding of knowledge for women (Davion, 1994). The popular feminist catchphrase 'the personal is political' stressed the need to appreciate the overlaps in the socio-cultural-political essence of women's personal experiences. As Mills (1997) stated, 'Those problems which many women once considered to be their fault... have come to be seen...as problems which are structural and therefore political'. Thus, women who have been touted as reservoirs of intuitive knowledge have often been historically dismissed, and their lived experiences disregarded. To contest this, voicing 'women's (un)lived experiences' was crucial for reconstructing knowledge and understanding the power dynamics within their experiences (Barbour, 2004).

Trauma and gendered knowing

Trauma stems from a sense of violation that causes extreme disturbance. It can remain embedded in cognitive patterns, impacting the cognitive function of those affected. This can further change how people enact their intuitive cognition. Our experiences profoundly shape intuitive cognition and trauma impacts this decision-making more than other forms of cognition. Let's consider some examples to understand how trauma manifests among women in the form of gendered negotiation with the world. Women in Delhi, for instance, might be very fearful of going out at night, given the high incidence of sexual harassment there. Moreover, women are subjected to constant catcalling, harassment, and molestation. Often, as a coping mechanism, women develop intuitive mechanisms to escape such stressful situations by taking a picture of a vehicle's license plate, calling their parents or friends, or using procedural knowledge to choose routes they feel are safer. Hence, women have heightened danger perception and perceive others as threatening, and their gut feelings might often be attuned to sensing danger. Intuitive judgment often allows trauma survivors to navigate difficult and unpredictable situations by identifying patterns in events.

Motherhood as embodied knowing

Motherhood is a deeply embodied experience. From conception, a woman's body begins to change and adapt to the growing foetus. She feels the baby's movements inside her womb and experiences the physical changes of pregnancy, such as weight gain, fatigue, and morning sickness. After birth, her body continues to change and adapt as she produces milk to feed her baby and learns to care for her newborn. Research on embodiment during pregnancy and post-pregnancy further underscores the importance of studying embodiment to learn more about gender, body, self, and society (Bailey, 2001). Holloway (2014) found that mothers often have their own set of tacit scripts and practices for caring for their children. These scripts may or may not align with professional medical advice, but they are often successful, which validates the embodied and tacit forms of knowing that mothers possess. These tactics are often described as 'the mother knows what's best for the child', associating motherhood with something more instinctual than experiential. Hence, it becomes important to understand this maternal instinct and discover its underlying mechanisms.

Maternal instinct in light of intuitive cognition

The essence of maternal instinct is deeply embedded in the 'good mother' ideology, which believes that a mother should have an organic knowingness of child-rearing from childbirth. This has become a common understanding across cultures. It presents itself as an essentialist notion that is seen as 'natural' among women and is considered common sense and common knowledge. The concept of 'institutionalised motherhood' promotes the idea that women have a natural maternal instinct rather than intelligence or selflessness, which is often a form of intuition (Adriienne Rich, 1976). This notion is often portrayed as a 'dramatised mother on stage', whose maternal self emerges from the 'good mother' ideal, which tells her what should come naturally to her.

Some thinkers argue that maternal instinct is embedded in primarily male-centric religious and philosophical texts (Henderson, 2018). However, women are by far the only ones who experience it. There is a universal understanding of the term 'maternal' that has been associated with attributes like nurturing, caring, and comforting (Aziza, 2020). The basis of maternal instinct lies in the 'shared embodiment' of the mother and her infant. Scholars Cusk and colleagues postulate that this sharing of bodies transcends to a metaphysical level, as Parker (1995) argue in *Torn in Two: The Experience of Maternal Ambivalence*, defining maternal instinct as a response to maternal ambivalence and the mothers' interpretation of these shared realities.

While many eminent feminist scholars, such as Nancy Chodorow (2012) posit that maternal instinct—often seen as a natural instinct—is a product of social conditioning. When a mother gives birth, she is often expected to bond immediately with her child. Conceptualising a bond between a child and the mother as inborn, instinctive, and natural has various implications, increasing expectations around the mother's supposed innate knowledge of the child. This further has numerous applications in developing mother-child relationships and the caring process with different age groups of children. Mothers who do not endorse the concept of maternal instinct believe that there is no such thing as an internal urge. Rather, the 'premonitions' that something is not right with their child are because of their knowledge as a mother. Constant monitoring of their child primes mothers to recognise 'micro signals', which assist them in knowing when something is not right (Borovska, 2015).

A study by Johnson (2009) found that mothers often value cultural knowledge that can act as a valuable resource. One form of this knowledge is that, instead of asking professionals, they seek help from other mothers and have also added the importance of integrating cultural practices such as 'removing the evil eye' with modern practices. This tacit knowledge about mothering, motherhood, and bodies is often communicated through culturally rooted metaphors called *consejos* (translated to 'suggestions' in English). For example, from a young age, girls are often told that they will be mothers someday and will naturally know how to care for their children. They also found that women often learn parenting from becoming a parental figure to their younger siblings, and often, such experiences help them navigate the difficult terrain of motherhood itself. Hence, it highlights that motherhood and mothering embrace a more pragmatic view in terms of adopting practices that feel 'real for us' and celebrate the intuitive, cultural, pragmatic, and embodied aspects of motherhood.

However, not all experiences are positive, as highlighted by the experience of the unknowingness of biological motherhood, which constitutes the overwhelming feelings of 'what is it to be a good mother?' (Miller, 2007). Most mothers experience 'embodied distress' and the 'fear of deviancy' during pregnancy and afterwards (Nash, 2015; Staneva et al., 2017). Often, women are asked to negate their own needs and prioritise the child's needs completely (Miller & Brown, 2005), stressing that women have a duty to love a child intensely beyond their own capacity as well. This in itself adds an expectation of prioritising the child at any cost as a sign of a mother, making it difficult to have a sense of self. This can be especially challenging for working women in contemporary times, who may have to negotiate their relationship with their children while working to support their families. Some practices of mothering emphasise performativity, or the social script during pregnancy and how one must be a mother. This can cause problems for mothers who do not fit these high ideals.

Women deal with psychic conflicts while conforming to these 'pressures' of being a good mother. A significant number of women experience distress when they struggle to feel unconditional, selfless love for their children and see themselves failing to perform the role of the perfect mother. This led Adrienne Rich (1976) to conclude that the mother is an incarcerated figure in her own maternal body.

Hardy (2010) also postulates that maternal instincts are primarily socially constructed instead of mere 'innate biological reactions'. She believes that the methods of examining maternal instinct should be revisited. Having a multi-dimensional approach can give us a broader picture of the phenomenon. Dissecting historical accounts of mothers in various cultures and across different stages of life can be useful, along with comparative studies. However, she also highlights that motherhood is not naturally instinctive, emphasising the role of common knowledge, which makes the instinct seem reflexive and automatic, often penalising mothers who do not abide by such ideals. Moreover, it raises the question of the presence of other family members, especially the father, who seems to escape the judgment of 'paternal instinct' that a mother is subjected to. There is also some evolutionary justification for this that highlights the role of parental investment, which remains higher for mothers and, hence, preference for kin selection. Women are more socially expected to have altruism as their intuitive response than men (Rand et al., 2016), mainly because it is believed that the behaviour of both men and women is governed and sustained through stereotyping of their social roles. This also relates to how motherhood has been construed and portrayed in movies and cinema in India, probably the most famous being *Mother India*, where a mother is willing to sacrifice her life for her child.

While intuitive cognition is seen as omnipresent, it can often lead to us endorsing violent stereotypes and penalising people who do not hold these Essentialised values. For example, women who feel an absence of maternal instinct are often seen as less of a woman and sanctioned for it. Frequently, what seems intuitive to people might be laden with years of violence, stereotypes, and control over bodies that dictate how one should feel. Often, this can lead to socio-emotional problems. We chose the film *Tribhanga* as a text to explore the contours of intuitive cognition, how trauma and social scripts shape our intuitive decision-making, and how the rejection of 'motherly instinct' is fraught with social sanctions and discrimination.

Tribhanga: The not so intuitive women

Tribhanga, the film, is written and directed by Renuka Shahane, an acclaimed Hindi and Marathi actress. Told through women of three generations, each with deviances and atypicality pertaining to their situatedness and temporal realities the film explored the themes of motherhood, daughterhood, and identity. All the characters discover themselves by navigating the space between their experiences and gendered notions, shaping their cognitive and emotional processes. It gives insights into the realities of mothering, which is comprised of all their flaws, mistakes, strengths, and weaknesses.

This film accounts for the remarkable journey of three generations of women—Nayan, Anu, and Masha—by exploring the intersectionality of their womanhood and their (un)lived motherhood realities. The complex relational dynamics of the mother and daughter dyad and the conflicts due to othering open the space for deconstructing gendered ways of knowing. Even if the three women seem distinctively different, there is a common quest for their own identity, as identity is heavily relationally linked to the mother, Nayan. This creates an emphasis on the role of the mother in their life and brings the script of 'good mother' which has been historically equated with the possession of a motherly instinct, into discussion. This film can help us understand the gendered ways of knowing of conforming and non-conforming women and how it guides their intuitive cognition. The authors intended to know the navigation across social roles to understand how their intuitiveness guided their cognition.

In *Tribhanga*, the first-generation Nayan is a passionate, talented woman with a desire to write. While she exhibits so much passion in the workspace, her relational spaces are neglected to prioritise her desire to write. There are scenes in which she shuts the door when she has heated arguments with her mother-in-law over her not following the social script of being a good mother and when she leaves the house with her children. This leads to the rejection of a social script of mothering that is positively sanctioned by society. We see a moment of action in which she makes an intuitive decision to leave based on her moral values and rejects her social position.

As an individual, Nayan had a strong feeling about her writing; she felt connected to her work and was able to experience the pain of being separated from it. Something usually represented as a maternal instinct in the mother-child relationship. She intuitively connects with her work, which she enjoys. She is quoted saying, '*Mujhe shanti se likhne do*' (trans: Let me write in peace), '*Mein bas likhte chali jaati thi*' (trans: I just used to keep writing). This can be seen as a violation of social heuristics attached to women, leading to negative sanctions in her relational space. She posits that writing is a calling that feels 'intuitively right' for her to engage in most of the time, which comes naturally to her. However, the film fails to highlight moments where Nayan engages reflexively in the maternal space and builds emotional space for the children during their childhood years. It was only retrospectively that she could see the damage her quest for identity might have brought to others. Here, she is seen to negotiate between her intuitive drive and her reflexive quest for her role and identity. Such a representation portrays how a woman's quest for identity may lead to othering of the relational or maternal space.

It is notable that, as a woman, Nayan's intuitive knowledge around her quest for identity was dismissed and often seen as less motherly. It was perceived as less womanly or selfish. This highlights the complicated nature of gendering intuitive knowledge and the convoluted terrain of when intuitive knowledge is valued and negated. A woman, in this case, Nayan, is dismissed when she expresses a natural intuitive desire for her work and rejects adopting the 'good mother' label and 'motherly instinct' or does not celebrate the notion of the naturalness of sacrifice. Such rejection is seen as a threat to the relational space, and here, society demands that women be intuitive in their relational spaces, understand the spouse's need before he has to ask, know the reason for crying, and know what every family member would want to eat. A lot of pressure is then placed on the woman to be relationally intuitive and reject any other need beyond the family's scope.

In fact, women are often asked to negate their own needs and prioritise the child's needs completely (Miller & Brown, 2005), stressing that women have a duty to love a child intensely, which complicates how wage-paying women negotiate their relationship with their child and often penalises their well-being. Usually, some practices stress the presence of performative mothering, which entails a social script of how one must perform mothering and pregnancy, which often causes problems for mothers who do not fit such high ideals.

Even in the movie, Nayantara was penalised for prioritising her passion for writing, as if focusing on that meant she was less of a mother and wife. The idea of a mother loving the child has been seen more in terms of constantly keeping the child at the center of their life. This was one of the central themes that made Nayan believe that she was not meant for married life since that involved giving up her own needs. Adrennie Rich (1976) in the study, highlighted the concept of 'Institutionalised motherhood', which propagates the embodiment of maternal instinct in women as opposed to intelligence and selflessness. This notion is conceptualised as a 'dramatised mother on stage' whose maternal self emerges from the good mother ideal, which connects her to what should come 'naturally' to her. Natural, which became a patterned process through social conditioning.

Nayan was blamed for things; for instance, if anything goes wrong, it's the mother's fault. The mother should have understood this. For instance, in this film, when Nayan's husband gets home from work, he finds his children eating with their grandmother. Nayan is present—absent in her mothering spaces—as she is engrossed in her writing work. Her mothering roles and responsibilities are being fulfilled by her mother-in-law, who is asserting her intuitive decisions about mothering on her, like reprimanding Nayan for being ignorant about her mothering responsibilities. As an intuitive prosecutor, the husband is quick to cast Nayan as a perpetrator and criminal for not doing the motherly duties that should come to her naturally and intuitively.

Anuradha, the daughter of Nayan, was also angry at her mother for having a desire for herself and reducing her space to that of a mother. There is a slight hint of intuition, which Nayan expresses in the scene where Anu is being sexually abused. A mother dismissing her intuitive knowledge has been a cardinal point of conflict between mother and daughter, as Nayan was unable to fulfil her role expectations as a mother, which were to make intuitive decisions and safeguard her daughter from abuse. Nayan is more often seen as a selfish woman than a mother or grandmother. Nayan's (un)knowingness can be deciphered from the nervousness on her face as she enters the room where Anu is being sexually abused. Her knowingness that something is not right is probably coming from her daughter's changed behaviour, as per Nayan's understanding. When she asked '*Kya hua*?' (trans: what happened?), there was some anticipation. It seemed that Anu somewhere knew about this intuitively, and she held grudges against her mother.

In personal life, trauma provides the basis for intuitive thought, as seen in Anu's character. The embodied knowledge that she carries from her childhood experience of sexual abuse is a figment of gendered learning in a woman. Anu's script of mothering is instinctive, wherein there are sufficient examples in the film that show that she is protective of her daughter, Masha. For example, in one conversation about Masha's child, she said, 'I didn't have a choice; *meri jethani ki itni betiyan hai*, (trans: my sister-in-law has so many daughters) so they didn't want to take a risk'. She can tell when something is not right with Masha. However, she may not feel those presumed maternal instincts as she navigates the various roles. The situation where Masha talked about her childhood in the mother's romantic relational space: Is this protectiveness coming from a biological maternal instinct or the trauma response of Anu's experience?

The movie *Conversations with Milan*, who was writing Nayan's autobiography, opened a space to witness the complex relationships between the women in the family—the love and support that they have for each other, as well as the pain and conflict that they experience. This opened the reflexive space between the three generations, widening the horizons of looking at the individual through multiple selves with multiple roles, identities, and desires. The struggles around balancing the personal and interpersonal space within a woman were a journey the movie helped to tap into, questioning the taken-for-granted assumptions about how a woman is supposed to be. When we glorify maternal instinct, we are somewhere enforcing the space to be still centered around motherhood, restricting the other selves. Psychologically, it is a form of intrapsychic violence where women, when unable to focus on their other spaces, feel othered in the maternal space, making them more overprotective and emotionally vulnerable. This further reinforces the stereotype of mothers as more emotional, less rational, and less intelligent. In the 21st century, this has very significant importance because children have started to perceive emotions as less rational and are trying to follow the script of becoming more rational, dismissing their exploration of emotions.

In the modern world, women seem to be even more conflicted, wherein the choices seem to be still somewhere enmeshed in the patriarchal script socially learned and reinforced while their intuitive self is navigating the unexplored spaces of their traditional selves while being absent-present in their modern intrapsychic spaces. Masha, for instance, a woman of contemporary times, is a defiant person, having been brought up by independent and opinionated women and having had unconventional life choices in a conventional socio-cultural template. Yet, she shares some familiarity with her grandmother's conservative and regressive schematic patterns, as she is fearful of the dysfunctionalities of her mother's and grandmother's relationship. She intuitively felt a danger of repeating such relational patterns, even though she shares an affectionate bond with her mother and grandmother. Her character reflects intuitiveness in social scripts; for instance, 'covering the head with a dupatta (trans: scarf) as a woman in front of elders', wherein she feels closer to her relational schemas by conforming to the social script. Even if a non-conventional script of women was raising her, the difference in society made her feel rejected, facilitating her to make conventional choices to find cohesion within society. This not only reflects on her as a character but also on how being on the rebel side of society can also feel isolating, further pushing an individual toward choosing traditional scripts. Nayan and Anu were similar in their desire to be agentic. However, the lack of space to acknowledge the differences and lack of dialogue on the choices and their repercussions made it possible for Masha to resonate more with spaces where there may be a lack of agency but also societal inclusion in relational spaces.

Initially, the movie lacked affective solidarity, wherein as the space of communication opened between the generations, it widened the space to see the person as an individual, wherein Anu could see all three through the lens of a woman and called the triad, defining it as '*Tribhanga—tedi medhi and crazy*', that is, three women who are defiant from the normal and filled with their own craziness. The dissonance around the beauty, with its own flaws, became more fine-tuned, giving her a sense of peace and acceptance.

The idea of what it means to be a 'woman who is intuitive' needs to be looked at through an interplay of multiple layers instead of socialisation. It becomes crucial to see how we identify the woman, which will shape their way of knowing. When we say the gendered construction of knowledge, it becomes important to rule out conditioning, trauma response, and the patriarchal script. What will make a 'woman feel fulfilled?'

Critique of the film

Nayan is engaging in perspective-taking but in retrospection. She is not emotive, so it has given a perspective of the script that is being herself or exploring. So, the director's intuitive cognition around Nayan's character construction also reflects the inbuilt schemas around women as either loving, protective, or ambitious. The combination of both and the presentation seems difficult to even envision in society. It is difficult for women to be exceptional, and it feels like roles are prerequisites to identity, reducing the lens of mother to identity. When it comes to intuitive cognition, it can be said that:

a Intuitive cognition is far more than a cultural pattern; gut feeling should be critiqued, coming from conditioning or something genuinely intuitive.
b Intuitive cognition is not just a cultural pattern but is rather discovering the self-oriented path. The film has also been credited with starting a conversation about the importance of female representation in Indian cinema. This film cannot be appreciated as representative of progressive women; rather, it's regressive at many levels.

Conclusion

The aim of this chapter was to examine the gendered shades of intuitive cognition in the context of motherhood. The researchers have used film analysis to understand how maternal instinct, which has been conceptualised as one of the prescriptive norms of motherhood, operates in each character of the film *Tribhanga*, which has been used for analysis. The study highlights major themes such as understanding the making of intuitive cognition of the female characters of the film, the intricacies around their conforming and non-conforming identities, facing social sanctioning owing to their violation of social heuristics, and lack of affective solidarity among the film characters.

It is imperative to understand that, in this context, intuitive cognition operates in multiple dimensions. It has shades of past trauma and gendered learning; however, it is essential to appreciate how the intuitive self forms at the core of our sense-making, whose overt manifestation is minimal yet pertinent. For instance, in the film, Anuradha hesitates to share her nightmare with her friend in which she gets flashbacks of her sexual abuse, owing to gendered intuitive knowing. With gendered knowing being the cardinal aspect of it, it is important to critically reflect on how maternal instinct is deemed to become an anchor for a woman in her mothering experiences and beyond. This analysis points out some of the limitations of intuitive cognition and how it can affect critical thinking, such as having a fixed image of a category or a group of people, which is highlighted by the social heuristics hypothesis. Moreover, intuitive cognition runs the risk of collapsing into other constructs and, importantly, enters an ambiguous territory where we cannot distinguish intuitive cognition from apprehension to trauma response, as all seem to be quite automatic and unconscious. This calls for a clinically sensitive understanding of intuitive cognition as well as for decision-making theorists to consider the implications and scope of intuitive cognition itself.

References

Aziza, N. (2020). Honing, loving, and nurturing: A study of mothers' role in family. *Martabat: Jurnal Perempuan Dan Anak*, *4*(2), 251–266.

Bailey, L. (2001). Gender shows: First-time mothers and embodied selves. *Gender & Society*, *15*(1), 110–129.

Bao, W., Wang, Y., Yu, T., Zhou, J., & Luo, J. (2022). Women rely on "gut feeling"? The neural pattern of gender difference in non-mathematic intuition. *Personality and Individual Differences*, *196*, 111720.

Barbour, K. (2004). Embodied ways of knowing. *Waikato Journal of Education*, *10*.

Belenky, M. F., Clinchy, B. M., Goldberger, N. R., & Tarule, J. M. (1986). *Women's Ways of Knowing: The Development of Self, Voice, and Mind*. Basic Books.

Borovska, V. (2015). Demystification of maternal ideologies–Maternal instinct. *Mind the Gap (s): Family, Socialization and Gender*, *i*, 125–126.

Buckwalter, W., & Stich, S. (2014). Gender and philosophical intuition. *Experimental Philosophy*, *2*, 307–346.

Chodorow, N. J. (2012). *Individualizing Gender and Sexuality: Theory and Practice*. Routledge.

Davion, V. (1994). Is ecofeminism feminist? In Karen Warren (Ed.), *Ecological Feminism* (pp. 8–28). Routledge.

Epstein, S., Pacini, R., Denes-Raj, V., & Heier, H. (1996). Individual differences in intuitive–experimental and analytical–rational thinking styles. *Journal of Personality and Social Psychology*, *71*(2), 390–405. https://doi.org/10.1037/0022-3514.71.2.390

Evans, J. St. B. T. (2008). Dual-processing accounts of reasoning, judgment, and social cognition. *Annual Review of Psychology*, *59*, 255–278. https://doi.org/10.1146/annurev.psych.59.103006.093629

Gelman, S. A., & Legare, C. H. (2011). Concepts and folk theories. *Annual Review of Anthropology*, *40*, 379–398. https://doi.org/10.1146/annurev-anthro-081309-145822

Gigerenzer, G., Galesic, M., & Garcia-Retamero, R. (2014). Stereotypes about men's and women's intuitions: A study of two nations. *Journal of Cross-Cultural Psychology*, *45*(1), 62–81.

Goldberger, N. R. (1996). Looking backward, looking forward. In N. R. Goldberger, J. M. Tarule, B. M. Clinchy, & M. F. Belenky (Eds.), *Knowledge, Difference and Power: Essays Inspired by Women's Ways of Knowing* (pp. 1–17). Basic Books.

Hall, G. S. (1904). *Adolescence in Literature, Biography, and History.*

Hardy, S. B. (2010). Mothers and others. Retrieved on December 19 2013: https://www.naturalhistorymag.com/features/11440/mothersandothers

Henderson, S. (2018). The blurring effect: An exploration of maternal instinct and ambivalence (Master's thesis). University of Kent.

Holloway, S. L. (2014). Reproducing motherhood. In *Geographies of New Femininities* (pp. 91–112). Routledge.

Johnson, L.R. (2009), Challenging "best practices" in family literacy and parent education programs: The development and enactment of mothering knowledge among Puerto Rican and Latina Mothers in Chicago. *Anthropology & Education Quarterly*, *40*, 257–276. https://doi.org/10.1111/j.1548-1492.2009.01044.x

Jäncke, L. (2018). Sex/gender differences in cognition, neurophysiology, and neuroanatomy. *F1000Research*, *7*. https://doi.org/10.12688/f1000research.13917.1

Kersey, A. J., Braham, E. J., Csumitta, K. D., Libertus, M. E., & Cantlon, J. F. (2018). No intrinsic gender differences in children's earliest numerical abilities. *npj Science of Learning*, *3*(1), 12.

Kruglanski, A. W., & Gigerenzer, G. (2011). Intuitive and deliberate judgments are based on common principles. *Psychological Review*, *118*(1), 97–109. https://doi.org/10.1037/a0020762

McRae, K., Ochsner, K. N., Mauss, I. B., Gabrieli, J. J., & Gross, J. J. (2008). Gender differences in emotion regulation: An fMRI study of cognitive reappraisal. *Group Processes & Intergroup Relations*, *11*(2), 143–162.

Miller, T. (2007). "Is this what motherhood is all about?" Weaving experiences and discourse through transition to first-time motherhood. *Gender & Society*, *21*(3), 337–358.

Miller, Y. D., & Brown, W. J. (2005). Determinants of active leisure for women with young children—An "ethic of care" prevails. *Leisure Sciences*, *27*(5), 405–420.

Mills, S. (1997). *Discourse.* Routledge.

Nash, M. (2015). Indulgence versus restraint: A discussion of embodied eating practices of pregnant Australian women. *Journal of Sociology*, *51*(3), 478–491. https://doi.org/10.1177/1440783312474357

Parker, R. (1995). *Torn in Two: The Experience of Maternal Ambivalence.* Virago Press.

Rand, D. G., Brescoll, V. L., Everett, J. A., Capraro, V., & Barcelo, H. (2016). Social heuristics and social roles: Intuition favors altruism for women but not for men. *Journal of Experimental Psychology: General*, *145*(4), 389.
Rhodes, M., & Chalik, L. (2014). The interplay between intuitive psychology and intuitive sociology. *British Journal of Developmental Psychology*, *32*(3), 248–251.
Rich, A. (1976). *Of Woman Born: Motherhood as Experience and Institution*. W.W. Norton & Company.
Sadler-Smith, E. (2011). The intuitive style: Relationships with local/global and verbal/visual styles, gender, and superstitious reasoning. *Learning and Individual Differences*, *21*(3), 263–270.
Staneva, A. A., Bogossian, F., Morawska, A., & Wittkowski, A. (2017). "I just feel like I am broken. I am the worst pregnant woman ever": A qualitative exploration of the "at odds" experience of women's antenatal distress. *Health Care for Women International*, *38*(6), 658–686. https://doi.org/10.1080/07399332.2017.1297448
Ward, S. J., & King, L. A. (2020). Examining the roles of intuition and gender in magical beliefs. *Journal of Research in Personality*, *86*, 103956.

Chapter 8

Myriads of intuitive cognition in the social world

Aritra Mukherjee and Ishita U. Bharadwaj

Myriads of intuitive cognition in the social world

Intuitive cognition is a way of thinking based on quick, instinctive, and gut-feeling-based reasoning rather than engaging in a deliberate, analytical process. It is logical and follows a deeper level of reasoning. Moreover, intuitive cognition is characterised by properties: it is effortless and experiential, i.e., it is based on the tacit knowledge gathered through one's life and done in combination with cultural intersubjective knowledge, i.e., knowing without knowing why. It could be classified in Polanyi's notion of 'tacit knowledge', i.e., the concept of judgement, experiences, insight, and intuition. Psychological studies have highlighted the crucial role of expert decision-makers, such as chess players, who can make complex moves in seconds for novice players to perform. This emphasizes on the importance of intuitive cognition in their expertise. Pattern recognition and decision-making are often so fast that they cannot give space for deep analytical thinking. Interestingly, the prevalence of decision-making styles finds that people rely on more intuitive cognition than analytical, and people feel greater satisfaction while engaging in intuitive cognition than analytical cognition. This highlights that cognitive theories must account for such knowledge and see how it functions in the social world.

The study of intuitive cognition in the social world is more complex due to its interdisciplinary terrain, as it has to consider both intuitive psychology and intuitive sociology (Shutts & Kalish, 2021). The classification of intuitive social psychology is complex as it falls in between intuitive psychology, which deals with beliefs, desires, and intentions (Wellman et al., 1990), and intuitive sociology, which highlights the role of social categories, norms, and social status (Shutts & Kalish, 2021). Hence, an intuitive cognition theory of decision-making would challenge the idea of the rational, unbiased man and highlight the development of folk social psychologists who make decisions rooted in history, which are tacit and formed through years of social negotiation. For example, a fight between two individuals from different religious communities can be viewed as a fight between individuals with personal

DOI: 10.4324/9781003377757-10

differences or between individuals due to religious differences. The decision-making will depend on folk psychological attributions based on people developing certain perceptual tendencies and expectancy biases or priming them to certain expectations. This constitutes the basic premise of Intuitive Social psychology.

From a young age, people can distinguish between groups and name them. They develop certain expectations about these groups based on their experiences and ascribe moral worth to them (Shutts & Kalish, 2021). Additionally, they assign norms for how each group should behave and what actions may violate those norms. This also influences how individuals are expected to act within their social category; for example, traditional gender roles dictate that women are more empathetic than men, and, therefore, the common belief is that women should take care of children (Goodnow & Delaney, 1989). From a young age, people can distinguish between groups and name them. They develop certain expectations about these groups based on their experiences and ascribe moral worth to them (Taylor et al., 2020).

Individuals often unconsciously absorb and internalize these norms about how different social groups—such as genders—are expected to behave. These intuitive frameworks shape automatic judgments and expectations, such that, for instance, women may be intuitively perceived as more empathetic and naturally suited to caregiving roles, like child-rearing, based on long-standing gender stereotypes.

People learn to associate categories with individuals, animals, or objects while receiving moral guidance regarding concepts like 'stranger danger' or distinguishing between 'good food' and 'bad food'. Additionally, our inherent bias leads us to view our group more favourably than others, supported by mere-categorisation experiments showing preference towards arbitrarily assigned in-group members even when no fundamental distinctions exist, also known as the mere exposure effect. Such preferences might be deeply embedded within our cognitive framework from an early age.

Intuitive sociology further emphasises how people form normative expectations about specific groups: defining their characteristics, determining their behaviours, detailing the information they process, and specifying how they interact with other groups (Shutts & Kalish, 2021). For instance, interactions between men and women in India differ from elsewhere due to cultural differences in societal norms. These intuitive cultural understandings influence individual behaviour, such as dictating how one should behave in a particular situation, also known as scripts and schemas (Bicchieri & McNally, 2018). However, it is essential to understand that constructs internalised in the psyche are recent constructions through social negotiation and patterns that appear intuitive, which also take years to come into shape and get accepted in society. For example, the concept of 'race' and its associated hierarchies are deeply entrenched in many societies. Moreover, the biological basis of race and racial categories was developed relatively recently, around the 18th century, during the peak of European colonization. Before that, differences were acknowledged but not held in such a rigid and hierarchical manner. Over time, the idea of some races being superior to others has led to the development of implicit biases, stereotypes, and systemic inequality that are still prevalent today. Hence, a concept such as 'race,' which feels like a 'natural' way to categorize people, is, in fact, a recent social product that is continually contested, negotiated, and established (Roth et al., 2023). Moreover, concepts such as collective emotions, i.e., the belief that groups and states often share a specific emotional climate (see Sullivan, 2015, for a detailed review), collective memory, i.e., the belief that groups usually understand the world through certain historical events usually serve as functional tools for decision-making in intergroup situations and in these moments we rely on our intuitions as a group rather than as rational, analytical beings (Tran, 2012).

While we can see that there is an appreciation and space for intuitive cognition in social psychology, one needs to understand the different theories that can be used to understand how social scientists can understand the prevalence of intuitive cognition in the world and how people use it judiciously. In this regard, we propose that intuitive cognition could be reasoned through the basic cognitive theory of the Dual Processing Model (Tversky & Kahneman, 1981), which states that people opt for quick and fast decisions because they wish to be cognitively frugal. The next are two theories. One is the symbolic interactionist perspective, which deals with how people understand everyday rules, regulations, and behaviour. Closely related to that is the social constructionist perspective, which states the importance of people's understanding of the world through historically situated understanding. Below is a brief description and synthesis of the theories and their usefulness in understanding intuitive cognition and how they operate in the social world.

Plausible social theories explaining intuitive cognition

Dual processing model and intuitive cognition

The concept of intuitive cognition in social theory is closely linked to the Dual-Processing model proposed by Tversky and Kahneman (1981). According to this model, people tend to be cognitively 'frugal' and rely on intuitive, peripheral routes in most daily activities. Tversky and Kahneman identified the presence of the availability heuristic, i.e., relying on information that has been available to us for a period of time, and representative heuristic, i.e., drawing judgements through a superficial understanding of patterns and action, the effect heuristic, i.e., drawing on emotions rather than information for making decisions was added to explain rapid peripheral reasoning. Other scholars, such as Goldberg et al. (1999), suggested that people act as intuitive prosecutors, seeking to understand reasons for others' behaviour, and also as intuitive statisticians, using a rough sense of statistics to aid decision-making. They emphasised that our understanding of cultural norms stems from the presence of a collective social other, where we do not see ourselves as active stakeholders. They also highlighted that our sense of meaning can be culturally determined; for example, the statement 'Arjun is cooperative' could be interpreted to draw comparisons with others or indicate a higher level of cooperativeness when in relation to others in the vicinity. The heuristic model also helps explain two fundamental biases about how people interpret other people's behaviour in society. The first is the fundamental attribution error and the actor-observer effect, where people tend to act as intuitive prosecutors and try to establish causal relations about others' behaviour and, in most cases, attribute dispositional reasons for others and situational and circumstantial reasoning for themselves. In addition, Paul Slovic et al. (2007) proposed that people often make decisions based on whether something feels good or bad to them, categorising it as negative or positive, also known as the affect heuristic. The understanding that emotions play a significant role in our decision-making processes often shapes our judgements about various subjects. Affect heuristics, for instance, describes how emotions rather than a thorough analysis can influence our attitudes or decisions. This is why many product companies aim to capitalise on feelings of joy or social status to enhance their popularity, even if their products are comparable to more affordable alternatives. Therefore, it is evident that cognitive theories have been employed in the social realm to comprehend how people make intuitive judgements about others' behaviour. While the concept of intuitive cognition in social theory provides a compelling framework for understanding decision-making and social interactions, it is essential to consider theories highlighting the importance of historical situatedness to understand the prevalence of these heuristics, advanced by the social constructionist and symbolic interaction perspective.

Social constructionist perspective and intuitive cognition

A theory that can help us understand intuitive cognition in the social world is the social constructionist perspective (Burr, 2015). The social constructionist perspective has four essential conditions to highlight that most interactions are socially constructed and that the world is not a direct reflection of objective reality and is shaped by various cultural and social forces such as language. Second, knowledge is created through interaction, which highlights that different interactions would produce different knowledge perspectives; for example, a plastic water bottle for an environmentalist can represent a biological hazard, and for a capitalist businessman, it could be a business opportunity, hence, highlighting that our intuitive leanings are shaped by our day-to-day and historical interactions. Third, meaning is not fixed but continuously shaped and reshaped through interactions, that both knowledge and intuitive thought are shaped by context and are open to transformation over time. For example the idea of good mother always stays at home and take care of home was once widely accepted. However, as societal conversations about gender roles and work-life balance has changed, many now intuitively have started accepting that a woman can also be a working professional highlighting how intuitive beliefs shift through social interaction.

Similarly, the intuitive belief that mental illness is personal weakness was once widespread. However, through changing public discourse and increased awareness society has gradually reconstructing this meaning now that mental health challenges are legitimate medical and psychological conditions than moral failings.

Thus, the social constructionist perspective allows us to understand the nature of intuitive cognition in a social world, and it highlights how specific intuitive patterns are more easily accessible and how some are not and need analytical skills. Social constructionism can help us understand how our social context shapes our intuitive thinking, and intuitive thinking can help us quickly understand the complex and ambiguous world around us. For example, research has shown that our cultural stereotypes often influence our intuitive judgements about people. This is because our stereotypes are part of our social context, shaping how we perceive and interpret the world. They are also rooted in history and transmitted through language (Hegarty & Pratto, 2004).

The social constructionist perspective is supported by newer research into intuition and intuitive reasoning. Some theorists, such as Volz and Zander (2014), posited that intuitive logic takes through tacitly informed cue-criterion relationships, i.e., certain cues trigger certain knowledge and trigger specific knowledge systems, i.e., like the ones of context-dependent memory. Thus, stressing the importance of experiences. Other scholars like Bowers et al. (1990) highlighted that specific environments trigger specific forms of tacit knowledge acquired through life, which is also furthered by Kruglanski and Gigerenzer (2011), who state that both intuition and deliberation revolve around the same principles of rules and information dependent on environmental conditions. Hence, intuitive cognition requires situatedness, cultural knowledge, and certain knowledge of being in the world.

A symbolic interactionist perspective for intuitive behaviour

Furthermore, theories such as symbolic interactionism help us understand that expectations are shared and then come into existence, forming common standards of behaviour. This, in turn, contributes to the development of our tacit knowledge and aids in our intuitive decision-making process. For instance, it guides the conduct of a police officer when interacting with regular individuals or individuals accused of serious crimes (Biddle, 2013). These standards establish the norms or unspoken rules of behaviour against which actions can be compared. Ridgeway and Correll (2004) state these rules are invoked through cultural scripts, which are automatic rules of thumb behaviour expected in a certain situation; intuitive cognition guides how to act, including knowledge of scripts and the development of schemas also referred to as cultural schemas (DiMaggio, 1997). It can also lead to role expectations related to profession, gender, and religion, among other factors (Srinivasan et al., 2019). For example, children internalise gender-specific scripts and develop ideas about who their friends should be from a very young age.

These norms can exist at functional and relational levels, meaning they have both a prescriptive and a descriptive role in guiding behaviour (Burke & Young, 2011). In one classroom exercise, the authors of this current study designed role-playing scenarios for conflict resolution in different situations. They observed that students naturally assumed various roles, adopted moral stances, and behaved in ways consistent with their assigned roles. This knowledge of normative roles helped the students navigate the uncertain and unfamiliar terrain of conflict resolution. These scenarios were necessary for the authors to have observed a different type of argumentation that diverged from the expected role-consistent behaviours the students had adopted. The students formed bonds based on their expected roles, showing a strong sense of solidarity within their groups while recognizing that their behavior were shaped more by situation than personal choice.

Further, this highlights that people negotiate through the social world with some knowledge referred to here as 'knowingness' about how the world operates. This is done through years of gathering tacit cultural knowledge and inhabiting a historically situated cultural place. Thus, it highlights that people often play out scripts, roles, and schemas through shared everyday processes situated historically and culturally, making intuitive thinking second nature and often better in interacting in society. Below, we shall look at a few domains in which intuitive cognition is best applied in the social world.

Embodied and affective knowledge and intuitive cognition

Researchers have posited that some knowledge is embodied (Ignatow, 2007), highlighting the potential of cultural and affective ways our bodies interact with the world. Moreover, according to Bourdieu, intuitive moral reasoning involves understanding the ethical boundaries between ourselves and other groups. Furthermore, people are accurately able to judge the emotions of others without having gone through an extensive reading list on the nature and type of emotions, which speaks of the level of theory of mind and its connection to intuitive, emotional decision-making and appraisals (Michalson & Lewis, 1985). For example, most people can accurately judge the expressions of universal emotions given by Ekman with high accuracy, which can be seen in young infants and children as well (Sauter et al., 2015). Sayer

(2005) draws attention to the meso-level, encompassing other actors, practices, and institutions that people engage with. When individuals apply ideas and methods of evaluating others from the available cultural repertoires, their actions are primarily driven by intuitions, emotions, and deeply ingrained beliefs regarding the human body. In addition, some emotions are socially and culturally built, operating only in specific contexts like the shades of embarrassment (Shweder, 2003) through *Lajja*, *haya*, and *Sharam*, where all have different shades and meanings, but their natural outpouring is socially conditioned. Hence, the cultural knowingness of how to act and behave and the appropriateness of certain behaviours can only 'intuitively' feel right. For example, we intuitively know not to laugh at a funeral, and it would be inappropriate to wail at a wedding. This cultural knowledge and intuitive rightness are what theorist Pierre Bourdieu called *Habitus* (Bourdieu, 2018). Understanding *Habitus* can be crucial to psychologists trying to unearth the workings of human minds and make accurate judgements in most situations in a social setting. *Habitus* refers to the phenomenon where our experiences, past experiences, and social positions shape how we feel, act, and present our thoughts. Bourdieu also talks about *Habitus* at a cognitive level, which he terms 'cognitive *Habitus*', which highlights how our social background affects how we think of a particular phenomenon.

For example, in a famous scene in the Oscar-winning Korean Film 'The Parasite' (2019), directed by Bong Joon-Ho, there is a moment when it rains heavily, setting the pretext for the story's climax. There is a difference in how the poor man whose house has been flooded cognises the rain and how the rich person understands the shower, which the rich woman deems as romantic and 'good weather', but the poor family's house gets flooded, creating sorrow and sadness. This disparity of understanding of the same event is caused by each individual's social position, which is shaped by their class and cultural position, such as one's family background, educational experiences, and social class, which shape *Habitus*, i.e., the different ways of knowing the world due to one's place in society. The theory of *Habitus* supports the idea of 'knowingness', which will be discussed later in the chapter as we dissect how we make intuitive judgements about people and class.

Intuitive cognition and stereotypes

Intuitive cognition can lead to the development of stereotypes and the use of stereotypes in action, such as making snap judgements about people. It can also impact decision-making, such as giving preference to some groups of people over others (Sierksma, 2022).In addition,intutiive cognition can be particularly valuable in navigating complex or unfamiliar situations where threats are uncertain and decision must be made quickly such as moving through crowded streets or having to make judgment under time pressure. For instance, when asked why we support a particular political stance or align with a specific side of protest, we often lack complete information or the time to research evert aspect. Yet, people frequently offer confident, seemingly well reasoned opinion that are largely shaped by their underlying moral intuitions. As Cheung et al. (2017) suggest, individuals often join social movements not for calculated personal gain but because they feel their social identity is at risk or they are motivated by shared hope of success. In these instances, actions are driven by a sense of collective purpose that transcends purely analytical reasoning.

The concept of 'knowingness' in intuitive cognition can be pretty valuable, especially in today's polarised society. We can observe that various groups are creating knowledge silos, bombarding individuals with biased information to encourage quick, heuristic-based judgements. A significant issue with intuitive cognition is that quick, intuitive judgements can trigger unconscious assumptions about certain groups, leading to unintended and serious consequences. For instance, research has shown that cultural stereotypes often influence intuitive judgements about people. This is because our stereotypes are part of our social context, shaping how we perceive and interpret the world, and are rooted in history and transmitted through language (Hegarty & Pratto, 2004). Intuitive cognitive reasoning can also lead to violence, especially in polarised and uncertain situations. In highly uncertain and dangerous situations, people often rely on what 'feels' right then. Intuitive cognition can bypass other thought processes and trigger a fight-or-flight response.

Essentialism and intuitive cognition

Another way intuitive cognitive reasoning and stereotypes go hand in hand is through Essentialist beliefs. Essentialism is a cognitive pattern that relies heavily on intuitive cognition and is used to make sense of categories of things. People tend to believe that there are hidden, underlying essences that make members of a type the same (Gelman & Hirschfeld, 1999). Hence, it provides the causal mechanism and the inferential potential to sort humans into social groups believed to have distinct essences. For example, the logic of individualistic Western people and collectivistic Indian people are Essentialised notions and are often used to reason out many behaviours. However, researchers know that there are factors such as urbanism, globalisation, and even class and gender privileges that dictate whether individuals are collectivistic or individualistic, yet classifying and sorting cultures and understanding individuals through these categories are as common as humanity itself.

Hirschfeld (1996, 2003) postulates that early Essentialisation about race could be thought of as 'folk sociology', which gives attribution to social groups (Kanovsky, 2007). This enables us to view race, caste class, and gender as categories with distinct ontological commitment, i.e., real in its implication in dictating how people ought and can behave. Hence, intuitive sociology can account for Essentialised beliefs about people as natural kinds, and these natural kinds carry with them a set of expectations that can be believed to originate from biological and psychological Essentialism, which is the belief that being part of a certain category leads to specific properties and attributes as mentioned above. Moreover, researchers have also argued that social Essentialism develops through the interaction of cognition and cultural input through generic language (Rhodes et al., 2012). Generic language is often used unknowingly but has strongly influenced Essentialist beliefs by stating general beliefs about a group rather than of a particular instance, like saying boys do not cry instead of saying 'he does not cry' (Gelman et al., 2010). Gelman (2003) also highlighted that children intuitively understand the essences of things and start deriving category judgements through Essentialist logic. Thus, the presence and application of intuitively driven Essentialist reasoning for people's behaviour are quite prevalent.

Another form of Essentialist thought that aids in explaining human behaviour quickly is social determinism (Rangel & Keller, 2011), i.e., the belief that people are culturally fixed at an earlier age. It is also important to acknowledge that what makes Essentialist reasoning so conducive to intuitive reasoning is the belief that these qualities are immutable, i.e., that they will not change, and that they are discreet, i.e., specific to that group only. This suggests that group members, due to their similarities, are treated with the belief that they have some inherently same qualities (Haslam et al., 2000), and there is a belief that these insights are not only fast but also, in most occasions, 'true'.

For example, caste and gender in India (Mahalingam, 2003) are frequently seen through this lens. A person's caste is typically identified by their surname and the traditional occupation of their parents, and children are expected to carry on this inherited social identity. Gender is also seen in this light that once one is born a male, they are destined to become a 'masculine man' and have specific attributes, and a failure to have them can lead to ostracism and prejudice. Thus, it indicates that while Essentialist thought can be powerful, it can also be problematic by establishing power dynamics and through stereotyped beliefs (Mahalingam, 2003, 2007).

Exercising inductive cognition and drawing on Essentialist thought can often cause harm once imbued with morals and status, such as caste in India, which can accrue different statuses and attributions of ability and warrant violating and crossing certain boundary thresholds. Mahalingam (2003) has differentiated between cognitive and social Essentialism; while the first is used just to provide reasoning for people's actions through their psychological makeup, the latter is used to justify power position in society by giving it moral and hierarchical underpinnings. The problem is not that humans are perpetually categorised, but these categorisations have social consequences through exercises of power, prejudice, and stereotypes (Mahalingam, 2003). For example, children's understanding of caste is established through understanding wealth, occupational roles, and the importance of these roles. Often, this results in the belief that people cannot change and they themselves are the reason for their struggle or hardships in life. Another historically famous example is the case of the Holocaust, where Jews were identified as a natural type (Kohl, 2011). At the same time, it is common knowledge that there were different kinds of Jews with varying affiliations to their religion. They were categorised as perverted, greedy, and anti-European, i.e., there was a fundamental attribution error. They were dehumanised and categorised into 'vermin' that needed termination. Hence, all of this led to the dehumanisation of this group of people, leading to the Holocaust. It then becomes recommended that people pay attention to social conditions that seem normal and natural and are seen as arbitrary, historically developed, and often false.

However, this does not imply that Essentialist thought should be shunned altogether. Often, through intuitive cognitive processes, one can make judgements about a particular person with reasonable accuracy, and it is cognitively far less taxing than having to make analytical judgements. In fact, in situations of uncertainty, people often have to make intuitive judgements to process vast amounts of information. Essentialist thought alongside intuitive cognitive reasoning aids in addressing the need for cognitive closure (Kruglanski & Webster, 1996). Hence, it reduces uncertainty, especially during information overload, and provides immediate explanations for novel and familiar situations. Furthermore, it can lead to a more orienting lens between two members of different groups when they come in contact. For example, an American who has encountered Indians in his school has some idea of what would be appropriate in India during his vacation. It could also be the other way around; John, having seen Indians on TV as 'smart' people, immediately categorises his new employee, Rajesh, an Indian, as 'smart'. Hence, Essentialised beliefs that aid in intuitive judgement that aid in the positive image of the outgroup can be a positive notion to study. Gelman (2004) points out that Essentialised beliefs have robust inductive richness and allow us to engage in deeper causal structure, i.e., drawing inferences about a person from a group and the person through knowledge of the group.

A case study on essentialism and intuitive cognition through the study of social class

In Indian society, a person's social status is determined by multiple factors, such as caste, class, gender, age, and skin colour. Moreover, it is interesting to understand how people generally understand social class and wealth. Often, people provide Essentialist reasoning to social status, such as judging that poor people are poor because of their nature (Kraus et al., 2012). More often, this type of reasoning is given by upper-class individuals. In contrast, poor people believe in contextuality and how multiple factors influence social class. Thus, poor people provide constructivist notions of social class to highlight the importance of material factors and the malleability of a specific category (Kraus & Keltner, 2009). The understanding of social class allows us to comprehend how people construe social class and the intuitive thought process that aids in these judgements, often providing social constructionist and often problematic Essentialist notions about social class, such as the inherent ability of rich people's minds. Therefore, we replicated Mahalingam's (2003) study on social class and tried to understand the logic of their response through content analysis.

Our research took a unique approach, using the same vignette Mahalingam (2003) employed to study how different castes held Essentialist notions of social class. However, we introduced an additional question, 'Why?' to explore the reasoning behind their beliefs about how a brain transplant would affect a person's behaviour. The vignettes were translated into Hindi, the spoken language in north India, and back-translated for accuracy. We collected data from 688 respondents, 344 class individuals (172 male and 172 female) and 344 class individuals (172 male and 172 female) in Delhi on the vignette below. A separate vignette of a similar nature was prepared for Kumar (rich person) as well. Responses were then coded into 'will change' or 'will not change' to the opposite class, such as that if Kathan were initially poor, then Kathan remaining poor would be marked as 'will not change', and Kathan changing to rich would be marked as 'will change'. The sample vignette is given below:

STORY A

Kathan is a poor man, and Kumar is a rich man. Someone takes Kathan's Brain, puts it in Kumar's head, takes Kumar's Brain, and puts it in Kathan's head. After the brain transplant, would Kathan act like:

a) a rich man,
b) a poor man.

Why?

Results and analysis

After analysing the responses, we found proof that people use intuitive psychology and intuitive sociology. In the Intuitive Psychology model, they highlight what poor people aspire to be, highlighting elements of desire and intuitive mental states to people. Intuitive sociology ascribes attributes like how they will spend their money, how they are likely to regain or lose their position in society, and what kind of capabilities are given to each group, highlighting the development of norms and social norms.

Moreover, we discovered that upper-class respondents tend to rely more on intuitive Essentialist responses. They believed that lower-class individuals have less ability and are judged less competent, while the rich are considered more competent. This suggests a tendency for people to intuitively ascribe more significant potential to the brains of wealthy individuals and underestimate the potential of those from poor backgrounds. This highlights how, intuitively, people may reproduce stereotypes and ascribe problematic values to different classes that can have moral and policy-level implications and provide logic for one's societal location (Mahalingam, 2003).

Our investigation involved content analysis to understand the reasoning behind these differences in response between both classes. The findings of this content analysis revealed a diverse range of reasons, broadly categorised into biological determinants (genes and body), psychological determinants (attributes and attitudes belonging to each class), transcendental attributions (such as karmic reasoning and destiny), class as caste notions (permanency and maintenance), social construction factors (habituated lifestyle, exposure or lack thereof to particular lifestyles), performativity, aspirations of upward mobility attributed to a group, and monetary/material determinants. We found that people intuitively provided reasons for how class gets maintained and how social mobility operates in society like; wealthier individuals were perceived as having the potential to maintain their status with an emphasis on competence; conversely, poorer individuals were seen through an aspirational lens. Additionally, attributes such as vigilance/incompetence were associated with being poor, while greed/competence was linked with wealth. Evidence also highlighted how transcendental Essentialist notions like *Karma* served unique cultural roles in shaping perceptions about deservingness within Indian society. The belief that people 'deserve' to be poor can impact welfare schemes and influence people's attitudes toward providing aid to them. For example, many people in our data give agency and the ability to reorient their lives to poor Kumar with a rich mind because agency and competence are associated with rich people. In contrast, some respondents highlighted the 'poor' brain. Kathan will squander away the money because he does not know what to do with that much money, and being lazy and wasteful are seen as poor men's traits who do not know how to utilise them well. Thus, people may intuitively be more inclined to judge rich people as kindly deserving of a 'second chance' while believing that the poor person has created the position for themselves (Ruggeri & Yu, 2023; Kraus et al., 2012). These results shed light on the complex interplay between Essentialist beliefs about social class, intuitive cognition, and the social consequences these beliefs can have. They suggest a deeper need to examine how beliefs about social class are formed, shaped, and transmitted through cultural artefacts and social contexts, i.e., aiding in the development of intuitive reasoning of the social world.

One interesting aspect of people's reasoning through intuitive cognitive reasoning highlights the 'knowingness' aspect, which assigns how people will intuitively act because of long-term familiarity and long-term automaticity of behaviour, which is also backed up by Pierre Bourdieu's theory of the *Habitus*. For example, in our data, we find that some people have argued that 'rich' Kathan will not be able to survive in the poor neighbourhood because he does not know how poor people live, he has not experienced 'poorness' whereas, the poor man must have encountered a rich neighbourhood, might have worked for them hence, know how rich people live. Consequently, poor and rich people are not cognised of the presence or absence of money but also of living poorly and richly. The theory of *Habitus* highlights the role of our culture, social positions, and status as a provider of information.

Summary of the study

Overall, the reasons provided by the participants highlight the presence of Essentialist thought and prejudiced assumptions in an activity that requires intuitive lay reasoning to understand social class. People also intuitively understand that they are products of society and historically situated and ascribe this understanding to fellow people as well, thus invoking the concept of '*Habitus*' and using a certain sense of 'knowingness' to help aid their reasoning as to how rich and poor people are made and how they can inhabit the other's space. However, it is important to note that in such situations of uncertainty like the 'brain transplant', people especially participants belonging to the upper-class bracket, endorse Essentialist beliefs that can become prejudiced and stereotypical; hence, it is essential to endorse more analytical reasoning and aid in building mechanisms that address that.

Conclusion

In this chapter, we have covered how intuitive cognition can be used to understand the way society functions. We have tried to establish the possible interconnection between intuitive sociology and intuitive psychology and how they can help in accounting for understanding how people become folk psychologists and folk prosecutors by not only trying to assign meaning to how people in group settings act. Moreover, we accounted for three perspectives from the Dual-Processing model, which is a cognitive model highlighting that humans are cognitively 'frugal' and prefer engaging in intuitive, heuristic-based cognition that aids in explaining people's behaviour. In contrast, two more interactionist theories of social constructionism and symbolic interaction highlight how language, culture, and historical situatedness help us understand our own '*Habitus*' and our own 'knowingness', which helps us navigate the world. It explains why some moral judgements have an intuitive appeal and how much of our decision is made on the appeals to our affective understanding of good and bad. Lastly, we focus on the perils of intuitive cognition and explore it with one phenomenon known as 'Essentialism', which is a philosophical position that highlights that people are born with certain essences that make them a part of that group, and this is often deployed in the fast-mode of thinking, intuitive mode of thinking to navigate complex social situations. We used a brain-transplant paradigm, swapped the brains of two individuals from two different social strata, and asked participants how they thought they would act.

Interestingly, we have found evidence of intuitiveness as 'knowingness' through our response, which validates the social constructivist and symbolic interaction take on intuitive cognition. Participants have highlighted that people will likely act poor or rich based on their 'knowingness' of their earlier lifestyle. People will continue to act the way they know, similar to the idea of *Habitus* given by Pierre Bourdieu and highlights the importance of tacit knowledge (Polanyi, 1969) and how people can 'intuitively' adapt or not adapt to certain places due to this knowingness. Overall, it highlights the vast potential of intuitive cognition in the social world and ways other things can proceed and consider engaging with this complex yet valuable concept.

References

Bicchieri, C., & McNally, P. (2018). Shrieking sirens: Schemata, scripts, and social norms: How change occurs. *Social Philosophy and Policy*, *35*(1), 23–53.

Biddle, B. J. (2013). *Role theory: Expectations, identities, and behaviors*. Academic press.

Bourdieu, P. (2018). The forms of capital. In *The sociology of economic life* (pp. 78–92). Routledge.

Bowers, K. S., Regehr, G., Balthazard, C., & Parker, K. (1990). Intuition in the context of discovery. *Cognitive Psychology*, 22(1), 72–110.

Burke, M. A., & Young, H. P. (2011). Social norms. In *Handbook of social economics* (Vol. 1, pp. 311–338). North-Holland.

Burr, V. (2015). *Social constructionism*. Routledge.

Cheung, W. Y., Sedikides, C., Wildschut, T., Tausch, N., & Ayanian, A. H. (2017). Collective nostalgia is associated with stronger outgroup-directed anger and participation in ingroup-favoring collective action. *Journal of Social and Political Psychology*, *5*(2), 301–319.

DiMaggio, P. (1997). Culture and cognition. *Annual Review of Sociology*, *23*(1), 263–287.

Gelman, S. A. (2003). *The essential child: Origins of essentialism in everyday thought*. Oxford University Press.

Gelman, S. A. (2004). Psychological essentialism in children. *Trends in Cognitive Sciences*, *8*(9), 404–409.

Gelman, S. A., & Hirschfeld, L. A. (1999). How biological is essentialism. *Folkbiology*, *9*, 403–446.

Gelman, S. A., Ware, E. A., & Kleinberg, F. (2010). Effects of generic language on category content and structure. *Cognitive Psychology*, *61*(3), 273–301.

Goldberg, J. H., Lerner, J. S., & Tetlock, P. E. (1999). Rage and reason: The psychology of the intuitive prosecutor. *European Journal of Social Psychology, 29*(5–6), 781–795.

Goodnow, J. J., & Delaney, S. (1989). Children's household work: Task differences, styles of assignment, and links to family relationships. *Journal of Applied Developmental Psychology, 10*(2), 209–226.

Haslam, N., Rothschild, L., & Ernst, D. (2000). Essentialist beliefs about social categories. *British Journal of social psychology, 39*(1), 113–127. https://doi.org/10.1348/014466600164363

Hegarty, P., & Pratto, F. (2004). The differences that norms make: Empiricism, social constructionism, and the interpretation of group differences. *Sex Roles, 50*, 445–453.

Hirschfeld, L. A. (1996). *Race in the making: Cognition, culture, and the child's construction of human kinds*. MIT Press.

Hirschfeld, L. A. (2003). On a folk theory of society: Children, evolution, and mental representations of social groups. In *Lay Theories and Their Role in the Perception of Social Groups* (pp. 107–117). Psychology Press.

Ignatow, G. (2007). Theories of embodied knowledge: New directions for cultural and cognitive sociology?. *Journal for the Theory of Social Behaviour, 37*(2), 115–135.

Kanovsky, M. (2007). Essentialism and folk sociology: Ethnicity again. *Journal of Cognition and Culture, 7*(3–4), 241–281.

Kohl, D. (2011). The Presentation of "self" and "other" in Nazi propaganda. *Psychology & Society, 4*(1), 7–26.

Kraus, M. W., & Keltner, D. (2009). Signs of socioeconomic status: A thin-slicing approach. *Psychological science, 20*(1), 99–106. https://doi.org/10.1111/j.1467-9280.2008.02251.x

Kraus, M. W., Piff, P. K., Mendoza-Denton, R., Rheinschmidt, M. L., & Keltner, D. (2012). Social class, solipsism, and contextualism: How the rich are different from the poor. *Psychological Review, 119*(3), 546.

Kruglanski, A. W., & Gigerenzer, G. (2011). "Intuitive and deliberate judgments are based on common principles": Correction to Kruglanski and Gigerenzer (2011). *Psychological Review, 118*(3), 522. https://doi.org/10.1037/a0023709

Kruglanski, A. W., & Webster, D. M. (1996). Motivated closing of the mind: "Seizing" and "freezing". *Psychological Review, 103*(2), 263. https://doi.org/10.1037/0033-295X.103.2.263

Mahalingam, R. (2003). Essentialism, culture, and power: Representations of social class. *Journal of Social Issues, 59*(4), 733–749.

Mahalingam, R. (2007). Essentialism, power, and the representation of social categories: A folk sociology perspective. *Human Development, 50*(6), 300–319. https://doi.org/10.1159/000109832

Michalson, L., & Lewis, M. (1985). What do children know about emotions and when do they know it?. In *The socialization of emotions* (pp. 117–139). Springer US.

Polanyi M. (1969). *Knowing and being*. Routledge & Kegan Paul.

Rangel, U., & Keller, J. (2011). Essentialism goes social: Belief in social determinism as a component of psychological essentialism. *Journal of Personality and Social Psychology, 100*(6), 1056.

Ridgeway, C. L., & Correll, S. J. (2004). Unpacking the gender system: A theoretical perspective on gender beliefs and social relations. *Gender & Society, 18*(4), 510–531.

Roth, W. D., Van Stee, E. G., & Regla-Vargas, A. (2023). Conceptualizations of race: Essentialism and constructivism. *Annual Review of Sociology*, *49*(1), 39–58.
Ruggeri, G. C., & Yu, W. (2023). *Human capital indicators: Atlantic Canada vs. Canada*. [Unpublished manuscript]. Department of Economics, University of New Brunswick.
Sauter, D. A., Eisner, F., Ekman, P., & Scott, S. K. (2015). Emotional vocalizations are recognized across cultures regardless of the valence of distractors. *Psychological Science*, *26*(3), 354–356.
Sayer, L. C. (2005). Gender, time and inequality: Trends in women's and men's paid work, unpaid work and free time. *Social Forces*, *84*(1), 285–303. https://doi.org/10.1353/sof.2005.0126
Shutts, K., & Kalish, C. W. (2021). Intuitive sociology. In *Advances in child development and behavior* (Vol. 61, pp. 335–374). JAI.
Shweder, R. A. (2003). Toward a deep cultural psychology of shame. *Social Research: An International Quarterly*, *70*(4), 1100–1129.
Sierksma, J. (2022). Children's intergroup prosocial behavior: The role of group stereotypes. PsyArXiv; 2022. https://doi.org/10.31234/osf.io/nsvfp
Slovic, P., Finucane, M. L., Peters, E., & MacGregor, D. G. (2007). The affect heuristic. *European Journal of Operational Research*, *177*(3), 1333–1352. https://doi.org/10.1016/j.ejor.2005.04.006
Srinivasan, M., Kaplan, E., & Dahl, A. (2019), Reasoning about the scope of religious norms: Evidence from Hindu and Muslim children in India. *Child Development*, *90*, e783–e802. https://doi.org/10.1111/cdev.13102
Sullivan, G. B. (2015). Collective emotions. *Social and Personality Psychology Compass*, *9*(8), 383–393.
Taylor, L. K., Dautel, J., & Rylander, R. (2020). Symbols and labels: Children's awareness of social categories in a divided society. *Journal of Community Psychology*, *48*(5), 1512–1526.
Tran, V. (2012). Emotions and decision-making processes in management teams: A collective level analysis. *Journal of Work and Organizational Psychology*, *28*(1), 15–24.
Tversky, A., & Kahneman, D. (1981). The framing of decisions and the rationality of choice. *Science*, *211*(4481), 453–458.
Volz, K. G., & Zander, T. (2014). Primed for intuition. *Neuroscience of Decision Making*, *1*, 26–34.
Wellman, H. M., Carey, S., Gleitman, L., Newport, E. L., & Spelke, E. S. (1990). *The child's theory of mind*. The MIT Press.

Chapter 9

Recognition to cognition

Changing roles of Sādṛśya in the process of making visual art

Sanjay Sen Gupta

The making of visual art is largely an intuitive activity. The drawing of lines, shaping of forms, choice of colors, application of pigments and tones, and even the finishing touches reflect upon the intuitive response of an artist to the call of the inner self. The process, however, also involves technique and skill accumulated through repeated action and observation – but a creative individual knowingly or unknowingly relies upon and hence submits himself/herself to his/her intuition only. This mechanism, being an important part of his/her cognitive process, is a kind of automaticity acquired by him/her that keeps evolving through lifelong practices. Obviously, this automaticity as a whole helps in constructing his/her own style of communication and is different from that of the identical bowl-making of a craftsman.

The artist, on the other hand, is often not aware of or concerned about the psycho-analytic details of art-making and often doesn't know what s/he does (Tagore 1961/2005, p. 36). S/he remains more engrossed in the various sources of inspiration, references, mediums, technicalities, applications, and the visual outcome of his/her art – while the happenings keep evolving around his/her intuitive responses helping to bring intended or unintended changes or instantaneously create a new form, pattern, or style. These responses, nevertheless, lead to newly formed gestalt with automatic re-organizations, but are primarily based upon multiple degrees of regular craftsmanship which emerge through a cognitive process. It is because of the pre-existed foreground of a long-practiced knowledge-base that the function of neuro-plasticity of the brain takes place by adding a new neural pathway to perform the same activity. Therefore, the affirmation to go with a new effort pops up in the mind with no hesitation, only when the intuitive process is initiated, unconsciously, by the process of recognition.

Introduction

A visual artist like any other human being comes to this world as a newborn animal with the primary instinct of thirst and hunger. Gradually s/he starts responding to internal and external experiences like taste, touch, smell,

DOI: 10.4324/9781003377757-11

sound, and light. With the awakening of sensory organs, s/he begins to 'copy' and internalize others, and the world around him/her, and in this process creates a unique internal representation of the environment which then finds an outlet in his/her responses, expressions, reactions, and behavioral mannerisms. This almost instinctual and fundamental cognitive process shapes the primary motifs and patterns of the child's functioning and behavior. The same instinct also drives each of them toward the replication of his/her perception of the visual world through the 'activity' of image-making – either in the form of drawing, painting, design, arrangement, model, craft, plaything, and so on.

With biological maturation, the child begins to explore his/her world more. This, facilitated by inputs from multiple environmental sources – coupled with the development of spoken language – leads to the reorganization of cognitive functioning. The child is then seen to step out of these primal sensory experiences and their crude replication in favor of matching their visual outputs with a projected idea of 'the real.' Many of them, nevertheless, often quit expressing or communicating through such visual art-making, as they resort to spoken language as their primary mode of expression and communication. This shift is often reinforced further by the socio-economic and cultural factors – specifically prejudices, and inhibitions. Only a handful, hence, retains and continues with their passion and instinct, and explores their aesthetic needs, sometimes to the extent of taking it up professionally, through various mediums of visual communication.

However, the sources of his/her technical and/or aesthetic learning also have their own agenda, intention, process, and limitation; and thus, often insist the student to follow his/her own projection of the 'ideal.' This form of structured learning, curated by different primary, secondary, and tertiary sources, pulls away the aspirant from the natural instinctual expression and experience of life as a whole. This process of cognitive restructuring is often difficult, challenging, and complicated and also necessitates – directly or indirectly – the would-be-artists to assimilate and accommodate this new information in the process, altering his/her own internal representations including their shape, form, color, and texture.

Thus the 'originality' claimed in the creative process, or the end-product, appears to be nothing but a 'copy' of the artist's schooling – that have variously been contextualized and named as Mimesis in Ion and The Republic, Anukaraṇa in Nāṭyaśāstra, Satya and Anukṛti in Viṣṇudharmottara Purāṇa, and so on. All these, however, are grossly shaped by his/her conditioning through the existing socio-economic and cultural paradigms, and together might be accommodated within the framework of Sādṛśya – as proclaimed by the Citrasūtra. Discovered all over India and Nepal in Devanagari, Sharada, Bengali, and Newari scripts, this widely followed Śilpaśāstra was discussed in adhyāya 35–43 of the third khaṇḍa of Viṣṇudharmottara Purāṇa. The term however means sym-visibility and con-similarity (Coomaraswamy, 1995, pp. 8–9) and thus appears to be aesthetically beyond the scope of

Naturalism – whose concept has variously been coined by both the Eastern and Western philosophies. The likeness being discussed here, between any content and its visual representation, may not always be natural – but rather be analogical, or exemplary, or even both. Because, the representation imitates the extract or idea or species of the content, by which it is internalized or personalized by the artist intellectually, rather than its substance as registered by his/her senses (Mukherjee, 2001, pp. xi–xiii).

This Sādṛśya, however, could be elaborated in multiple features of Rūpasādṛśya, Kalpasādṛśya, Bhāvasādṛśya, and Rasasādṛśya – whose nature and appearances as reflected in the theory of Ṣaḍaṅga would be discussed in the following pages. The term as a whole thus summarizes the significance and importance of cognition in the creative process that could finally be recognized in the manifestation of the end-product. This book chapter aims to review and recognize the role of Sādṛśya in the context of time, space, and the person concerned – with a special emphasis on the experience of a visual artist in the process of making his/her work of art.

Recognition: The artistic experience

Human eyes usually are the last set of sensory organs to be activated in their fullest competence – though they take over immediately as the most active medium of capturing the worldly experiences. Visual signals provide us the most convincing perception of the 'real' in comparison to others like taste, touch, smell, and sound. Perhaps for this reason 'eye witness' has always been considered to be one of the most comprehensive pieces of evidence in the court of law. It's only in the case of people blind from birth that the other modes of human experiences evolve to be more sensitive and powerful.

However, in general, visual experiences constitute a major part of the human memory that is fed by multiple sources of introduction and registration. A person gets to know his/her immediate surroundings by their color, shape, form, and texture – with or without a name – though obviously things that s/he can touch appear with an added dimension of surface and volume. All these memories, stored in various layers of the human brain, help the individual to identify any of them during their next encounter. An individual once registered with the look, touch, smell, taste and the name of an apple, for example, relates its memory immediately when s/he experiences the fruit next time in any form of its appearances. Even for a name-not-known flower or a fish or a bird, a human brain initially registers and later identifies the content by repeating the same process whatsoever. Thus, it initiates and mobilizes the course of recognition and gradually develops a general perception by comparing the latest experience of the same objects/subjects repeatedly with their prior experiences and memories. Such comparisons, whatsoever, provide him/her with a sense of Sādṛśya that could be traced in a primitive form though – for the first time in the cognitive process.

Thus, a visual artist – be s/he untrained or trained – comes to know what an average 'tree' looks like, or what an average 'man' looks like. Such generalizations are imbibed in him/her through the collective memory of people around that follows the prevailing markers of registration and recognition. This perception becomes more intense only through a series of close encounters with the subject/object – leading toward a more personified observation and understanding of the same. The artist thus needs to study the variety of appearances of various species of trees to know which of them is mango, for example, or which of them is fig. This study, however, is closely associated with the cognitive foundation already instilled in him/her in various degrees and dimensions and thus may vary between one artist and the other. Even the same specimen of a mango tree may be experienced from different angles, in different seasons, at different times of the day, in different perspectives, and in different contexts – resulting in a more intimate dialogue between the observer and the observant. This process of apperception, as it is known, is equally true for the other sources of human experience that feed the human mind together in various degrees and at various levels.

This journey from registration to apperception for a visual artist is extremely important and instrumental in constituting his/her repertoire of images. Even the experiences of taste, touch, smell, and sound for him/her are majorly transliterated with a visual code as s/he is routed to the visual language as his/her primary mode of the cognitive process. This storage, however, expanded throughout the multiple layers of the conscious and subconscious mind, takes an important role in triggering and hence influencing the process of art-making. This trigger may happen with the sudden click of an idea, or being absorbed in a series of thoughts, by seeing a visual or experiencing a group of visuals in regular intervals, or just looking at the blank space on a wall, paper, canvas, etc. The moment, whatsoever, s/he intends or decides to draw/paint/model/sculpt an image, it immediately refers him/her back to the repertoire of images in his/her conscious and subconscious – from where appearances are transmitted into different kinds of visual shapes and forms. Thus, we can identify Sādṛśya once again in the process of making visual art, which could be found equally active in the rendering of imaginary contents and abstract ideas.

Recognition and Sādṛśya

The cognitive process in the human mind, as we have already seen, begins with the registration of information received from various primary, secondary, and tertiary sources – in the form of visual, sound, smell, taste, and feel. It's only in the case of a second encounter with any of them that Sādṛśya as an integral part comes into play for the first time to guide our mind in recognizing the same against the primary body of registered contents. Such formal similitude between two experiences centering on the same visual content may

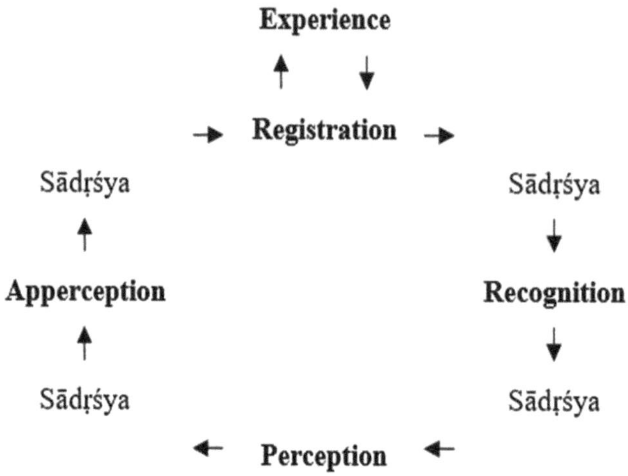

Figure 9.1 Role of Sādṛśya in the cognitive process.

be identified as Rūpasādṛśya. Thus a repertoire of recognized contents is gradually built in our minds, generating a kind of value system, which guides us in prioritizing one of them over the other. Thus it is correctly said that – 'The way we see things is affected by what we know or what we believe' (Berger, 1972/2008, p. 8). This indeed is an important stimulant for an artistic mind to indulge itself in imitating the valued content/s with the help of lines, patches, and layers of available pigments on a desired surface chosen by the same values and priorities (Thakur, 1354/1407, p. 346).

However, the contents restored in this way are often recollected – with or without a specific purpose – where Bhāvasādṛśya could be identified functioning as a catalyst by taking similitude of type or emotion of the two into consideration. These happen obviously in parallel to the new registrations that keep on pouring from a variety of direct and indirect sources, variably influencing the subconscious of the receiver and its ever-changing construct. A third encounter with the same content, nevertheless, opens up another degree of Sādṛśya that instigates a personalized understanding of the same leading toward a holistic discernment known as Perception. Such cognition deepens the memory of the content – while its degree varies against the rest of the recognitions and registrations continuing in their variable paces, under the variable conditions. Further connection/s whatsoever with the same or similar content, beyond the limits of perception, keeps Sādṛśya alive and active as an integral part of cognition leading toward the sharing of identity between the receiver and the received. This on the other way could be recognized as Apperception, which for an artist is developed in contributing to the dynamic construct of reasoning with variable influences on cognition as a whole.

Such repetitions take place quite frequently in the practice of visual art, where the artist looks at the source image and the one replicated by him/her on the chosen surface. This act of imitation nevertheless doesn't supplement the job of a camera – which, apart from its choice of frame, adjustment of focus and fixing of light, is an un-analytical reproduction of the source. On the contrary, the content in front of a visual artist is translated by the apperception of a human mind and delivered through a Bhāvasādṛśya in respect to his/her own repertoire. A comparison of an artwork with the source, or a comparison among various artworks delivered from the same source, would prove this matter evidently (Thakur, 1354/1407, pp. 347–349).

In parallel to all these, another form of recognition could be traced in different dynamics when a content is recollected and/or described from memory and/or imagination be it through auditory, visual or in a combined mode. Kalpasādṛśya takes the lead in such a case bringing the memory and/or imagination close to its/their recollection and/or description, both for the deliverer as well as the receiver. Besides this, similar kind of recognition or registration may also take place, when any content is delivered by emphasizing on its core value or essence through a somewhat suggestive manner. Rasasādṛśya refers to this kind of similitude, by pushing Rūpasādṛśya to the back-seat, where the deliverer and the receiver are connected by their respective apperception of the same content. Even a blank space or a piece of canvas or paper could trigger the artistic recapitulation of acquired imageries and guide the artist's apperceived intent to indulge in Kalpasādṛśya. The process, however, continues through a repetitive cycle of cognition and representation till the aesthetic ego is satisfied, though temporarily, by resulting in Rasasādṛśya between the image and the imagination. Thus it is rightly said that –

> An image is a sight which has been recreated or reproduced. It is an appearance, or a set of appearances, which has been detached from the place and time in which it first made its appearance and preserved for a few moments or a few centuries.
>
> (Berger, 1972/2008, pp. 9–10)

Sādṛśya in image-making: The cognitive experience

Art-making is a human activity. No other creature on earth 'creates' art, though many of their works/activities, or that of nature at large, have been and still are being identified by us humans as successful 'art forms.' But the creature/s concerned do/es not appear to be aware of any phenomenon like this.

The journey of human behavior on the other hand takes conscious route/s of variable degree and intensity, in general, to invent/create/make something effective/important to themselves – primarily material and then aesthetic. However, the source of this urge is essentially not known to the artist – the creator/maker of art – but that doesn't stop him/her from coming up with the

Figure 9.2 Role of Sādṛśya in the making of art – cognition and execution.

'pleasing forms' (Read, 1931/1961, p. 14). In most cases, s/he responds to the urge with impulsiveness and spontaneity, though later on improvises and/or manipulates through a synthesis of various constructs that arise from his/her artistic ambitions.

The process of art-making thus is initiated in the human mind – that of the artist – instigated by a vision/sense of void/vacuum against variable sources of his/her experience, knowledge, and recognition. At times it happens in front of an empty visual space – may be a flat wall, a bare ground, an unfilled object-surface, or a blank piece of paper/canvas. Apart from this, however, such creative impulse is also generated through a pattern/series of thoughts in mind or a pattern/series of information gathered from various sources. In any case, the possible art form thus unfolds itself gradually and appears either in parts, or in layers, or as an impression of close-to-the-whole. At times, it comes sparkling as an idea, or a theme, or a form, or a structure, or a texture, or a line, or a patch of color – from which the artist builds up the work gradually with his/her experience and expertise by adding, removing, applying and rejecting visual contents following the method of trial-and-error.

In all such cases, Sādṛśya plays an important role in each and every step of the creative process that eventually is a dynamic construct conditioned by various phenomena. Some of the major conditions are:

- Direct experience from primary sources
- Information and/or opinion from secondary sources
- Desire to create
- Success and/or failure in rendition as per standards set by others

- Knowledge of artworks done by the others – in past or/and present
- Learning of mediums and techniques
- Study work and practice
- Success and/or failure in rendition as per standards set by the self
- Accumulation of skills desired by the self or the other
- Visual apperception based on overall inputs.

We have already seen how direct experiences are cognized through Rūpasādṛśya, Bhāvasādṛśya, Kalpasādṛśya and Rasasādṛśya – while information and/or opinion from secondary sources also play a key role in this process. The latter guides the receiver's mind up to variable extent through a continued methodology of check and trial, in which the subconscious keeps on comparing the real with the projections and expectations from the other. Thus, the desire to create does not always appear in similitude with an apperceived desire/idea/imagery of the artistic mind, rather the apperception itself grows like a multi-layered construct reflecting multiple intents of the other in various degrees. Even the appreciation of the view of a sunrise, for instance, is thus restricted for the onlooker by various taboos provided by his/her cultural capital that s/he inherits, accumulates, represents, and delivers up to a great extent. Hence Sādṛśya in a broader sense, with all its possible dynamics, keeps on supplying various models – gross and subtle – for him/her to follow all throughout.

Experience for a visual artist thus plays a significant role in determining the content of his/her art – along with its form, medium, surface, scale, appearance, element, composition, drawing, color, technique, light-and-shade, and so on. As a beginner, his/her success and/or failure in his/her aesthetic rendition largely follows the standard set by the others – including family-members, neighbors, friends, relatives, teacher/s, peers, etc. Especially the teachers and peers have a long-lasting influence in shaping the cognitive construct of the budding artist. Rūpasādṛśya and Rasasādṛśya overpower his/her gross apperceptions and insist him/her in reaching closest to the desired standards set by them. Even accumulation of knowledge and information about the artworks done by the others – including artists of the past or/and the present and other contemporary fellow citizens – comes up with a similar set of choices aiming to the desired visuals. These choices automatically narrow down the artist's desire, observation, understanding and quest – and thus restrict him/her gradually within a repertoire of limited patterns and archetypes. S/he remains under the spell of Bhāvasādṛśya and Kalpasādṛśya, repeating similar group of visuals and contents, while his/her aesthetic journey evolves to be well-destined and predictable.

Learning of different mediums and techniques also pulls the artist into certain affection, preferences, and advantages that get equally reflected in his/her visual study-works and other relevant practices. As a result, his/her choice of medium gets limited, color palate becomes defined, and technique gets perfected and hence stereotyped. This time, however, his/her success and/or failure in the making of 'his/her' art majorly imitate/s the standards set by the self as a matured practitioner. This standardization also includes variable desire to be viewed by the possible onlookers – gauging their expected remarks and reviews. Even the accumulation of skills is guided or streamlined by a projected standard that is aspired by the self or/and inspired by the other. Sādṛśya thus could be traced as a constant companion in all stages of the creative process – leading toward the visual apperception of the artists based on the overall inputs.

Cognition: The artistic apperception

In a continuous process of cognitive cycle, the creative urge for an artist is always initiated at a deeper level and with a personal note. In comparison to others, his/her aesthetic perception takes a more intimate approach toward the contents provided by registration and recognition. A tree or a dog, for example, thus become a subject of an artist's individual claim, while the same subjects may be apperceived by another on a different note altogether. Even the gross perception of a mango tree or a German shepherd for that matter could be registered, recognized, and cognized by those two artists with an enforced claim of their own 'real' understanding. As a result, their approach to the same subject happens to be different since both consider their individual perception to be closer to the original-duplicate, and thus wishes to give shape to their desired output.

The artistic apperception thus instigates the selection of medium – which usually is determined by the artist's inclination and expertise, along with the requirement of the subject or the prevailing trends. An artist may choose watercolor for a particular painting – either if s/he has special interest or/and skill in the same, or the desired subject/object itself is envisioned to be demanding the medium in particular. In any of these cases, the key role whatsoever is played by the guidance from experts or subject-teacher/s, suggestion from the seniors, work of the fellow colleagues and many more that influence the artist's choice up to a great extent. Even the style of execution in each piece of work equally reflects the cognitive status of the artist's mind that is constantly being fed by the lessons of art history and exposure to the works of other artists. Initially, during the formative stages, the artist grossly accumulates a wide range of variety and keeps on trying this or that, since his/her visual apperception and aesthetic vocabulary are yet to be crystallized. Later on, however, their ambitious ego settles down through a series of encounter with his/her own reflection of abilities and thus narrows down to a range of style – either homogeneous or heterogeneous. The panorama of this range hence varies according to their sources of inspiration, their capacity of containment, and their embodiment of execution.

The viewer, nevertheless, is expected to enjoy a reverse journey up to the source but may indulge in a different route to a variably different form and degree of experience as a whole. Even the overall aesthetic appeal happens to be different in two different art works done by the same artist or in two similar paintings done by two different artists. Perhaps for this reason a Caravaggio differs widely from Raphael, a Rajput miniature differs from a Persian, or a Japanese woodcut differs widely from that of a Tibetan Thangka. In all such cases, apperception has always taken the most important role in their artists' cognitive process – being clearly reflected in their artworks and thus identified as the markers of 'uniqueness.'

Recognition to cognition: The changing role of Sādṛśya

We have seen how the aesthetic exposure for an artist is closely associated with Sādṛśya – all in terms of the visual appearance, emotion, imagination, and essence of a subject or object. Various parameters of beauty are thus constituted gradually through a curious mix of personal encounter/s, secondary or tertiary description/s or/and opinion/s, individual or/and collective idea/projection/imagination of the ideal, and the desire to create something closest to that (idea/l) for making it recognizable. The visual perception of each individual/group is thus developed through the identification of Sādṛśya in between the idea of ideal and the reality of the real. This however leads to a personalized and intimate interaction that gradually evolves into various creative thoughts and aspirations – and varies in this process as per differences in place and time. The same face, for example, may appear with a different look at various times of the day, difference of light, place (both foreground and background), season, mood, situation, and so on.

References also take an important role in the discovery of Sādṛśya – especially when the artist/viewer is exposed to a wide range of visual contents. Thus, a smile may look similar to the moonlight, a dance performance to a storm, or a sunrise to the work of Monet, and so on. This however constitutes the personality of an aspiring/matured artist, who refers to the relevant variety of Sādṛśya and receives all visual information through a looking glass of his/her cognitive construct. Even the process of initiation to create an aesthetic representation begins with an inspirational push by the desire to be like something/someone or/and connect with the other/s. This desired effect – structural, tonal, and textural – gets reflected in the choice of medium that is connected with Sādṛśya at various levels with a variety of degree and intensity. Similar markers could be identified in the choice of technique, which in turn is reflected upon the appropriation of the process and selected preferences. Thus, a fabric color in certain cases may be more appropriate than oil paint, while the latter may be preferred instead for the convenience and skills of the artist/s concerned.

With the initiation of such a process, Sādṛśya begins to remain agile, alert, and active till the completion of the work at last. Each of the lines drawn, each of the strokes applied, each of the patches of pigment, and each layer of color/lacquer/polish thus passes through a continuous check and balance guiding the artist in proceeding through a series of trials and errors. Drawings are thus erased and corrected, paints are covered and left, brushstrokes are directed and controlled, chisels are pushed and restricted, and so on. Each of these steps thus focuses on maintaining either of Rūpasādṛśya or Bhāvasādṛśya or Kalpasādṛśya or Rasasādṛśya or multiple of them together through Pramā or sense of proportion (Thakur, 1354/1407, pp. 31–32). It is this Pramā that simultaneously extracts from and contributes to the cognitive process for keeping it alive and productive. The process of making visual-art, however, continues till the evolving output appears to be closest to the artists' apperception, ideal, imagination, desire, habit, ability, mannerism, and limitation.

References

Berger, J. (2008). *Ways of Seeing* (pp. 45–64). British Broadcasting Corporation and Penguin Books. (Original work published 1972).

Coomaraswamy, A. K. (1995). The theory of art in Asia. In K. Vatsyayan (Ed.), *The Transformation of Nature in Art* (pp. 8–9). IGNCA & Sterling Publishers.

Mukherjee, P. D. (Ed.). (2001). *The Chitrasūtra of Viṣṇudharmottara Purāṇa*. IGNCA & Motilal Banarsidass Pub (P) Ltd.

Read, H. E. (1961). *The Meaning of Art*. Penguin Books & Faber and Faber. (Original work published 1931).

Tagore, R. (2005). *On Art & Aesthetics: A Selection of Lectures, Essays and Letters*. Subarnarekha. (Original work published 1961).

Thakur, A. (1354/1407). *Bhārataśilpera Ṣaḍaṅga*. Visva Bharati BS 1401. Bāgeśwarī Śilpa Prabandhāvalī.

Chapter 10

The bond invisible

Reflection on intuition and expression with special reference to the artworks of Rabindranath Tagore

Swati Bhattacharya

Introduction

Creativity and intuition are the two sides of the same coin. If creativity leads to a creative expression, visual, literal, or audio-visual, it is intuition that guides one throughout the process. Yet intuition, though at the core of creative expression, is somewhat enigmatic in nature, it is easier to feel its presence than to verbally define it. Intuition is one of the major internal determinants that not only manipulates the conception and visualization of an artist but also triggers his creative imagination into the execution of the vision. This is a highly personal quest that starts with the artist's encounter with the shapes, colors, and different sights in the outer world, and once it becomes part of his creative perception, intuition takes up the rein quite inexplicably. It amalgamates emotion, insight, and imagination, leading to a creative expression. This surprisingly capricious and private pathway is integral to the formation of shapes and substances. The mind of the creative artist offers a virtual space where an emotive reconstruction of forms, and their specific interaction with the pictorial space germinate within the shadowy depth of intuition. The work of art, though, seems to be created only by exploiting technical expertise, but it has a more pervasive and formative underpinning.

Of course, there is not a single definite way in which intuition 'directs' the artist in search of 'the expression'. There are indeed different layers of perception that are integral to any creative journey. Finally, forms, composition, and application of colors of creation have contextual relevance. However, the underlying intuitive process remains inexplicable due to the implicit nature of the intuitive process. Intuition, perhaps, is the synthetic integration of multiple dimensions. The complexity and multiplicity of intuition have prompted philosophers, psychologists, and art theoreticians to define creative intuition from different angles.

Intuition originates from the Latin 'intueri', which implies 'to look at' or 'to contemplate'. The dictionary meaning of the word is 'power or faculty of attaining direct knowledge or cognition 'without evident rational thought

DOI: 10.4324/9781003377757-12

and inference' (M & W Dictionary, 2021) or 'the ability to understand something instinctively, without the need for conscious reasoning' (Oxford English Dictionary, 2021).

It has also been defined as 'a spontaneous, immediate perception of truth that does not rely on the intermediary of rational thought processes or overt, external physical evidence' (Hague, 2003). This definition runs somewhat parallel to the Indian concept of '*pramatrichaitanya*'[1]...or the inborn consciousness/faculty that makes one aware of *prama*[2] (*pra*[3] that is perfect and *ma* that is value or *maan*[4]). The unconscious awareness that is active in the creative artist's mind helps him in his conscious effort to give expression to his emotion in a unique way that transports the *Rasika*,[5] or connoisseur to the world of transcendental bliss.

According to Carl Jung, 'creative intuition is a communication between the conscious mind and the collective unconscious, that suggests possibilities inherent in a subject or situation. Referring to unconscious knowledge as "absolute" knowledge, a perception through images or "subjectless simulacra"' (Jung, 1926). 'Jung argues that the healthy, creative psyche responds to the unification or integration of its conscious and unconscious contents, which involves a kind of transcendental function so necessary for creative expression' (Hardman, 2011). For Croce (1866–1952), the aesthetician, intuition, being an organic whole, can never be analyzed and broken into abstract components. It is innate, natural, and a priori to creative perception. For him, 'intuit' is to express (1909); therefore, a painting or, so to speak, any work of art is nothing but the expressed intuition, which is intrinsically connected to feeling. In *Essence of Aesthetic*, he writes:

> ...what gives coherence and unity to the intuition is feeling: the intuition is really such because it represents a feeling and can only appear from and upon that. The feeling is what confers upon art the airy lightness of a symbol: an aspiration enclosed in the circle of a representation—that is art; and in it, the aspiration alone stands for the representation, and the representation alone for the aspiration.
>
> (Croce, 1921)

His conviction is that intuition is the cognitive form of the unifying currents of feeling that trigger artistic expression. This is in complete contradiction to Stein's views, who defines it as 'a method of formulating or solving a problem in which the person has no conscious awareness or knowledge of how he arrived at the answer or what stimuli led him to it' (Stein, 1974, p. 203). For Croce, an intuitive presentation is a 'complete conscious manifestation' just as it is, preceding the application of definite concepts. The French philosopher Gilles Deleuze's (1991) ideas are also closer to Croce's views because, according to him, intuition is 'neither a feeling, an inspiration, nor a disorderly sympathy, but a fully developed method, one of the most fully developed methods in philosophy' (Deleuze, 1991, p. 13). In Sanskrit terminology, the synonym for intuition is *swagna*,[6] that is *swa*[7] (own) *gna*[8] (from *jnan*[9] that is knowledge). This knowledge is what controls the artist till he acquires *prajna*[10] (perfect knowledge), that is, he reaches the point where he is a master of his creative world, where he can play with the pictorial elements according to his own unmediated thought, coming from the vision of the future and not from the experience of the past.

Prajna is defined as '*naba-naba-unmeshshalini-pratibha*'.[11] It is the latent potential of an artist. When a creative self reaches the pinnacle in the appraisal of his creation, it prompts an artist to be constantly innovative. This can be attained only when one's intuition, or the power of indulging in a pre-subjective venture, finds its freedom at the highest level of concentration. Without this intuitive perception, all his accumulated skills would be in vain. In one of the oft-quoted *sloka*s, it is said that 'to someone who lacks prajna, the knowledge of shastras is of no avail' (*Chanakya Neeti*: *sloka* 27).

Views of the master artists

Intuitive consciousness can thus be said to be at the core of the creative process. The role of creative intuition has not been chartered in great detail, especially by the master artists. Despite being aware of the role of this internal component of creativity, which according to Indian aestheticians leads one to explore the rasa, the sap, or the essence of creation, the practicing artists have hardly ever tried to specify its nature.

Yet quotes from some of the iconic painters from the Western world have helped us to get some practical insights regarding the interrelation of intuition and creative expression, especially in the field of visual arts. To be precise, these references are used as determinants for postulating the psychological and philosophical aspects of the continuous process, where intuition and imagination blend in a creative expression. Let us begin by referring to the views of Leonard da Vinci (1452–1519), for whom experience was much more important than intuition. Experience can be accepted as the cognition of the outer world. For him, painting was the soul imitator of all the visible world of Nature. Hence, for him, it was observation, perception, and cognition of the inner rhythm of the natural world that were more important than any intuitive composition. Repeatedly, he had stressed practicing and studying but had advised the budding artists to follow the methods only after understanding the inner logic of things, which presumably he realized to be an essential and integral aspect necessary for attaining artistic acumen. Yet asserts Leonardo da Vinci, 'Whatever exists in the universe, whether in essence, in act, or in imagination, the painter has first in his mind and then in his hands' (Goldwater & Treves, 1947), thereby proclaiming the role of the process within. It indeed forestalls the view of Croce that 'The intellect presupposes the intuitive mode' (Croce, 1921).

Van Gogh (1853–1890), who always relied on his intuition, has identified the intuitive urge to create, with a flood of emotion/inspiration and in a letter written from Arles (1888) to his brother Theo, he writes:

> If the emotions are so strong that one works without knowing one works when sometimes the strokes come with a sequence and coherence like words in a speech or a letter, then one must remember that it has not always been so and that in the time to come there will again be heavy days empty of inspiration.
>
> (Goldwater & Treves, 1947)

But in another letter written in the same year, he advises that they (the artists) would do well to learn a little to be 'primitives' (Goldwater & Treves, 1947). The integrative message from these two statements confirms that the intuitive process is not in contradiction with technical knowledge of painting, the flow guided and chartered by intuition is so natural that one gets completely relaxed and absorbed in his task, oblivious to any external stipulations. Here, primitive implies natural, where the sole beacon of light guiding his hand is his intuition. This is the highest state of absorption in creative meditation, where to echo the words of Abanindranath Tagore, the pen, the ink, and the mind, the trio indulge in creation.

Wassily Kandinsky (1986–1944) assumes that cognition, or 'the choice of object (i.e., one of the elements in the harmony of form), must be decided only by a corresponding vibration in the human soul' (Goldwater & Treves, 1947). This corresponding vibration can be identified as intuition, especially because he begins his chapter 'Art and Artists' (Kandinsky & Sadleir, 1914) with the assertion that 'The work of art is born of the artist in a mysterious and secret way. From him it gains life and being' (Kandinsky, 1977, p. 53). Paul Klee (1879–1940), one of the pioneers of the Bauhaus movement, wrote in the Bauhaus Prospectus of 1929 that

> We construct and construct and yet intuition still has its uses. Without it we can do a lot, but not everything...When intuition is joined to exact research, it speeds the progress of exact research.
>
> (Dessau quoted in Goldwater & Treves, 1947, p. 444)

They emphasized this synthetic integration of the inside–outside of the self in a holistic milieu. The Bauhaus movement had a holistic approach at its core; it wanted to eradicate the boundary between art and craft and emphasized minimalistic design, which in its turn necessitated an intuitive cognition, a harmonized vision of the inner potential and the outer expression.

Pablo Picasso (1881–1973) in a conversation (1935) with Christian Zervos (editor of Cahiers d'Art), commented that a painter 'paints to unload himself of feelings and visions'. He talks of sensations that come to him from afar. He

Figure 10.1 Study for sluice by Wassily Kandinsky (Google Image Result for https://paintingz.com/media/catalog/product/cache/dff63637c3986eef73a2638cb3a80daa/1/7/178423.jpg)

apparently can smell it and see it and paint it because he must 'get rid of' the sensation, but he confessed that he was often clueless about his creation on the very next day. Thus, for him, art is a spontaneous expression of the intuitive cognition of the world around him, or the sensations, as he calls them. These are as natural and as intuitive as 'the songs of birds' or 'the love of night-flowers or everything around one', and art should be accepted as a resonance in the senses, and one should not make any attempt 'to understand' (Goldwater & Treves, 1947). Jean Arp (1886–1966), an artist of the twentieth century associated with the Dadaist movement who made intuition, random strokes, and chance findings an innate part of his artistic creations, mentioned in this context that despite having professional training, as an artist he relied more on intuitive and instinctive artistic expressions.

However, it can never be denied that rational planning for composing and harmonizing different pictorial elements like 'marrying form and color' and the use of skills are definite requirements, though the artistic expression is triggered to a great extent by cognitive intuition, and (Van Gogh) definitely an artist's 'need to train his soul' (as suggested by Kandinsky, 1977), but as

Monet (1840–1926) has suggested, he should also be 'sure of his method and composition' for communication of the intuitive cognition.

Views of the young practicing artists

These are the thoughts the master artists have shared as an afterthought or when they felt the need to offer some explanatory note to illustrate their creative ideology. On a creative spree, the practicing artists are not bothered with these types of theoretical discussions but enjoy the formative role of intuitive thinking in their creative journey.

During our conversations with some practicing artists (both trained and untrained), it was found that all of them attached huge importance to intuition as far as their creative endeavors are concerned. To some of them, intuition is the guiding force, something that comes from within and dictates to them while they are working; to others, it is like the compass that gives direction to their work.

As per one of the young artists, the metamorphosis of an expression—imagined in mind, intangible in state—to a piece of expression—often tangible in a form essentially holds within moments of intuitive engagements with the medium according to his practice and understanding. In the case of painting, intuition to him may play a large role in the choice of medium, tone, and space, ultimately making up the very piece of expression. To say that this happens in the void is again half in its spirit and expression. He feels for a practitioner artist to be able to rein over the withheld intuitive gestures, a large role is also played by the predisposition to memory and a priori set of knowledge—physical, cognitive, and cultural—a core seat of the intuitive network. Spontaneity, intuition based on a priori knowledge, walk into a relay of interplay making spaces, dialogues, and expression.

While, according to a young painter professor, our conscious mind is always exposed to the outer world. Intuition helps him to communicate between him and the medium with which he is working, waves of different thoughts cross his mind. Intuition helps him to hold on to a thought which inspires him to create something.

For a senior artist in his 50s, intuition is something on which one doesn't have any control while s/he is going to create her/his artwork. It's always a part of his paintings. Before starting a painting, he has a rough idea of what it will look like at the time it is finished. But painting has its own way, its own language, which may reflect his thoughts, emotions. While creating, the creator becomes an observer of his creation, having no hold on his ongoing creation. He needs to go with both techniques and creative exploration as his paintings want to go. there is concept of no mistake, no expectations, no fear while one is absorbed in creative process; instead it is a state of joy and serenity while playing with mysterious forms, shapes, and paints. To him, each and every artist should have intuition…

A young art teacher and artist opined that in his art-practice intuition plays a significant role. Not all his subjects or visual nuances are consciously chosen or critically selected. Even while in between the processes, he intuitively juxtaposes images which later, appear to be producing a coherent meaning.

For another lady practicing artist, who eventually doesn't have any formal training, intuition is something which comes involuntarily. It's a feeling that needs no preponderance. Intuition helps her to communicate between herself and the medium with which she is working.

Such astute exposure by the artists to the inner process and their realization apropos the presence of intuition as the reinforcement of their artwork offers a definitive cognizance of the creative process. Of course, the artists who share these views are speaking unswervingly about their very own and exclusive creative drive. These can be considered more subjective internal bases experienced during the creative progression. Still, the quest is difficult to articulate, even by a trained artist. Their pursuit and its liaisons with abstract conceptions such as intuition, motivation, and imagination may be perceived by an artist but are impossible to translate in an analytical setting. This also is largely due to the fact that art educators and art students rarely ponder on or feel any urge to analyze the psychological mechanisms and philosophical crux of creativity. Creative expression for them is a natural way to de-burden them of their emotion, a place to play with imagination and experiment with diverse styles and stimuli.

Accordingly, for most of them, intuition is something vital and integral to their visual chronicle and, therefore, is of a highly personal nature. For many of them, it is an unconscious, spontaneous expression that goes beyond plan. However, these intuitive strokes or expressions in the pictorial space, though unpremeditated, are far from inadvertent. These may be spontaneous with origins on the subconscious plane but have their triggers in training, observation, perception, and in emotion. Again, in a painting, a large part can be planned yet what harmonizes the pictorial elements is the intuition—that is, the cognition that initiates and integrates the creative expression. It is the self-knowledge (and not the knowledge of the self) that appears to be at work here.

The process of painting or any creative expression, thus can be summed up as the achievement of the intricate blend between the practical or technical capacity developed and nurtured through training, and experience to manipulate the brush, mix paint, and compose a work of art and the intuitive faculty to communicate the feelings, /thought/ideas of the artist as 'perfectly' as possible. Perfection, here, naturally implies the closest approximation to his visionary manifestation formulated in his mind, which has intuition at its core. What an artist intuitively visualizes in abstraction, is concretized through this intertwined weaving of intuition and imagination, which is acknowledged as creative expression. Of course, this is no linear journey, as has been substantiated by the sayings of the different artists and artist-teachers quoted above. Neither is the journey the same for all the works by the same artist. Intuition is responsible for creating the variance in the works of different artists and different works of the same artist. It nurtures and matures the knowledge, the *prajna*, which is designated as being capable of generating something unique every single time the artist is at work. Other Eastern philosophies, like Zen Buddhism and Taoism, also enumerate somewhat similar concepts (Tagore, 1947).

Case study: Rabindranath Tagore's paintings

The concept of intuition as an important facet of creativity may best be studied with reference to Tagore's paintings. Tagore never had any formal training in art and had taken up art only in the last two decades before his death in 1941. This lack of formal training liberated him, as formal teaching is usually restricted to the handing down of procedures, skills, and techniques, in addition to the awareness of some typical cognitive processing. Nandalal Bose, the master artist who has seen the poet working, remarked: 'Majority of the artists begin the creative process with the subject or idea, but Rabindranath, it seems, often begins creating before the subject has taken any conscious form in his mind' (Bose, 1936, p. 31). 'Because they represent no preconceived subject'. As suggested by Nandalal, he never felt any urge to 'explain' his images:

> People often ask me about the meaning of my pictures. I remain silent even as my pictures are. It is for them to express and not to explain. They have nothing ulterior behind their own appearance for the thoughts to explore and words to describe.
>
> (Tagore: My Pictures, 1930, Neogy, 1961)

With his exposure to the works of both contemporary European and Asian art, he had developed an instinctive affiliation with art. At the same time, he was evidently interested in the new trends in contemporary Indian art. Initially, it all started as a free play of mind. The strange world of fantastic animals and figures, and geometrical and architectural designs started to emerge from his doodling on the discarded portion of his writings, or while 'filling up the spaces on the manuscripts'. These 'self-contained and resilient shapes' born out of unconscious scribblings/crossings over writings on the pages of his manuscripts are nothing but intuitive, as if they sprout from some innermost core of the artist's mind and assert themselves (to borrow the artist's own words), saying, 'Hey, I am here'.

> With prodigal abandon, Tagore had explored during the brief period of (1928–1930) his discovery of the world that was not sentiment, not thought, not utterance—pure form, fashioned of light.
>
> (Drawings and Paintings of Rabindranath Tagore, Neogy, 1961)

It was perhaps due to his love for these pure intuitive forms, he had refused to add titles to his paintings. He also did not date most of his works. He painted briskly, finishing each picture in one sitting. He would paint with whatever color he could lay his hand on, in case the color he had been using was finished because it was impossible for him to stop once he had started working on a painting (Bandopadhyay, 1982, p. 55). The forms and figures portrayed in his paintings seem to emerge from some dark, mysterious corner of his mind; technically, it might be called the subconscious. The artist would term it imagination, but the technical knowledge or an absolute lack of it did not matter once these bizarre-looking forms became a part of the world of his intuitive cognition. He, like Croce, believed that expression and not the latent cognition or perception is enough in the absence of expression. In a lecture delivered at the inauguration of an exhibition of his paintings in Calcutta in 1932, he claimed that he did not 'create' the paintings they have 'become', and jokingly added that it's their only claim to their existence in this world. How did they 'become'? He had told Rani Mahalanobis in 1928:

> First there is the hint of a line, and then the line becomes a form. The more pronounced the form becomes, the clearer becomes the picture of my conception...The only training which I had from my younger days was the training in rhythm in sound. I had come to know that rhythm gives reality to which is desultory, insignificant in itself.
>
> (Neogy, 1961, p. 101)

This intuitive understanding of 'the rhythm' lurking underneath the veil of forms has been the generative force in his artistic outbursts at the dusk of his life.

> The drawings and paintings of the poet had richly traced the extraordinary inner journey of a complex individual leading to a convinced cognition of individuated imagery.
>
> (Neogy, 1961)

A quote from a letter he had written to William Rothenstein in the thirties (the one is preserved in Rabindra Bhavan), might help to show that he was quite aware of this inner cognition:

> My pictures certainly possess a psychological interest, being products of untutored figures and untrained minds. I am sure they do not reveal a strangeness born of my utter inexperience and individual limitations.
>
> (Rothenstein et al., 1972)

He had sought peace and enlightenment in his songs, did he try to explore darkness and mystery in his drawings? or did they turn out to be the manifestation of the same with a palette full of colors dark, dense, and deep? 'The world speaks to me in colors', he said he and they found their rhythmic resonance in his works because his soul claimed he 'answers in music'.

In the spring of 1930, during a tour to France, Tagore was advised by some friends and connoisseurs to hold an exhibition of his works in Paris. Thus, the first public and international exhibition of his paintings was organized in Paris in May 1930. Through a series of exhibitions in Paris, London, Berlin, Moscow, and New York, the world discovered the poet Rabindranath as an important modern painter. Subsequently, his works continued to be exhibited both in India and internationally.

Tagore, in a letter, illustrated his views on his paintings in 1941:

> When I turned to painting at once found my place in the grand cavalcade of the visual world. Trees and plants, men and beasts, everything became vividly real in their own distinct forms. Then lines and colors began revealing to me the spirit of the concrete objects in nature.
>
> (Neogy, 1961)

The various aspects of nature—the silhouetted trees, the curved lines of creepers, the flowers and foliage always inspired him, he did not follow any particular style or technique but indulged in a visionary exploration of what he terms as the 'great procession of forms', and aspired to intone the 'spirit'.

The entire visual journey for him was essentially coordinated by an organic and spontaneous evolution. It appears as if his paintings are not products of any analytical cogitations. The quickly moving lines scratching the paper, the hurried strokes of dark colors, the gloomy brooding expressions on the faces of the women, the introspective looks of the male figures, and even the strange animals and birds that frequent his oeuvre all point to a flux of mind and are intense yet thriving with an overwhelming vitality. The forms are strange and mystical, often verging on the eerie. The paintings in ink and watercolor speak of calmness and depth that refract equally in his portraits and landscapes. Yet this exterior calm seems to pulsate with an inner angst, a silence 'evocative of a conversation where the onlooker perceiving the image is initiated into an inquisition, a dialogue with the visual image touched and forwarded by emotional endowment and appeal' (Ghosh, 2011, p. 338).

The resultant feels of the mystery that is associated with Tagore's painting can be explained to some extent if one thinks of the philosopher William James's (1929) exploration of intuitive consciousness. James refers to potential doorways to other types of experience and perceptions that are impossible in the 'sunlit' areas of everyday conscious activity and calls this dimension of the psyche a 'trans marginal field' or 'wider self' that embraces aesthetic, mystical, religious, and metaphysical events. (Hague, 2003, p. 29) James calls this state of consciousness the 'B-region' and claims that it is as real as our 'daylight' one because it has effects in the natural world.

> Our ideal impulses originate in this region... and we belong to it in a more intimate sense than that in which we belong to in the visible world, for we belong in the most intimate sense wherever our ideals belong.
>
> (James, 1929; Hardman 2011)

Like James, Jung also sees a connection between the openness to subliminal states of mind and creative activity; for him, they can get interlinked,

> and completely new thoughts and creative ideas can also present themselves from the unconscious, thoughts, and ideas that have never been conscious before. They grow up from the dark depths of the mind like a lotus and form the most important part of the subliminal psyche.
>
> (Jung, 1964, p. 25)

Tagore's paintings reflect this sense of belonging in this 'B region'. They invite the viewer to delve deeper into the dense darkness of the mind, where raw emotion and metaphysical sensitivity mix and merge to create an intimate space. The palette, comprising of deep browns, blood-stain reds, greenish black, and intense blue with sparse touches of yellow, contributes to creating a dusky mood. The bright yellow patches peeking out from behind the elaborate maze of dark brown or black trees, the sporadic blue bordering the blurry geometrical heads of women in conversation impede the atmosphere even more, by penetrating the overlapping hues and communicating the 'mystical susceptibility'.

One is again reminded of Croce's views:

> To give artistic form to content of feeling means, then, impressing upon it the character of totality, breathing into it the breath of the cosmos. Thus understood, universality and artistic form are not two things but one.
>
> (Croce, 1966, p. 262)

Croce's idea resonates with Tagore's expressions in 1930, especially in the following quote, where, discussing his paintings, he comments: 'The world of sound is a tiny bubble in the silence of the infinite'. His paintings, felt Tagore, were an act of salvaging the emotions hidden deep within his mind. In the last few years of his life, he was finding it more and more difficult to stick to his ideal of truth and beauty. The aggressive attitude of the West, the experience of the world wars, and the political ambivalence among the leaders of the freedom movement in India, along with the prevalent social discrepancy and continuous economic crisis he had been facing to run the institution of his dream, caused a suppressed anger, frustration, and disillusionment in his mind. The outcome was what Abanindranath Tagore has termed the 'volcanic eruption'. In a strange coincidence, John Dewey (1934) used the same imagery to explain such creative outbursts:

Figure 10.2 A landscape by Rabindranath Tagore. (Google Image Result for https://www.sanctuarynaturefoundation.org/uploads/Article/1714717195165_1.jpg)

> Even the volcano's outburst presupposes a long period of prior compression and if the eruption sends forth molten lava and not merely separate rocks and ashes, it implies the transformation of original raw materials.
>
> (Dewey, 1934/2005, p. 75)

The thousands of paintings Tagore had done within this short period are evidence of his reaction formation.

His own remarks in 1930 correspond to this idea of aesthetic sublimation, resulting in a spontaneous upsurge of creative splurge.

> In the process of this salvage work I came to discover one fact that in the universe of form there is a perpetual activity of natural selection in line and only the fittest survives, which has in itself the fitness of cadence.
>
> (Neogy, 1961)

In Tagore's artworks, one catches a growing vision of a world, where the common and mundane, the ugly and bizarre, change place with the expected transcendental/ideal images of existence, which is apparent in his poems. This has been explained as the expression of the repressive forces dominating his subconscious. The most primitive and raw emotions evoked by these images can be read as subtle expressions of regressive impulse.

(a)

Figure 10.3a An imaginary animal. (https://www.pinterest.com/pin/primitivism-malaganmask-from-new-ireland--293508100691846256/)

One can seek the explanation by referring to Freud (1958), who had 'explored the idea of creativity as a "defense mechanism" rooted in the unconscious' (Hardman, 2011).

The mask-like self-images done with the quick lines on his printed photographs indicate not how he visualized his own outward appearance but how he optically projected his inner self in his mind. As if through these portraits, he wanted to establish a new cognitive parameter of his identity.

This might be explained with reference to the Jungian concept of the collective unconscious. According to Jung, the mind consists of three psychic levels: the conscious, the personal unconscious, and the collective unconscious. It is the last, which according to Jung is the domain of intuition and instinct. The collective unconscious for Jung is a

> ...boundless expanse, a place of unprecedented uncertainty, with apparently no inside and no outside, no above and no below, no here and no there, no mine and no thine, no good and no bad. It is the world of water, where all life floats in suspension; where the realm of the sympathetic nervous system, the soul of everything living, begins; where I am indivisibly this and that; where I experience the other in myself and the other-than-myself experiences me.
>
> (Jung & Hull, 1959, pp. 21–22)

(b)

Figure 10.3b The woman's face. (https://in.pinterest.com/pin/530580399823665715/)

The surreal content of some of the images of human faces (mainly the faces of women), with their grim visages and harsh geometrical contours, conveys a deep sense of foreboding. The grim eyes, with their hypnotic yet dispassionate stare and crooked, downturned, cynical smiles, have something primordial about them. The primitive and the archaic in his painting so often identified by critics, might be clarified, or put into perspective by tagging the following theoretical framework:

> Without delving too deeply into the different memory systems that exist within the brain, suffice it to say that our representations of self and the world are complex precisely because they combine perceptual and conceptual processing of space and time with an emotional memory system. This system is housed in the amygdala and related areas and may be aroused by the activation of consciously or unconsciously proceeded stimuli.
>
> (Oppenheim, 2005, p. 110)

In Tagore's case, the stimuli perhaps were the result of the incongruity he experienced between his ideal world or inner representational world and the actuality of his perceptual cognition. For K.G. Subramanyan, the artist, this way of expressing oneself is very similar to the expression of the folk artists, and he

Figure 10.4 A self-portrait of Rabindranath Tagore. (https://i.pinimg.com/736x/1f/76/c0/1f76c0b69a9f526e654abbcc2a0f0796.jpg)

clarifies his point by saying, 'The decorative arabesque assumes various aspects of man and beasts that rise directly from the unconscious. They came unsolicited' (Subramanyam, 2006, p. 65). Although this comment was made in the context of his doodles, it is also applicable to most of his paintings.

Again, Rabindranath's presence in Europe in 1921 was of immense importance 'so when he embarked on his painterly activity, it has to be believed that though technically he was a novice, he had a rich visual experience of modern painting...' (Parimoo, 1973, p. 119).

It was between 1920 and 1924 that the French Dada movement was pronouncedly active in publicizing its ideas, and it was quite natural that Tagore, during his frequent visits to Europe and exposure to the experimental artworks of European and American artists, would be highly intrigued by their new ideas. He had also visited Weimar, the center of the Bauhaus movement, and got acquainted with them, and he made no secret of his admiration for their artworks. In fact, many later critics have found much similarity between his works and that of Nolde one of the artists in the group (Parimoo, 1973, p. 119). These could be considered markers of 'Rabindranath's conscious intent upon adopting the automatic as a process in his art' (Ghosh, 2011, p. 333). This appears all the more relevant because in his paintings, 'Categorical frontiers dissolved and the nascent inner world was peopled with self-generating entities that belonged as much to the state of awakening as to that of dreaming' (Neogy, 1961, p. 12).

Finally, it can be said that Rabindranath's paintings perhaps offer the closest approximation to the intuitive expression of art, in the Indian context. A.K. Coomaraswamy, in his introduction to Tagore's catalog of paintings (1930) showcased in America, had eulogized them as 'publication of a private correspondence'. Truly enough, Tagore's paintings bear in them a suggestion of an instinctive impulse that transforms the familiar/expected into the unfamiliar with a touch of surreal, individualistic, yet at the same time bordering on the universal.

Once again, one is reminded of Croce's comment:

> In intuition, the single pulsates with the life of the whole, and the whole is in the life of the single. Every genuine artistic representation is itself and is the universe, the universe in that individual form, and that individual form as the universe. In every utterance, every fanciful [imaginative] creation, of the poet, there lies the whole of human destiny, all human hope, illusions, griefs, joys, human grandeurs and miseries, the whole drama of reality perpetually evolving and growing out of itself in suffering and joy.
>
> (Croce, 1966, p. 262)

The above quote is almost an echo of Tagore's observation in 1926:

> Art represents the inexhaustible magnificence of our creative spirit, it is generous in its acceptance, generous in its bestowal it is unique...and universal in its appeal.
>
> (Neogy, 1961, p. 62)

That his paintings never cease to intrigue the viewers with their complexity and cadence, the intricacy of design, sign, and brilliance of mystifying colors bear testimony to the veracity of the above remark.

Conclusion

The concept of intuition as an important part of creativity is hardly ever considered, especially for academic ponderings or critical appreciation of artworks. Prominence is more on the stylistic novelties and the experiments with techniques applied, but the cognitive state principal to it is hardly ever paid attention to or chosen as an area of reflection, especially in the case of visual art. Naturally, the individual intuitive thought or the non-rational and insentient features of the creative progression are rarely deliberated as a pertinent subject of dialogue. The classification of artworks as per some 'ism' often supplants the need for a greater perceptive approach. A search for creative intuition or generating stimuli behind the artwork is generally neglected as insignificant. This only leaves the viewer with a partial grasp of the creative process and leaves the artist unaware of the full potential of his creative energy. That this search is relevant as it is complementary to the applied, cogent, and scientific considerations of creative cognition, has been proved in the above discussion. With the help of some of the relevant theories of psychologists and philosophers, along with the analysis of Rabindranath's paintings, several principles underlying creative intuition can be identified. These theories and approaches are further validated by statements from famous artists themselves, who, from their experiences, have commented on the role of intuition in their creative journeys. In doing so, they establish its significance in the discovery of a visual language that is intense and intriguing.

Notes

1 Pramatrichaitanya: this Sanskrit word means consciousness as knowing; the source of knowledge; proof.
2 Prama: highest or top or perfect.
3 Pra: perfect.
4 Maan: value, worth.
5 Rasika: connoisseur, graceful.
6 Swagna: intuition, clairvoyance.
7 Swa: own.
8 Gna: knowledge.
9 Jnan: knowledge.
10 Prajna: transcendental wisdom or supreme knowledge.
11 Abanabaunmeshshalinipratibha.

References

Bandopadhyay, S. (1982). *Rabindra chitrakala: Rabindra sahityer patabhumika*. Dey's Publication.
Bose, N. (1936). The paintings of Rabindranath. *Visva Bharati Quarterly*, *1*(14), 31.
Croce, B. (1921). *The essence of aesthetics* (D. Ainslie, Trans.). Heinemann
Croce, B. (1966). *Philosophy, poetry, history: An anthology of essays* (C. Sprigge, Trans.). Oxford University Press.
Deleuze, G. (1991). *Bergsonism*. Zone Books.
Dewey, J. (1934). *Art as experience*. Penguin Group.
Freud, S. (1958). *On creativity and the unconscious*. Harper.
Ghosh, N. (2011). Extension of the self: Doodles to painting. In *The art of Rabindranath Tagore', appreciation of Indian art: Selected writings*. The Ramakrishna Mission Institute of Culture.
Goldwater, R., & Treves, M. (Eds.). (1947). *Artists on art: From the XIV to the XX century*. Pantheon Books, Kegan Paul.
Hague, A. (2003). *Fiction intuition and creativity* (1st ed.). The Washington Catholic University of America Press.
Hardman, T. (2011). Understanding creative intuition. *De arte*, *46*, 22–32.
James, W. (1929). *Variety of religious experiences*. Modern Library.
Jung, C. (1926). *Psychological types* (G. Baynes, Trans.). Routledge & Kegan Paul.

Jung, C. G. (Ed.) and after his death Franz, M.-L. (1964). *Man and his symbols*. Random House.
Jung, C. G., & Hull, R. F. C. (1959). *The archetypes and the collective unconscious C. G. Jung* (R. F. C. Hull, Trans.). Pantheon Books.
Kandinsky, W. (1977). *Concerning the spiritual in art* (M. T. H. Sadler, Trans.). Dover Books.
Kandinsky, W., & Sadleir, M. (1914). *The art of spiritual harmony, by Wassily Kandinsky; tr. with an introduction by M.T.H. Sadleir*. Constable and Company Limited.
Neogy, P. (Ed.). (1961). *Rabindranath Tagore on art and aesthetics: A selection of lectures, essays and letters*. Inter-National Cultural Centre by Orient Longmans, New Delhi Publisher.
Oppenheim, L. (2005). *A curious intimacy: Art and neuro-psychoanalysis*. Routledge.
Oxford Dictionary. (2021). *Oxford English Dictionary*. Oed.com. https://www.oed.com
Parimoo, R. (1973). *The paintings of the three Tagore's, Abanindranath, Gaganendranath, Rabindranath, chronology and comparative study*. Maharaja Sayaji Rao, University of Baroda. https://www.indianculture.gov.in
Rothenstein, W., Lago, M., & Tagore, R. (1972). *Imperfect encounter; letters of William Rothenstein and Rabindranath Tagore, 1911–1941, edited with an introd. and notes by Mary M. Lago*. Harvard University Press.
Stein, M. (1974). *Stimulating creativity* (p. 203). Academic Press.
Subramanyam, K. G. (2006). *Moving focus*. Lalit Kala Akademi.
Tagore, A. (1947). *Bharatshilper sadanga*. Visvabharati Granthanbivhag.

Chapter 11

Intuitive linkage

Interface between artistic expression and mental illness

Samadrita Bhattacharya

Artistic creations have long been captivated by the offering of researchers glimpses into the depths of human expression and creativity. The act of creating art, starting from literature, music, painting, or sculpture, has been an intriguing subject of exploration in various disciplines, including psychology. But, defining art and who is an "artist" has been a challenging and controversial task, perplexing artists, philosophers, musicians, and scientists for centuries. The subjective nature of art and its reliance on individual creative instincts have contributed to the debate surrounding their definition.

The word "art" traces its origin to the Latin word *ars*, denoting "skill" or "craft." Throughout history, the definition and classification of art have undergone significant transformations influenced by socio-cultural, political, and technological changes that have resulted in an expansion of its scope. Despite varying perspectives, most agree that art is an act of expression created through the manipulation of formal tools, presented in a unique style, and capable of evoking emotional responses in its audience. This conceptualization encompasses all recognized art genres, including 2D forms like drawing or painting, where artists visually express themselves through the manipulation of visual tools such as line, contour, shading, etc. The term "artist," on the other hand, can be traced back to the terms used in Ancient Greece such as "technē" which referred to individuals with mastery over any craft or the term "artista" that emerged over time to differentiate craftsmen and art students. In modern times, the definition of an artist has become more commercialized, influenced by technology, media, and entertainment. Currently, the term artist is used broadly to encompass anyone engaged in activities that are considered as works of art. While some argue that formal education in art is necessary, others, like Picasso and Courbet, believe that painting cannot be taught. It is increasingly recognized that artists do not have to be professional image-makers nor is artistic production the sole proprietorship of only those who have gone through a rigorous art training curriculum and understood all the intricacies of the grammatical aspects of art. Indeed, there is a wide variation in well-versed creative groups who do not fit

DOI: 10.4324/9781003377757-13

into the categories of "professional artists" nor do they fit into the "normal" group. In spite of that, they are powerful and creative image-makers who produce such exciting work that takes on a life of its own, at times separating it away from its producer and at other times blending it in with the producer. This is the realm of "outsider art" a term coined by Roger Cardinal (Cardinal, 1972).

This essay considers and uses the term "artist" in the broadest sense to denote anybody, skilled or unskilled, capable of expressing through the medium of drawing and painting and thereby includes in its realm the outsider artists as defined above. It considers as a sample not only the "professional image-maker" but also those who create an image for its sake, for the sole purpose of communication and creation.

Art, as a form of human behavior, encompasses various mental processes. Similar to other behaviors, it serves the purpose of satisfying needs. The human desire to communicate and express oneself has been evolutionarily linked to meeting fundamental biological needs, ensuring safety, seeking social connections and a sense of belonging, as well as satisfying self-actualization and aesthetic needs as defined by Abraham Maslow (1954). This innate drive significantly influences the process of image-making which is seen to comprise complex patterns, symbols, and figures with very personal or specific meanings, even without formal training. Human beings have been evidenced, historically, to draw, to document their life struggles, their fantasies (often very biological), significant events, and important places and instructions they wanted to be passed on. They seem to possess an innate capacity to convey their thoughts and emotions in a visual language. It is as if they have an almost intuitive grasp of how to effectively communicate their ideas and sentiments through their artistic expressions. Often in clinical settings and mental hospitals, it is observed that individuals suffering from serious mental disorders "refuse" to "talk" or "communicate" within therapeutic settings. But, these very individuals would spontaneously produce images, scribbles, and symbols, either with provided materials or in the absence of formal tools, whatever they can lay their hands on, at times, using "walls" as their canvas.

This raises a few intriguing questions. The first is whether there is an "intuitive" basis to art, and if so, what does it involve? Second, does analyzing artwork provide insights into these underlying psychological functioning, personality traits, and potential pathological changes, if so, what is the extent to which these can be reliably and validly established? And finally, what is the impact of mental illness on this process?

From a clinical point of view, it's crucial to find answers to these questions. This exploration is important not only for its research implication but also because it helps open up closed dialogues and allows working through therapeutic resistance. This, in turn, allows for deeper exploration and understanding of the underlying psychodynamics resulting in effective symptom reduction. This would not have been vital, had the patient been an "object" that could be put under a microscope, or observed "objectively" from different angles. But, as researchers in the field of psychiatry and clinical psychology point out (Fried et al., 2016), sticking to a strictly "symptomatic approach" "taking seriously only what one could observe and verify" (Kaplan, 1964, p. 9) would mean leaving out the most crucial aspect of the treatment—the patient himself, his inner world, his subjective experience—the very foundation of the pathological process. Additionally, exploring the intricacies of the art-making process and understanding the degree to which it involves conscious deliberation versus being primarily driven by unconscious intuition, or a combination of both, is also crucial for several reasons. First, it allows one to better comprehend how the individual conceptualizes, plans, and executes their work, thereby knowing correctly how to facilitate and further the process appropriately and plan any changes to be made therein to suit therapeutic goals. Second, it allows therapists to guide individuals in accessing their intuitive abilities and using art as a means of self-expression, healing, and personal growth. Third, it would allow to minimize subjectivity that is inherent in art-based assessments by avoiding the overemphasis or neglect of any element included in the creation. This approach, thus, would ensure a more balanced and meaningful analysis of the artwork.

The present chapter explores the fascinating relationships and parallels between intuitive processes and drawing or painting, focusing on how they shape, influence, and orient the paintings created by diverse categories of individuals, patients suffering from different types of mental illness, and both trained and untrained artists.

Method

This study compares and contrasts the theoretical views of different psychology schools on artistic creation, autobiographical testimonies from proclaimed artists (some obtained through one-on-one interviews), and data from analyzing artworks and narratives created by individuals living with mental health conditions. The research aims to shed light on parallels and commonalities in their creative processes, focusing on interconnections and overlaps with intuitive processes.

It is within these intricate brushstrokes, vibrant colors, and evocative compositions that the present discourse seeks to discover the profound impact of intuition on artistic expression, extending beyond artistic expertise and limitations imposed by mental illness. It also hopes to uncover in this process, the unspoken language of the artist's hand and delve into the unique perspectives of individuals with mental illness, highlighting how their artworks serve as a profound means of self-expression and reflection thereby broadening the understanding of the human psyche, creativity, and the transformative power of art.

Theoretical perspective: Conceptualizing intuition

Intuition has been defined in various ways by different disciplines, each drawing on the concept to explain specific behaviors within their respective domains. A quick literature review of the varied conceptualization, also reveals, that, it had quite frequently been used synonymously and interchangeably with terms such as insight, imagination, ideation, priming, etc. Proposed definitions were found to range from broad simplistic conceptualizations to denote a sense of "knowing without being able to explain how we know" to more perspective-specific definitions. The multitude of entries for the word "intuition" attests to the complex and multifaceted nature of its study, and therefore, a brief deliberation is needed on the different perspectives to set a meaningful context for the selection of a particular angle for the purpose of the study.

As a psychodynamic psychologist, Carl Gustav Jung was one of the earliest researchers to formulate a conceptual framework of intuition from a psychological perspective. He recognized its role and importance in therapy and patients' testimony (*PathologischeEinfalle*) which often involved patients *Vorahnungen* or "premonitions," precognitive dreams, and vision. According to him, intuition was a very natural process, much like a revelation, that after "falling into your head" is processed by the receptive under-conscious, as conceptualized by Jung, resulting in an "uncontrolled automatism" which redirects intuition, either to the unconscious through the *Anschauung* or "intuition", thereby casting an unconscious impression on the present conscious functioning or directly to consciousness to become manifest intuition. Tracing the origin of the word to Latin *Intueri* meaning to "look at or into," he said that as a basic psychological function, it mediates perception unconsciously and though it may appear in the form of sense perception, feeling, or intellectual inference, it is none of these. In intuition, a complete and whole content presents itself, without a clear explanation of how it came to be. Intuition is akin to an instinctive apprehension, capable of perceiving various types of content. Like sensation, it is an irrational aspect of perception, that is primitive and infantile and a precursor to ideas. It is experienced as "given" and "true" and possesses an intrinsic certainty and conviction and on a definite state of psychic "alertness" of whose origin the subject is unconscious much like the "physical foundation" of the sensory world (Pilard, 2018, ch. 1).

Jung further classified intuition into subjective and objective, as well as concrete and abstract forms. Subjective intuition involves perceiving unconscious psychic data within the subject, while objective intuition involves perceiving subliminal data associated with external objects and the thoughts and emotions they evoke. Concrete intuition mediates the perception of actual things, while abstract intuition mediates the perception of interconnections between objects. Jung emphasized that there is no inherent predisposition toward an "intuitive type" and anyone who relies on intuition and is oriented toward it can be considered an intuitive type. In abnormal cases, the intuitive process becomes deeply intertwined with the collective unconscious, often leading to seemingly irrational and incomprehensible behavior.

Researchers investigating the cognitive mechanisms and mental representations underlying intuitive judgments (Bolte & Goschke, 2008) indicated that intuitive processes underlying gestalt judgments, or perceptual tasks, rely on the unconscious activation of conceptual object representations. Additionally, the experiments demonstrated that unrecognized coherent fragments produced reliable priming of correct object names in a lexical decision task, providing further evidence of the activation of unconscious semantic representations (Bolte & Goschke, 2008). These findings, they state, support the theory that intuition involves implicit memory. This memory, although not consciously accessed, influences judgments even when the gestalt or the sense of "wholeness" is disrupted. Further, as a sub-component of long-term memory, it encompasses various types of knowledge and skills acquired from previous tasks, such as procedural memory for actions like brushing, modeling, and composing. It also includes priming, which involves unconscious cues from past experiences that affect current tasks, and associative learning through repeated connections between stimuli and responses, as seen in classical and operant conditioning.

Recent research has linked implicit memory to intuition and tacit knowledge, with the latter considered a subset of the former, and tacit knowledge in its turn has widely been linked to intuition. Polanyi (1967), who introduced the term formally, defined tacit knowledge as "a power to know more than we can tell" ("Michael Polanyi and tacit knowledge," n.d.), while Ambrosini and Bowman (2001), more recently, conceptualized it as "non-codified, disembodied know-how." They identified the main characteristics of tacit knowledge as (1) people with tacit knowledge are unable to articulate the decision-making process that guides their performance, (2) tacit knowledge is a form of personal knowledge, and (3) tacit knowledge is practical and describes a process through which the capabilities, i.e., the technical know-hows of a person is utilized. Studies on skill acquisition have shown that tacit knowledge becomes more effective and automatic with repetition.

Previous research, aimed at establishing the neural basis of intuition, implicated the Orbitofrontal cortex (OFC) to be crucial to its mechanism. But the exact role has remained unclear. More recent research using Magnetoencephalography (MEG)proposed that the OFC acts as an integrator of incomplete stimulus information, providing a coarse representation of the overall gist of the information and that it was independent of the physical characteristics, tasks at hand, and participants' explicit recognition of the stimulus. This representation is subjectively perceived as a gut feeling, which biases decision-making, at least in the initial phases. Additional findings suggest that there are specific neural pathways, particularly the white matter tracts mentioned, involved in transferring information between different brain regions during intuitive processing. This connectivity is crucial for the integration of incomplete stimulus input and the formation of a coarse representation of the information's gist. These neurological findings are important in that they help to address the criticism that the study of intuition is a pseudoscience at best.

Westcott and Ranzoni (1963) viewed intuition as a mode of thought that involves making judgments and predictions based on limited information. Other researchers suggest that intuition is the result of mental routines triggered by stimuli, the unconscious matching of perceived patterns to stored patterns in memory, the synthesis of isolated bits of data into a coherent whole, or the organization of experiences and facts into a new condensed pattern. Intuition is seen as a process of relating different elements of information, including external stimuli, memory (particularly implicit memory), emotions, and subconscious concerns (Shirley & Langan-Fox, 1996). It also involves implicit learning and is an associative process. These processes involve encoding environmental cues and various cognitive abilities like reasoning, empathy, emotional resonance, and metaphorical and analogical thinking. Subconscious associations are important in intuitive thought and help integrate our internal and external experiences seamlessly.

In contrast to insight, intuition is often described as a vague, emotional, gut feeling. According to Bruner (1960), the intuitive thinker may struggle to provide a clear explanation of their thought process and might not even be conscious of the specific aspects of the problem they responded to. Intuitive thinking relies on familiarity with the relevant knowledge domain and its structure. On the other hand, analytic creative thinking, of which insight is an outcome, albeit unconscious, proceeds step by step, with explicit and reportable steps. In such a form of thinking, thinkers are usually aware of the information and operations involved in their thinking process and can report it as such (Bruner, 1960, p. 57). Imagination, on the other hand, serves as a wellspring for artistic creation, enabling artists to mentally construct images, ideas, and concepts that go beyond immediate sensory perception. It is through the power of imagination that artists can envision new possibilities, explore alternative realities, and manifest their unique artistic vision. Imagination fuels creativity, allowing artists to transform abstract ideas into tangible artistic expressions and again can be reported almost in every detail and is even susceptible to manipulation, unlike intuition. Inspiration, while distinct from the aforementioned concepts, is also deeply intertwined with artistic creation. It refers to a state of being mentally stimulated or influenced, which propels artists toward meaningful creations. Inspiration can arise from various sources, such as nature, emotions, experiences, or the works of other artists, and is almost always conscious. It ignites the creative spark within artists and provides the motivation and energy to bring their artistic visions to life.

In the realm of artistic creation, intuition, insight, imagination, and inspiration play integral roles. Intuition grants artists access to profound insights, while insights lead to transformative understandings. Imagination fuels the creative process, allowing artists to envision and manifest their artistic vision. Again, in contrast, inspiration provides the driving force, motivating artists to explore new territories and create meaningful works of art.

The theoretical discourse on the nature and properties of intuition, as distinct from these concepts, allows to form a conceptual background of the specific processes underlying the course of art creation and to gain a deeper understanding of the complicated interplay that characterizes the artistic path.

The psychology of art

Despite the universality of art, significantly less effort has been directed toward understanding the various facets of art and how it relates to those who create, i.e., the artist. With the dawn of the twenty-first century, the focus has been on increased exploration and development of this interdisciplinary arena. Initially met with skepticism, the involvement of unconscious psychological processes in artistic creation gradually gained acceptance among art psychologists, historians, and artists.

Although Germany was the birthplace of art psychology as a discipline, it soon began to spread, expand, and transform in the USSR, England, France, and the USA, thus becoming increasingly popular in use for the purpose of assessment and therapy.

Currently, there are multiple approaches to art therapy as there are multiple drawing tests that are being popularly used worldwide: Goodenough Harris Draw–A–Man Test, (Goodenough, 1940) with its many modifications, the House–Tree–Person technique, constructed in 1948 by Buck, which was later modified by Burns (1987) into Kinetic-House–Tree–Person test, to overcome limitations of the previous version (Malchiodi, 2005), the Silver Drawing test, developed by Silver (2003) and the Diagnostic Drawing Series, which for the first time was attuned to the diagnostic protocol of Diagnostic Statistical Manual. The reason behind the effectiveness of drawing as a diagnostic tool is that it is "less threatening" and provides the patient with a safe and comfortable way of expressing themselves that may otherwise not be possible for them to verbalize. The process of creating an artwork, as well as the outcome, viz., the final product, the artwork itself, provides invaluable insight into the underlying psychological processes of the individual, his inner conflicts, wishes, needs, etc., that might not be revealed as clearly in other more verbal tests (Oster, 2016). This act, along with structured interviews, facilitates treatment planning by providing critical information about the focus and goal of the treatment. In the case of children, it often acts as an active instrument in establishing rapport and interest in the testing procedure.

The different schools of psychology have developed their conceptualizations and theorizations as regards the underlying psychological dynamics of art, whether at all it is decipherable, and the approach that should be followed in art-based analysis including its applicative efficacy. They also hold different views as to the definition, nature, origin, characteristics, and the role of intuition therein, of the term "symbol" as used in artwork, the very fundamental unit of art analysis. Therefore, a brief deliberation is needed on the concepts put forth by the approaches, especially concerning the construct of symbols as used in art. This is because it is also fundamental to this chapter which is primarily analytical and also to form a firm theoretical grounding and context.

Neuroscientists like Zeki (2010), Alland (1977), and Cavanagh (2005), among others, took a pivotal standpoint by claiming that both the neuroscientist and the artist aim at an exploration of the "potential and capacities of the brain" albeit by their own distinct methods. As per Cavanagh (2005), it is the intentional deviations from the set rules of physics, made by the artist in creating the works of art, is what makes them so interesting to the study of neuropsychology. He termed these as "alternative physics" or "internal physics" that is used by our visual brain, which not only influences the appreciation of painting but also enables a rapid and perhaps more efficient perception of the real world. Uncovering and identifying these deviances in a work of art is possible, not merely to find faults or slip-ups, but to understand the workings of the brain that created it. This, he posits is what makes art, a "found science." He contends that art creation relies on the brain's information processing and abstraction abilities, wherein various cortical centers abstract particulars into general concepts, culminating in unconscious knowledge acquisition, with only the abstracted concepts accessible to consciousness. Researches looking into the neuroscience of artistic activities have found that damage to specific brain regions does not fully explain artistic abilities. These studies have analyzed the effects of brain damage on skilled artists and the connections between different brain regions and artistic skills, techniques, styles, talents, and creativity. The findings suggest that artistic cognition cannot be solely attributed to a specific hemisphere or area of the brain. These artistic skills can persist for many years, even in the presence of severe cognitive deficits caused by neurodegenerative diseases like dementia (Fornazzari, 2005). Also, the observed changes are not limited to artists alone, suggesting that they reflect the cognitive and perceptual specialization of the human brain, which are intimately involved in the creation of art (Drago et al., 2008).

For instance, they also reported that damage to the right parietal lobe, which is specialized for topographical memory and spatial perception, can result in a condition known as "neglect drawing." This means the inability to complete drawings on the left half of a page. Even when the outline drawing is complete, neglect can still be observed in the coloring process. These findings suggest that there may be a "resistance" to some of the cognitive processes involved in creation and that it involves a broader and more complex cognitive network.

The Gestalt theory of visual perception suggests that artists use principles of perception to create coherent and meaningful artwork. These principles, taught in art schools, involve manipulating visual elements like line, color, and medium. However, the final artwork goes beyond mere composition and often reflects the artist's thoughts, emotions, and inner world. This adds depth and meaning that cannot be fully explained by technical aspects alone. It is a phenomenon that goes beyond the mechanical manipulation of visual tools. As an explanation. Gestaltists like Golomb (2003) and Arnheim (2004) propose that art reflects humans' innate drive to shape and reconfigure familiar elements, allowing the integration of personal experiences with external expression. This process, facilitated by holistic, analog, and self-organizing brain mechanisms, a theorization that was later established empirically, as discussed in the preceding segment, enables artists to use perceptual abstraction and intuition, to transform past elements into novel syntheses, fostering therapeutic insights and new emotional approaches through visual thinking. Intuition helps artists go beyond linear or sequential analysis, allowing them to grasp the underlying essence and meaning of a subject and convey a sense of unity, coherence, and aesthetic meaning in their work.

Thus, expression, the central theme of the psychology of art, as a special facet of perception, discloses the cognitive connections between objects which arise from an intricate interaction of various centers in a perceptual field rendering the work of art a composite of interfacing forces. According to Arnheim (2004), expressiveness is the result of the internal "stresses" and "strain" that characterize the underlying process of visual perception. In addition, he also held that all perceptual expressions are intrinsic to any manifest object or processes and that the connection between internal experience and external expression may be presented in the form of a metaphor, symbol, or tangible creation.

The Gestalt psychologists, such as Hornbostel, believe that metaphors and symbolism begin with comparing stimuli from different senses and finding similarities between them. These similarities provide the basis for creating symbols, which are more abstract than the objects they represent. The resulting pictures created through manipulating symbols are more concrete than the symbols themselves, but still higher in the hierarchy of symbolism compared to the underlying thoughts that influenced their creation.

Proponents of this view, also hold that art-making is essentially developmental and changes and developments in perceptual and cognitive processes over lifespan result in consequent changes in the artistic style of the artist, just as psychopathology or any disturbance. In the case of the latter, this causes a breakdown of the "gestalt" of the artwork, and works of art become increasingly representational either loosely integrated or integrated too formally, as being closer to the medium and increasingly less concrete in nature as evidenced in Schizophrenic art or schizoid art (Verstegen, 2006).

J.P. Guilford's creativity test (Guilford, 1966), also revealed, that creativity comprises various component abilities rather than a single skill, emphasizing the importance of divergent thinking and recognizing connections and similarities between objects in the creation of art.

The Cognitivists, on the contrary, denied the explicit role of intuition and held that the act of creating a drawing or painting involves conscious problem-solving, where the artist selects forms, shapes, lines, colors, and arrangement to achieve their desired goal while considering formal elements and the syntax of visual arts. However, future theorists criticized this view for its narrow focus and stressed that the creative process combines reason and intuition, akin to sudden insight that occurs during the incubation phase of creative problem-solving. Cognitivists, however, acknowledge the influence of talent, the elusive factor that have traditionally been used to distinguish artists from non-artists, despite its lack of empirical conceptualization. According to them, talent represents a predisposition to excel in a specific skill, such as the visual arts and its associated symbol systems, although its precise nature remains difficult to define.

Like the Gestaltists, the cognitivists too observed that symbols play a fundamental role in human thought processes, enabling individuals to operate meaningfully within specific contexts and that artists engage in artistic activity to recreate the world in their own symbolic image. They however differed in their emphasis on the conscious engagement of creators in cognitive processes, including problem generation, meaning comprehension, and creative problem-solving, as they use and create symbols to perceive, understand, and construct their experiences of the world.

Although research in the cognitive era of psychological understanding tried to empirically establish the role of intuition in art-making, Carl Jung was the first person to stress the role of intuition in art. Unlike his predecessor, Sigmund Freud (1900), the father of Classical Psychoanalysis, as he viewed artworks not merely as a riddle to be deciphered and analyzed, but as an entity that needed to be understood from both cultural and psychological standpoints.

Freud and other psychoanalysts of his time were primarily concerned with eliciting unconscious conflicts and phantasies as symbolized in a work of art. They believed that repression plays a significant role in the symbolism expressed. They conceptualized symbol formation as the process through which hidden thoughts and desires find symbolic expression in various forms like dreams and art, stemming from both conscious and unconscious levels of the mind. Freud emphasized that beneath the manifest content of art and dreams lies a latent content expressed through symbols, which can be personally subjective or culturally shared, originating from both conscious and unconscious aspects of the mind.

Carl Jung emphasized that two forms of thinking, directed and non-directed, contribute to the creation of symbols in dreams and art, with symbols being affect-infused, subliminal images that defy simple verbal explanations and possess deep, individualistic connotations.

Jung states that there are four functions of consciousness—thought, feeling, intuition, and sensation. These resources enable the observer to perceive, analyze, and respond to the wide array of stimuli he is bombarded with every moment from "within" and "without." The unconscious not only harbors the memory of that which had once been conscious, but it can also, by virtue of its dynamism, give rise to completely new thoughts and creative ideas—ideas that are born from the depth of the consciousness and from an important part of the subliminal psyche. Not only this, the unconscious may also color conscious experience, giving it an undertone, that may at the time of recall of that once-conscious object "extend and confuse the conventional meaning" thereby transforming it into a symbol that is highly individualistic.

As regards the process of creation, Jung, who himself was an artist of sorts, stated that the process of creating a work of art is also an exceedingly personal activity. Extreme anxiety and resistance may forgo the initial task of putting "brush to paper" or "hand to clay." Once this is surmounted the maker, so to say, makes a conscious decision to interact and forge a "relationship" with the medium even though he may still falter in his efforts to amalgamate and give expression to the aforementioned stimuli. This is more difficult in the case of a patient because in them the conscious and the unconscious are broken or split, and the ego boundaries are more permeable and often dissipate. What follows, thereafter may hardly kowtow to "will or expectation." Even the most skilled and trained artist may find his work developing its own personality distinct from his plan or layout. The objects of art interact, manipulate, and are in turn manipulated by the artist as the work proceeds. What emerges finally, therefore, is infused by a feeling of "otherness" that is different from yet belongs to the individual who made it. For those "away from the normal" working with images in an unstructured way may often bring into action a different hidden aspect of his personality and will result in a unique collection of forms, emotions, and configurations that in order to be fully meaningful in understanding the client, should be approached non-judgmentally without any preconceived notions. As Edith Wallace, psychiatrist and Jungian analyst, puts it, this process can be conceptualized as a "dialogue" between the conscious and the unconscious (Junge, 2010).

Like Jung, Object Psychologist, Susan Deri also considers artwork to be a "dialogue" between the creator and the created, and as resulting from the projection of "dialectical tensions" that occurs in the space between the artists' inner world (me) and the outer world (not me).

All this said, it is important to note however that none of these theories are without criticism and much is still left to be understood about the exact nature of the psychological functioning underlying art. But it would not perhaps be erroneous to infer on the basis of the above discussion that the process of art-making not only involves the manipulation of formal visual elements guided by certain grammar or principles, but it also involves a deeper, less explainable, conscious, or deliberate process. While artists may adhere to certain techniques, rules, or conventions, the act of creating art often goes beyond explicit reasoning and involves intuitive, subconscious, and spontaneous elements.

This complex interplay brings forth unique expressions that may not be fully expressed or consciously controlled, but nonetheless, contribute to the richness and diversity of artistic expression.

In sum, the different perspectives show that processes, that are not always conscious, or readily available to consciousness, do play an important role in artistic activities. It underlines that artists engage in both directed thought (logical and objective) and undirected thought (subjective and imaginative) to create works of art, much akin to the processes that underlie intuition. Convergence was also seen in that intuition, whether they used the term or not, is considered as an essential aspect of the creative process allowing artists to use their innate understanding of the visual world. In the creation of art, a dialogue takes place between the conscious and the unconscious, and the finished artwork often has personal, symbolic, and emotional meaning. Further, the psychological process of art is not determined only by specific brain regions or hemispheric specialization but involve a broader cognitive network further providing es empirical support to the claim. Overall, the process of creating art goes beyond explicit thinking and includes intuitive, unconscious, and spontaneous elements that contribute to the richness and diversity of artistic expression.

Autobiographical testimonies

As elucidated above it may at least be theoretically acknowledged that intuition plays a significant role in the creative process, and many artists have been influenced consciously or unconsciously by it. The famous artist Pablo Picasso, who according to Art historian Patricia Failing was "very properly trained in the grand tradition of painting" created many works that were experimental that explored form and structure, romanced with the material, and contained individuals from Picasso's history, his lover, and his daughters. Picasso would do and redo many of his paintings, sometimes completely painting them over, sometimes adding color and then removing all of them. In fact, many of his drawings were found to be much more expressive than the final outcome (Behind the Art, 2023). When asked about his process, Picasso said, "To draw you must close your eyes and sing. I begin with an idea and then it becomes something else" (Itani, 2020). Vincent Van Gogh said that he envisioned his artwork in his dreams and then brought those dreams to life on canvas. He claimed that even in the humblest of surroundings, he found inspiration that drew him in with an unstoppable force (Van Roojen, 2019).

In interviews conducted by the author, prior to the research, a selected sample of artists trained in various art schools as well as those not trained as such, about the process they usually follow in creating their works. I found that every artist had a unique story to tell. Some of the most revealing insights from the current exploration are presented below.

As participant-1, an eminent artist and Professor of Indian painting, stated during her interview session in 2010 that:

> I never think or feel that I am creating the piece, some idea just appears... Mostly they are complete, some vaguely so... Then I do it. Hindrances pop up, at times the product deviates while under process, may be due to the intricacies and complexities within the technical process I am trained in... the product will manifest spontaneously through you, without its deliberate efforts ... you will then see the obstacles dissolve on their own and the pattern unfold automatically within you.
>
> (Interview with author)

Participant-2, a self-taught painter, recounts in a personal interview in 2007 with the author stated that:

> I generally do not begin with any specific subject in mind. I just paint. It often takes its own course. Colors and subjects often mimic my psychological state and thought at a given time. What satisfies me today may not be so tomorrow, so, many times it so happens that I completely discard my entire work, by applying white and begin anew, or make changes in the old picture that I might not have thought of adding at the beginning...a picture manifest itself.
>
> (Interview with author)

Cartoonist (Participant-3) states in a personal interview with the author that:

> When one goes on to write a novel or even merely expresses oneself, through theatre, one has to proceed keeping the respective grammar in mind. But through overt and covert practice that involves deep deliberation, leads to spontaneous expression that has been imprinted in the mind. Like that, when I begin expressing, such as through a light stroke, or a medium line, or a deep line, then automatically the knowledge as if in a "free flow" converts into the pictures, and consequently the specific techniques, what I have learnt, for example, in which position to hold the pencil or brush to produce the medium line or else become immaterial as they come all together in the act of expression as a coherent whole. How they come together is the magic.
>
> (Interview with author)

Analysis of these interviews, and many others, all of which could not be included for the sake of keeping the chapter concise, also, revealed that though many of them have had an experience similar to that described above, of having ideas unexpectedly pop into their heads or some unknown internal process that influenced the final outcome, not all had that experience. Others reported starting working with their medium without having a specific idea in mind and relied on the behavior of the paint or other material to guide them toward a subject of study. It was also revealed that once people got to work, their original layout of what they intended to create frequently changed and had to be redone, as it did not "feel right" or had some "error in them that was not previously noticed" and this was true even when they were creating commissioned works (interview with the author).

However, the problem with such testimonies, as Policastro (1995) states, is that (1) it may be inaccurate and difficult to establish empirically and (2) the artists may not be able to verbalize the process exactly as he/she experienced it at the time he was creating. Despite its limitations, there is no denying the valuable insight the interviews stated above provide into the art-making process. It reveals how the act of creation serves as a conduit for artists to express their unconscious thoughts, emotions, and experiences. It also demonstrates and provides a compelling case as to how the creative process develops through a series of representational transformations, moving from imprecise, syncretic, and implicit forms of knowledge to more distinct, comprehensive, and explicit ones. And, the final result, the artworks produced, often showcase a profound depth and meaning that goes beyond the artists' conscious intentions. However, as Perkins (1981) points out, it should be interpreted with caution.

Clinical findings

Focusing on paintings created by patients diagnosed with chronic schizophrenia, bipolar affective disorder, and obsessive-compulsive disorder, my investigation concentrated on analyzing their artwork to gain insights into their distinct personality traits and psychological functions. All participants included in this research had undergone long-term exposure to psychotropic drugs as part of their treatment regimen and included both individuals with previous training in art as well as untrained ones. Results revealed that individual styles of drawing were preserved in patients who were previously trained or learnt drawing in a particular style pre-morbidly, as revealed by case history, and was minimally changed perhaps in terms of impulsively adding an unnecessary or inconsistent detail (in the Bipolar Disorder group) or more hesitant stroking (in the obsessive-compulsive group) or creating bizarre internal detail in human figures (schizophrenic group).

It was found that irrespective of training, the majority of the patients (95%) diagnosed with Schizophrenia were found to be decisive (with decisive being defined as being resolute and definite resulting in a meaningful goal-directed behavior), as obtained from the analysis of their drawings. This unexpected finding is in sharp contrast to the conventional understanding of schizophrenia raises intriguing questions about the nature of decision-making involved in individuals with this disorder while making paintings. Traditionally, ambivalence has been considered a core symptom of schizophrenia, characterized by conflicting thoughts, emotions, and difficulties in making choices something that was not revealed from an analysis of their works. Observation of the process revealed average to below average reaction time in beginning the work, and sustained effort at the completion of work, a phenomenon not observed when they were responding to the Rorschach Inkblot test, also used in the same research, for external validation of findings. In Rorschach, there were long reaction times, and frequent rejection of cards, and around 28% were revealed to have marked ambivalent tendencies. Again, no lack of confidence was noted in this group. In patients belonging to this group even when they had significant thought or perceptual disturbance color usage was seen to be appropriate though the majority used cool colors and tended to sparsely color the picture. This indicates that at least part of the psychological process underlying the process of art-making remains largely preserved even in the presence of psychological disorders that influence conscious decision-making.

During the data collection process in my research, as well as while conducting art therapy, I would ask the patients how they decided what to draw when I asked them to "draw anything you like" after they finished drawing. Often, almost like a pattern, enough to call it a finding even, they would look at the just completed drawing, as if seeing it for the first time, and say "you know, when you told me to draw I drew the first thing that came to my mind, and when I drew that, I *felt* something else needed to be added (pointing to another figure/object, relevant or irrelevant)." Patients suffering from Obsessive Compulsive Disorder were observed to be rubbing out major details or even complete drawings before restarting again because it did not "feel" right, but what questions about what "did not feel right" were met with "I don't know ...you know." In Bipolar patients, it was observed that they would often draw a big centralized figure and would add something around it to indicate a background, they would look for some time and add something more, going on drawing apparently unrelated details but which would come together as a whole meaningful composition. For example, Patient Mr. B first drew a "Shivling" to a little right to the page, then drew the "trishul," then added the "banyan tree," then drew the house around the "Shivling." Then, he stopped, looked at the picture, and drew the lines on the ground, wrote, and then added the birds. When asked to elaborate he just discussed the items he drew but not the relation or why he placed them where he did. He recollected in session "when I was outside I saw something like this Shiva" but why he chose to draw that now in the free drawing session, was something he could not explain.

Another interesting thing that was revealed was that many patients who were supplied with colors chose not to use them, when given a choice, because they stated "I don't want to.... It looks ok," but usually they colored appropriately if specifically instructed too.

It was observed that both the untrained group and the trained group exhibited specific drawing techniques learnt many years ago, despite not regularly using them. The trained group, even when instructed that there was no right or wrong way to draw, still relied on the styles they had learnt in Art College. Some women without formal drawing lessons drew cultural religious motifs like "Dhaner-chora" or "alpona," which are associated with Bengali Hindu worship and include colored motifs, patterns, and symbols.

In my therapy session with children, it was frequently observed that they would just slap one color next to another in no definite sequence, worked absolutely absorbed, till they finished it, would hold it up, and happily would display it to say "this a treasure map," "a volcano," sometimes this was observed even when I would instruct them to symbolize the feeling of the day like "happy," "sad," etc. When depicting happiness or a "good mood" they would use bright colors like shades of blue, green, yellow, and red—a kaleidoscope of colors, while if a child is disturbed, he/she would inevitably use colors such as black, small tucked away in a corner, or in the center, sometimes with other bright colors, when asked to draw the "mood of the day." This was true of both children who were going to art classes and those who were not. This use of colors is not "taught" anywhere in traditional art school and indicates a process that goes beyond the taught, trained, that is unconscious, but with the potential to become conscious or at the very least guide conscious behavior.

Another patient suffering from a complicated grief reaction, during an art therapy session, drew an ambiguous, abstract figure to depict what her current emotional state was. On inquiry, she used statements such as

> Well... I have shaded this region because *I* wanted the region to be dark. You know shading makes a thing appear darker. It gives this sense of deariness, pain and so I mixed this black with blue, to give it a tinge.
>
> (Interview with the author)

When asked where she learnt that she could use shades in this manner, mixing blue and black to color such compositions, or whether she had learnt it specifically to do abstract paintings, she replied that she learnt Indian painting in art school and was taught that shading gives gradient to picture, how to mix colors to make a new one, but she never was trained in abstract painting and saw them only in exhibitions. For this drawing, specifically, when instruction was given, she stated that she just knew she did not want to make any form with a definite outline and felt that abstract art might be a better option and that the combination of these two colors would do justice to what she wanted to express through the painting.

In all, the clinical findings suggest that some form of complex decision-making process underlies the creation of artwork. It entails a journey from implicit to explicit, unconscious to conscious, and is similar across creators of different mental conditions, age, and sex. Similar to the autobiographical testimonies given above, it also underscores the fluid and spontaneous nature of the creative process, wherein they often feel an impetus to include or modify components in their artwork, sometimes even after completion.

Discussion

Thus far, I have reviewed the theoretical perspectives and relevant research findings therein, autobiographical testimonies of artists both contemporary and historically prominent, and findings from clinical research and therapy to see whether actually intuition, as defined earlier, does underlie the process of creation and, if at all, how and to what extent. Earlier research on creative intuition was mostly conducted in laboratories or based on autobiographical accounts or through retrospective analysis of works by famous painters who were not present when the analysis was conducted. This, I felt, necessitated discourse from the present angle where all the major sources come together to bridge the subjective with the objective and to find the overlaps, the interconnections, and conjunctions among them.

As is apparent, from the preceding discussion, irrespective of the language used, and the perspective taken, the process of art-making is strikingly similar to the processes involved in intuition and, therefore, it would not be perhaps fallacious to state that intuition does have a significant role to play in the creation of artwork; however, simple or complicated, commissioned or free creation. Previous researchers have referred to this as "creative intuition" (Policastro, 1995; Shirley & Langan-Fox, 1996). As conceptualized by Goldberg (1983) this function of intuition involves generations of options and opportunities some of which might be superior to others rather than being right or wrong. In keeping with the accounts of the creative process given by both patients and non-patients, both trained and untrained, it was revealed that even when they do create layouts prior to actual creation, these though based on technicalities are more than just grammar. They then modify it, not *correct* it in the sense of correcting grammatical errors, erase it out, until it "feels right," or they "just feel that it is what I want to create." Almost all agree that these feelings cannot be put in words nor are they an outcome of a conscious reasoning process but rather "spontaneous," and prompt absolutely similar to the "feeling" aspect of intuition which has also been corroborated by Vaughan (1979). In fact, Vaughan claims that intuition may manifest itself and gain access to consciousness in the form of emotions or feelings. John Furlong also, among others, in the opening chapters of his book, referred to it to be a nebulous emotional gut feeling that is often accepted without question as valid. Research across various fields repeatedly shows that this "gut feeling" is closely connected to action (Fischbein, 1975) as it results in a sense of immediacy. This "gut feeling" when precedes the action, enabling the creator to see the artwork from different perspectives at the time of inception proper, influences the whole process of art-working at a subliminal level, akin to the "operative intuition" as stated by Goldberg (1969). This is the condition in which individuals often find themselves doing things that they cannot explain "for no apparent reason." The accounts and findings reveal that the artist is fused with his work during the process of creation, as if in dialogue, immersed, engaged, which is also in sync with the spiritual aspect of intuition as conceptualized by Vaughan which provides him with a holistic view of reality that transcends cognitive processes and offers the person a true transpersonal encounter (Shirley & Langan-Fox, 1996).

The argument that this process is both universally applicable and valid for trained, untrained, and special populations is not unfounded, especially when considering the existence of diverse forms of intuition and various intuitive typologies that have been identified through standard psychometric evaluations like the Myers–Briggs Type Indicator test (MBTI) and the Types of Intuition Scale. The types of intuition scale identify three different types of intuition which may be used in conjunction, or one preferentially over the other: holistic, inferential, and affective. Holistic intuitions are conclusions reached by the integration of several, disparate inputs into a totality that may or may not be explicitly stated—a finding seconded by Baylor who referred to it as "sensing relationships." On the other hand, decisions made through automated inferences are known as inferential intuitions. These decision-making techniques were initially analytical but have since evolved into intuitive ones with experience. These two forms of intuition are what, it appears from the preceding discourse, I believe, is at play in the case of artists with previous experience in the creation of art.

As Baylor (2001), points out, in contradiction to the existing popular notion that experience is counterintuitive rather than being pro-intuitive. With experience, what was once an immature intuition, prior to training becomes mature intuition. Mature intuition is characterized by an immediate and intuitive understanding of complex situations that may be too intricate for analytical processing. and is the outcome of the initial impact of training with immature intuition. Thus, with training "intuitive" basis of art is not lost rather the nature of the base changes with and accommodates the changing skills.

Affective intuitions, conversely, are conclusions primarily based on emotional responses to decision-making circumstances and may be considered akin to immature intuition as theorized by Baylor. This form is more prominent in children and, I feel, also in individuals with mental illnesses, especially in the case of psychotic disorder where regression is culminating in impulsivity and emotional reasoning.

Conclusion

Contradictory findings, poor methodological research approaches, and a skewed skeptic approach to the subject have made the scientific inquiry of the links between art-making and intuition almost impossible and challenging. But as this chapter points out, albeit, at a very primary theoretical level, such inquiry is pregnant with immense possibility not only for the sake of future research scope but also in terms of its application to therapy and art education. By recognizing the role of intuition, educators and artists can develop strategies that harness intuitive processes in the creative journey, thus enabling more profound and authentic artistic expression that transcends linguistic and cultural boundaries. Thus, this attempted exploration hopes to not only enrich our comprehension of the creative process but also open doors to enhanced pedagogical approaches and more profound artistic experiences.

References

Alland, A. (1977). *The artistic animal: An inquiry into the biological roots of art.* Anchor Books.

Ambrosini, V., & Bowman, C. (2001). Tacit knowledge: Some suggestions for operationalization. *Journal of Management Studies, 38*(6), 811–829. https://doi.org/10.1111/1467-6486.00260

Arnheim, R. (2004). *Art and visual perception: A psychology of the creative eye* (2nd ed.). University of California Press.

Baylor, A. L. (2001). A U-shaped model for the development of intuition by level of expertise. *New Ideas in Psychology, 19*(3), 237–244. https://doi.org/10.1016/s0732-118x(01)00005-8

Bolte, A., & Goschke, T. (2008). Intuition in the context of object perception: Intuitive gestalt judgments rest on the unconscious activation of semantic representations. *Cognition, 108*(3), 608–616. https://doi.org/10.1016/j.cognition.2008.05.001

Bruner, J. S. (1960). *The process of education.* Harvard University Press.

Burns, R. C. (1987). *Kinetic-house-tree-person drawings (K-H-T-P): An interpretative manual.* Brunner/Mazel.

Cardinal, R. (1972). *Outsider art.* Littlehampton Book Services Ltd.

Cavanagh, P. (2005). The artist as neuroscientist. *Nature, 434*(7031), 301–307.

Drago, V., Finney, G. R., Foster, P. S., Amengual, A., Jeong, Y., Mizuno, T., Crucian, G. P., & Heilman, K. M. (2008). Spatial-attention and emotional evocation: Line bisection performance and visual art emotional evocation. *Brain and Cognition, 66*(2), 140–144. https://doi.org/10.1016/j.bandc.2007.06.005

Fischbein, E. (1975). *The intuitive basis of scientific reasoning.* Academic Press.

Fornazzari, L. R. (2005). Preserved painting creativity in an artist with Alzheimer's disease. *European Journal of Neurology, 12*(6), 419–424. https://doi.org/10.1111/j.1468-1331.2005.01128.x

Freud, S. (1900). *The interpretation of dreams*. Basic Books.
Fried, E. I., Van Borkulo, C. D., Cramer, A. O., Boschloo, L., Schoevers, R. A., & Borsboom, D. (2016). Mental disorders as networks of problems: A review of recent insights. *Social Psychiatry and Psychiatric Epidemiology*, *52*(1), 1–10. https://doi.org/10.1007/s00127-016-1319-z
Goldberg, L. R. (1969). The search for configural relationships in personality assessment: The diagnosis of psychosis vs. neurosis from the MMPI. *Multivariate Behavioral Research*, *4*(4), 523–536. https://doi.org/10.1207/s15327906mbr0404_7
Goldberg, P. (1983). *The intuitive edge*. Putnam.
Golomb, C. (2003). *The child's creation of a pictorial world*. Psychology Press.
Goodenough, F. L. (1940). *Measurement of intelligence by drawings*. World Book Company.
Guilford, J. P. (1966). Measurement and creativity. *Theory Into Practice*, *5*(4), 185–189. https://doi.org/10.1080/00405846609542023
Infed. (n.d.). *Michael Polanyi and tacit knowledge*. Retrieved August 5, 2024 from https://infed.org/mobi/michael-polanyi-and-tacit-knowledge/
Itani, O. (2020, March 3). 10 Picasso quotes that will inspire the creative artist in you. *Medium*. Retrieved August 5, 2024 from https://medium.com/swlh/10-picasso-quotes-that-will-inspire-the-creative-artist-in-you-1d4d0c0faa27
Junge, M. B. (2010). *The modern history of art therapy in the United States*. Charles C. Thomas Publisher.
Kaplan, B. (1964). *The inner world of mental illness: A series of first-person accounts of what it was like*. Harper & Row.
Malchiodi, C. A. (2005). Art therapy. In C. A. Malchiodi (Ed.), *Expressive therapies* (pp. 16–45). Guilford Press.
Maslow, A. H. (1954). *Motivation and personality*. Harper & Row.
Oster, G. D. (2016). *Using drawings in clinical practice: Enhancing intake interviews and psychological testing*. Routledge.
Perkins, D. N. (1981). *The mind's best work*. Harvard University Press.
Pilard, N. (2018). *Jung and intuition: On the centrality and variety of forms of intuition in Jung and post-Jungians*. Routledge.
Polanyi, M. (1967). *The tacit dimension*. Anchor Books.
Policastro, E. (1995). Creative intuition: An integrative review. *Creativity Research Journal*, *8*(2), 99–113. https://doi.org/10.1207/s15326934crj0802_1
Shirley, D. A., & Langan-Fox, J. (1996). Intuition: A review of the literature. *Psychological Reports*, *79*(2), 563–584. https://doi.org/10.2466/pr0.1996.79.2.563
Silver, R. A. (2003). The silver drawing test of cognition and emotion. In *Handbook of art therapy* (pp. 410–419). Brunner-Routledge.
Van Roojen, P. (2019). *Vincent van Gogh*. Pepin Press.
Vaughan, F. E. (1979). *Awakening intuition*. Anchor Press.
Verstegen, I. (2006). *Arnheim, gestalt and art: A psychological theory*. Springer Science & Business Media.
Westcott, M. R., & Ranzoni, J. H. (1963). Correlates of intuitive thinking. *Psychological Reports*, *12*(2), 595–613. https://doi.org/10.2466/pr0.1963.12.2.595
Zeki, S. (2010). *A vision of the brain*. Wiley-Blackwell.

Part III

Intuitive Cognition

From Knowledge to Practice

Chapter 12

Metacognitive strategies in fundamental skill acquisition

Shazia Hasnain and Santoshi Halder

Introduction

Language learning is an arduous task (Barin, 2011, Larsen-Freeman & Cameron, 2008) that calls for a variety of cognitive and linguistic skills and abilities (Larsen-Freeman & Cameron, 2008). Different theories and ideas regarding how children learn their first and second languages have been put forth by linguists. Nativist theory propounded by Chomsky (1964) stressed that a child is born with a Language Acquisition device (LAD) that aids in acquiring language. The Nativist theory states that children generally have a biological predisposition to learn languages, which facilitates language acquisition and mastery with minimal effort (Lightbown & Spada 2013). In contrast to the nativist view, there were other theories, such as the interactionist hypothesis, which maintained that social interaction with other people has a major role in a child's linguistic development (Brown, 2000). Vygotsky's sociocultural theory placed a strong emphasis on the intermediary role of the human mind. According to Vygotsky, we modify the nature of our interactions by mediating and regulating them with others and with ourselves through the use of "symbolic tools or signs" (Lantolf, 2007). Children gain more control over mediational tools like language as they get older, both for inter- and intrapersonal goals (Mehrpour & Forutan, 2015). Another viewpoint that has gained traction in recent years is the idea that learning to speak a language involves the same principles as learning to ride a bicycle or play an instrument and therefore "language acquisition is a skill acquisition" (Chater & Christiansen, 2018). This implies that consistent practice and social exchange aid in learners' language development.

Needless to say, learning a second language necessitates the use of particular strategies, whereas learning one's native tongue comes naturally through imitation and observation as well as some innate tendencies. While language acquisition is influenced by cognitive structures, recent research in cognitive neuroscience has distinguished between two levels of cognition: the first is characterized by more conscious mental processes involving explicit knowledge and deliberate focus, and the second is characterized by unconscious

DOI: 10.4324/9781003377757-15

processes that are more "embodied, pattern-based, and intuitive" (Shaules, 2018). Since both conscious and unconscious processes are involved in learning a foreign or second language, both implicit and explicit instruction are required for mastery. "Deep learning"—the process by which complex language knowledge is integrated with cognition—requires a number of unconscious learning mechanisms, including pattern recognition, trial-and-error experimentation, and habit development (Shaules, 2018).

Unconscious cognition: Intuition

Just as intuition works well in first language learning, a similar development of intuition for second and foreign languages will be helpful for learners. In research conducted by Stancuna and Craciun (2011) on foreign language acquisition in kindergarten children, various activities were used, and it was concluded that an intuitive form of language teaching (verbal and non-verbal tasks) was effective for the young kids. Repetition and interesting tasks were key to the progress in children's language.

Since intuition is considered to be an unconscious cognitive process, learning languages can be aided by techniques like association and pattern recognition. According to Pi et al.(2008), the fundamental ability or intellect of humans is pattern recognition, which underpins many of our daily tasks. One of the most important portals to gaining an understanding of human psychological activity is the recognition of patterns. It has strong links to mental functions like perception, memory, learning, and reasoning. Pattern recognition in humans is comparable to a conventional perceptual process that depends on previous information and experience. Pattern recognition, therefore, involves repetition and making connections that facilitate language learning. There are different theories for pattern recognition, the main ones being: *template matching* which assumes every perceived object is stored as a "template" into long-term memory (Shugen, 2002); unlike one-to-one matching, *prototype matching* compares incoming sensory data to an average prototype (Shugen, 2002). Other theories are *top-down and bottom-up processing*, *feature analysis*, and *recognition-by-components theory*. In the process of learning a language, pattern recognition will enhance intuitive knowledge.

Teachers' role in language learning is therefore important as different strategies for language learning must be developed to activate the cognitive and linguistic aspects which will also help them develop the intuition that they have in their first language. According to Shaules (2018), language teachers must have an extensive knowledge of the "unconscious cognition" or the intuitive mind as that will help them to follow a pedagogy where learners can have "deep learning" whereby complex patterns of knowledge are integrated with the intuitive mind.

Intuition, according to Hammond (1996, p. 60), is a cognitive process that generates a response, idea, or solution in some way without employing a deliberate, logically sound, methodical process. To attain this intuitive level of language acquisition, several cognitive and metacognitive strategies may come to the rescue in place of conventional methods of teaching-learning. The learners will develop "metalinguistic awareness," which will enable them to compare their native and target language and also correct themselves (Gass, 1983), and it will eventually facilitate their command over the English language. Native speakers undoubtedly rely on their intuition to distinguish between correct and incorrect language construction and even research coerces this claim. But there is no denying the vital role of intuition when learning a second language (Iqbal et al., 2021).

For intuitive learning, students need to be given autonomy and individual pace to learn a language rather than following a generalized method of learning. According to Oxford (2003), there should be more learning autonomy in language classes, with students being able to use a range of various learning strategies to maximize their learning. Oxford maintains that one of the key elements determining how successfully our students pick up a second or foreign language is their preferred method of language acquisition.

Strategies for language learning

Every learner has a different learning style (Shah et al., 2013), and all approaches and methods may not benefit them (Kumaravadivelu, 1994). Therefore, in order to effectively acquire a second or a foreign language the learners need some strategies at their disposal. It is vital to understand how to learn, which entails mastering efficient learning strategies and language teachers must be aware of the strategies to be able to prepare and upskill the learners. Learning strategies, according to Brown (1980), are those processes that can directly contribute to learning. Learning techniques increase learning's effectiveness, self-direction, and transferability to other contexts, according to Oxford (1990, as referenced in Ghufron, 2017). Ghani (2003) claims that it serves as a facilitator to promote learning.

According to Scarcella and Oxford (1992), learning strategies are behaviors, actions, or procedures that students employ to improve their own learning. Examples of these include encouraging oneself to take on a challenging language task or looking for conversation partners. Students can build their strategies or learn strategies from their teachers, which will enhance their learning process. Some students learn better with strategies than others due to the different strategies they apply (Rubin, 1975; Stern, 1975). Chamot et al. (1996) state that while some second language learners employ strategies randomly which results in ineffective learning, other learners use them systematically in their second language learning, which produces effective learning. Learners should be able to "recognize their cognitive style," according to the "Common European Framework of Reference for Languages," which acts as a primary source for national pedagogical documents for language teachers (CEFR, 2001, p. 149 as cited in Straková, 2013). Thus, it was deemed that the learner-centered approach implies not only making the learners active and involved in activities but also making them understand some strategies that may assist or boost their language skills.

Both social constructivism and cognitivism serve as the foundation for learning strategies. McCombs BL (2017) states that research on "study skills and memory strategies," such as those done by Atkinson and Shiffrin (1968), Belmont and Butterfield (1969), Hagen and Kingsley (1968), and Hare (1963), is where the term "learning strategies" originated. Ausubel's cognitive theories (1960, 1963, 1968) also contributed to the development of learning strategies by emphasizing the role of "advanced organizers" in supporting learning. In addition to reflecting social constructivism, the suggested learning strategies placed a strong emphasis on collaborative problem-based learning to support students' growth in critical thinking, cooperation, and teamwork as they worked through real-world problems in interactive and cooperative learning environments that foster peer engagement and support. As part of the social constructivist learning theory, Driscoll (2002) emphasized that learning is boosted when students are engaged in learning and that analytical thinking is fostered through applied and reflective activities. Thus, the theories of constructivism and cognitivism aim at making the learners independent critical thinkers and problem solvers.

Categories of learning strategies

According to Brown (2007), language learning strategies can be categorized based on the awareness of the strategies used by the learners. The three categories of strategies that Brown (2007) and O'Malley and Chamot (1990) first proposed are cognitive, metacognitive, and socio-affective strategies. A socio-affective technique is one that focuses on social-meditating with others, according to O'Malley and Chamot (1990). Cooperation and asking clarifying questions are examples of socio-affective strategies.

Cognitive strategies require the material of the tasks to be manipulated for better understanding. The learner can directly manipulate the language material through cognitive strategies such as reasoning, analysis, taking notes, summarizing, synthesizing, outlining, and reorganizing information to develop stronger schemas (knowledge structures) and formal practice of structures and sounds in naturalistic settings. The ability of humans to construct language with cognitive functions including perception, memory, and attention allocation has been highlighted by cognitive psychologists (Schmid, 2017). The process of learning and producing language involves the method of storing knowledge in long-term memory and retrieving it (Schmid, 2007). Cognitive strategies are those in which the learner manipulates the content consciously (e.g., by creating mental representations) or physically (e.g., by grouping and taking notes) (O'Malley and Chamot, 1990, cited in Saks and

Leijen, 2018). In her taxonomy, Oxford (1990) differentiated compensatory and memory strategies from cognitive strategies. According to her taxonomy, memory techniques serve a very specific purpose in helping students retain and recall new information. Learners can use a variety of cognitive methods to understand and produce new language, while compensatory strategies help them overcome limitations in their language abilities. Certain taxonomies (e.g., O'Malley & Chamot, 1990) combine these strategies into a single category as cognitive strategies.

Planning, observing, and assessing one's learning process are all aspects of metacognitive methods (Brown et al., 1983). Metacognition emerged in the 1970s as a part of the "cognitive theory revolution" (Livingston, 1997). It has been reported that when learners apply metacognitive strategies effectively, they can learn more quickly and efficiently than any other strategy because they allow students to regulate and assess their own learning process since they are aware of how they are learning (Anderson, 2003). Language learning effectiveness emerges from how well the learners know the characteristics of the tasks that they are to work on and the strategies that will best help in accomplishing or solving the task (Mahmoudi et al., 2010) and also the excellence and pace of the learners when they are engaged in the cognitive process (Rahimi & Katal, 2011). Fewell (2010) emphasized that learners who employ metacognitive strategies are more likely to engage in self-directed learning.

Importantly it has been specified by O'Malley and Chamot (1990) that there are no specific strategies for second-language learners and the same strategies can be used for both first and second-language learners. Further, Oxford (1993) added that foreign language learners can use the same strategies while learning a language.

Oxford (1990, 1996) proposed a different taxonomy of learning strategies, arguing that there is a system of techniques that complement one another in direct and indirect learning strategy categories. Memory, cognitive, and compensatory strategies are examples of direct strategies in this system; social, affective, and metacognitive strategies are examples of indirect strategies. Oxford (1990, p. 37) states that "mental processing" of the language is necessary for all direct strategies. Oxford (1990) also noted that indirect tactics promote language learning by employing various techniques such as organizing, focusing, evaluating, exploring possibilities, and reducing nervousness.

Purpose of the present study

All four language acquisition skills—reading, writing, speaking, and listening—are essential. The present study limited itself only to reading and speaking skills as it was reported in studies that there are profound difficulties faced by second and foreign language learners when it comes to reading (e.g., Wuit,

2012; Wallace, 2014) and speaking (Hinkel, 2005, cited in Nazara, 2011; Zhang, 2009). A lot depends on the approaches and strategies used by teachers in the classroom as well as the competence of the language teachers in informing and applying the strategies in the classrooms. The current study aims to determine the techniques used in earlier studies to enhance the reading and speaking skills of English language learners who are second or foreign language learners. The study also intends to determine whether the participants in the previous studies were aware of the cognitive and metacognitive techniques they could use while learning to read and speak in the second language.

Research questions

1 What strategies do second language learners most frequently employ to acquire the skills necessary to read and speak a second language?
2 How was the effectiveness of strategies assessed in the studies?
3 Are there differences in the strategies based on the proficiency level of students?

Methodology

Criteria for selecting the studies

The research papers were reviewed spanning 2012–2023 and based on certain criteria the studies were selected for the present review. The criteria set for the review were that the papers had to be about learning of English language as a second and foreign language. Second, only those studies were selected that were related to the strategies of language learning and had the details about cognitive or metacognitive strategy. Studies that were both quantitative and qualitative were chosen. Furthermore, not all the research could be included because only those articles that were available and accessible through open-access portals were included. Theoretical publications about general language learning strategies and other language skills were also omitted, as were meta-analytical research.

Strategy for searching and selecting studies

A search was conducted from 2012 to 2023 for empirical and review-based publications and theses in the journal databases of Sage, Elsevier, Eric, Springer, Shodhganga, ProQuest, etc. Phrases used while searching the databases were: strategies for language learning; cognitive strategies for English language learning; metacognitive strategies for English language learning; cognitive strategies for speaking skills, cognitive strategies for reading skills; metacognitive strategies for speaking skills; and metacognitive strategies for reading skills.

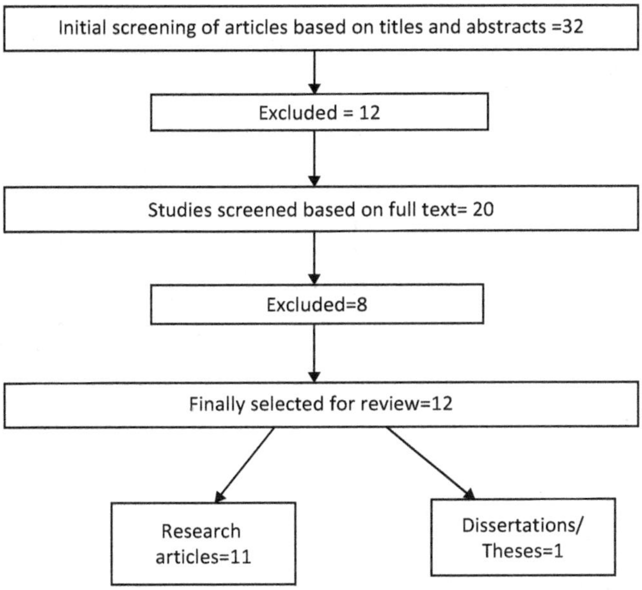

Figure 12.1 Flow chart of the study selection process.

In the initial stage, duplicate articles and non-English articles were removed. The study titles were reviewed, and irrelevant articles were removed. After this, the abstract was studied to decide if it matched the selection criteria. The articles selected for the "full article" stage were all focused on the strategies used for speaking and reading skills (Figure 12.1)

Two experts coded and selected the studies initially and subsequently, the full articles were also selected by them. Minor disagreements related to the theoretical and metanalytic studies were resolved with discussion. As shown in Table 12A.1 (appendix), the included empirical studies were then categorized and analyzed under the following headings: (a) name of author and year of publication, (b) publication source, (c) the area where the study was conducted, (d) the nature and size of the sample, (e) interventions/tools used, and (f) findings.

Findings and discussion

Twelve studies were selected for the present review whereby six were based on speaking skills and six on reading skills. The findings and discussion that emerged after the review have been presented in this section.

Strategies mostly used by learners for reading

The learners in the study of Mehrdad et al. (2012) employed about twenty different cognitive and metacognitive techniques like *planning, monitoring,*

Table 12A.1 Cognitive and metacognitive strategies used for reading and speaking skills

S no.	*Author and year*	*Journal*	*Place*	*Objectives*	*Sample*	*Intervention/tools*	*Findings*
1.	Uysal and Tezel (2020)	*RumeliDE Dil ve Edebiyat Araştırmaları Dergisi*	Turkey	To identify the effects of language learning strategies instruction based on learning styles on reading comprehension of EFL learners.	52 preparatory school students.	Two cognitive learning strategies, namely, note-taking and summarizing, were taught for 5 weeks.	Effective results were seen in the reading skills of students taught with cognitive skills.
2.	Mehrdad et al. (2012)	Procedia Social and Behavioral Sciences	Iran	To investigate whether students at different proficiency levels equally benefit from teaching cognitive and metacognitive strategies.	180 BA students from Azad University.	90-minute sessions of reading instruction. Both cognitive and metacognitive, were taught to the students in the experimental groups. Strategies such as monitoring, evaluating, skimming, scanning, planning, etc.	Cognitive and metacognitive strategies affect different readers differently depending on their level of language proficiency. Elementary students were not able to benefit.

3.	Maasum and Maarof. (2012)	Procedia – Social and Behavioral Sciences	Malaysia	To explore metacognitive reading strategies employed by a group of ESL undergraduates when reading academic texts at a public university.	41 undergraduate students studying at a university in Malaysia. 26.8% were male and 73.2% were female.	Metacognitive Awareness of Reading Strategies Inventory (MARSI) which was designed by Mokhtari and Reichard (2000).	Students were conscious of their cognitive process during reading and were able to utilize a wide array of metacognitive reading strategies to achieve comprehension.
4.	Kasimi (2012)	ELT Research Journal	Turkey	To find out the relationship and differences between two groups of participants' reports on the use of cognitive and metacognitive reading strategies at English Language Teaching Departments in Iran.	461 participants: first-grade students of English at ELT Departments of seven different universities. The average age of participants was 21 and their ages varied from 17 to 34.	Metacognitive Reading Strategies Questionnaire (MRSQ) of Taraban et al. (2004) and Cognitive Strategies Questionnaire (CSQ) of Maghsudi and Talebi (2009).	Significant and mutual relationships between the use of cognitive and metacognitive reading strategies were found.

(Continued)

Table 12A.1 (Continued)

S no.	*Author and year*	*Journal*	*Place*	*Objectives*	*Sample*	*Intervention/tools*	*Findings*
5.	Ahmed (2020)	Arab World English Journal (AWEJ) Volume 11. Number3	Oman	To explore the awareness and use of cognitive and metacognitive reading strategies of Omani EFL (English as a Foreign Language) students studying different disciplines.	375 undergraduate students. 246 were females, and 129 were males.	Survey of Reading Strategies (SORS) as the instrument.	Omani EFL learners have greater awareness and used cognitive strategies more frequently than the other two categories of reading strategies.
6.	Asmara (2017)	Advances in Social Science, Education and Humanities Research (ASSEHR)	Indonesia	This study is to investigate which cognitive reading strategies frequently used by first-grade senior high school students in Rancaekek to enhance their reading comprehension.	30 students in first grade of senior high school.	The questionnaire was adapted from Ozek and Civelek (2006).	The result from the questionnaire shows that only four strategies belong to cognitive reading strategies that have been frequently used by more than half of the students.

7.	Sari and Omolu (2021)	Journal of Foreign Language and Educational Research	Indonesia	Analyzing the students' strategies in speaking English as a foreign language.	36 10th-grade students	A questionnaire with 15 statements containing strategies that have been proposed by several experts: Rubin (1987), O'Malley (1985), Oxford (1990), and Stern (1992): Interviews.	Strategies used by students were: cognitive strategies, metacognitive strategies, communication strategies, social strategies, and socio-affective strategies.
8.	Basalama et al. (2020)	Jambura Journal of English Teaching and Literature	Indonesia	To elaborate on the kinds of students' learning strategies in the English-speaking class and to identify the factors that caused students to choose that learning strategy.	107 students in the fourth semester from the English department.	Questionnaire: 19 items plus an interview. Adapted from Oxford and Nyikos (1989).	Students used metacognitive, cognitive, and socio-affective strategies while learning speaking. The most used strategy by students was note-taking and the least strategy was a translation.

(*Continued*)

Table 12A.1 (Continued)

S no.	*Author and year*	*Journal*	*Place*	*Objectives*	*Sample*	*Intervention/tools*	*Findings*
9.	Wang et al. (2023)	Asian Englishes (Routledge)	China	To analyze learning strategies used by Hong Kong university students for learning English.	A total of 101 students (31 male and 70 female) studying at The Education University of Hong Kong.	Strategy Inventory for Language Learning (SILL) taken from Oxford (1990) Questionnaire with 50 items.	The use of cognitive strategies was significantly associated with grade level, with fourth-year students using cognitive strategies more often than fifth-year students.
10.	Alang (2017)	Thesis Alauddin State Islamic University of Makassar	Indonesia	To find out the kinds of cognitive strategies used in English-speaking classes.	90 students in the second semester majoring in the English Education Department. 4 were interviewed.	Observation and interview.	There are several kinds of cognitive strategies that students used in learning speaking: practicing, receiving and sending messages, analyzing and reasoning, and creating a structure for input and output.

11.	Ghufron (2017)	Indonesian Journal of English Teaching	Indonesia	To find language learning strategies used by EFL fluent speakers in EFL-speaking classes and to reveal the fluent speakers' awareness of the benefits of the language learning strategies.	6 students in the EFL-Speaking Class of the English Education Department.	Questionnaire on strategy and interview.	The students were aware of certain cognitive, metacognitive, and social affective strategies and they used it in speaking skills effectively.
12.	Gani et al. (2015)	Studies In English Language and Education	Indonesia	To study the learning strategies used by both low and high-performance speaking students in developing their speaking skills as well as the differences between the learning strategies used by both groups of learners.	16 second-year high school students (with low and high speaking performance).	Questionnaires and interviews were the main instruments used: The Strategy Inventory for Language Learning (SILL) version 7.0 containing 50 items (Oxford, 1990).	High speaking performance used more learning strategies than those with low speaking performance. Low performers used support and compensation strategies while high performers used cognitive, metacognitive, memory, and social and affective strategies in a balanced manner.

evaluating, skimming, scanning, and so on. The most used cognitive strategies by the advanced-level university students in Kasimi's (2012) study were *guessing meaning by using clues, re-reading details to answer questions*, and *guessing unknown words*. The least used cognitive strategies were checking comprehension, making inferences after reading, and using punctuation. Metacognitive strategies used most by advanced learners in the same study were *re-reading for better comprehension, determining the meaning of critical words, and underlining to remember*. The least used metacognitive strategies were checking understanding of current information, using margins for notes, and noting the readability of text. Maasum and Maarof (2012) found that among undergraduate ESL (English as a second language) learners, the most used global strategies were *previewing text before reading*, problem-solving strategies mostly employed were re-reading, paying close attention to what they are reading, and speculating on its meaning. There was moderate use of support strategies like the use of dictionaries.

According to Ahmed (2020), students studying English as a foreign language (EFL) preferred cognitive strategies including *reading slowly to ensure comprehension and, when a text gets tough, paying closer attention to what they are reading*. Support strategies such as highlighting words and assessing information in both mother tongue and English were employed. Using tables, figures, and pictures to improve understanding when new information is available was the most popular metacognitive technique. The learners in Asmara's (2017) study mostly employed the following cognitive strategies—*picturing the text in mind, inferring the text's meaning from its title, determining a word's meaning from its context, and looking up keywords in dictionaries*. In the experimental study by Uysal and Tezel (2020), two cognitive strategies were used for five weeks that is *note-taking and summarizing* and the outcomes were effective.

Strategies used by learners for enhancing speaking skills

Six studies were reviewed for speaking skills, and it was discovered that learners employed a variety of strategies to improve their speaking. In the study by Sari and Omolu (2021), students in the tenth standard used management and planning strategies, such as using a dictionary and body language that involved hand and body gestures to speak, to help them as foreign language learners direct their learning speaking strategy. According to the study, in addition to direct strategies (memory and compensation), indirect strategies (affective), and planning techniques, a significant amount of cognitive and metacognitive strategies were employed. Another study conducted on second-year high school students was by Gani et al. (2015). Students with both high and low speaking performance results were included in the study. The strategies used by both categories of speakers were similar and yet different in many ways. For instance, high performers while learning pronunciation used *repetition, imitation, listening to native speakers* and watching English movies, reading books. Low performers usually *consulted friends and some practiced and learned pronunciation from movies*. For vocabulary, both low and high performers used memorization. Another difference between them was that high performers employed new words in their social interactions, whereas low performers did not. Grammatical patterns are memorized by high performers while low performers approach friends for help and also learn from their mistakes. Thus, compensation and social strategies were used by low performers while the high performers used cognitive, metacognitive, memory, compensation, and social strategies in a balanced way.

Basalama et al. (2020) had fourth-semester students of English department as subjects and the survey showed that most of them used *notetaking* as a cognitive strategy while speaking. The translation was the least used and the reason given was that translation takes time and therefore it is best suited to be used in writing skills but not speaking (Bagheri & Fazel, 2011 cited in Basalama et al., 2020). Among the metacognitive strategies, *self-monitoring* was used largely by the students. In Alang's (2017) study the second-semester students of the English Education department used several cognitive strategies for speaking including rehearsing, receiving and delivering messages, evaluating and reasoning, and structuring input and output.

The university students of English in the study by Wang et al. (2023) largely used cognitive strategies yet there were differences in the way they used the strategies. Social and affective strategies were used less comparatively. While fourth-year students used the cognitive strategies effectively and largely, fifth-year students showed instability in the use of cognitive strategies owing to the fact that they had other engagements like applying for jobs, etc. It was also found that giving sufficient time for homework and practice of language increased the use of cognitive strategies compared to those who gave insufficient time for study. All in all, memorization-oriented teaching as followed in Hong Kong was unsuccessful in improving English language skills and therefore the employment of cognitive and other strategies seemed to be a welcome change for the students. The same holds true for Asian countries such as Indonesia, Arab countries, and India where rote memorization and examination-oriented methodology are followed in English language classrooms.

In a case study by Ghufron (2017), EFL learners used cognitive and metacognitive strategies for speaking skills. The participants disclosed that they were cognizant of the techniques and tactics they were employing. However, all the strategies were not known to them. Consequently, Ghufron (2017) suggested that teachers provide students with the strategies so they can apply them in the classroom. The successful strategies for the EFL learners in the study can be applied to EFL students in different nations.

Learning strategies and their relationship with the proficiency level

Reading strategies according to proficiency level. Out of the studies reviewed for strategies used in reading skills, all age groups of learners were found. Mehrdad et al. (2012) conducted a study on undergraduates of different proficiency levels. Subjects were undergraduates and it seemed that cognitive and other strategies did not work on the beginners and advanced learners but the intermediate students were able to make use of the strategies while reading and the study concluded that linguistic knowledge and other factors play a role in how effective the strategies are in the learning of a language. Contrarily the advanced first-grade ELT (English Language Teaching) students from the universities in Turkey and Iran in Kasimi's (2012) study had certain preferences in cognitive and metacognitive strategies whereby some strategies were used more than others effectively. In Ahmed's study (2020), first-year EFL diploma students from various fields employed a greater number of cognitive strategies, followed by support strategies, and a lower number of metacognitive strategies. The diploma students in this study were from different disciplines like business, engineering, biology, etc., which indicates they were not advanced learners of English. There was a lack of training in metacognitive strategies that made them use cognitive and support strategies. The study pointed out the need for informing students about metacognitive strategies as they can be more effective in improving reading skills. Maasum and Maarof (2012) conducted a study on second language learners who were undergraduates to know whether they used cognitive and metacognitive strategies. The study reported that ESL learners used metacognitive strategies while reading and were well aware of the strategies to be used. Asmara (2017) found that first-grade high school students who had problems in reading comprehension used only four cognitive strategies indicating they were unaware of strategies to use while reading. Uysal and Tezel (2020) had EFL learners who were at the preparatory stage and were intermediate learners. Two cognitive strategies were used in the experimental study: summarizing and note-taking and the experimental group performed well.

Speaking strategies for different proficiency levels. Most of the studies reviewed for speaking skills do not mention the proficiency level of the learners except for one study which is Gani et al. (2015). Gani et al. (2015) showed persuasively that students who speak less proficiently employ different strategies that are different from high-proficiency speakers. This information is significant as it indicates that all strategies may not be effective for all age groups and also all proficiency levels. Therefore, language teachers must take cognizance of this finding and accordingly segregate and implement the strategies in the classrooms. The "one-size fits all" approach, therefore, needs to be abandoned by the teachers.

Type of study designs and tools used

Studies on reading strategies. The studies analyzed in this review are mostly surveys with only two studies being based on intervention (i.e., Mehrdad et al., 2012; Uysal & Tezel, 2020). Studies with intervention indicate clearly whether a particular cognitive strategy is effective and whether it can be used on similar students in another situation. Survey studies provide an insight into what the learners think and apply in classrooms while reading and this has been done with questionnaires that differed in each study. Again, none of the studies employed the interview which could have been a useful tool for getting specific information about how the learners use the strategies related to reading. The use of interviews for gaining more information could have provided supporting details about how the learners use the strategies (Asmara, 2017).

Studies on speaking strategies. The studies related to speaking skills have used varied designs effectively. A case study was used by Ghufron (2017) whereby data were collected employing observation and a questionnaire. Similarly, Gani et al. (2015) used field notes, questionnaires, and interviews in the study that gave a comprehensive view of the results. A mixed study design was also found in the studies conducted by Sari and Omolu (2021) and Basalama et al. (2020). Wang et al. (2023) employed a questionnaire to as certain techniques used by language learners while Alang (2017) conducted a qualitative analysis in his thesis using observation and interviews of learners. The questionnaire used in a few studies (Gani et al., 2015; Wang et al., 2023) was SILL (The Strategy Inventory for Language Learning) developed by Oxford (1990) and comprised 50 items. Sari and Omolu (2021), used a tool with 15 statements taken from experts like Rubin (1987), O'Malley et al. (1985), Oxford (1990), and Stern (1992).

Conclusion and implications

The reviewed studies indicate that the students with an idea about the language learning strategies applied them to their advantage in the process of their learning. One noteworthy finding from the studies was that almost all the studies were conducted on mature and adult learners. It remains intriguing to find out whether cognitive strategies can be applied at the beginner level or at the secondary school stage. One of the studies (Mehrdad et al., 2012) showed that beginners were not utilizing cognitive strategies and the reason could be that they were not aware of them or were not trained to use them. This implies that learners must be given enough time to get acquainted with the strategies so they will use them naturally while reading and speaking. Another gap found in the review was that Indian studies were hardly found related to the topic. All of the studies in this review are from Asian countries (six studies from Indonesia) and since English is a second or foreign language for students in these nations, strategies for them will be equally beneficial as those for first-language learners. There are no distinct strategies for second and foreign language learners, as stated by O'Malley and Chamot (1990). Consequently, second- and foreign-language learners can benefit from the application of effective tactics.

The *implications* of this present review are that it will aid the language teachers in making themselves aware of the various cognitive and metacognitive strategies that can be used in the classrooms to make the language learners more independent in their learning and to add effectiveness to the language learning process. Teachers will also comprehend the relationship between cognitive and metacognitive skills, and how the use of cognitive techniques will affect the application of metacognitive strategies (Kasimi, 2012). Furthermore, the present study highlights the way strategies differ according to the proficiency level of the learners. This will help teacher educators inform and train the pre-service teachers in the usage of strategies while teaching speaking and reading skills to learners of varying proficiency levels.

Teachers will understand the need to undertake certain tests like Grammaticality Judgement tests to understand how much intuition the learners have developed in identifying and using the correct forms in the second language and it will be indicative of how well they know the language (e.g., Gass, 1983). Second Language teachers can fathom ways to help the students reach the "metalinguistic awareness" stage by providing them with enriching experiences in the language through strategies and games like "word games, puns, translation tasks" (Gass, 1983). Thus, implicit and explicit methods of teaching a language must be used by teachers to develop the intuitive aspect of language learners.

In conclusion, it is crucial to develop children's intuitive skills by enhancing their experiential learning with the use of various learning methodologies. These techniques are simple, more experiential, support the learner's autonomy, and ultimately, the intuitive nature of the method will flourish if the knowledge is robust and drawn from a range of experiences.

Limitations and future direction

The study was limited to only 12 studies (six studies on reading and six on speaking), and it was also limited to only speaking and reading skills. Further research and review on cognitive strategies and metacognitive strategies used in language learning need to be conducted. More importantly, studies with intervention can help understand the effectiveness of the strategies. Also, more studies need to be conducted on language teachers in different countries regarding their awareness and knowledge of cognitive and metacognitive strategies. Future studies must explore the effectiveness of cognitive and metacognitive strategies in developing linguistic intuition among language learners.

References

Ahmed, R. M. (2020). Investigating EFL learners' awareness of cognitive and metacognitive reading strategies of students in different disciplines. *Arab World English Journal*, *11*(3), 294–304.

Alang, A. N. (2017). *A study of cognitive strategies in learning speaking used by the second semester students of English education department at Alauddin State Islamic University* (Doctoral dissertation, Universitas Islam Negeri Alauddin Makassar).

Anderson, N. J. (2003). Meta-cognitive reading strategies increase L2 performance. *The Language Teacher*, *27*, 20–22

Asmara, N. I. (2017). An analysis of cognitive reading strategies used in reading comprehension. *Proceedings of the ninth international conference on applied linguistics (CONAPLIN 9)* (pp. 304–307). Atlantis Press. https://doi.org/10.2991/conaplin-16.2017.69

Atkinson, R. C., & Shiffrin, R. M. (1968). Chapter: Human memory: A proposed system and its control processes. In K. W. Spence, & J. T. Spence (Eds.), *The psychology of learning and motivation* (Vol. 2, pp. 89–195). New York: Academic Press.

Ausubel, D. (1963). *The psychology of meaningful verbal learning*. New York: Grune& Stratton

Ausubel, D. P. (1960). The use of advance organizers in the learning and retention of meaningful verbal material. *Journal of Educational Psychology*, *51*, 267–272. https://doi.org/10.1037/h0046669

Ausubel, D. P. (1968). *Educational psychology: A cognitive view*. New York: Holt, Rinehart & Winston.

Bagheri, M. S., & Fazel, I. (2011). EFL learners' beliefs about translation and its use as a strategy in writing. *Reading Matrix: An International Online Journal*. *3*(4), 292–301.

Barin, M. (2011). An evaluation of university level preparatory class students' feelings in terms of foreign language anxiety [yabancı dil KaygısıAçısındanÜniversiteHazırlıkSınıfıÖğrencilerininDüşüncelerininDeğerlendirmesi]. *Atatürk ÜniversitesiSosyalBilimlerDergisi*, *11*(47), 1–14.

Basalama, N., Bay, I. W., & Abubakar, A. (2020). Student's learning strategies in English speaking class. *Jambura Journal of English Teaching and Literature*, *1*(1), 27–39.

Belmont, J. M., & Butterfield, E. C. (1969). The relations of short-term memory to development and intelligence. In L. C. Lipsitt & H. W. Reese (Eds.), *Advances in child development and behavior* (Vol. 4, pp. 29–82). New York: Academic.

Brown, A. L., Bransford, J. D., Ferrara, R. A., & Campione, J. C. (1983). Learning, remembering and understanding. In J. H. Flavell, & E. M. Markman (Eds.), *Handbook of child psychology: Cognitive development* (Vol. 3, 4th ed.). New York: Wiley.

Brown, D. H. (2000). *Principles of language learning and teaching*. (4th ed.). New York: Longman

Brown, D. H. (2007). *Principles of language learning & teaching*. (5th ed.). Pearson: Longman.

Brown, H. D. (1980). *Principles and practices of language learning and teaching*. Englewood Cliffs, NJ: Prentice Hall

Chamot, A. U., Barnhardt, S., El-Dinary, P., & Robbins, J. (1996). Methods for teaching learning strategies in the foreign language classroom. In R. Oxford (Ed.), *Language learning strategies around the world: Cross-cultural perspectives* (pp. 175–188). Manoa: University of Hawaii Press.

Chater, N., & Christiansen, M. H. (2018). Language acquisition as skill learning. *Current Opinion in Behavioral Sciences*, *21*, 205–208.

Chomsky, N. (1964). The development of grammar in child language: Discussion. *Monographs of the Society for Research in Child development*, *29*(1), 35–42.

Council of Europe. (2001). *Common European framework of reference for languages: Learning, teaching, assessment*. Cambridge: Cambridge University Press.

Driscoll, M. (2002). *Web-based training: Creating E-learning experiences* (2nd ed.). San Francisco, CA: Jossey-Bass/Pfeiffer.

Fewell, N. (2010).Language learning strategies and English language proficiency: An investigation of Japanese EFL university students. *TESOL Journal*, *2*, 159–174.

Gani, S. A., Fajrina, D., &Hanifa, R. (2015). Students' learning strategies for developing speaking ability. *Studies in English Language and Education*, *2*(1), 16–28.

Gass, S. (1983). The development of L2 intuitions. *Tesol Quarterly*, *17*(2), 273–291.

Ghani, M. (2003). Language learning strategies employed by L2 learners. *Journal of Research (Faculty of Languages & Islamic Studies)*, *4*, 31–36.

Ghufron, M. A. (2017). Language learning strategies used by EFL fluent speakers: A case in Indonesian context. *IJET (Indonesian Journal of English Teaching)*, *6*(2), 184–202.

Hagen, J. W., & Kingsley, P. R. (1968). Labeling effects in short-term memory. *Child Development*, *39*, 113–121. https://doi.org/10.2307/1127363

Hammond, K. R. (1996). *Human judgment and social policy. Irreducible uncertainty, inevitable error, unavoidable injustice*. New York: Oxford University Press.

Hare, R. M. (1963). *Freedom and reason*. Oxford: Oxford United Press.

Hinkel, E. (Ed.). 2005. *Handbook of research in second language teaching and learning*. New Jersey: Lawrence Erlbaum Associates, Inc.

Iqbal, A., Rahman, G., & Hamid, A. (2021). The role of intuition in the acquisition of complex structures. *Pakistan Social Sciences Review*, *5*(1), 278–290.

Kasimi, Y. (2012). Cognitive and metacognitive strategies employed by Iranian and Turkish EFL readers. *ELT Research Journal*, *1*(3), 159–174.

Kumaravadivelu, B. (1994). The post method condition: Emerging strategies for second/foreign language teaching [J]. *TESOL Quarterly*, *28*, 27–47.

Lantolf, J. P. (2007). *Sociocultural theory and second language learning*. Oxford: Oxford University Press.

Larsen-Freeman, D., & Cameron, L. (2008). Complex systems and applied linguistics. *The Modern Language Journal (MLJ)*, *92*, 644–645. https://doi.org/10.1111/j.1540-4781.2008.00793_5.x

Lightbown, P. M., & Spada, N. (2013). *How languages are learned*. (4th ed.) Oxford: Oxford University Press.

Livingston, J. A. (1997). *Metacognition: An Overview*. Available at: https://gse.buffalo.edu/fas/shuell/CEP564/Metacog.htm

Maasum, T. N. R. T. M., & Maarof, N. (2012). Empowering ESL readers with metacognitive reading strategies. *Procedia-Social and Behavioral Sciences*, *69*, 1250–1258.

Maghsudi, M., & Talebi, S. H. (2009). The impact of lingualuity on the cognitive and metacognitive reading strategies awareness and reading comprehension ability. *Journal of Social Sciences, 18*(2), 119–126.

Mahmoudi, E., Khonamri, F., & Rafeie, M. (2010). The relationship between metacognitive awareness of reading strategies and comprehension monitoring in reading ability of EFL learners. Paper presented at *The 8th international TELLSI conference*, AlZahra University, Tehran, Iran.

McCombs, B. L. (2017). Historical review of learning strategies research: Strategies for the whole learner: A tribute to Claire Ellen Weinstein and early researchers of this topic. *Frontiers in education*, 2, 1–21.

Mehrdad, A. G., Ahghar, M. R., & Ahghar, M. (2012). The effect of teaching cognitive and metacognitive strategies on EFL students' reading comprehension across proficiency levels. *Procedia-Social and Behavioral Sciences, 46*, 3757–3763.

Mehrpour, S., & Forutan, A. (2015). Theories of first language acquisition. *Journal of Language, Linguistics and Literature, 1*(2), 30–40.

Mokhtari, K. & Reichard, C. (2000). *Development of the metacognitive-awareness-of-reading-strategies inventory* (MARSI). Unpublished manuscript, Oklahoma State University, Stillwater, Oklahoma, USA.

Nazara, S. (2011). Students' perception on EFL speaking skill development. *Journal of English Language Teaching, 1* (1), 28–43

O'Malley, J. M., & Chamot, A. U. (1990). *Learning strategies in second language acquisition*. Cambridge, U.K.: Cambridge University Press.

O'Malley, J. M., Chamot, A. U., Stewner-Manzanares, G., Russo, R. P., & Küpper, L. (1985). Learning strategy applications with students of English as a second language. *TESOL Quarterly, 19*(3), 557–584.

Oxford, R. L. (1990). *Language learning strategies: What every teacher should know*. New York: Newbury House.

Oxford, R. L. (1993). *Style analysis survey (SAS)*. Tuscaloosa: University of Alabama. [Reprinted in Reid, 1995.]

Oxford, R. L. (1996). *Language learning strategies around the world: Cross-cultural perspectives*. Manoa: University of Hawaii Press.

Oxford, R. L. (2003). *Language learning styles and strategies: An overview*. Oxford: GALA.

Oxford, R. L., & Nyikos, M. (1989). Variables affecting choice of language learning strategies by university students. *The Modern Language Journal, 73*(3), 291–300.

Ozek, Y., & Civelek, M. (2006). A study on the use of cognitive reading strategies by ELT students. *The Asian EFL Journal, 14*(1), 1–26.

Pi, Y., Liao, W., Liu, M., & Lu, J. (2008). Theory of cognitive pattern recognition. In P. Y. Yin (Ed.), *Pattern Recognition Techniques, Technology and Applications* (pp. 433–462). BoD-Books on Demand.

Rahimi, M., & Katal, M. (2011) Metacognitive strategies awareness and success in learning English as a foreign language: An overview. *Procedia – Social and Behavioural Sciences, 31*(2012), 73–81

Rubin, J. (1975). What the "Good Language Learner" can teach us. *TESOL Quarterly*, 9(1), pp. 41–51.

Rubin, J. (1987). Learner strategies: Theoretical assumption, research, history, and typology. In A. Wenden, & J. Rubin (Eds.), *Learner strategies in language learning* (pp. 15–30). Englewood Cliffs, NJ: Prentice-Hall.

Saks, K., & Leijen, Ä. (2018). Adapting the SILL to measure Estonian learners' language learning strategies: The development of an alternative model. *The Language Learning Journal*, *46*(5), 634–646.

Sari, C. N., & Omolu, F. A. (2021). The strategies in speaking English at grade X students. *Journal of Foreign Language and Educational Research*, *4*(2), 25–37.

Scarcella, R. C., & Oxford, R. L. (1992). *The tapestry of language learning: The individual in the communicative classroom*. Boston: Heinle & Heinle.

Schmid, H. J. (2007). Entrenchment, salience, and basic levels. Retrieved from https://www.anglistik.unimuenchen.de/personen/professoren/schmid/schmid_publ/2007_entrenchment.pdf

Schmid, H. J. (2017). *Entrenchment and the psychology of language learning: How we reorganize and adapt linguistic knowledge*. Washington, DC, US: American Psychological Association; Boston, MA, US: De Gruyter Mouton.

Shah, K., Ahmed, J., Shenoy, N., & Srikant, N. (2013) How different are students and their learning styles? *International Journal of Research in Medical Sciences*, *1*(3), 121–215.

Shaules, J. (2018). Deep learning: Unconscious cognition, the intuitive mind, and transformative language learning. *Juntendo Journal of Global Studies*, *3*, 1–16.

Shugen, W. (2002). Framework of pattern recognition model based on the cognitive psychology. *Geo-spatial Information Science*, *5*(2), 74–78. https://doi.org/10.1007/BF02833890

Stancuna, L. A., & Craciun, A. I. (2011). A multiple intelligences approach: Intuitive English learning – A case study for k-1 students. *Procedia-Social and Behavioral Sciences*, *11*, 72–76.

Stern, H. H. (1975). What can we learn from the good language learner?. *Canadian Modern Language Review*, *31*(4), 304–319.

Stern, H. H. (1992). *Issues and options in language teaching*. Oxford: OUP.

Straková, Z. (2013). Developing cognitive strategies in foreign language education. *Journal of Language and Cultural Education*, *1*(1), 37–50.

Taraban, R., Kerr, M., & Rynearson, K. (2004). Analytic and pragmatic factors in college students' metacognitive reading strategies. *Reading Psychology*, *25*(2), 67–81.

Uysal, N. M., & Tezel, K. V. (2020). The effects of language learning strategies instruction based on learning styles on reading comprehension. *RumeliDE Dil ve Edebiyat Araştırmaları Dergisi*, *21*, 697–714.

Wallace, C. (2014). *The Cambridge guide to teaching English to speakers of other languages*. Cambridge, UK: Cambridge University Press.

Wang, C., Zhu, S., & Ma, B. (2023). A study on English learning strategies of university students in Hong Kong. *Asian Englishes*, *25*(3), 376–390.

Wuit, A. J. (2012). Reading in a second language: A reading problem or a language problem. Retrieved from https://www.accessmylibrary.com/article-lGl-102749284/reading-second-languagereading.html

Zhang, S. (2009). The role of input, interaction, and output in the development of oral fluency. *English Language Teaching*, *2*(4), 91–100. https://doi.org/10.5539/elt.v2n4p91

Chapter 13

Metacognitive and intuitive strategies in children's learning

Nandita Babu and Radhika Khurana

Researches on "metacognition" emerged in the 1970s in studies by Flavell (1971, 1976, 1979). He defined metacognition as "active monitoring and consequent regulation and orchestration of these processes (information processing activities) in relation to the cognitive objects or data on which they bear, usually in service of some concrete goal or objective" (Flavell, 1976, p. 232). Thus, while cognition stands for mental processes, metacognition stands for cognition about cognition. Metacognition is usually understood in terms of two abilities, metacognitive knowledge and metacognitive regulation. Metacognitive knowledge is the awareness of thoughts, feelings, and desires of self. For example, Rama knows that she is feeling nervous before exams, or Raghav knows that he doesn't want to go to his friend's house. Metacognitive regulation (Nelson & Narens, 1990) refers to scrutinizing and controlling one's cognitive processes with feedback from metacognitive knowledge. These abilities are complementary and dependent on each other. For example, because Rama knows that she is nervous before the examination, she is practicing some relaxation strategies to ease her mind before the exams, or Raghav will make up a plausible excuse in order to avoid going to his friend's house.

Metacognition can be seen as related to intuition. Intuition is "the intellectual technique of arriving at plausible but tentative formulations without going through the analytical steps by which such formulations would be found to be valid or invalid conclusions" (Bruner, 1960, p. 13). Intuition and creativity are important parts of the history of natural science. Intuition has led to many scientific discoveries. Archimedes' famous "eureka!" moment is an example.

Different conceptualizations of the relationship between metacognition and intuition

The association between metacognition and intuition has been conceptualized in various ways by various theorists. The section discusses the dual process theory of reasoning (Wason & Evans, 1975), Two Mind Theory (Evans

DOI: 10.4324/9781003377757-16

& Stanovich, 2013), the perspective on the mutual incompatibility of intuition and metacognition (Baylor, 1997; Mandler, 1995; Schön, 1982) and Baylor's U-shaped model of the development of intuition (2001).

Dual process theory of reasoning

The association between intuition and metacognition has been proposed through the Dual Process Theory of Reasoning (Wason & Evans, 1975). It conceptualizes reasoning as comprised of two types of processing, type 1 (intuitive) and type 2 (reflective or analytical). Evans (2011) defines type 1 processing as "fast, high capacity, independent of working memory and cognitive ability." Like the name suggests, intuitive processing is an autonomous process and thus, engages the working memory of a person to the bare minimum. Further, it doesn't require central or controlled processing capacities. It requires tacit and innate learning along with repeated and acquired associations (Evans & Stanovich, 2013). An instance is a pilot making a fast-paced decision in the face of a complex, time-bound situation of successfully landing a plane in near-zero visibility due to extreme fog. Controlled processing is not required here as there is a short span of time to make the decision. Type 2 processing, is defined as "slow capacity, heavily dependent on working memory, and related to individual differences in cognitive ability" (Evans, 2011). This process is based on reflective thinking and is used in those circumstances where careful decision-making is required. An example of this is planning a raid to apprehend dangerous criminals. This requires a deliberate series of thoughts and reflections on the team's and the criminals' strengths, weaknesses, and resources.

Two mind theory

Another way of conceptualizing these two systems (metacognition and intuition) is in the form of the Two Mind Theory. As inferred from above, intuitive thinking seems evolutionarily old, unconscious, and related to animal cognition, while analytical thinking seems to be more recent, conscious, and related to human cognition. Thus, there are "two minds" with each mind being a family of systems in itself. Some key differences can be highlighted between the two. Both minds have different and distinct sources of information to generate behaviors. Thus, the intuitive mind relies on experiential learning to produce spontaneous and innate behaviors, like landing the plane in fog, while the reflective mind relies on working memory to produce carefully informed, analyzed, and reflected decisions, like criminal raids. The latter is based on higher-order mental processes, including meta-representations (Evans, 2010). Overall, reasoning has been said to be jointly determined by both minds (Evans & Stanovich, 2013).

Mutual incompatibility of intuition and metacognition

Some theorists believe that intuition and metacognition are mutually incompatible. Baylor (1997) argues that metacognition, which restricts free thought, may hinder intuitive thinking. Intuition, according to Schön (1982), is a direct but passive perception of reality, made possible by the mind's ability to perceive reality without effort. Thus, awareness hinders the usage of unconscious material and the creation of a new relatively simple series of ideas (Mandler, 1995). Further, metacognition is needed to become an expert in a subject. After learning a few concepts, a student can self-monitor and analyze her performance to metacognitively assess her progress: "How well am I performing in my studies?" "How can I get good marks?" However, a lot of times, they will learn a concept or answer a question intuitively, which is fundamentally a different mental process than metacognition.

U-shaped model of development of intuition

Baylor (2001) proposed that intuition develops along a U-shaped trajectory, with the amount of intuition initially starting at a relatively higher level and thereafter decreasing and increasing with the level of skill. This argument is based on the assertions made by a few studies. Within a certain field, the term "available intuition" refers to the possibility for intuitive thought to exist at a specific stage in the growth of a person's degree of competence. In particular, it is contended that initially young children have intuitive knowledge (such as in kindergarten). However, the analytical method taught in schools clashes with these processes. This is seen by the second graders' slower response times as compared to kindergarten children in an intuitive task (Choi, 1993). In a similar vein, Schön (1982) contends that young infants initially possess intuitive understandings that allow them to provide accurate responses. Later, school disrupts intuitive thinking by teaching children, models, and processes that are at odds with their intuitions. As a result, the children make errors as these models and procedures take precedence over their intuitions. Later, children obtain more sophisticated knowledge via education making them to respond accurately once again. Overall, the model contends that when intuition levels rise, a person's ability to simply answer properly again is accompanied by an increased capacity for higher-order intuitive connections and understandings. Therefore, the model proposes that the "U" curve reflects two forms of intuition that are different from one another. These two types of intuition are immature intuition and mature intuition. The distinction between them refers to the person's underlying skill (and associated knowledge structure) in a particular subject area.

While Baylor's model (2001) provides a reasonable difference between the intuition used by children and that used by, say, scientists, it assumes that when the level of expertise is mediocre, the intuition is at its lowest level. According to the model, the reader must assume that during the period of mediocre expertise, the child is in school and is technically in the knowledge acquisition stage. The model appears to assume that the stages of knowledge acquisition and using that knowledge for intuitive thinking are mutually exclusive and do not overlap. However, knowledge and intuition are ever-changing processes. Further, the role of metacognition in intuition is not discussed in the model. Finally, assuming this model, all pedagogical techniques to encourage intuitive thinking in classroom settings will be futile because school years are assumed to only aid in knowledge acquisition.

The perspectives described above propose a segmented view of the relationship between intuition and metacognition. While other models do talk about the relationship between intuition and metacognition, most of them conceptualize the two as seemingly independent cognitive faculties. Further, only Baylor's (2001) U-shaped model focuses on the knowledge component required for intuitive thinking (Baylor, 2001). In that model too, the aspect of metacognition is completely ignored. Therefore, a comprehensive model to elucidate the relationship between knowledge, intuition, and metacognition is needed. Thus, a model on the quadratic and cyclical process of knowledge, intuition, metacognition, and inference, is proposed below.

The quadratic process of knowledge, intuition, metacognition, and inference in problem-solving

Take an example. In a physics class in grade 8, a physics teacher has given the students a tricky problem to solve. Just then, a student gets up and gives the correct answer. When the teacher asked, why this was the correct answer, she said "I don't know." She was not able to reason well, but then she gave the correct answer. The proposed model can help to understand this.

A figure depicting four stages of problem-solving, knowledge, intuition, metacognition, and inference

The proposed model has four components.

1 **Knowledge:** It refers to the skills, facts, and information that are acquired through education or experience, along with the conceptual grasp of a subject matter. For instance, the student in the physics class was already familiar with physics-related topics discussed in class. Assuming it was a question on gravity, she was previously aware of the formula for gravity and the ideas around it before the question was asked.
2 **Intuition:** The student's answer was based on her use of intuitive thinking. The answer was not the product of deliberate thinking or reasoning on the speaker's part. When she was confronted with the challenge, her subconscious brain might have made an attempt to retrieve the previously stored thinking patterns from her previous experiences and relate them to the

problem at hand. This is where knowledge implicitly helps in intuitive thinking (Baylor, 2001; Hogarth, 2001; Myers & Myers, 2002). It seems as if the answer was derived from some fundamental understanding. Even though decisions like this are commonly made on the spur of the moment and may seem illogical at first glance, they are not. It is not apparent, yet it makes sense. The inability to articulate the reasoning behind her response shows that the process was occurring on an implicit level. This is similar to the participant child not being able to give justification for her answer in a standard cognitive task even after getting it right.

3 **Metacognition:** If the student gives the right response at the previous level and stops there, the answer will be deemed illogical and produced by "hit and try." However, if she thinks about why she provided the response and reflects on those thoughts, she will be able to reason that it was due to specific prior knowledge she had about a related topic, which made it easier for her to solve the problem. Thus, the objective of metacognition is to make the process of implicit thought explicit, which contributes to the benefits of intuitive thinking. The process of developing one's own metacognition is an essential stage in the creation of valid, trustworthy, and rationally derived new information.
4 **Inference:** After the student has known the possible concepts related to the novel problem through metacognition, the next step is to draw inferences about the problem and its solution. This gets incorporated into the explicit knowledge structures. Here metacognition and inference connect both intuition and deliberate thinking. Thus, inference allows the thinker to validate and refine the initial intuitions through the application of logical reasoning and critical thinking.

The model proposes that even though intuition is unconscious and implicit, it is still a cognitive process. Once reflected upon metacognitively, this implicit process of associating different nodes of knowledge by brain becomes explicit, uncovering how that supposed "hunch" came into mind. This information helps the thinker to infer that such problems can be solved in "this" particular way. With regard to Baylor's U-shaped model (2001), the acquired knowledge does generate intuition. However, employing metacognitive thinking after that can make implicit intuitive thinking conscious and integrate it into one's knowledge structure.

Development of intuition in children

The ability to reason progressively develops throughout cognitive development. While it may reflect that this acquisition undermines the innate intuitive talents of children, theorists like Piaget, see it as the pinnacle of human progress. Let us recapitulate Piaget's theory briefly. Piaget (1936) described four phases of cognitive development. First is the sensory-motor period (from birth to 18 months or 2 years), where children use their natural abilities, such as seeing, sucking, grabbing, and hearing, to explore their surroundings. They learn by exploring with their senses and motor activities. Then, in the preoperational stage (between the ages of 2 and 7 years), symbols, ideas, and pictures start to represent actual things and occurrences and may be used while "thinking" on a very basic level. Intuition is the key aspect of these two phases. Children start to manipulate mental constructs when they reach the stage of concrete operations (about 7–11- or 12-year-old). Less egocentric, the child now identifies the reasons over and above the 'self' for seen occurrences. Finally, they may think about abstract things and connections when they reach the stage of formal operations (between the ages of 11 and 15 years). They may evaluate a proposition's reliability based on how it is presented in an argument. Additionally, they have the capacity to consider speculative ideas, formulate hypotheses, reflect on their own thinking, and approach challenges methodically by formulating plans before acting.

In recent years, Piaget's theory has been challenged in different ways. According to research (Bickart, 2013), preoperational children may be more rational than Piaget thought, but this is not evident as children are unable to vocally communicate their thinking. In contrast to what Piaget's paradigm would suggest, children in the formal operational stage sometimes exhibit less reason. Additionally, higher states of awareness and the potential for developing intuitive abilities have no place in his work. The formal logic stage cannot be hypothesized as lacking intuition due to the dominance of logical thought. If intuition and logical thought are not seen as polar opposites, one can reason that children who are older do not lack intuition as these two abilities are coexisting and are dependent on each other. In fact, formal operations might be seen as an extra source of intuition, offering more data, novel symbols and notions, broader applications, and a thorough means of vetting the output. This is unlike the intuition of younger children's intuition, which is based on imprecise sensory data as well as simple pictures and symbols.

Another challenge to Piaget's theory comes from the study of intuitive inferences. The study project by Stavy and Tirosh (2000) looks closely at intuitive thinking in the context of education. They went into great length on the creation and use of intuitive principles in several scientific and mathematical fields. They found that characteristics of an activity led kids to depend on a domain-general rule that is automatically used to provide a response. An example is intuitive rules, which are the operations that take one feature of the problem and generalize it to draw conclusions about another property. For instance, an intuitive rule like more of A indicates more of B (for example, weight, height, volume, breadth, density, size, area, time, or distance) is extended to produce an assessment of another property (e.g., a perimeter). These rules may shed light on how children intuitively give answers to problems. However, children might use these rules and give incorrect answers too.

An example of this is the standard conservation task of Piaget. The children determine if two rows with the same number of coins in a one-to-one correspondence are equal. After the children confirm this equivalence, one of the rows is lengthened by increasing the distance between the coins. Children under the age of 6–7 years think that changing an object's spatial arrangement alters its numerosity. As a result, they assume that the longer the line, the more coins there are, using the intuitive rule more A-more B. It highlights that intuitive rules, especially for 6–7-year-olds, do not always help them to solve problems (Osman and Stavy, 2006).

Children's prior knowledge and instincts also come into play while learning from an informant, which differs with the child's age. Preschoolers often do not believe in evidences that are not aligned with their own experiences, such as when adults tell them that an item is a different color or someone is a different person (e.g., Lane et al., 2014). In fact, the more the testimony contrasts with the children's own understanding, the more skeptical they become. Children may be skeptical not just of paradoxical assertions about the identification of objects but also of counterintuitive claims regarding the reality or possibility of events. Furthermore, using their intuition, they can also identify whom to trust and whom not to trust. Lane and Harris (2015) studied the relationship between children's intuitions and the knowledge level of their informants. Children aged 3–8 years saw movies in which biology or physics specialists made assertions that were either intuitively congruent or paradoxical about little-known creatures or items. Younger children, in particular, believed adults who claimed to have relevant knowledge than those who claimed to know nothing about the topic at hand. Further, children tended to believe those assertions that made sense to them. This distinction became stronger as children grew older and had more solid intuitions about what is often the case. In conclusion, children's faith in evidence is affected by both the skill of the witnesses and the maturity of the children themselves. Throughout their growth, children's intuitions tend to increase, which might affect their openness to statements that go against their intuition. Lee et al. (2002) showed an incident to child participants in which a girl reported to her mother that a ghost had leaped out of her book and shattered a glass. Children aged 5–6 were more inclined to conclude that it was the girl, rather than the ghost, who shattered the glass, compared to those aged 3–4. Children's growing doubt about ghosts seems to be a key mediator of this age-related rise in skepticism.

Some theorists believe that the traditional school system is a hindrance to the development of intuitive thinking in children since the acquisition of factual information and the right response are prioritized in school grades. For them, using a new grading scale could promote intuitive thinking in children. Other theorists feel that it is a common misapprehension that children have superior or unique ways of knowing. People who criticize the bad education system usually posit such arguments. However, according to Goldberg

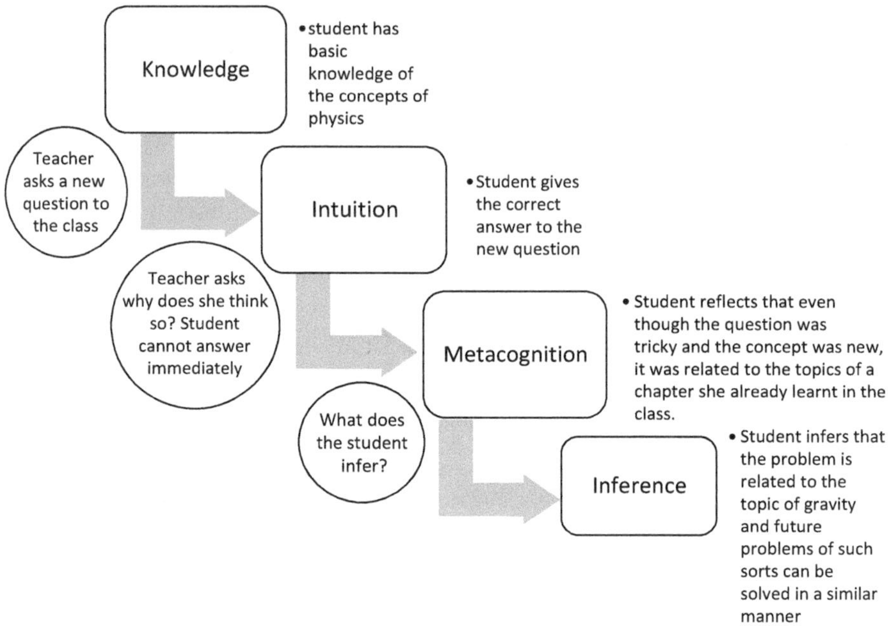

Figure 13.1 Model of the quadratic process of knowledge, intuition, metacognition, and inference in problem-solving.

(1983), this is an absolute over-celebration of children's "wisdom of childhood." As compared to logical thought, children might use intuition more than adults. However, less reasoning does not imply greater intuition and vice-versa, as then, intuition and reasoning incorrectly seem like diametrically opposite abilities (see model in Figure 13.1).

During the school years, the educational system fosters both the acquisition of new knowledge and intuitive thought. Despite the fact that educational systems encourage students to gain knowledge, the schools should focus on cultivating an environment that is more conducive to the development of intuitive skills.

Development of intuition in classroom settings

As observed from the studies and theories mentioned above, children have the ability to tap into their intuition. They also have some "innate" attributes (such as curiosity, receptivity, innocence, and wonder) that may help their intuition. When faced with a new situation, children have a natural tendency to give in to whatever comes their way, without the burden of the desire to prove their point. Regaining such characteristics is beneficial since they encourage the use of intuition and lead to discoveries that cannot be explained by logic alone. Going with one's gut feeling and making judgments swiftly based on instinctive cognitive processes, are examples of intuitive thinking. Students should be encouraged to think in a varied way through this way of thinking. The student's cognitive approach, which they use to make sense of many circumstances in life, is improved through intuitive thinking (Harlan, 1986).

Almost all of today's students are pushed to study by using punishment or the promise of rewards. This places severe constraints on the mind's innate capacity for intuitive cognition, especially its creative function, which thrives in an atmosphere devoid of external pressure and true motivation. Students are penalized for expressing assumptions, half-formed sentiments, and hazy hunches from an early age, despite the fact that these are the same things that lead to discovery the majority of the time. The message this sends to them is that taking chances is not worthwhile. They develop a supposedly "healthy" fear of expressing ideas that may deviate from the teacher's expectations or that are "off-topic." When it comes to their instincts, they learn to play things safe, which is the biggest mistake of the traditional educational system (Waks, 2006).

It is argued that formal education suppresses students' innate creativity and intuition (Harlan, 1986). Overly methodical, analytical ways of thinking are expected, and intuition is not just disregarded but actively discouraged. In many ways, we convey to kids that their inner monologue is useless. For example, directing the class to guess the "right answer," snubbing different ways of solving the same mathematical problem, and encouraging children to stick to the prescribed course books. This teaches children that their knowledge isn't complete unless they can articulate it and show others how they figured it out for themselves. Of course, that's not the case for kids, who are not able to express as much as they know. Nonverbal forms of thinking are essential to intuition and clearly natural to a child's brain processes, yet this outlook discourages them. An example of this can be seen in cognitive tasks created in the field of developmental psychology. It often happens that children know what the correct response is but are not able to justify it. For example, children are not able to reason why in standard false-belief tasks, the protagonist would search for a particular thing in a particular place they pointed to. Here, a child will be scored a zero for the justification question. However, the reason for pointing at the right place might be their intuition. It may happen that once they are encouraged to metacognitively think about their motivation for the answer, they might justify it too.

To pursue this line of thinking, we may give kids a deeper appreciation for intuitive and creative thinking by making these traits the focus of academic pursuits. This "may be taught" both intellectually and experientially by providing pupils with greater room for experimentation and improvisation. Not all "free" or alternative educational models have to compromise on traditional learning goals. Pedagogical approaches related to math and science by acting out the roles of real-world mathematicians and scientists, from brainstorming ideas to carrying them through to completion, should be supported (Panbanlame et al., 2014). Everything else, including the humanities, may be treated in the same way. Students of all ages may develop a more attuned sixth sense by learning about and witnessing intuitive behavior.

With the aid of a few unfinished phrases, assignments, or scenarios, teachers should urge students to ponder and draw inferences. Though students' intuition may be accurate or inaccurate, it should still be encouraged. False guesses shouldn't be discouraged by teachers since only by speculating can you increase learners' capacity for intuition (Harlan, 1986). Below are some pedagogical techniques teachers can use to develop the intuitive thinking abilities of children in the classroom.

Pedagogical techniques

1 **Ensure a safe and threatless environment:** The teacher should establish a secure environment in which children may explore and communicate their innermost thoughts. Children learn to suppress their innate understanding because they know it is no longer advisable to place their reliance on it. They may find it troubling to trust their intuition while being constantly taught what they should believe and do, in addition to the pressure to be responsible and "practical." For example, if the child doesn't give the supposedly "right answer," teachers should not say, "You did not study your book well." Rather, they should say, "Let's explore more about why you feel like that." Downgrading a child because their answer is different from the textbook version may hinder the development of intuitive thought, especially if it happens in front of the whole class. Teachers must ensure that children are not getting demotivated to follow their intuition.

2 **Give attention to one's own intuitive thoughts:** Teachers should appreciate answers that are distinct from what is usually considered the "correct" answer to a question. When teachers are more attentive to their own self, they will naturally be more attentive to the children. Children are acutely aware of the moment their teachers are not present with them mentally. As a result, it is important that teachers have the ability to listen to them and participate in their world without feeling the need to impose their will on them in order to foster their trust in us and their innate sense of knowing. Thus, even if the teacher does not get the answer she expected, she should maintain eye contact, nod, and smile while the child is talking. If children are good at intuitive thinking, their intuition also helps them to read others' nonverbal behavior to know if they are being listened to.

3 **Allow children to be inquisitive:** Teachers should motivate children to be inquisitive. This helps children to reflect, introspect, and be better informed by their emotions, knowledge, purpose, and ambitions. In this way, they learn to depend on their own ingenuity and ability to make

choices for themselves. Teachers should put aside their rigid way of enforcing knowledge and experience in order to have curiosity. They should see them as capable of determining what is best for themselves. Questions with no predetermined answers engage more intuitive faculties. For instance, "What would you do if you met a Jinn? Why?" "What would you make if you had a magic pencil?" How will you feel using it? Suppose, you get the power to fly, where would you fly?

4 **Give value to child's unique characteristics:** Children's particular ideals and goals are intricately related to their intuition. They guide them toward their "interests," promoting a balanced life with a purpose. Teachers may discern this by paying attention to the times when a child is most engaged and excited by a task. If honed properly, such intuitive acts may become a unique aspect of a child's personality. Attending to and facilitating the child's intuitive inclinations may aid in the development of that unique skill. For instance, a child who makes good drawings and becomes engrossed in the process may be encouraged to draw imaginary situations, like a person from another planet or a human bird, to facilitate artistic imagination.

5 **Give students control in decision-making:** Teachers should give children the opportunity to actively participate in the decision-making process and enable them to develop a "sense of self" and listen to their intuition. This is irrespective of whether the goal is for academic or non-academic activities. To be successful at co-creating, teachers have to give up some amount of control on their end and acknowledge that children are active, intentional, and intuitive agents who can shape their own environment. For example, while making an assessment, children can be asked about the method of their own assessment. Do they want a traditional pen-and-paper assessment or a pairwise debate on the topic, or do they want to make models, charts, or posters on the topic? This would facilitate intuitive thought in choosing their desired mode of assessment and then doing the task itself.

6 **Encourage articulation of self:** Teachers should inspire children to find imaginative methods for their thoughts to be communicated. Like the Reggio Emilia Approach to Early Childhood, pioneered by Loris Malaguzzi, teachers should assist children with identifying a means of expression that is most comfortable to them, such as creating art, telling stories, making music, acting, or dancing. An instance is encouraging children to draw and explain an event or engage them in role plays, depending on their comfort. This way, the teachers can assist them in expressing themselves more and strengthening their connection with their learning and with themselves.

7 **Use language mindfully to encourage intuitive thinking:** Certain terms and instructional phrases make it easier to encourage children to use their intuition faculties. The teacher should allow students to use terms like "I feel this would be the right answer" or "what I can sense from this topic

is..." and later encourage them to think about "why they feel so". Helping children with metacognition along with intuitive thinking will help them to crystallize their understanding of that particular concept so that they don't think that their answers are a product of mere guesswork. Using different terms for standard tasks, like "Funsheets" rather than worksheets or brain boosters instead of class tests can also encourage children to think outside the standard pedagogical. In asking questions too, teachers can phrase them to encourage intuitive thinking in children. For example, asking "What do you feel the answer should be?" as opposed to "What is the correct answer to this question?"

8 **Don't shut the wrong answers:** The teachers should make sure to acknowledge and appreciate children's creative contributions and self-expressions. They should honor them as expressions of the student's own learning, and development. Keeping children's intuitive energy flowing and their sense of self-worth intact requires being attentive to, appreciating, and including children's ideas without putting them down by labeling them as incorrect. One way to ensure this is to use the phrase "Yes and?" rather than "no" or "wrong." Usually used as a means to communicate with children and encourage them to finish the tasks at hand without giving excuses, saying "Yes and?" in the classroom allows children to come up with inventive ways to expand upon their answers, and experimenting on them playfully to see where it leads you. This helps with more brainstorming and, thus, more intuitive thoughts.

9 **Encourage unstructured play:** An unstructured play is a child-directed play activity in which a child is encouraged to play without any purpose or explicit rules. Such type of play enhances children's capacities for creativity, spontaneity, and adventure. Teachers should encourage children to explore the wide outdoors or their own imaginations without being forced to follow a strict rule or method of play. This type of explorative, non-directive, and unstructured play might help children maintain a connection to the voice of their intuition. A few examples of unstructured play are playing with blocks, coloring and drawing on blank paper, forming new outdoor games to play with friends, or exploring a garden.

10 **Discuss hypothetical situations:** In order to encourage intuitive thinking, teachers can ask children about the actions they may undertake in certain hypothetical situations. Children may learn to develop faith in their own intuition and decision-making by engaging in conversation about hypothetical scenarios, which can also empower them to act on those choices in the event that they present themselves in real life. This development of intuition might spill into classroom interactions when discussing a particular topic because children will now be confident about their own intuitive thoughts. For example, "What would you do if you were alone in a forest?" "What would you do if you were stuck in Charlie's Chocolate Factory?"

Intuition is important in classroom as it makes learning more engaging for kids. The ability to think differently is enhanced, enabling pupils to consider all relevant parts of a topic. Children's ideas should be respected and supported by teachers by inspiring them.

In conclusion, the relationship between intuition and metacognition is proposed by different researchers in a variety of ways. However, due to some or the other shortcomings in these perspectives, the authors proposed a consolidated and comprehensive model of "The Quadratic Process of Knowledge, Intuition and Metacognition." The authors suggest that both intuition and metacognition are essential components of cognition. Even though intuition may not be viewed explicitly as a cognitive process, it is a component of tacit cognition. Sometimes intuition aids in problem-solving, while other times it hinders it. For instance, the intuition of the girl in grade 8 helped her solve the physics problem. However, the intuitive rule of "more A, more B" caused children under 6–7 years of age to fail the task involving coins. When intuition impedes problem-solving, rational thought (or metacognition) is advantageous. Thus, using the intuitive rule, the children could not separate the number of coins and their spatial extents in arrays. Doing this would require rational thought. Sometimes rational thought alone is not sufficient to solve a problem. The physics question could not have been solved through rational thought because it was novel and had never been taught. However, because the child was knowledgeable about the problem's subject, this knowledge became the foundation for intuitive thinking, which implicitly formed connections and worked on the problem. Nonetheless, it is important to consider how and why the answer came to mind. The task of metacognition is to make the implicit process explicit. Intuition should be followed by metacognition in order to correctly grasp the underlying concept of the problem at hand. Future studies and interventions based on the model may be fruitful in enhancing children's problem-solving skills using intuition and metacognition.

References

Baylor, A. L. (1997). A three-component conception of intuition: Immediacy, sensing relationships, and reason. *New Ideas in Psychology*, *15*(2), 185–194. https://doi.org/10.1016/S0732-118X(97)00016-0

Baylor, A. L. (2001). A U-shaped model for the development of intuition by level of expertise. *New Ideas in Psychology*, *19*(3), 237–244. https://doi.org/10.1016/S0732-118X(01)00005-8

Bickart, J. (2013). *The possible role of intuition in the child's epistemic beliefs in the Piagetian Data Set* (dissertation). *The possible role of intuition in the child's epistemic beliefs in the Piagetian data set*. ProQuest LLC. https://eric.ed.gov/?id=ED558820

Bruner, J. (1960). *The process of education*. Harvard University Press.

Choi, K. S. (1993). Developmental changes in intuitive thinking of Korean children. *Early Child Development and Care*, *85*(1), 89–95. https://doi.org/10.1080/0300443930850110

Evans, J. S. B. T. (2010). Intuition and reasoning: A dual-process perspective. *Psychological Inquiry*, *21*(4), 313–326. https://doi.org/10.1080/1047840X.2010.521057

Evans, J. S. B. T. (2011). Dual-process theories of reasoning: Contemporary issues and developmental applications. *Developmental Review*, *31*(2), 86–102. https://doi.org/10.1016/j.dr.2011.07.007

Evans, J. S. B. T., & Stanovich, K. E. (2013). Dual-process theories of higher cognition: Advancing the debate. *Perspectives on Psychological Science*, *8*(3), 223–241. https://doi.org/10.1177/1745691612460685

Flavell, J. H. (1971). First discussant's comments: What is memory development the development of? *Human Development*, *14*(4), 272–278. https://doi.org/10.1159/000271221

Flavell, J. H. (1976). Metacognitive aspects of problem solving. In L. B. Resnick (Ed.), *The nature of intelligence* (pp. 231–235). Lawrence Erlbaum.

Flavell, J. H. (1979). Metacognition and cognitive monitoring: A new area of cognitive–developmental inquiry. *American Psychologist*, *34*(10), 906–911. https://doi.org/10.1037/0003-066X.34.10.906

Goldberg, P. (1983). *The intuitive edge: Understanding and developing intuition.* J.P. Tarcher.

Harlan, D. (1986). *The role of intuition in the teaching/learning process.* Doctoral Dissertations 1896 – February 2014. https://scholarworks.umass.edu/dissertations_1/4090

Hogarth, R. M. (2001). *Educating intuition.* University of Chicago Press.

Lane, J. D., & Harris, P. L. (2015). The roles of intuition and informants' expertise in children's epistemic trust. *Child Development*, *86*(3), 919–926. https://doi.org/10.1111/cdev.12324

Lane, J. D., Harris, P. L., Gelman, S. A., & Wellman, H. M. (2014). More than meets the eye: Young children's trust in claims that defy their perceptions. *Developmental Psychology*, *50*, 865–871. https://doi.org/10.1037/a0034291

Lee, K., Cameron, C. A., Doucette, J., & Talwar, V. (2002). Phantoms and fabrications: Young children's detection of implausible lies. *Child Development*, *73*(6), 1688–1702.

Mandler, G. (1995). Origins and consequences of novelty. In S. M. Smith, T. B. Ward, & R. A. Finke (Eds.), *The creative cognition approach* (pp. 9–25). The MIT Press.

Myers, D. G., & Myers, D. G. (2002). *Intuition: Its powers and perils.* Yale University Press.

Nelson, T. O., & Narens, L. (1990). Metamemory: A theoretical framework and new findings. In G. H. Bower (Ed.), *Psychology of Learning and Motivation* (Vol. 26, pp. 125–173). Academic Press. https://doi.org/10.1016/S0079-7421(08)60053-5

Osman, M., & Stavy, R. (2006). Development of intuitive rules: Evaluating the application of the dual-system framework to understanding children's intuitive reasoning. *Psychonomic Bulletin & Review*, *13*(6), 935–953. https://doi.org/10.3758/BF03213907

Panbanlame, K., Sangaroon, K., &Inprasitha, M. (2014). Students' Intuition in mathematics class using lesson study and open approach. *Psychology*, *05*(13), Article 13. https://doi.org/10.4236/psych.2014.513161

Piaget, J. (1936). *Origins of intelligence in the child.* Routledge & Kegan Paul.

Schön, D. A. (1982). 9 – Intuitive thinking? A digression stimulated by U-shaped curves. In S. Strauss (Ed.), *U-shaped behavioral growth* (pp. 227–247). Academic Press. https://doi.org/10.1016/B978-0-12-673020-3.50016-1

Stavy, R., & Tirosh, D. (2000). *How students (mis-) understand science and mathematics: Intuitive rules*. (Ways of knowing in science series). Teachers College Press.

Waks, L. (2006). Intuition in education: Teaching and learning without thinking. *Philosophy of Education*. https://doi.org/10.47925/2006.379

Wason, P. C., & Evans, J. S. B. T. (1975). Dual processes in reasoning? *Cognition*, *3*(2), 141–154. https://doi.org/10.1016/0010-0277(74)90017-1

Chapter 14

Inception and manifest of intuitive cognition in children

Mouma Nag, Ananya Sengupta and Pritha Mukhopadhyay

Introduction

Piaget, in his theory of life-span development, incorporated an "intuitive substage" that ranges from four to seven years in the preoperational period of cognitive development. The children, at this stage, comprehend various phenomena from their own unique perspectives. Consequently, they establish cause–effect relationships between different phenomena or different events in their own way. The flow of thought in children that paves the way for their plausible understanding of the world differs from that of an adult thought process. Despite the apparent limit of their factual knowledge owing to their tender age, children act upon the environment based on their understanding within the span of their knowledge. Piaget, in one of his works with children, once asked a six-year-old child "Does the sun move?" in which the child answered, "Yes, when one walks, it follows. When one turns round it turns round too," (Airenti, 2018). In other instances, the child explains the causality of the brightness of the sun as "God has put a lot of light bulbs in it" (Schlottmann, 2001). In both cases, it is evident that the child is relating a distant natural phenomenon, like the sun's movement with human movement, which is not so easy and not a mere random response at that age. It emerges from the inner understanding based on his the-then cognitive status that depends on the knowledge he derives from his experience-based percept rather than the underlying concept which is beyond his comprehension. Though it appears simplistic and less complex way of thinking, it is age-appropriate considering his level of cognitive maturation at this developmental stage. However, there is no bar to substantiate that intuitive thinking is inner knowledge, based on one's level of understanding encountering his bottom-up experience.

In explaining intuitive thinking, Piaget also referred to the child's attribution of animism to inanimate objects, at this stage, as they fail to recognize definite boundaries between the animate and inanimate (Boyer, 1996). They regard a lot of objects as possessing living properties, which are inert. All these would indicate that the child makes extensive use of assumptions, which could

DOI: 10.4324/9781003377757-17

be considered faulty from the perspective of the adult mode of thinking. However, as has already been stated from the child's perspective, these types of thoughts are age-appropriate, as they derive this knowledge, based on the perception-based experiential data, beyond which developmentally their cognitive mechanic is yet to develop. It is evident that children have an innate capacity to learn automatically utilizing the natural way of learning, when they are neither mature enough nor educated or trained with the underlying conceptual frame of the natural and social phenomena, like, though the sun moves, it is not an animate entity. The point is whether this cognitive style, with which they are endowed with naturally can be effectively used to design learning paradigms to help them move toward a mature level of thinking.

It is so stated as that the deliberate mode of thinking process needs formal training. Second, in the intuitive process, the child gets the scope to learn through the process of assimilation, be it whether it's right or wrong, finally making it easier to relate it to the mature deliberate process of thinking. Intuition is a faster, parallel processing of information that organizes the relevant data with simultaneous processing of information in a holistic manner, which can be nurtured during teaching-learning sessions. For example, a teacher tries to explain the concept of momentum to a child. If he asks the child, "throw stones in water and check how far it can go," the child while performing the act will discover that the heavier the stones are, the stronger the force needed to throw the stones further. Through this exploration, he can relate the overall concept of mass and velocity, which can give him a sense of mastery of the learned concept. The positive affect associated with the whole process of learning for knowledge formation, can make the learning and subsequent generalization pleasurable and automatic through the activation of the process of assimilation.

The importance of this assimilation is evident from the report of a science class demonstration (Bickart, 2013). Children were introduced to an experiment using a candle. The children were shown a candle with its wick lit. The children started describing it in terms of its brightness and comparing it with the radiance of the sun. Midway, the teacher started asking questions about the characteristics of a candle, the color of the flame, the burning of the wick, and so on to understand whether the children's responses were based on the concept of light, that is, to record the testable facts in a child's mind. This untimely intrusion of analytical query broke the children's sense of continuity of relating the phenomenon of the candlelight with sunlight. Intuition seems to be this holistic understanding with self-involvement. If the teacher's query could be an open-ended question to encourage the children to think in an intuitive fashion to reach the decision beyond the scope of right or wrong, it could widen their perspectives and ease their journey from the immature to mature intuition. If support and acknowledgment from the teacher could be provided to "learn to express in one's own way, beyond the boundaries of right and wrong" the learning could be more spontaneous, experiential, and strongly integrated in cognitive-affective process through the mechanism of association.

It can be inferred that the knowledge is gained through the trajectory of a holistic approach to a more segmented approach. The intuitive child remains embedded and interconnected with the external world having an all-inclusive perception of the world. Gradually, all the children complete the journey of their learning by segregating the information into parts, logically analyzing them, and finally, getting encouraged to think of the whole, which has been broken down into parts for understanding (Bickart, 2013).

The discussion leads to the question of whether logical reasoning and intuitive learning stand in mutual contradiction. However, it can be explored following the process of Lev Vygotsky. Vygotsky showed a constructive way of child-learning by introducing the term "zone of proximal development" (1978). He stated it as "the distance between the actual developmental level that is determined by independent problem-solving and the level of potential development as determined through problem-solving under adult guidance, or in collaboration with more capable peers" (Vygotsky, 1978).

For example, Kumon is a very popular mathematics learning method started in Japan, where the teacher tries to scaffold students in an adaptive way to make them better realize the level of their learning without any explicit rule impositions. There are no theoretical explanations or lectures given by the teachers, rather the material itself through different examples allows a student to discover their own rules (Orcos et al., 2019). Therefore, the learning itself creates a sense of autonomy, a sense of freedom and the teachers provide the required assistance by performing the same act, if necessary. The intrusion of teacher assistance is such that it is not perceived as imposition, rather it appears as an aid in learning the steps. Children also get the opportunity to exercise their creativity at different levels of learning. In that way, learning experiences with the provided the freedom of thoughts become more enjoyable to the children because of a proper balance between the challenges and skills. This is the root of experiencing the state of flow (Csikszentmihalyi, 2009).

Precisely, this chapter aims to explore such a journey of learning from a child's immature epistemic beliefs to more mature intuition by nurturing their ability to think impossible, providing them with an adaptable assistance and finally connecting the immature intuitive thought with the more mature one, with the aim for easy assimilation with deliberate thinking.

Method

This is a naturalistic observational study method to find out the basic factors underlying immature intuition in early life, which has the possibility to develop into a more mature process of thinking to enhance a better understanding of the world. The study includes a thematic analysis of the observations noted in the study.

Research questions of the study

1 Whether intuitive thinking has any relevance in the learning process.
2 Whether nurturance of intuitive process facilitates the process of deliberate learning and reasoning.

To reach these objectives of understanding the intuitive process, different observations have been conducted on children between five and seven years of age in different sets of situations. All the situations are considered as different cases.

Participants

Three children of five, six, and seven years of age, belonging to the preoperational stage of Piaget's theory of cognitive development (Berk, 2009), participated in this study. Purposive sampling was used in the present study all children are of middle- and high SES, Bengali speaking, and currently attending an institution of primary education in Kolkata. Therefore, participants are considered as a relatively homogenous sample.

Ethical consideration

Consent was taken from their parents whether they would allow their children to participate in the study and the willingness of the children was also assured regarding participation. The demographic and background information were secured from the parents.

Situations designed for concept formation

Situation 1: Learning law of gravitation

In this intervention, the group of children were asked different questions to reach toward the conception of the law of gravitation while playing a ball. Questions were asked by the researcher "why the ball falls down" and they confirmed that they know that heavy things fall. Then the problem of a magnet was introduced in the next step. The placement on the top of the magnet was not disclosed to them. Here they were asked, "if heavy things come down, then why the piece of iron which is apparently heavy, moved towards the given object?"

Situation 2: Learning force

A steel glass used for drinking was placed at different distances and children were asked to throw the ball into the glass.

A steel glass was kept at varying distances at different times. The children were instructed to hit the glass with the ball. While one was throwing the ball, others were enjoying the activity by watching the moves of another participant, who could effectively hit the glass with the ball before them. However, everybody experienced the episode himself.

Observations are based on informal conversations with children, where all the children in a week participated in one episode each day, comprising two different playful situations in sequence, with 14 observations in totality in two weeks. Data saturation was reached by the first week of each individual playful situation, and two additional observations were conducted to verify data saturation.

Rationale for thematic analysis of observations

Data of the three children observed in the naturalistic observations were submitted for thematic analysis. The dataset has been obtained from the child's answers to some questions during the incubation of some concepts out of interaction with the researcher. The situation was monitored to help children relate the "to be developed" concepts of gravitational force to evolve from their existing epistemic beliefs about natural phenomena, through the intuitive process of thinking. Different domains of intuition could emerge from this kind of qualitative analysis by which underlying intuitive skill, which is natural to us but needs nurturance, could be explored.

Triangulation

Three sources of data are included in this study: the initial observational data enhanced by member reflections and memoing. In addition, the literature and theory used to support the findings obtained in the study, can be considered as a source of data. Multiple sources of data allow the researcher to verify and support findings, or potentially find contradictions that can bring richness and depth to findings (Carter et al., 2014). Thus, triangulation of data can be used to increase validity and reliability of findings.

Data analysis

Coding

Open coding, axial coding, and selective coding were used in this study. The process initiated with the intricate reading of every line of the transcripts, notes of observational data, and analytic memoing to highlight each piece of data, cluster them to categorize in separate codes and use the constant comparative approach to minimize any bias. The categorization revisiting the process of coding remained until the researchers were satisfied with the fact that all the data had been utilized. This repetition gives rise to different codes explaining the core phenomenon of intuitive cognition that emerged from the conversation of the children.

Result and discussion

The aim of the study was to find out whether intuitive thinking has any relevance in the learning process and whether the nurturance of an intuitive process facilitates the process of deliberate learning and reasoning. During this study, many broad categories emerged from the data. Two interventions have been provided during the observation. Interventions were created to make them learn the concepts of gravitation and force with distance.

Intervention 1: Learning the concept of law of gravitation

Three of the children during the first phase of intervention where they were made to learn the law of gravitation by throwing the ball up, where they were involved in a discourse with each other. The act of playing together emerged as a cue for understanding the concept of gravitation.

Immediacy and collective positive experiences

When they threw the ball in the sky, the researcher asked, "why does it come down." The first thing they uttered was "it is not cloud, cloud is light, but the ball is thick." From these collective responses, it was assumed that they have a basic understanding of the fact that cloud due to its lightweight flow away, which they have gathered from their experience. On the contrary, the ball with its greater weight in comparison to clouds, falls toward the floor. Therefore, it is visible that their initial understanding of weight in explaining the falling of the ball in connection with the lightness of the cloud was neither taught by the researcher nor given in the problem. It indicates their natural sense is more of a part of the intuitive process (Baylor, 1997) than that of the logical derivation of deliberate reasoning. Most interestingly, the six-year-old boy, who belongs to the intuitive sub-stage of preoperational development, first uttered the relation between the weight and the object. It may be assumed that the child, who is in this stage, may have the freedom of thinking, which has not yet been overshadowed by the imposition of formal training that strengthens the deliberate thinking and suppresses the intuitive query. The rest of the children spontaneously endorsed the decision. Exposure to formal training that encourages deliberate thinking could have an inhibitory effect on the spontaneity of thinking, making one apprehensive of the accuracy of response. However, children in this study belonging to the intuitive sub-stage of development made more natural responses promptly that justifies the immediacy factor of intuitive thinking. Seven days later, after their first session on the initial problem of asking about the reason for the falling of heavy things, another problem of a magnet was placed before them. They could promptly connect the magnet with the idea of weight. Here, a piece of iron was held opposite to a magnet and was shown to them. The magnet was placed on the iron piece, and they were misled intentionally by asking "if the heavy thing comes down, then why is the iron moving up to the given object." Immediately they responded that "definitely here is a superpower you hold opposite to the iron, it's a super magnet." It reveals that they were acquainted with the term and the attracting power of the magnet. It may be inferred from this statement that they could identify the existence of a superpower against the given weight. Four days later, in the next session of ball throwing, when the ball came down after throwing high, they said "it may be there is a superpower in the floor." This series of events also indicates that they are traveling from one episode to another without failing to link the events together. Initial natural sense of falling of heavy weight got connected with the idea of F, where they identified the attraction ability of the magnet irrespective of the object weight. The researcher's induction of contradiction in the second session by asking "if the heavy thing comes down, then why the iron is moving up to the object" led them toward making the connection. Four days later, it was found that they automatically said that "the falling of the ball to the ground may be because of the fact that there is the superpower in the floor." Therefore, they connect the magnetic force lying down somewhere in the ground, in the earth, from a general discourse out of playing with a magnet. When the problem of magnet was placed before them, they clearly stated that "This is a super power, super magnet, which drags the thing towards it." Later, they associate the idea of magnetic force with the ground, where the things fall. Most interestingly, it is not a mere hunch, rather they reached toward a decision by their own where different information was collected experientially over a course of time. This assimilation incited the development of the idea of magnetic force in the children. It indicates that they understood its the presence of magnetic force everywhere and generalized the already generated schema of bigger magnetic force. All this understanding is implicit. The schema of the "falling down of a ball connected with the idea of falling due to magnetic force" could form in a short span of time spontaneously, based on experiential learning, which has both the visuospatial and temporal plane. Episodic learning is right hemispheric (Tulving et al., 1994). This resonates with the function of parallel distributed processing, where different information from different time periods stored in different nodes, keep connected according to their potency to subserve the situational need. In the present scenario, the children from Day 1 keep weaving the information when they were asked about the reason behind the fall of the ball. Consequently, the idea of falling related to the magnetic force and they finally associated it with the presence of a bigger magnetic force of the earth. It is a constant weaving of episodes, which is not very explicit or deliberate. They came up with an experiential process in every episode spontaneously. Most importantly, when they were challenged with the question that if the heavy things come down then why the piece of iron not held under the certain object come down, increases the potency of the situational need to think immediately. All the information keeps distributing in the parallel nodes during the seven days of playful activity, being assimilated with the understanding the bigger magnetic force. Finally, they could generalize the idea of a bigger magnetic force by saying that "super magnet is there in the road, in my uncle's house also."

Therefore, immediacy was found to be one of the visible components of this cognition, where the constant interlacing of experiences in a child's mind is evident. Whatever they experience, they keep connecting the facts in some or the other way, in an effortless manner due to the parallel distributed processing in our brains. It is different from the deliberate reasoning that requires more time to get functional. If intuitive thinking can be nurtured, then it is assumed to reduce the load in our working memory system that is bombarded with a lot of information. It stops processing each information as a separate entity, rather information from different nodes is constantly assimilated in relevant categories of every individual information by constantly categorizing the information from different nodes. The activation of parallel networks is evident during experience in a casual set-up, where the thoughts are not constricted by the so-called territory of right and wrong. However, it does not imply that there is no necessity of right and wrong rather it highlights the fact of nurturing the young minds to think freely in their early years of learning.

Figure: Model of PDP from first intervention

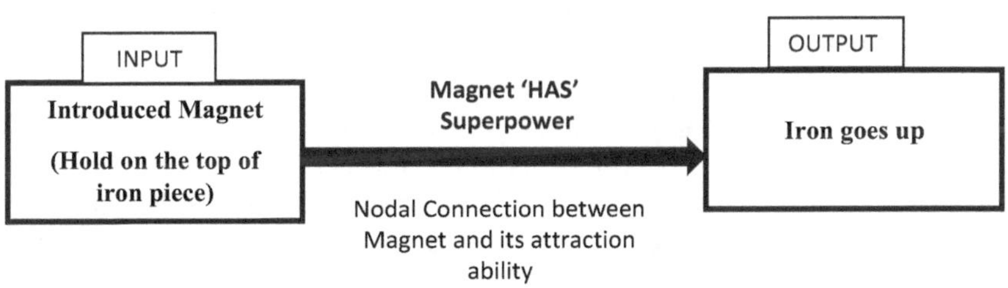

Figure 14.1 A magnet held on top of the iron (input), iron goes up; magnet has superpower (output). The nodal connection between the magnet and its attraction ability (HAS).

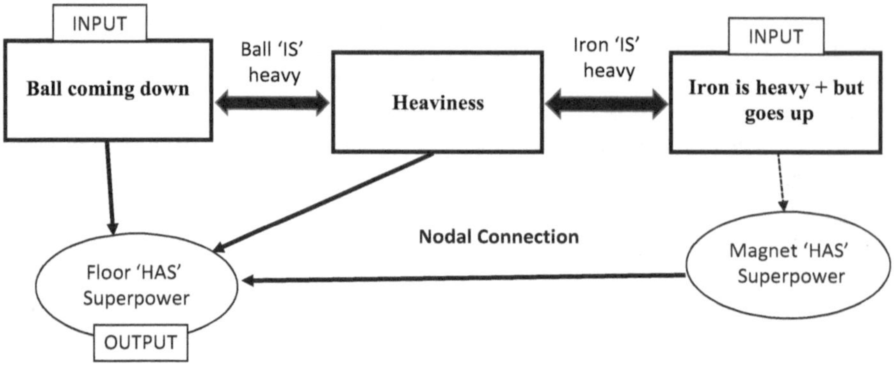

Figure 14.2 Ball is coming down (input), associating with heaviness (IS). Iron is heavy but goes up (input). The nodal connection between the magnet and its attraction ability (HAS) and the ball is heavy (IS) but coming down leads to the conceptualization that floor has a super magnet (output). Finally, learning the concept of gravitation happened.

Intervention 2: Learning the law of force in relation to distance

In this intervention, children were asked to throw the ball into a glass placed at different distances. It was observed that just like the example of throwing the spoon, children were repeating the same posture and move after the first successful attempt. It is not a primary circular behavior rather children were assumed to enjoy the implicit connection between force and distance. They also stated "look, if I throw this in this way (showing a particular pattern of holding the ball) it will go into the glass." They were not able to verbalize the connection of given force to the ball with distance but acted out the pattern of holding the ball implying that they are associating the connection between force and distance. Considering this conversation, we found in literature that it is possible to acquire tacit knowledge (Nonaka and von Krogh, 2009) through observation, imitation, and practice (e.g., master–apprentice relationship) without the support of verbal language. It resonates with the function of parallel distributed processing that we have already discussed in the first intervention. But here, the parallel processing of every information over the course of learning got associated with the act of imitation. The children were continuously imitating the researcher, and one another, until they succeeded to reach the goal. Children implicitly weaved every successful move in relation to different distances by imitation. Finally, the information regarding every successful move for different distances being stored in different nodes easily got assimilated by increasing the weightage of every successful move. Since, they understood the relation between force and distance, therefore, they felt an inner satisfaction to repeat the behavior.

In the present study, it was seen that the children were referring to the thoughts of one another while generating the ideas. Almost every phase of their activity they collectively reached a conclusion implying the fact that playful activity becomes more enjoyable and helpful in the presence of more people. It is an act of collective cue generation, which was observed in the present study at every step of the activity. Therefore, collective experience is found to have an impact on intuitive thought. Co-experience is found to facilitate the formation of a common perspective and as a result, the thought transforms into words and phrases from tacit knowledge, which ultimately assimilate into explicit concepts (Nonaka, 1994). It was a playful condition that itself increases the positive affective potency of every experience while learning. It helped them to be better absorbed in the situation. Later, they seemed to generalize the idea of force with distances in different domains. After these sessions, one day they were playing tennis game on their mobile when the researcher was unable to do the moves. Suddenly, the six-year-old boy showed by saying that "you have to drag your finger backward very slowly if you want to shoot closer," From researcher's reflection, it can be stated from this scenario that once the schema of the relation between force and distance formed, they could easily generalize all the information from the same network in their visuo-spatial faculty of mind.

In summary, parallel distributed processing in both examples acted as a core mechanism in forming the knowledge base, which is not deliberate. But it can reduce the unnecessary load of deliberate reasoning thus enhancing the skill of knowledge acquisition. A few domains or themes that have emerged in both interventions are as follows.

Sense of autonomy

Here, from the researcher's reflection, it was revealed that they found a sense of autonomy in executing the act due to the praise from the researcher for their understanding. It was also noted that the collective participation in intellectualizing the connection of weight with the object through this playful activity made them emotionally connected with the act, which brings task involvement. In the intervention of connecting force with distance, performing acts on their own also brought a sense of autonomy. The six-year-old child stated after consequent failing that "I want to do it once more, please give it to me." Even when succeeded, he did not stop practicing with another glass on his own. Even the facial expressions depicted the same sense of satisfaction, which might have been generated from the sense of autonomy. A sense of autonomy gave the children the privilege to be involved in their learning in a more intense way. From self-determination theory (Ryan & Deci, 2017), it was observed that the more the stake of making a decision a person gets, the more it enhances their understanding. Here also, all the children because of enjoying autonomy, learned all the experiences in a sense of being authorized, which led them to act beyond the constrictions of rules and regulations standardized by the society. It essentially proves that the feeling of autonomy is required while they are in the stage of learning, understanding rules is necessary but learning should be given in a way where rules do not displace their enjoyment of freedom. Autonomous activity helps to feel the interoceptive cues by active participation. Our data also resonate with the fact.

Novelty

Data reveal that the children who were engaged in the playful activity to learn the concept of gravitation, concept of force using the natural method of observation, imitation, and their collective activity of playing ball, manifested new ways of framing new ideas in understanding the concept. It was observed in the first episode of ball throwing, they automatically generated their own logic by saying that "If the ball comes toward the floor, it means a magnet in the floor drags it towards it." It implies that they were not only associating the information from different episodes, rather they were constructing their own logic in their own way despite not knowing the concept of gravitational force. In addition, it was found from the second intervention that the children generalized their experientially acquired knowledge of force in relation to distance. When they were playing tennis video games or bottle flipping, they were making their own strategy and stated, "please drag the finger slowly to shoot closer and drag faster to shoot to the back player of the opponent."

They have not only acquired the knowledge but, over the course of time, also used the knowledge and formulated their own strategy in different places. Most importantly, all these generalizations are effortless once the basic knowledge has been formulated. This is assumed to be the intuitive flow that can occur if the learning has been done with hands-on experiences. It also paves the way of becoming intuitive with all its essence. In a similar vein, Tsoukas (2005) argued that tacit knowledge only manifested in our behavior, it cannot be converted to explicit knowledge.

Knowledge of application

Children's knowledge acquisition was not restricted to the given situation only. Throughout their conversation and playful activities, they remembered consciously what they observed while learning of the activity and reasoned out the solution on their own through self-reflection. They could apply this concept later in totally different situations. A set of underlying processes that supervises the outcomes of intuitive processes subsequently determines the depth of rational thinking. Intuitive process generates two distinct outputs: first is the content of the initial answer and the accompanying sense that the answer can be right for the given situation (Wang & Thompson, 2019). This Feelings of Rightness (FOR) is predicted to vary in strength across a set of problems and provides a compelling cue to accept the correct alternative. Here the children's statement that "I know it works" is the feeling of confidence that they had while generalizing the idea of force in relation to distance.

Based on the study a predictive model of intuition can be framed as follows:

Predictive model of intuition

Intuitive flow of thoughts = natural endowment (Frequency of event × situational need × immediacy) + positive affective valence.

Natural endowment = It is the constant in the formula which implies that it is constant amongst people as we are born with this natural gift.

Frequency of events = It implies the proportion of how frequently we experience a particular event that helps to form a pattern.

Situational need = It implies the problem at hand.

Immediacy = It implies the proportion of chances of how fast an integrated form of thoughts will emerge to fulfill situational needs.

Overall, the formula provides a predictive model from our observations that along with other factors, if the weightage of an experience is increased by frequent divergent exposure through scaffolding, it enhances the capacity to perceive a problem from different perspectives through strengthening different relevant nodes of knowledge through associative process. Subsequently, a stream of intuitive thoughts emerges to fulfill the requirement of the problem. Educational training following this formula may help educationists nurture the supple mind to learn through a mature intuitive thinking process. It will facilitate the function of deliberate thinking.

Conclusion

The study denotes that the factor of immediacy, hands-on experiences beyond the formal set-up of learning experiences, and reasoning reduce the cognitive load. Parallel distributed processing enables a person to integrate the information in one trajectory over the course of time. Subsequently, it is assumed to help in strengthening their formal training of deliberate reasoning in later life.

Future Directions

All these domains emerged as different domains of intuition. If intuitive thinking is nurtured along with formal training of deliberate processing in the educational set-up, learning will be less burdensome and more enjoyable for the children.

References

Airenti, G. (2018). The development of anthropomorphism in interaction: Intersubjectivity, imagination, and theory of mind. *Frontiers in Psychology*, *9*. https://doi.org/10.3389/fpsyg.2018.02136

Baylor, A. L. (1997). A three-component conception of intuition: Immediacy, sensing relationships, and reason. *New Ideas in Psychology*, *15*(2), 185–194. https://doi.org/10.1016/s0732-118x(97)00016-0

Berk, L. E. (2009). *Child development*. Pearson/Allyn & Bacon.

Bickart, J. (2013). The possible role of intuition in the child's epistemic beliefs in the Piagetian data set. In *ProQuest LLC eBooks*. https://eric.ed.gov/?id=ED558820

Boyer, P. (1996). What makes anthropomorphism natural: Intuitive ontology and cultural representations. *Journal of the Royal Anthropological Institute*, *2*(1), 83. https://doi.org/10.2307/3034634

Carter, N., Bryant-Lukosius, D., DiCenso, A., Blythe, J., & Neville, A. J. (2014). The use of triangulation in qualitative research. *Oncology Nursing Forum*, *41*(5), 545–547. https://doi.org/10.1188/14.onf.545-547

Csikszentmihalyi, M. (2009). *Flow*. HarperCollins.

Nonaka, I. (1994). A dynamic theory of Organizational Knowledge Creation. *Organization Science*, *5*(1), 14–37. https://doi.org/10.1287/orsc.5.1.14

Nonaka, I., & von Krogh, G. (2009). Perspective: Tacit knowledge and knowledge conversion: Controversy and advancement in Organizational Knowledge Creation theory. *Organization Science*, *20*(3), 635–652. https://doi.org/10.1287/orsc.1080.0412

Orcos, L., Carrera, R. M. H., Espigares, M. J., & Magreñán, Á. A. (2019). The Kumon method: Its importance in the improvement on the teaching and learning of mathematics from the First levels of early childhood and primary education. *Mathematics*, *7*(1), 109. https://doi.org/10.3390/math7010109

Ryan, R. M., & Deci, E. L. (2017). Self-determination theory: Basic psychological needs in motivation, development, and wellness. *Basic Psychological Needs in Motivation, Development, and Wellness*. https://doi.org/10.1521/978.14625/28806

Schlottmann, A. (2001). Perception versus knowledge of cause and effect in children: When seeing is believing. *Current Directions in Psychological Science*. https://doi.org/10.1111/1467-8721.00128

Tsoukas, H. (2005). Do we really understand tacit knowledge. *Managing Knowledge: An Essential Reader*, *107*, 1–18.

Tulving, E., Kapur, S., Craik, F. I., Moscovitch, M., & Houle, S. (1994). Hemispheric encoding/retrieval asymmetry in episodic memory: Positron emission tomography findings. *Proceedings of the National Academy of Sciences*, *91*(6), 2016–2020. https://doi.org/10.1073/pnas.91.6.2016

Vygotsky, L. S. (1978). Mind in society: The development of higher psychological processes. https://ci.nii.ac.jp/ncid/BA03570814

Wang, S., & Thompson, V. (2019). Fluency and feeling of rightness. *Psihologijske Teme*, *28*(1), 37–72. https://doi.org/10.31820/pt.28.1.3

Chapter 15

The role of intuition in psychotherapy

Insights into reflective practices

Piya Saha, Kaustav Manna and Pritha Mukhopadhyay

Introduction

Decision-making is the foundation of psychotherapeutic processes for diagnosis, interventions, and rehabilitation. Efficient clinical judgment and decision-making play a vital role in therapeutic outcomes. Clinical decision-making involves the ability to think and act systematically to solve problems (Tanner et al., 1987). Like decision-making in any other domain, in a psychotherapeutic setting too, the cognitive process includes addressing the problem through the process of identification of cues and clinical features, data gathering, integration, analysis, and evaluation with an aim to resolve the problem (Clack, 2009). Witteman and Koele (1999) found that treatment decisions were better predicted by the therapist's theoretical knowledge of the orientation and approaches of psychotherapy. Critical thinking, reflective practice, problem-solving, and judgment are the core dynamics underlying this complex process of decision-making (Standing, 2005). Zuber (2000) observed that patients' own problem formulation is a dimension to consider in treatment planning and in recommendation for the suitable mode of psychotherapy. He observed that for directive psychotherapies like cognitive and cognitive behavior therapies, patients tend to formulate their problems in terms of symptom formulations; and for insight-oriented psychotherapies, like, psychodynamic and expressive therapies, relation-formulations are prioritized.

In the United Kingdom, the Department of Health promotes the concept of "evidence-based practice" that requires clinical decision-making based on evidence that has been systematically investigated and established as a valid one. According to the American Psychological Association, evidence-based practice (EBP) in psychotherapy combines best available research evidence with clinical expertise in the context of patient characteristics, culture, and preferences (APA Presidential Task Force, 2006, p. 273). EBP involves conscientious, explicit, and judicious use of the best available evidence in making decisions (Sackett et al., 2000). In EBP, practitioners evaluate, sort, and prioritize relevant information (e.g., research evidence, assessment data) and

DOI: 10.4324/9781003377757-18

subsequently use this information to optimize their decisions and practices (Webb, 2001). However, clinical expertise is more than just textbook knowledge and treatment manuals; it includes the ability to use the most relevant available information in an unbiased manner and to convert this information into knowledge (Mayer-Schönberger & Cukier, 2013). Though acquired knowledge is useful during the therapeutic process, a seasoned therapist uses clinical experience that develops based on one's intuition, personal experience, clinical training, and supervision (Gyani et al., 2014). However, a study indicates cognitive behavior therapists are more likely to use research-based evidence than therapists with other theoretical orientations like that of psychodynamic, humanistic, and eclectic (Gyani et al., 2014). Moreover, studies revealed that decision-making in complex, high-stake task environments, such as aviation and firefighting, proficient decision-makers often benefit from using their intuition (Bingham & Eisenhardt, 2011; Klein, 1995). Scientists and mathematicians also reported that they sensed that there was a solution before knowing its contents (Hadamard, 1945). In psychotherapy, clinical intuitions are experienced mainly in uncertain or ambiguous circumstances; when there is inadequate information; situations of urgency, time pressure; or in situations of intense arousal, and heightened emotionality (Marks-Tarlow, 2014c).

Role of intuition in decision-making process in psychotherapy

In clinical practice, mental health professionals have to make rapid decisions. Deductively derived sequential decision-making does not always work in the psychotherapeutic process. Mental health professionals are not always conscious of how the underlying process is working while making decisions in a clinical setting. They become aware only when they look into the decision-making process while reflecting on their clinical decision (Higgs & Jones, 2008). Perhaps this decision is based on one's implicit knowledge system derived from different sources, like clinical experience, textbook knowledge, and personal perceptions. When the experiential knowledge integrates, it culminates in a holistic pattern implicitly, leading to clinical decision-making. This may be termed intuitive knowledge. Reflective practice is the way a professional stops to think and reflect on their experiences either at the moment or afterward, which prompts a particular response, or particular judgment. It is also important for medical practitioners to develop their intuition, as theoretical or technical knowledge and skill alone is not enough in clinical decision-making (Mickleborough, 2015).

Decision-making has features of both intuitive and deliberative modes (Kahneman, 2011; Stanovich, 2010). Psychotherapy has the demand for fast, automatic, solution-based decision-making in the course of therapy, following the paradigm of an automatic experiential-intuitive system that operates implicitly and provides holistic analysis of organism–environment interactions based on parallel channels of associative memory and affective valence. However, the slow, deliberate, and conscious decision that requires intentional effort is also important in psychotherapy, thereby deliberation and intuition complement each other in the therapeutic setup. One constantly switches between these two modes. Where clinical intuition facilitates the art of psychotherapy, conscious deliberation facilitates science of the empirical approach. In decision-making, intuitive process leaps into the unknown, and deliberate process checks their impact and relevance (Marks-Tarlow, 2014a, 2014b).

Intuitive response has been considered as a crucial component of patient–therapist interactions in all schools of therapy (Shapiro & Marks-Tarlow, 2021). The psychoanalytic conceptions of intuition date back to Carl Jung where he describes it as the core of psychoanalysis. The therapist uses analytical intuition to reach unknown psychic realities (Williams, 2006). Jung proposed the experiential-intuitive system, he referred to it as a second psychic system coexisting with consciousness, and it has everything that consciousness has but in subliminal form (Williams, 2006). Eric Berne was the first to describe "clinical intuition" as an important phenomenon in therapy (Berne, 1949). Berne describes that through intuition, therapists gain knowledge implicitly within the therapeutic encounter and it arises without conscious thought (Bove & Rizzi, 2009). Rogers describes that clinical intuition arises from a deep empathy and attunement toward a client, this allows the therapist to connect with different aspects of the client, which was unexplored (Kirschenbaum & Henderson, 1989). So, clinical intuition develops through therapeutic alliance where the therapist connects with clients; recognizes the sense of the client's dynamics, their situations, and understands the patient's subjective experience which remains hidden beneath the words.

Neuroanatomical basis of intuitive cognition

Clinical intuition has been of great importance in the therapeutic process and it is theorized to be a part of the therapeutic process across psychotherapies. Clinical intuition can be a skill that therapists and counselors use to connect empathically with their clients (Edwards, 2013; Jeffrey & Stone Fish, 2011). Schore (2011, 2012) has primarily delineated an integrative neurobiological theory of clinical intuition, emphasizing the primacy of the right brain networks in empathic attunement and clinical intuition. The vertical axis facilitates affective-emotional processing from "low-right" subcortical-limbic to "high-right" anterior cingulate and orbitofrontal systems. The vertical axis is complemented by the horizontal axis of right-to-left symbolic processing that enables conscious verbal capacity and rational-analytic functions of emotion and self-awareness. The right hemisphere is crucial for implicit attention whereas the left hemisphere plays an important role in expressing explicit knowledge (Chen & Hsiao, 2014). Imaging studies also have shown activation of the ventromedial-prefrontal cortex in tasks involving intuitive cognition (Horr et al., 2014; Volz & von Cramon, 2006), which is implicated in emotion and social interaction (Bar et al., 2001; Gazzaniga et al., 2002).

Social intuition is another type of intuition discussed often in literature and is crucial in psychotherapy. The intuition process is a mediation of social and emotional cues below the threshold level of awareness (Marks-Tarlow, 2014c). The neural basis of social intuition, theory of mind (ToM), and empathy is linked with the mirror neuron mechanism (MNM) that enables quick understanding of others' actions and gestures solely by observing them (Jellema et al., 2024; Mathon, 2013; Rajmohan & Mohandas, 2007; Rizzolatti & Craighero, 2004), that plays an immense role in therapeutic effectiveness, beyond the exchange of dialogue. A review study illuminates that mirror neuron tracks the emotional flow, movements, and intentions of those with whom we are interacting, and match this state by stimulating the same parts of our brains that are active in them and make a brain-to-brain link with others (Malhotra & Sahoo, 2017), where the intuitive process is rooted. As a result, the MNM related to the unconscious processing of others' actions gestures, and emotions results in transference in therapy (Malhotra & Sahoo, 2017).

In psychotherapy, this understanding of others' emotions occurs through an empathy network and gets linked to the self-reflection process during intuitive decision-making through an associative process. It has been proposed that empathy is mediated by at least three neural systems—the mirror neuron system (MNS), the affective empathy system, located in the anterior insula and midcingulate cortex, and the cognitive empathy system of ToM that almost overlaps with the default mode network (DMN) (Li et al., 2014; Walter, 2012). ToM is a multidimensional process, comprised of both the ability to understand others' beliefs and knowledge (cognitive ToM) and to infer others' emotions (affective ToM). The "Cognitive ToM" is a prerequisite for affective ToM. In complex social situations as in psychotherapy, efficacious affective ToM processing requires the integration of cognitive ToM and empathy processing (Białecka-Pikul et al., 2017; Sebastian et al., 2011). The DMN nodes interact with MNS to produce a mental mapping of social and cognitive input to create a coherent representation of self and other (Buckner et al., 2008; Molnar-Szakacs, & Uddin, 2013), which are crucial in the intuitive connection between client and therapist in therapeutic practice. These aspects of self are associated with grounded awareness mediated by the interoceptive process (Davey & Harrison, 2018; Fingelkurts & Fingelkurts, 2011). Greater activity of the DMN during automated decision-making was noted in a functional magnetic resonance imaging (fMRI) based study with cognitive flexibility task (Vatansever et al., 2017), which is one of the important features in clinical intuition. Thus, the therapist's intuitive decision-making in psychotherapy may be facilitated by the integrated activity of empathy network, mainly MNS, and DMN that help to develop a therapeutic alliance and provide a healing environment to the client promoting therapeutic outcome.

However, clinical intuition has remained unexplored as intuitive insights in therapy. It is mostly related to implicit meaning with cognitive and emotional salience rather than to observable cognitions and behavior. In this study, we will explore the decision-making process among clinicians in the therapeutic process.

Methods

Aims: The present study attempts to understand the experience of intuition by psychotherapists during the therapeutic process and its role in clinical decision-making. To reach the objective, the case-study method was adopted. The data analysis was done using a qualitative approach (Arya, 2020).

Participants: The study participants were three female clinical psychologists between the age range of 29 and 37 years, residing in West Bengal, India. They are registered with the Rehabilitation Council of India (RCI) with Master of Philosophy (M.Phil.) in Clinical Psychology and are actively engaged in the therapeutic process. The participants follow different psychotherapeutic approaches like Cognitive-Behavioral Therapy (CBT), Eclectic approach, Narrative Therapy, and Mindfulness (shown in Table 15.1) for working with clients. Informed consent was taken from all the participants to participate in this study.

Table 15.1 Socio-demographic details of the participants

Participants	*Age*	*Gender*	*Years of experience*	*Qualification*	*Therapeutic orientation*
Therapist-1	33	Female	7 years	M.Phil., Ph.D.	CBT, Eclectic approach, Mindfulness
Therapist-2	37	Female	More than 10 years	M.Phil., Ph.D.	CBT, Narrative Therapy, Mindfulness
Therapist-3	29	Female	5 years	M.Phil., Doctoral Research Fellow	Eclectic approach, Mindfulness

Tools used:

- **Information schedule:** A semi-structured interview was designed for this study to elicit information pertaining to each individual's age, education, years of experience, and details of therapeutic orientation.
- **In-depth interview:** This was conducted to enable the participants to share their experiences with the therapists and to explore their psychotherapeutic experiences during clinical decision-making. The interviews were coded following the guidelines of Charmaz (2006) and thematic analysis was carried out.

The semi-structured interview schedule was designed keeping in mind issues related to the psychotherapy process and to understand the role of clinical decision-making in the therapy outcomes. Typically, each interview lasted for about 30–45 minutes. The interviews for each participant were conducted till theoretical saturation was achieved.

For example,

- What are the factors associated with diagnosis and effective therapy?
- What do you do when you are stuck in a particular therapeutic session?
- Have you ever taken any decision in the therapeutic session without conscious awareness and did it work? Can you elaborate on such an experience?
- What have you sensed after the satisfactory therapeutic experiences?

An in-depth interview has been conducted for a comprehensive understanding of the participants- such as,

- Their experiences of a particular phenomenon
- How they have made sense of these experiences, and
- The meanings they attach to them.

The main focus of the study was on:

- Participant's meaning-making (interpreting her own experience),
- The researcher's sense-making (interpreting the participant's account), and
- Initiating a circular process of questioning, uncovering meaning, and further questioning to reach saturation.

Procedure

Triangulation of Data: The data were transcribed and coded by the two authors independently and finally interpreted by all the authors. The codes and themes that corroborated with each other, amongst the three authors, were finally retained.

Major findings

In this qualitative study, clinical decision-making in practicing psychotherapists was explored. A number of themes emerged inductively from the transcripts and data saturation was achieved. After the qualitative analysis, the following themes were considered-

Factors important for diagnosis: How therapist diagnose client?

The therapeutic treatment process often requires instantaneous decision-making. Understanding the role of therapists in the recognition and management of mental disorders among their clients is important for therapeutic progress. In this study, participants elaborated the importance of biopsychosocial information for the diagnosis of cases. It is also important to record a detailed history of illness from the client and their family members. Understanding the patient's sociocultural background, personality, family dynamics, and duration of illness are important factors for the diagnosis of cases. Moreover, they also stated that therapist's existing knowledge base, which they gained from academic knowledge and clinical training as well as years of experience is important for the diagnosis and therapy of cases. The combination of theoretical orientation and clinical training helps to develop clinical expertise.

Subtheme: Decision-making when the therapist stuck in a therapeutic session

Therapists are expected to make decisions in the clinical process to maximize the positive therapeutic outcome. Such decision-making is typically deliberate and analytical in nature (Patterson & Eggleston, 2017). Also, at times application of existing therapeutic methodology does not work for a client, and the therapist gets stuck with no therapeutic progress. In this situation, the therapist informed that, initially they discuss the case with senior faculty, supervisors, or other members of the therapeutic forum to get different perspectives, which they might be missing. However, when this process did not work, all participants mentioned that the temporary pause of a few days or weeks between therapy sessions was found extremely beneficial for both the client and the therapist as it helps in developing self-reflection. The self-reflection helps both the client and the therapist in in-depth exploring, clarifying, identifying cues, and a better understanding of the issues so that the situation can be seen from a new perspective. The participants reported that they often come across cases, where the symptom manifestations may be pointing towards a certain diagnosis but the therapists felt that there is more to the case than meets the eye. As reported by Therapist-1 (case example-1) a client came with the presenting complaints of rebelliousness, being uncooperative, defiant, and hostile toward parents that easily points to the diagnosis of Oppositional Defiant Disorder (ODD). But she felt that some link is missing.

Therapist-1 reported that "*When I feel that something is lacking and stuck in a particular session, I don't focus on a strict diagnosis rather I prefer to slow down, take some time and explore and gather more information regarding the case*". She pointed out that time helps me in self-reflection and the establishment of a deeper sense of rapport with the clients which helps in developing the therapeutic alliance. As discussed earlier, the DMN plays an important role in self-reflection (Davey & Harrison, 2018). This engrossment resulting from the integration of data obtained from various self-relevant sources and related interoceptive awareness, automatically activate the DMN that facilitates the automatic pattern recognition. This pattern recognition is generated at the unconscious level keeping relevance to the situation. In this case, Therapist-1 sensed some hidden patterns particularly emotional distress, apprehension, and hesitation in the client when discussing her feelings and thoughts toward the parents and the reason for excessive aggression toward them, during clinical interactions. This generates the feeling of "*something else is there*" in Therapist-1. This experience in a therapeutic session kindles a feeling almost intuitively. This instantaneous negative affect aroused from the apprehension of "*something else is there*" acted as a warning bell to the therapist (Otto & Greenway, 2016) that guided the Therapist-1 toward searching and recognizing the possible patterns of psychopathology underlying the client's sense of helplessness and fear. In the session, the therapist sensed the actual reason for the client's symptom manifestation without knowing its exact content. However, it was during temporary pauses between the sessions through the self-reflection process that the intuitive understanding of the therapist hinted at the possibility of exploitation or abuse. With a gradual progression of the sessions, the history of abuse was confirmed by the client also. So, this pattern recognition is not devoid of knowledge but rather develops from experiential knowledge-based nodes of the associative process of thinking. On the other hand, in therapy, a positive affect on the client might signal the therapist to "go-ahead" with their intuitive experience and it may benefit therapeutic outcomes as it happens in the case of decision-making in any other field like entrepreneurship (Otto & Greenway, 2016).

The study participant (Therapist-3) also stated that in a sexual abuse case "*sixth sense develops*", this sense develops from different pattern recognitions, mainly, the client's facial expressions, intonations, or the way the client modulates his voice ending up in concealing information, which enlightens the therapist with the feeling that "*something is missing*". This sixth sense helps the therapist to attenuate information, which the client willingly or unwillingly is unable to disclose. This process probably helps the therapist to acknowledge clients' non-verbal gestures, which act as cues that probably encourage intuitive decision-making during therapy situations. In line with our study findings, Hassani et al. (2016) also revealed that the nurses who participated in their study represented their professional understanding as a sixth-sense feeling that comes when they work with patients. They comprehended intuition as a sixth-sense feeling. Further, the therapeutic alliance helps to establish a relationship based on trust and provides a sense of collaboration between the patient and the therapist (Greenson, 1965). The patient, on the other hand, experiences the therapist as one non-threatening agent, who enables them to follow the therapist's perspective.

Experiencing intuition in therapeutic process

In a therapeutic session, it is common for therapists to experience a gut-level feeling about a client, although not knowing the basis or source of their knowledge that encourages therapists to self-reflect and explore their personal thoughts and feelings within their professional roles. This conscious awareness helps both the therapist and the client to consider the problem from a new perspective to make the best decisions during therapy.

To explore the clinical intuition phenomenon, it is necessary to understand how participants define and view intuition. Participants expressed that they didn't know how to express this phenomenon and had difficulty in finding the appropriate words to articulate a definition of intuition. Rather they opt to give descriptions of intuition. Therapists explained intuition in different ways based on their own experience of it. Therapist-1 stated that "*A flow develops automatically, not being aware of how this flow or unstructured things arise in therapeutic situation*". Therapist-2 said "*It's really hard to define because it's so mingled with our own experiences...and our unconscious thinking*", and stated it as "*an Aha feeling*". Therapist-3 defined "Intuition" (the term she used herself) as basically "*clinical eye*". "*It is a curiosity to know what else and what could have happened*". It was further illustrated by Therapist-3 as it is like an implicit network which develops from the acquisition of information which helps us to predict things and facilitate our thinking. Perhaps it is intuition. It gives us the sensation of mismatch and missing something. "Intuition" develops from one's existing knowledge base which is gained from academic knowledge, years of experience, and also develops from years of clinical practice. Sharpe (1938) explained that our unconscious has a repository of memories and experiences, which may have been forgotten but have never been lost and this intuitive knowledge is derived from experiential knowledge. In therapy, intuitive information may prove significant in conceptualizing cases and developing interventions (Jeffrey & Stone Fish, 2011).

Simultaneous intuitive insight experience between therapist and client

In clinical practice, the therapist develops an implicit level of relationships with clients that has a great impact on the therapeutic process. In a psychotherapeutic setting, both therapist and client share intense emotions, mutual understanding, and empathy. This involvement facilitates a spontaneous intuitive experience between the client and the therapist.

In qualitative research, it is important to evaluate the researcher paradigm. In this study, the first author's personal reflexivity shed light on her intuitive experiences in a clinical setting. When the first author reflected on one of her interactions with a client, she recalled a session during which she sensed simultaneous intuitive experiences with the client in the clinical setting. In the clinical session, a lady, aged 42 years (case example-2), married, housewife, and having two children came with the chief complaints of headache, low energy, sleeplessness, no interest in pleasurable activities, irritability, and low mood, for a duration of almost more than two years. She was diagnosed with a persistent depressive disorder by a psychiatrist and psychologist according to the Diagnostic and Statistical Manual of Mental Disorder-5. (DSM-5; American Psychiatric Association, 2013). The case history was taken in the first session, but there was no clear explanation for symptom manifestations. During the psychometric testing, the Thematic Apperception Test (TAT) (Bellak, 1954) was administered. In the 13MF card of TAT (heterosexual relationship card), findings revealed attachment conflicts with opposite-sex figures and emotional turmoil in past romantic relationships. Immediately following the response to 13MF card, the client suddenly makes eye contact with the therapist (first author) for a few seconds and blushes uncomfortably, it appears as if the client is suddenly aware of the reasons for her inner conflicts. This non-verbal communication between the therapist and the client simultaneously enlightens sudden intuitive insight in them about the root cause of the client's problems. Affective engrossment during the psychometric testing creates a flow state in the client which intuitively guides both the therapist and the client toward the client's emotional distress (Marks-Tarlow, 2014c). This state facilitates self-reflection and guides her toward the personal discovery of her own experiential knowledge and the reason for her emotional distress. This shared flow state helps the client and the therapist (first author) to discover the inner conflicts that result from the client's inclination toward her past romantic relationship and the reason for dissatisfaction in the present marital relationship. The non-judgmental environment, mutual understanding, and empathy facilitate the active engrossment of intense emotions resulting in shared moments of flow between therapist and client (Riva et al., 2016). Consequently, both the client and the therapist gain an intuitive understanding of the client's conflict. Flow can be considered as a shared experience when it is developed in more than one person simultaneously in a situation (Aube et al., 2014; Delle Fave & Bassi, 2009), a state in which "things are *clicking* or in *sync*" and wherein everything seems to come naturally.

According to the Interpersonal Synchrony (In-Sync) Model of psychotherapy, alliance emerges from the coupling of the neural activity of the patient and therapist (Koole & Tschacher, 2016) justifying the notion that intuitive understanding of others' emotions in psychotherapy may be facilitated by the integrated activity of the affective empathy system of MNS and cognitive empathy system of ToM and the DMN network (Li et al., 2014; Walter, 2012). In psychotherapy, states shared between the client and therapist occur via synchrony, and this mechanism underlies emotion transmission, affective reciprocal exchange, physiological linkage, and empathy (Koole & Tschacher, 2016). A case study revealed that in a therapeutic session when simultaneous cardiac activity was recorded using a sensor attached to the chest of the therapist and the client, the cardiac patterns dynamically changed during the session. However, cardiac activity becomes synchronized mainly during rapport building and empathetic interaction (Kodama et al., 2018).

Further, Hasson et al. (2012) stated that the implicit visual, auditory, and tactile nonverbal emotional transmissions shared face-to-face between two right brains communicating at ultra-rapid rates. Schore (1994, 2012) in the review study stated that in "heightened affective moments" the empathic therapist follows the patient's affect, and rapidly shifts out of the left brain into a right brain state of evenly suspended attention during therapeutic interaction. The clinician's right orbitofrontal cortex implicitly monitors the patient's changing emotions (Schore, 1994). This way, the clinician with years of experience intuitively responds to the patient's moment-to-moment shifts in emotional arousal and affective states during therapeutic interaction effortlessly without even conscious awareness. In line with this discussion, a functional near-infrared spectroscopy (fNIRS) investigation was done by Zhang and her colleagues (2018) on a patient's and a therapist's brain functioning during a face-to-face psychotherapy session in the laboratory. During the session, increased cortical blood flow (hemoglobin oxygenation) and interpersonal brain synchronization of the right temporoparietal junction were evident in both the clinician's and the patient's brains. This increased right-lateralized interbrain synchronization was related to subjective ratings of the affective bond or positive personal attachments between dyads. Therapists reported being attentive to "moment to moment cues" of emotional expression and body posture of the client and offered emotional feedback to the client. So, interbrain synchronization plays an essential role in building up a therapeutic alliance which promotes an intuitive understanding of the client's conflict with the therapist. Another review study postulated that high Interpersonal Synchrony during therapeutic interaction promotes positive therapeutic outcomes (Sened et al., 2022) and symptom reductions (Bilek et al., 2017). An fMRI study (Bilek et al., 2017) during the performance of a joint attention interaction task, revealed lower synchronized neural coupling in right temporoparietal junctions (rTPJ) in the dyads of borderline personality disorder patients (BPD)-healthy participants (HP) as compared to HP dyads. However, in the remission phase, while doing a similar task, the BPD-HP dyads' synchrony of neural coupling was at par with that of the HP dyads in the rTPJ, the region crucial for ToM ability. It indicates that the psychotherapeutic sessions for extended periods of time facilitate inter-brain synchrony between the therapist and the patients by enhancing neural plasticity in the patients that transfers gradually in other interpersonal relationships, eventually resulting in symptom reduction (Bilek et al., 2017; Sened et al., 2022).

Also, Therapist-1 shared some clinical experiences of spontaneous intuition experience that develops between therapist and client simultaneously. In a clinical session, a couple came to Therapist-1 who was undergoing in-vitro fertilization (IVF) treatment but failed thrice to conceive a child (case example-3). During one of the sessions, Therapist-1 suddenly, without any prior planning shared a personal experience regarding adoption where her close family member went for adoption and they are now satisfied with the decision. In this particular moment, the idea suddenly "*clicked*" the therapist and the client simultaneously. The utterance of this experience by the therapist might be based on self-reflections which has developed in response to the client's conflicting situation through an associative process after gathering information in the course of the discussion related to the client's pregnancy-related problem. When the therapist narrated the example, she mentioned it unintentionally, but it "*clicked*" the client spontaneously. Thereafter, the client decided to go for adoption instantly, which the couple had avoided initially. So, this client's inability to consider alternative solutions and changing the response from non-acceptance to acceptance regarding the adoption process can also be discussed using Hull's theory of drive reduction.

Hull believed behavior occurs in response to "drives". The reduction of the drive acts as a reinforcement for that behavior. When the goal of the drive is attained, the drive is reduced. This constitutes reinforcement of the behaviors that lead to the drive reduction and ultimately attaining a behavior through creating an excitatory potential. Thus, Hull developed a theory of learning that could be expressed mathematically, he developed a "formula" to explain and understand human behavior scientifically (Hergenhahn & Olson, 1997). Hull believed that this formula could account for all behaviors:

The Mathematical Deductive Theory of Behavior is as follows:

$$\mathbf{sEr} = (\mathbf{sHr} \times \mathbf{D} \times \mathbf{K} \times \mathbf{V}) - (\mathbf{sIr} + \mathbf{Ir}) \pm \mathbf{sOr}$$

where, sEr = reaction potential; D = drive; sHr = habit strength; K = incentive motivation; V = clarity of the stimulus (stimulus dynamics); sIr = conditioned inhibition; Ir = reactive inhibition; sOr =other identified variables.

In this particular example the couple did not have any option of adoption in their mind initially but the spontaneous desire to adopt a child emerged after a few therapy sessions following the therapist's abrupt sharing of personal adoption experience. It can also be explained from Hull's drive reduction theory. In this example, we can consider the need for satisfaction of maternal instinct as the inner drive (**D**) of the female client and at the same time she had the fear to face the distress of pregnancy. The Habit strength (**sHr**) of intense desire to be a mother reaches the apex due to own maternal instinct interacting with the societal belief that motherhood is crucial for being a complete woman. When this positive desire to be a mother that was hindered by the apprehension of pregnancy-related complications, was removed by the decision to adopt a baby, this relief of anxiety acted as a Reinforcement (**k**) and facilitated the desire to be a mother by overcoming the inhibiting factors (**Ir**); and strengthened the client's acceptance of adoption process. Moreover, when the therapist shares a personal experience which gives clarity to the situation that can be considered "V" as Par Hull's theory.

The therapeutic process ignited the inner drive that helped the client to overcome the inhibition, creating excitatory potential to the desire of satisfying her inner drive of maternal instinct. The "adoption" idea clicked instantly with the client and created a "shared flow state" between the therapist and client which gave immense satisfaction to both. This decision is the outcome of the intuitive process that played a role in the therapeutic session. Intuition is a very efficient way of decision-making (Slovic et al., 2007) though it is based on a heuristic process (Tversky & Kahneman, 1975), and is well-accepted in literature for efficient decision-making in different domains of life during complex, uncertain situations demanding rapid decision-making. This "Moment of experience" where things are *clicking* or in *sync*" at an implicit level helps the client to resolve the emotional turmoil within the unconscious level, which promotes therapeutic progress. Participant explained this spontaneous simultaneous intuitive thinking as an "*Aha! Moment*" and it gives a feeling of assurance to the therapist that it will work for this client.

How do therapists become aware of the intuitive experience?

Vaughan (1979) discussed intuition as a source of knowledge that can present itself at various levels of awareness: physical, emotional, and mental.

- Intuition at the physical level consists of gut feelings or other bodily sensations.
- The knowledge received intuitively at the emotional level comes through sensitivity to one's own and others' feelings.
- Mental intuition is an ability to make in-the-moment decisions and conclusions based upon associative knowledge with partial acknowledgment in the declarative plane knowledge or without evident rational thought. Intuition on the mental level often comes into awareness through mental images.

Therapists in this study expressed intuitive awareness in therapeutic interactions in the following ways:

Therapist-1 expressed that during a therapeutic session when the intuitive feeling is experienced both by the client and the therapist simultaneously, she felt internal satisfaction. She further explained that this feeling of simultaneous intuitive insight where both can connect with the problem and reach the resolution with this gives an immense satisfaction like "*when one eats an ice-cream on a hot summer day*". Therapist-2 stated that

"It's like someone telling from inside to go with this unknown feeling, it's like multiple modalities working together like eyes, nose, and ear working simultaneously. At this moment I don't miss any information and consider every minute detail, it helps to maintain the flow".

Therapist-3 explained that "*when we get information, we start to visualize gradually the information in our mind. When a mismatch occurs with the visual representation of this information we search for missing links*". So, the therapist experiences these unknown intuitive feelings with all the visual, auditory, and kinaesthetic modalities at the physical level and also with the mental level of absorption in the therapeutic process. However, through self-reflection, the therapist becomes aware of these unknown intuitive experiences.

Experiencing intuition: Types of cases where intuition was felt strongly

All three therapists specified a common response regarding the specific type of clinical cases where they strongly experienced intuition. They mentioned that they felt the clinical intuition mainly in critical cases of child abuse, self-harming, substance abuse, and marital disharmony. Jeffrey and Stone Fish (2011) and Carson (1999) reported that intuitions play an important role in marriage and family therapy. It provides a unique source of relation-based information and guidance that may be difficult to reach through other ways of knowing. The therapists rely mostly on their intuition when seeking to understand problematic relationships and facilitate change in family systems.

In this study, Therapist-1 sensed a strong feeling of "*something else*" when an eight-year-old girl came with a behavioral problem like opposing parents, arguing, showing aggression, and temper tantrums (case example-1). The excessive aggression of the child towards her parents through both verbal and non-verbal gestures provided the therapist with the feeling of "*something else*". Finally, in the fifth session with further exploration of this negative emotion, the client shared that "*I don't like the way my father loves me*". Her mother also knew that the client's father abused her, but didn't do anything to stop this incident. Similarly, Therapist-3 also shared her experience that in a particular case where the child showed passive aggression toward her parents, verbally presented her parents as perfect, cooperative, and loving. The therapist felt some mismatch between the verbatim and the behavior. She felt that there must be something and said "*inconsistency in the findings or mismatch in the calculations*". This searching guides her toward an intuitive feeling. Later in the fourth session, it was revealed that negative emotions toward parents developed as parents has failed to protect their child from sexual abuse.

Loye (1983) describes types of intuition: cognitive inference that is "rapid and subliminal visual and verbal cues contribute to a final decision", and Gestalt intuition that is a process in which missing data and gaps in information are detected and hidden relationships are identified. So, in the case examples, the participant's verbatim like "*something is missing*", "*something else*", and "*picking up the cues*" indicates the important role of intuition. This gestalt intuition helps them to identify the true nature of the problem or conflicts in the client. In challenging cases when searching is required due to pattern mismatch, the therapist sensed the intuition strongly. They unconsciously pick up the subliminal cues in the clinical setting which guides them to understand the dynamicity of the client's problem. In this way, intuition helps to clarify problems, identify feelings, read subtle, nonverbal behaviors, and pick up on what is not even communicated by clients (Carson, 1999). These experiences of therapists indicate that in a therapeutic process, when searching is required mostly in case of pattern mismatch, the therapist sensed the intuition strongly. They unconsciously identify the cues in the clinical setting which guides them to understand the dynamicity of the client's problem. The type of problem clients come with also influences intuition thinking.

Clinical expertise and decision-making in psychotherapy

Another important theme that came out in clinical decision-making is "clinical expertise" which is considered to be one of the important factors of clinical intuition. Participants stated that years of experience and expertise help formulate the knowledge base to make spontaneous decisions. We cannot totally deny our feelings of "*something else*". But as symptoms cannot come "*out of the blue*", similarly, our therapeutic stances also cannot come "*out of the blue*". It should be differentiated from impulsive decision-making which directs one to faulty decision-making. Similarly, deliberate thinking can also be biased and erroneous if it is used without considering the other important subtle information or cues during the psychotherapeutic process. Experiential learning (Benner et al., 2008) from particular cases is the foundation of good clinical judgment and clinical wisdom.

In the book "*From Novice to Expert*", Benner (2001) explained that novices (who are in a training period) have little experience in clinical decision-making or critical analysis, and rely mostly on guidelines and rules for direction. The expert can make decisions based on both abstract and concrete information, which has been obtained through individual experience and skill acquisition. Converting data and information into knowledge and wisdom usually requires years of clinical practice when one is overwhelmed with multiple sources of information (Mayer-Schönberger & Cukier, 2013). Experts are more competent to differentiate relevant from irrelevant cues and easily form intercorrelations between cues. When one has a lot of experience or expertise in certain area, the brain has more information to match from the current experience against prior experience, this makes the intuitions more reliable.

Rumelhart (1989) proposed a feed-forward parallel distributed network of information processing. The network consists of three units—input, hidden, and output units. Each of these units projects onto the other through weighted connections. Although the initial connections may be weaker in strength, through training such connections strengthen over time. Decision-making will be precise if the distance between the target and current output activation is reduced. People process information in a parallel fashion, matching the present experience with previously laid down patterns of related experiences or events and adding new information to it, enriching the existing node and creating a new node of the network. Reduction in error is related to the activation of the relevant nodes and increase in error is linked to decrement in the inter-connectedness among the related nodes during information processing. Similarly, a novice therapist when start to acquaint themselves with all the symptoms of disorders and to discriminate between disorders, the therapist is also forming connections. In example-1, in the initial phase, the connections are weak and random which leads the novice therapist to make less precise clinical decision-making (shown in Figure 15.1). However, when the therapist acquires expertise, such connections become strong which develops gradually as the therapist gathers extensive clinical experience (shown in Figure 15.2).

The hidden layer facilitates the smooth transmission of activated input units to the output layers making it possible to reach a conclusion or decision. These hidden units comprise a large set of parallel distributed information which combines together and associations are formed amongst sets of information. With experience, the therapist gradually learns to identify mismatches in patterns of activation and uses intuition to draw upon previous experience and knowledge to make clinical decisions to make less erroneous clinical decisions. In a previous example of a child abuse case, it can be understood that when the therapist is a novice, she is able to connect the presenting complaints with obvious probable factors—temper tantrums could result due to ODD/conduct disorder (CD) features, or excessive parental pressure, etc. (shown in Figure 15.1). Although they are able to identify the discrepancy between verbal and non-verbal cues since these patterns of activations are weak and random the clinician misses the hidden layers of the

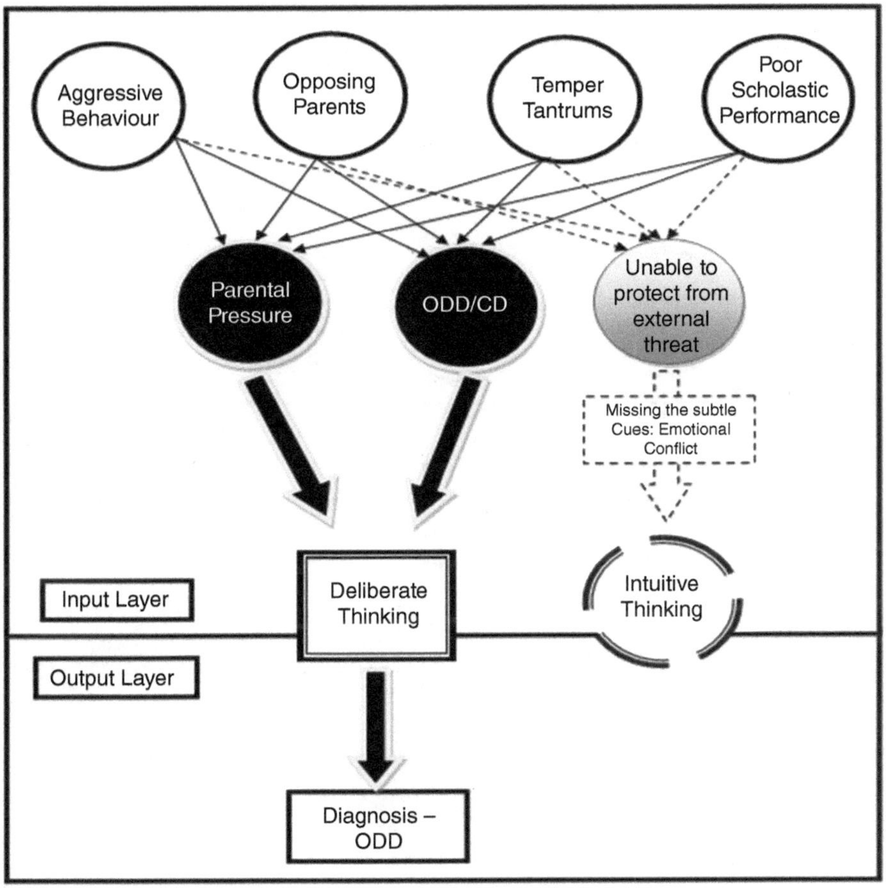

Figure 15.1 Connectionist model of clinical decision-making for Novice Therapist for a case example-1 depicting two units—input and output. Dotted lines indicate weaker connections and solid lines indicate strengthened connections in information processing.

* Oppositional defiant disorder (ODD) and conduct disorder (CD).

client's problematic behavior which a therapist with years of expertise reaches easily and makes the precise and accurate decision-making, which might remain unrecognizable to a novice therapist.

As the therapist gains more experiential knowledge with training, the activation pattern of nodes becomes more stable (shown in Figure 15.2). The therapist is able to intuitively connect between experiential associations with a knowledge base, decrement the activation of nodes for irrelevant information through efficient pruning, and reach a precise decision. In the example (shown in Figure 15.2), the therapist with expertise can easily link the

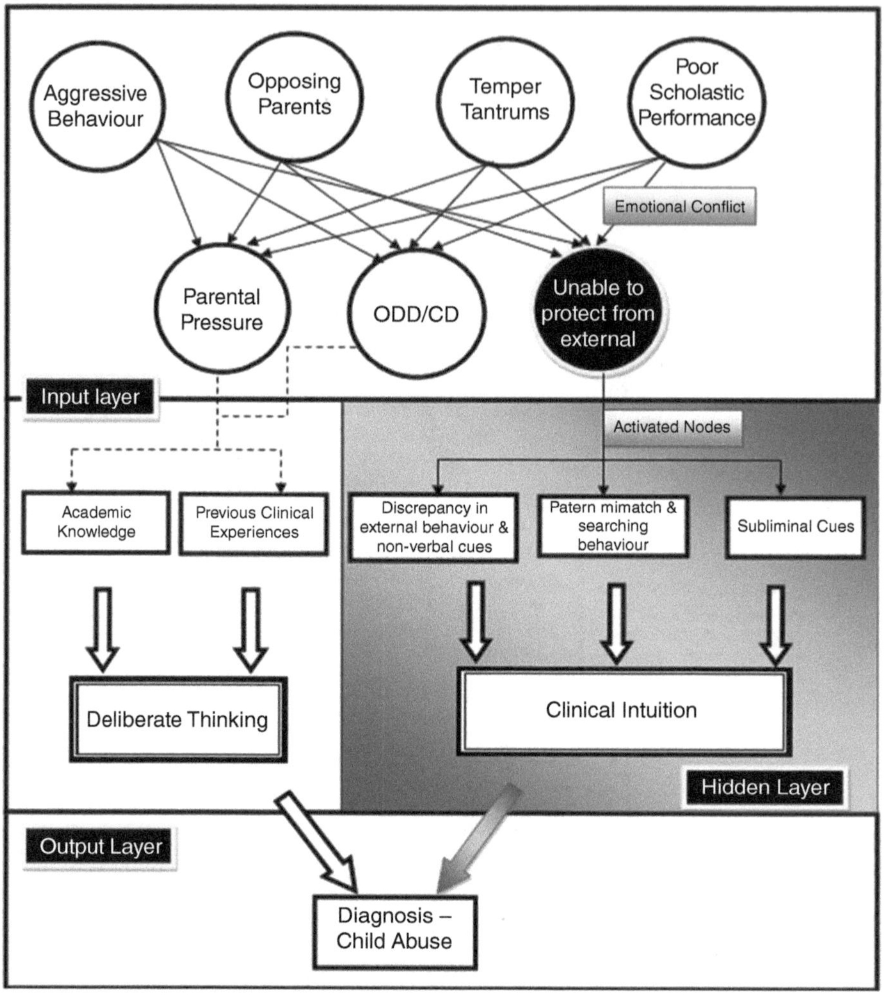

Figure 15.2 Connectionist model of clinical decision-making for Expert Therapist for case example-1, depicting three units—input, hidden, and output units. Dotted lines indicate weaker connections and solid lines indicate strengthened connections during information processing.

* Oppositional defiant disorder (ODD) and conduct disorder (CD).

aggressive behavior toward the parent with temper tantrums, and poor scholastic performance to the parents' inability to protect the child from external threats and to make the diagnosis of child abuse. This stability in pattern activation leads to the development of expertise in the therapist.

Further, with experience, an expert can gather easily subliminal messages. Subliminal messages exert great influences on one's thoughts and behavior

(Hassin, 2013; Ruch et al., 2016; van Gaal et al., 2012). Subliminal stimuli are signals below the absolute threshold level of human conscious perception (Elgendi et al., 2018). The human unconscious can perform various high-level cognitive functions that enable decision processes to benefit from subliminal messages (Hassin, 2013; van Gaal et al., 2012). Through subliminal received information, an expert can semantically integrate and rapidly store unconscious pieces of novel information into long-lasting associative memories that can be retrieved if it is relevant to the context of clinical decision-making. In line with our discussion, an fMRI study (Hruska et al., 2017) was done on a medical practitioner where they observed activation of similar brain areas in both medical students (novices) and practicing gastroenterologists (experts), but differences in hemispheric activation while they diagnose clinical cases. For diagnosing difficult clinical cases, novice clinicians have shown greater activations in the left anterior temporal cortex and left ventral lateral prefrontal cortex whereas expert clinicians had greater activations in the right dorsal lateral, right ventral lateral prefrontal cortex, and right parietal cortex. However, no hemispheric differences in activation were observed between novices and experts to diagnose easy clinical cases. The study points out that novices' activations of left hemisphere neural regions are associated with factual rule-based knowledge and retrieving semantic representations from memory. Whereas, in expert's right hemisphere activation in neural regions associated with experiential knowledge, supports abstract or holistic processing of information.

Moreover, intuition in clinical practices is closely related to empathetic feeling, the ability to pick up on others' emotions, whether conscious or nonconscious, expressed or latent (Marks-Tarlow, 2014c). In a therapeutic setting, the accuracy of clinical intuition depends on the therapist's inclination toward the kind of empathetic matching—whether it has a cognitive or an emotional aspect toward the client's unregulated emotional state. In this study, Therapist-2 revealed that during the initial days of therapeutic interaction, she scolded a teenage client for hitting her mother. In the course of clinical practice, Therapist-2 realized that she must not have acted in that way and could have dealt with the client more efficiently. During the therapy session, Therapist-2 developed emotional empathy for the client's mother, which prompted scolding behavior. Emotional empathy is useful in therapy for understanding the subjective experience of the client's state. However, novice therapists with less affect monitoring ability may have difficulty separating themselves from others' overwhelming emotional states which might develop counter-transference in therapeutic sessions. This affective state would often upsurge their emotional weightage and lead to emotional burnout, personal distress, and impulsive behavior. Utilizing cognitive resources to adopt the other's perspective, recognition of client's experiences from their point of view using theory of mind, better interoception for intuitive understanding, and efficient monitoring of affective content for decision-making requires cognitive empathy (Marks-Tarlow, 2014c), which a therapist acquires through years of clinical experiences. A neuroimaging study revealed that the DMN plays a significant role in the self-modulation of cognitive and emotional empathetic states (Oliveira Silva et al., 2018). The study observed a positive correlation between cognitive empathy assessed from "The Interpersonal Reactivity Index" (IRI scale) and activation of the bilateral superior medial frontal cortex nodes of the DMN. However, a negative correlation was found between emotional empathy and the same bilateral superior medial frontal cortex nodes of DMN. This finding revealed that the nodes of DMN, particularly the superior medial frontal cortex, are involved in regulating emotional reactivity facilitating cognitive empathic processes (Oliveira Silva et al., 2018). Consequently, an expert therapist with efficient modulation of DMN nodes is likely to develop cognitive empathy, allowing to maintain a distinction between the client's feelings and self-related feelings, which enhances the chances of accuracy of intuitive decision-making in psychotherapy.

Conclusion

The current study suggests that therapeutic decisions are influenced by several factors which include deliberate and analytic thinking such as theoretical orientation, research evidence, client characteristics, therapist schema, and professional expertise. It is equally important to explore the unknown to develop a therapeutic alliance, and for better therapeutic outcomes. The blending of theoretical information with the associative intuitive process gives direction to therapeutic progress. Clinical intuition emerged from an engrossed state during the moment-to-moment interactions between therapist and client, which creates a synchronized state between them, where everything comes automatically without conscious awareness and a natural flow of emotion, and empathetic bonding develops. Moreover, in seasoned therapists' knowledge-based nodes become activated spontaneously leading to clinical intuitive insight through parallel processing. In psychotherapy, it is crucial for both therapist and client to be aware of one's intuitive feelings and bring implicit level thoughts and feelings into the conscious plane through self-reflection to develop a better perspective of conflicting thoughts and situations. The present study will help in understanding the new emerging concepts of intuition in psychotherapy from a broader and holistic perspective that will promote better clinical decision-making skills in future therapeutic practices.

References

American Psychiatric Association. (2013). *Diagnostic and statistical manual of mental disorders* (5th ed.). https://doi.org/10.1176/appi.books.9780890425596

American Psychological Association, Presidential Task Force on Evidence-Based Practice. (2006). Evidence-based practice in psychology. *American Psychologist*, *61*(4), 271–285. https://doi.org/10.1037/0003-066x.61.4.271

Arya, P. (2020). Case study methodology of qualitative research: Key attributes and navigating the conundrums in its application. *Sociological Bulletin*, *70*(1), 94–110. https://doi.org/10.1177/0038022920970318

Aube, C., Brunelle, E., & Rousseau, V. (2014). Flow experience and team performance: The role of team goal commitment and information exchange. *Motivation and Emotion*, *38*,120–130. https://doi.org/10.2139/ssrn.3464409

Bar, M., Tootell, R. B. H., Schacter, D. L., Greve, D. N., Fischl, B., Mendola, J. D., Rosen, B. R., & Dale, A. M. (2001). Cortical mechanisms specific to explicit visual object recognition. *Neuron*, *29*(2), 529–535. https://doi.org/10.1016/s0896-6273(01)00224-0

Bellak, L. (1954). *The thematic apperception test and the children's apperception test in clinical use*. Grune & Stratton.

Benner, P., Hughes, R. G., & Sutphen, M. (2008). Clinical reasoning, decision making, and action: Thinking critically and clinically. In R. G. Hughes (Ed.). *Patient safety and quality: An evidence-based handbook for nurses*. Agency for Healthcare Research and Quality. https://www.ncbi.nlm.nih.gov/books/NBK2643/

Benner, P. E. (2001). *From novice to expert: Excellence and power in clinical nursing practice*. Prentice Hall.

Berne, E. (1949). The nature of intuition. *Psychiatric Quarterly*, 23, 203–226. https://doi.org/10.1007/BF01563116

Białecka-Pikul, M., Kołodziejczyk, A., & Bosacki, S. (2017). Advanced theory of mind in adolescence: Do age, gender and friendship style play a role? *Journal of Adolescence*, 56, 145–156. https://doi.org/10.1016/j.adolescence.2017.02.009.

Bilek, E., Stößel, G., Schäfer, A., Clement, L., Ruf, M., Robnik, L., Neukel, C., Tost, H., Kirsch, P., & Meyer-Lindenberg, A. (2017). State-dependent cross-brain information flow in borderline personality disorder. *JAMA Psychiatry*, *74*(9), 949–957. https://doi.org/10.1001/jamapsychiatry.2017.1682

Bingham, C. B., & Eisenhardt, K. M. (2011). Rational heuristics: The "simple rules" that strategists learn from process experience. *Strategic Management Journal*, *32*(13), 1437–1464. https://doi.org/10.1002/smj.965

Bove, S., & Rizzi, M. (2009). Listening to intuition: Reflections on unconscious processes in the therapeutic relationship. *Transactional Analysis Journal*, 39(1), 39–45. https://doi.org/10.1177/036215370903900105

Buckner, R. L., Andrews-Hanna, J. R., & Schacter, D. L. (2008). The brain's default network: Anatomy, function, and relevance to disease. *Annals of the New York Academy of Sciences*, *1124*, 1–38. https://doi.org/10.1196/annals.1440.011

Carson, D. K. (1999). Intuition in marital and family therapy. *Annals of the American Psychotherapy Association*, 2, (5), 4–10.

Charmaz, K. (2006). *Constructing grounded theory: A practical guide through qualitative analysis*. Sage.

Chen, L., & Hsiao, J. (2014). Right hemisphere dominance in nonconscious processing. *J Vision*, *14*, (10), 1313. https://doi.org/10.1167/14.10.1313

Clack, G. (2009). Decision making in nursing practice: A case review. *Paediatric Care*, *21*(5), 24–27. https://doi.org/10.7748/paed2009.06.21.5.24.c7078

Davey, C. G., & Harrison, B. J. (2018). The brain's center of gravity: How the default mode network helps us to understand the self. *World Psychiatry*, *17*(3), 278–279. https://doi.org/10.1002/wps.20553

Delle Fave, A., & Bassi, M. (2009). Sharing optimal experiences and promoting good community life in a multicultural society. *The Journal of Positive Psychology*, *4*(4), 280–289. https://doi.org/10.1080/17439760902933716

Edwards, S. D. (2013). Intuition as a healing modality: Historical and contemporary perspectives. *Journal of Psychology in Africa*, *23*(4), 669–673. https://doi.org/10.1080/14330237.2013.10820686

Elgendi, M., Kumar, P., Barbic, S., Howard, N., Abbott, D., & Cichocki, A. (2018). Subliminal priming – State of the art and future perspectives. *Behavioral Sciences*, *8*(6), 54. https://doi.org/10.3390/bs8060054

Fingelkurts, A. A., & Fingelkurts, A. A. (2011). Persistent operational synchrony within brain default-mode network and self-processing operations in healthy subjects. *Brain and Cognition*, *75*(2), 79–90. https://doi.org/10.1016/j.bandc.2010.11.015

Gazzaniga, M. S., Ivry, R. B., Mangun, G. R., & Gazzaniga, R. A. (2002). *Cognitive neuroscience: The biology of the mind*. W. W. Norton & Company.

Greenson, R. R. (1965). The working alliance and the transference neurosis. *The Psychoanalytic Quarterly*, *34*(2), 155–181. https://doi.org/10.1080/21674086.1965.11926343

Gyani, A., Shafran, R., Myles, P., & Rose, S. (2014). The gap between science and practice: How therapists make their clinical decisions. *Behavior Therapy*, *45*(2), 199–211. https://doi.org/10.1016/j.beth.2013.10.004

Hadamard, J. (1945). *The mathematician's mind: The psychology of invention in the mathematical field*. Princeton University Press

Hassani, P., Abdi, A., Jalali, R., & Salari, N. (2016). Use of intuition by critical care nurses: A phenomenological study. *Advances in Medical Education and Practice*, *7*, 65–71. https://doi.org/10.2147/AMEP.S100324

Hassin, R. R. (2013). Yes, it can: On the functional abilities of the human unconscious. *Perspectives on Psychological Science*, *8*(2), 195–207. https://doi.org/10.1177/1745691612460684

Hasson, U., Ghazanfar, A. A., Galantucci, B., Garrod, S., & Keysers, C. (2012). Brain-to-brain coupling: A mechanism for creating and sharing a social world. *Trends in Cognitive Sciences*, *16*(2), 114–121. https://doi.org/10.1016/j.tics.2011.12.007

Hergenhahn, B. R., & Olson, M. H. (1997). Clark Leonard Hull. In *An Introduction to theories of learning* (5th ed.). Prentice Hall.

Higgs, J., & Jones, M. (2008). Clinical decision making and multiple problem spaces. In J. Higgs, & M. Jones (Eds.), *Clinical reasoning in the health professions* (pp. 3–17). Butterworth Heineman Ltd.

Horr, N. K., Braun, C., & Volz, K. G. (2014). Feeling before knowing why: The role of the orbitofrontal cortex in intuitive judgments-An MEG study. *Cognitive, Affective & Behavioral Neuroscience*, *14*(4), 1271–1285. https://doi.org/10.3758/s13415-014-0286-7

Hruska, P., Hecker, K. G., Coderre, S., McLaughlin, K., Cortese, F., Doig, C., Beran, T., Wright, B., & Krigolson, O. (2017). Hemispheric activation differences in novice and expert clinicians during clinical decision making. *Advances in Health Sciences Education*, 22(4), 1047–1047. https://doi.org/10.1007/s10459-017-9787-9

Jeffrey, A. J., & Stone Fish, L. (2011). Clinical intuition: A qualitative study of its use and experience among marriage and family therapists. *Contemporary Family Therapy*, *33*(4), 348–363. https://doi.org/10.1007/s10591-011-9161-7

Jellema, T., Macinska, S. T., O'Connor, R. J., & Skodova, T. (2024). Social intuition: Behavioral and neurobiological considerations. *Frontiers in Psychology*, *15*, 1336363. https://doi.org/10.3389/fpsyg.2024.1336363

Kahneman, D. (2011). *Thinking, fast and slow*. Farrar, Straus and Giroux.

Kirschenbaum, H., & Henderson, V. L. (Eds.). (1989). *The Carl Rogers reader*. Houghton Mifflin.

Klein, G. A. (1995). A recognition-primed decision (RPD) model of rapid decision making. In G. A. Klein, J. Orasanu, R. Calderwood, & C. E. Zsambok (Eds.), *Decision making in action. Models and methods* (2nd ed., pp. 138–148). Ablex Publishing.

Kodama, K., Tanaka, S., Shimizu, D., Hori, K.& Matsui, H. (2018). Heart rate synchrony in psychological counseling: A case study. *Psychology*, *9*, 1858–1874. https://doi.org/10.4236/psych.2018.97108

Koole, S. L., & Tschacher, W. (2016). Synchrony in psychotherapy: A review and an integrative framework for the therapeutic alliance. *Frontiers in Psychology*, *7*, 862. https://doi.org/10.3389/fpsyg.2016.00862

Li, W., Mai, X., & Liu, C. (2014). The default mode network and social understanding of others: What do brain connectivity studies tell us. *Frontiers in Human Neuroscience*, *8*, 74. https://doi.org/10.3389/fnhum.2014.00074

Loye, D. (1983). *The sphinx and the rainbow: Brain, mind and future vision*. Bantam Books.

Malhotra, S., & Sahoo, S. (2017). Rebuilding the brain with psychotherapy. *Indian Journal of Psychiatry*, *59*(4), 411–419. https://doi.org/10.4103/0019-5545.217299

Marks-Tarlow, T. (2014a) The interpersonal neurobiology of clinical intuition. *Smith College Studies in Social Work*, 84(2–3), 219–236.https://doi.org/10.1080/00377317.2014.923712

Marks-Tarlow, T. (2014b). *Awakening clinical intuition: An experiential workbook for psychotherapists*. W.W. Norton & Company.

Marks-Tarlow, T. (2014c). The nonlinear dynamics of clinical intuition. In F. F. Orsucci, & N. Sala (Eds.), *Chaos and complexity letters*, (pp. 147–170). Nova Science Publishers, Inc.

Mathon, B. (2013). Les neurones miroirs: de l'anatomie aux implications physiopathologiques et thérapeutiques [Mirror neurons: From anatomy to pathophysiological and therapeutic implications]. *Revue neurologique*, *169*(4), 285–290. https://doi.org/10.1016/j.neurol.2012.10.008

Mayer-Schönberger, V., & Cukier, K. (2013). Big *data: A revolution that will transform how we live, work and think*. Houghton Mifflin Harcourt

Mickleborough, T. (2015). Intuition in medical practice: A reflection on Donald Schön's reflective practitioner. *Medical Teacher*, *37*(10), 889–891. https://doi.org/10.3109/0142159X.2015.1078893

Molnar-Szakacs, I., & Uddin, L. Q. (2013). Self-processing and the default mode network: Interactions with the mirror neuron system. *Frontiers in Human Neuroscience*, *7*, 571. https://doi.org/10.3389/fnhum.2013.00571

Oliveira Silva, P., Maia, L., Coutinho, J., Frank, B., Soares, J. M., Sampaio, A., & Gonçalves, Ó. (2018). Empathy by default: Correlates in the brain at rest. *Psicothema*, *30*(1), 97–103. https://doi.org/10.7334/psicothema2016.366

Otto, J. S., & Greenway, P. (2016). The integrative functioning of aspects of cognitive, affective and somatic processes in the experience of intuitive style. *Personality and Individual Differences*, *88*, 129–133. https://doi.org/10.1016/j.paid.2015.08.042

Patterson, R. E., & Eggleston, R. G. (2017). Intuitive cognition. *Journal of Cognitive Engineering and Decision Making*, *11*(1), 5–22. https://doi.org/10.1177/1555343416686476.

Rajmohan, V., & Mohandas, E. (2007). Mirror neuron system. *Indian Journal of Psychiatry*, *49*(1), 66–69. https://doi.org/10.4103/0019-5545.31522

Riva, E., Freire, T., & Bassi, M. (2016). The flow experience in clinical settings: Applications in psychotherapy and mental health rehabilitation. In L. Harmat, F. Ø. Andersen, F. Ullén, J. Wright, & G. Sadlo (Eds.), *Flow experience: Empirical research and applications* (pp. 309–326). https://doi.org/10.1007/978-3-319-28634-1_19

Rizzolatti, G., & Craighero, L. (2004). The mirror-neuron system. *Annual Review of Neuroscience*, *27*, 169–192. https://doi.org/10.1146/annurev.neuro.27.070203.144230

Ruch, S., Züst, M. A., & Henke, K. (2016). Subliminal messages exert long-term effects on decision-making. *Neuroscience of Consciousness*, *2016*(1). https://doi.org/10.1093/nc/niw013

Rumelhart, D. E. (1989). The architecture of mind: A connectionist approach. In M. I. Posner (Ed.), *Foundations of cognitive science* (pp. 133–159). The MIT Press.

Sackett, D. L., Straus, S. E., Richardson, W. S., Rosenberg, W., & Haynes R. B. (2000). *Evidence-based medicine: How to practice and teach EBM* (2nd ed.). Churchill Livingstone.

Schore, A. (2011). The right brain implicit self lies at the core of psychoanalysis. *Psychoanalytic Dialogues*, *21*(1), 75–100. https://doi.org/10.1080/10481885.2011.545329.

Schore, A. N. (1994). Affect regulation the origin of the self. In *The neurobiology of emotional development*. Lawrence Erlbaum Associates, Inc.

Schore, A. N. (2012). *The science of the art of psychotherapy*. W. W. Norton & Company.

Sebastian, C. L., Fontaine, N. M. G., Bird, G., Blakemore, S.-J., De Brito, S. A., McCrory, E. J. P., & Viding, E. (2011). Neural processing associated with cognitive and affective Theory of Mind in adolescents and adults. *Social Cognitive and Affective Neuroscience*, 7(1), 53–63. https://doi.org/10.1093/scan/nsr023

Sened, H., Zilcha-Mano, S., & Shamay-Tsoory, S. (2022). Inter-brain plasticity as a biological mechanism of change in psychotherapy: A review and integrative model. *Frontiers in Human Neuroscience*, *16*. https://doi.org/10.3389/fnhum.2022.955238

Shapiro, Y., & Marks-Tarlow, T. (2021). Varieties of clinical intuition: Explicit, implicit, and nonlocal neurodynamics. *Psychoanalytic Dialogues*, *31*(3), 262–281. https://doi.org/10.1080/10481885.2021.1902744

Sharpe, E. F. (1938). *Dream analysis; A practical handbook in psychoanalysis*. W.W Norton & Co.

Slovic, P., Finucane, M. L., Peters, E., & MacGregor, D. G. (2007). The affect heuristic. *European Journal of Operational Research*, *177*(3), 1333–1352. https://doi.org/10.1016/j.ejor.2005.04.006

Standing, M. (2005). *Perceptions of clinical decision-making skills on a developmental journey from student to staff nurse*. [Doctoral dissertation, University of Kent]

Stanovich, K. E. (2010). *Decision making and rationality in the modern world*. Oxford University Press.

Tanner, C. A., Padrick, K. P., Westfall, U. E., & Putzier, D. J. (1987). Diagnostic reasoning strategies of nurses and nursing students. *Nursing Research*, *36*(6), 358–365. https://doi.org/10.1097/00006199-198711000-00010

Tversky, A., & Kahneman, D. (1975). Judgment under uncertainty: Heuristics and biases. In D. Wendt, & C. Vlek (Eds.), *Utility, probability, and human decision making* (pp. 141–162). Springer. https://doi.org/10.1007/978-94-010-1834-0_8

van Gaal, S., de Lange, F. P., & Cohen, M. X. (2012). The role of consciousness in cognitive control and decision making. *Frontiers in Human Neuroscience*, *6*, 121. https://doi.org/10.3389/fnhum.2012.00121

Vatansever, D., Menon, D. K., & Stamatakis, E. A. (2017). Default mode contributions to automated information processing. *Proceedings of the National Academy of Sciences of the United States of America*, *114*(48), 12821–12826. https://doi.org/10.1073/pnas.1710521114

Vaughan, F. E. (1979). *Awakening intuition*. Anchor Books.

Volz, K. G., & Von Cramon, D. Y. (2006). What neuroscience can tell about intuitive processes in the context of perceptual discovery. *Journal of Cognitive Neuroscience*, *18*(12), 2077–2087. https://doi.org/10.1162/jocn.2006.18.12.2077

Walter H. (2012). Social cognitive neuroscience of empathy: Concepts, circuits, and genes. *Emotion Review*, *4*, 9–17. https://doi.org/10.1177/1754073911421379

Webb, S. (2001). Some considerations on the validity of evidence-based practice in social work. *British Journal of Social Work*, *31*(1), 57–79. https://doi.org/10.1093/bjsw/31.1.57

Williams, S. (2006). Analytic intuition: A meeting place for Jung and Bion. *British Journal of Psychotherapy*, *23*(1), 83–98. https://doi.org/10.1111/j.1752-0118.2006.00010.x

Witteman, C., & Koele, P. (1999). Explaining treatment decisions. *Psychotherapy Research*, *9*(1), 100–114. https://doi.org/10.1093/ptr/9.1.100

Zhang, Y., Meng, T., Hou, Y., Pan, Y., & Hu, Y. (2018). Interpersonal brain synchronization associated with working alliance during psychological counseling. *Psychiatry Research: Neuroimaging*, *282*, 103–109. https://doi.org/10.1016/j.pscychresns.2018.09.007

Zuber, I. (2000). Patients' own problem formulations and recommendations for psychotherapy. *Journal of Psychotherapy Integration*, *10*(4), 403–414. https://doi.org/10.1023/a:1009431217143

Chapter 16

Intuition cognition balance in the capacity building of entrepreneurship

Ipsita C. Patranabis, Shrestha Chakrabarty and Sharmistha Banerjee

Introduction

Indian social structure has always considered job-oriented career planning to be a softer option rather than business. Though India has produced entrepreneurs of international fame and created multinational companies of repute, the stories of first-generation entrepreneurs mostly record intuitive stories rather than planned ones. This observation is starkly true for women entrepreneurs. Narratives on women entrepreneurs are far less recorded as compared to women working professionals in corporate India. The recent pandemic has brought forth many women who have ventured into businesses either driven by family needs, financial challenges or the need for an identity. These needs may not be listed in a hierarchical model, but they can be identified when one listens to their stories about the drivers behind their businesses. In most cases, circumstantial wants and individual requirements have triggered the development of these businesses. Hence, decision-making played a crucial role for these entrepreneurs. As work-from-anywhere gave a lot of flexibility and freedom in managing time, many working professionals started exploring newer avenues where they could have independence of responsibility and authority and pursue their passion in an economically gainful manner. Against this backdrop, this chapter highlights the need for effective decision-making in all stages of business, from the inception of ideas to their execution, stabilization and growth. The current study attempts to explore how decision-making styles (intuitive and or cognitive) influence entrepreneurial abilities and consecutively result in business growth.

Review of literature

In *Entrepreneurial Decision-Making*, Veronica Gustafsson (2004) mentioned that according to Shane and Venkataraman (2000), the core concept in any entrepreneurial venture is the identification of opportunity. According to Casson (1982), opportunities can be defined as situations in which the transaction of goods and services can be done in a profitable way. Suitable SWOT

DOI: 10.4324/9781003377757-19

(strength, weakness, opportunity, threats) analysis of the business environment is done by an effective entrepreneur who has the right competencies not only to identify an opportunity but also to evaluate the potential of a product or service in the market and to simultaneously explore and exploit the market opportunity. According to past researchers, entrepreneurs may differ in their ability to identify a business potential, so, decision-making skills, which entrepreneurs demonstrate to create and exploit an opportunity, is an issue worth researching (Gustafsson, 2004). Additionally, Mintzberg and Westley (2001) suggested that the way entrepreneurs collect and process data for a prospect reflects their cognitive or rational approach while the distinguishing features of potential entrepreneurs as compared to others mostly reflect their intuitive styles of decision-making. They also mentioned that preferences toward decision-making style may differ but in most occasions, the approaches are not mutually exclusive. With decision-making being an integral part of the entrepreneurship process, the current study explores the relationship between entrepreneurship ability in business advancement and decision-making style. Decision-making is vital for all entrepreneurs as the entrepreneurial process involves a lot of risk and uncertainty. Therefore, behavioral researchers have suggested that a strong motivational trigger is needed to drive such processes where potential entrepreneurs are stimulated to pursue opportunities with persistence and to intensify their efforts for the sustenance of their businesses (Bartol & Martin, 1998). Thus, passion in business is what differentiates one entrepreneur from another. In this fast-changing competitive business environment, prompt action always gives the advantage of a first mover. The present environment relies on the speed of decision-making as a response to environmental dynamism (Baum & Wally, 2003; Eisenhardt & Martin, 2000; Judge & Miller, 1991). Along with the speed of making decisions, entrepreneurs also need to rely on the quality of the decisions made. Hence, they must depend on the traditional decision-making process of data collection, generation of alternatives and choosing the best possible alternative. The first two steps may be cognition-driven whereas the third step relies on intuition that is based on their experiences (Eisenhardt, 1989). Past research even suggests that the speed of making decisions increases for young decision-makers (Forbes, 2005), who recognize opportunity heuristically (Bingham & Eisenhardt, 2011), utilize routines to guide their decision-making (Helfat & Peteraf, 2003), trust in their own intuition (Miller & Ireland, 2005; Wally & Baum, 1994) and rely on past experiences (Forbes, 2005). Thus, a combined effect of intuition and cognition is observed in entrepreneurial decision-making, from the past literature. Though data-driven actions are mostly secure and offer less risk, it is time-consuming, and the present business environment makes room for the initiator. Thus intuition-driven action makes it fast and may set the opportune moment to be the pioneers and creators of a business. There may be controversy as research also suggests that decisions based on experience may not be fruitful as situations keep on evolving. However, the present researchers feel that learning from earlier experiences and molding the intuitive thought process as per the present demand can lead to greater success. With this as the background, this essay explores the research gap in identifying the decision-making styles influencing the business progression of women entrepreneurs.

Research gap

Identify the influence of decision-making style based on intuition and cognition on an entrepreneur's journey toward advancement.

Objectives of the study

- To assess the influence of decision-making style on entrepreneurial ability.
- To investigate the relationship between entrepreneurial ability, decision-making styles and thereby growth of the business.

Methodology

An online and offline survey of women entrepreneurs was conducted through snowball sampling from November 2022 to March 2023 and responses were received from 112 women entrepreneurs. The questionnaire had two parts. The first part was an Entrepreneurial Self-Assessment Survey (ESAS) consisting of 20 statements, based on the *Quiz Developed by the Women's Initiative for Self-Employment*. The total score of ESAS was obtained by calculating the sum of the ratings corresponding to each statement. The entrepreneurial ability was assessed with the help of the range of scores provided in the questionnaire which is 80–100 (Outstanding ability to be an entrepreneur), 60–79 (Satisfactory ability to be an entrepreneur), 40–59 (Self-employment may not be an appropriate career) and 0–39 (Should probably avoid entrepreneurship).

The second part was a self-reported measure of decision-making style consisting of 10 items (5 each): the intuitive-experiential style, as measured by Faith in Intuition (FI), and the analytical-rational style, as measured by Need for Cognition (NFC).$$ Epstein and his colleagues (1996) developed a self-report measure named the "Rational-Experiential Inventory" (REI), which consists of two scales: NFC for rationality and FI for experientiality (Epstein et al., 1996; Pacini & Epstein, 1999), which has been used here. The NFC is a shorter version of Cacioppo and Petty's (1982) scale with the same name, and the FI scale is a new scale constructed by Epstein and his colleagues (1996). All thirty items of the questionnaire were rated on a 5-point Likert scale ranging from "Strongly disagree" to "Strongly agree". With the exception of the reversely scored items indicated by (R), "Strongly disagree" was assigned 1 point, "Disagree" 2 points, "Neutral" 3 points, "Agree" 4 points and "Strongly agree" 5 points. To obtain overall scores for FI and NFC, all relevant individual scores were added up. Hence, the maximum (minimum) scores for both FI and NFC were 25 (5). The Cronbach alpha coefficient value, that is the measure of the internal consistency of the scale, was found to be 0.908. Hence, the questionnaire has been used for data collection for this research study. Demographic information of the respondents in terms of their age, qualification, type of business, mode of business, years in business, change in sales, change in asset, change in loan, scale of the business, scope of the business and employee strength have also been recorded. The data has been analysed using descriptive statistics with the help of SPSS Version 26.

Findings and analysis

Sample demographics

According to Table 16.1, among the 112 women entrepreneurs surveyed in this study, 75 have shown "outstanding ability" to be an entrepreneur, 33 have "satisfactory ability", but the remaining 4 did not show any compelling characteristics of an entrepreneur. The respondents are in the age group of 19–65 years. Their educational qualification varies from high school to postgraduate degree. The entrepreneurs are engaged in the service sector, production or trade and they operate both in online and offline mode.

Entrepreneurial ability and decision-making style

The respondents were further categorized according to their decision-making styles (Table 16.2): FI indicating experientiality and NFC depicting rationality (Epstein et al., 1996; Pacini & Epstein, 1999). The respondents have been divided based on their respective scores of FI and NFC in four quartiles, namely, 5–10 (Low), 11–15 (Moderate), 16–20 (High) and 21–25 (Very High). The research sought to probe any possible relationship between their

Table 16.1 Entrepreneurial Self-Assessment Survey (ESAS) revealed four categories of entrepreneurs as a career choice

Entrepreneurship as a career choice	*Number of respondents*
Avoid entrepreneurship	1
Self-employment may not be an appropriate career	3
Satisfactory ability to be an entrepreneur	33
Outstanding ability to be an entrepreneur	75
Total	**112**

Source: Primary data.

Table 16.2 Type of decision-making style of the entrepreneurs

Decision-making style	*Low*	*Moderate*	*High*	*Very high*	*Total*
Faith in intuition (FI)	2	13	49	48	112
Need for cognition (NFC)	5	34	50	23	112

Source: Primary data.

decision-making styles: based on faith in intuition/NFC and their entrepreneurial ability.

Following the above results and the distribution of respondents across their career choice to be an entrepreneur, it has been observed that only 3.5% (four respondents) of them are not in their most suitable profession. The four respondents showing no convincing potential of a successful entrepreneur have been kept out of the scope for further analysis. They may re-evaluate their choice and move on to an alternative career for better outcome. Consequently, the research will focus on the decision-making styles of the 108 respondents who belong to the satisfactory and outstanding category of entrepreneurs. Thus Table 16.3 has been designed to portray the levels and combinations of FI and NFC in their decision-making styles for career growth and business advancement.

From Table 16.3, among the 33 respondents who were found to have a "satisfactory ability to be an entrepreneur", 26 have high to very high FI and 17 have high to very high NFC. However, in this "satisfactory" category of respondents, there are 7 entrepreneurs who have shown low and moderate FI whereas 16 entrepreneurs have revealed low and moderate NFC. Similarly, among the 75 respondents who were found to have "outstanding ability to be an entrepreneur", 71 have high to very high FI and 56 have high to very high NFC. However, in this "outstanding" category of respondents, there are 7 entrepreneurs who have shown low and moderate FI whereas 16 entrepreneurs have revealed low and moderate NFC.

Now to locate the interface of the decision-making styles of each entrepreneur, Table 16.3 has been split into Tables 16.4 and 16.5 depicting the "satisfactory" and "outstanding" cohorts, respectively. The tables clearly depict that individuals cannot solely depend on FI or NFC; a combination of both leads to stability.

Figure 16.1 shows 15 entrepreneurs in the satisfactory cohort of 33 having high scores in both FI and NFC. This indicates approximately 45% of the entrepreneurs belonging to this group have high scores on both FI and NFC. Thus, for these 15 entrepreneurs, the decision-making style is influenced by the combined effect of intuition and cognition. The authors posit that such combinations of high FI and NFC may be a precursor of entrepreneurial success.

Figure 16.2 shows 54 entrepreneurs in the outstanding cohort of 75 having high scores in both FI and NFC. This indicates that 72% of the entrepreneurs

Table 16.3 Type of decision-making style of successful entrepreneurs

Decision-making style of successful entrepreneurs	*Satisfactory (33 entrepreneurs)*		*Outstanding (75 entrepreneurs)*		*Total*
	Low & moderate	*High & very high*	*Low & moderate*	*High & very high*	
Faith in intuition (FI)	7	26	4	71	108
Need for cognition (NFC)	16	17	19	56	108

Source: Primary data.

Table 16.4 Type of decision-making style of entrepreneurs in the "satisfactory" cohort

Decision-making style of successful entrepreneurs	*Satisfactory (33)*	
	Low & moderate	*High & very high*
Faith in intuition (FI)	7	26
Need for cognition (NFC)	16	17

Source: Primary data.

Table 16.5 Type of decision-making style of entrepreneurs in the "outstanding" cohort

Decision-making style of successful entrepreneurs	*Outstanding (75)*	
	Low & moderate	*High & very high*
Faith in intuition (FI)	4	71
Need for cognition (NFC)	19	56

Source: Primary data.

belonging to this group have high scores on both FI and NFC. Thus, for these 54 entrepreneurs, the decision-making style is influenced by the combined effect of intuition and cognition. Hence, it may be mentioned here that in both cohorts, which include potentially successful entrepreneurs, a striking percentage have high scores in both intuitive and cognitive abilities influencing their decision-making styles. This substantiates the previous observation of high FI and high NFC driving success in entrepreneurship. This skewed behavior of entrepreneurs to have high combinations of both decision-making styles (Figures 16.1 and 16.2), is also tested statistically.

The hypothesis evolved is H_0. There is no association between the choice of decision-making style and entrepreneurial ability.

NFC

Need for Cognition (NFC)	High & Very High	17	**15**
	Low & Moderate	XX	26
		Low & Moderate	High & Very High
	Faith in Intuition (FI)		

Figure 16.1 "Satisfactory" entrepreneurs with both high and very high FI and NFC.
Source: Primary data.

Need for Cognition (NFC)	High & Very High	56	**54**
	Low & Moderate	XX	71
		Low & Moderate	High & Very High
	Faith in Intuition (FI)		

Figure 16.2 "Outstanding" entrepreneurs with both high and very high FI and NFC.
Source: Primary data.

The hypothesis has been tested using a chi-square test which has rejected the null hypothesis thus confirming the association between choice of decision-making style and entrepreneurial ability to be significant which has been further explained in the following section.

Association between entrepreneurship as a career choice and decision-making styles

To test the hypothesis, of whether the association between entrepreneurship as a career choice and the decision-making styles of the women entrepreneurs are statistically significant, chi-square tests have been conducted as shown in Tables 16.6–16.9. According to the results, the associations have been found to be significant (Tables 16.7 and 16.9). Hence, it can be concluded that the ability of a potential and successful entrepreneur is closely related to their decision-making style among ordinary (satisfactory) and outstanding entrepreneurs.

Table 16.6 Distribution of the number of respondents with entrepreneurship as a career choice and faith in intuition as the decision-making style

		Entrepreneurship as a career choice		
		Satisfactory	*Outstanding*	*Total*
Faith in intuition	Low	0	1	1
	Moderate	7	3	10
	High	19	30	49
	Very high	7	41	48
Total		33	75	108

Source: Primary data.

Table 16.7 Significant association between entrepreneurship as a career choice and faith in intuition as the decision-making style

Chi-square tests			
	Value	*Df*	*Asymptotic significance (2-sided)*
Pearson Chi-square	15.104[a]	3	.002
Likelihood ratio	15.413	3	.001
No. of valid cases	108		

Source: Primary data.

[a] Three cells (37.5%) have an expected count of less than 5. The minimum expected count is .31.

Table 16.8 Distribution of the number of respondents with entrepreneurship as a career choice and need for cognition as the decision-making style

		Entrepreneurship as a career choice		
		Satisfactory	*Outstanding*	*Total*
Need for cognition	Low	2	1	3
	Moderate	14	18	32
	High	15	35	50
	Very high	2	21	23
Total		**33**	**75**	**108**

Source: Primary data.

Table 16.9 Significant association between entrepreneurship as a career choice and the need for cognition as the decision-making style

Chi-square tests			
	Value	*Df*	*Asymptotic significance (2-sided)*
Pearson Chi-square	9.656[a]	3	.022
Likelihood ratio	10.592	3	.014
No. of valid cases	108		

Source: Primary data.

[a] Two cells (25.0%) have an expected count of less than 5. The minimum expected count is .92.

Hence, significant associations ($p < .05$) between *entrepreneurship as a career choice* and *faith in intuition* as well as the *need for cognition* as a decision-making style indicate that entrepreneurship as a career choice can be determined by the decision-making styles of individuals.

Entrepreneurial scores indicating "satisfactory" and "outstanding", as used in the essay so far, is the entrepreneurs' self-assessment. Hence, to corroborate the relationship of business success with the decision-making styles, this essay hereafter uses more concrete measures of business success, namely, growth in scale and reach of the market, as collected from the responses.

Relationship between the advancement of business and decision-making style

As mentioned in the methodology, the study has considered two measures of business advancement: the scale of the business and the scope or market reach of the business. The scale of the business is indicated by micro, medium and small size of the business and the scope of the business is indicated by the local, regional or national level business. Table 16.10 is a schematic representation of the business advancement with respect to their scale and scope within the satisfactory and outstanding clusters of the entrepreneurs.

From Table 16.10, it is evident that not all the entrepreneurs (108 as in the sample) could expand their business either in scale or scope or both scale and scope. It may be submitted that market opportunities or business resources are not the only criteria for growth. This should be complemented by an entrepreneur's ability to optimally explore and utilize the business strengths and environmental prospects by making the right decision at the right time. So, the study further analyses the influence of FI and NFC on the decision-making style of those 14 entrepreneurs who have expanded their business as per both the categories combining the satisfactory and the outstanding cohorts (Table 16.11).

Table 16.10 Business advancement of successful entrepreneurs with respect to scale and scope of the businesses

Advancement of the businesses with respect to	*Satisfactory*	*Outstanding*
Scale	4	12
Scope	5	9
Both scale and scope	4	10
Total	**13**	**31**

Source: Primary data.

Table 16.11 Influence of FI and NFC on entrepreneurial decision-making in the category of business advancement in both scale and scope

Sl. No.	*Advancement in the scale of the business*	*Advancement in the scope of the business*	*FI decision-making style*	*NFC decision-making style*
11	Micro to small	Regional to national	High	Very high
22	Micro to small	Regional to national	Very high	Medium
23	Micro to small	Local to regional	High	Medium
44	Micro to small	Local to regional	High	Medium
55	Micro to small	Local to regional	High	Medium
66	Micro to small	Local to national	High	Medium
77	Micro to small	Local to national	High	Medium
88	Micro to medium	Local to national	High	Medium
99	Micro to medium	Local to national	Very high	Very high
10	Micro to medium	Local to regional	Very high	Medium
11	Micro to medium	Local to regional	High	High
12	Small to medium	Regional to national	High	Medium
13	Small to medium	Local to regional	High	High
14	Small to medium	Local to national	Very high	Medium

Source: Primary data.

Note: Very high, high and moderate categories of FI and NFC are based on quartile divisions of the scores.

Table 16.11 is graphically represented in Figure 16.3 for effective data visualization and a clear understanding of the influence of FI and NFC in the decision-making styles of those entrepreneurs who could advance in their business both in scale and scope. The x-axis in Figure 16.3 indicates the scale and scope of the business corresponding to the serial number of each entrepreneur, as mentioned in Table 16.11, while the y-axis indicates the FI and NFC scores. An overall observation reveals that FI has been a dominating influencer indicated as *High* and *Very High* in the decision-making styles for this cluster of "successful" entrepreneurs (Table 16.11). This has also been clearly revealed in

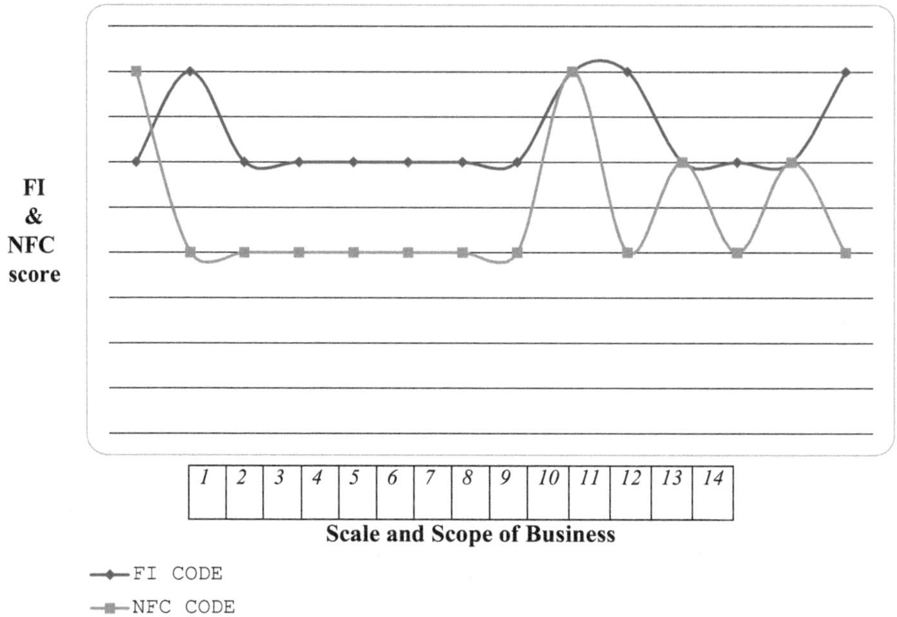

Figure 16.3 Influence of FI and NFC on entrepreneurial decision-making in the category of business advancement in both scale and scope.

Source: Primary data.

Figure 16.3 where the line graph of FI (indicated by blue) overrides the NFC line (indicated by red). A keen examination of Table 16.11 and Figure 16.3 shows that 10 out of 14, that is, 71% of the successful entrepreneurs have advanced both in the scale and scope of their businesses despite *Medium* NFC but *High* or *Very High* FI. This *High-Medium* combination in 10 out of 14 cases suggests that a balanced approach of intuition and cognition can facilitate appropriate decisions and help business goals to have a sustainable approach.

Conclusion

From the above interpretation, it may be inferred here that for significant performance in business ventures high or very high FI is a decisive trait than that of NFC. Entrepreneurs with medium NFC but high or very high FI have demonstrated higher potential of achieving a successful entrepreneurial career. It is important to note here that, though FI is the principal decision-making trait for success and sustainability in entrepreneurial careers, NFC also shows its presence because only intuition may not drive stability in the competitive business world. A thorough study of the data also reveals that entrepreneurs who have expanded both in scope and scale of their businesses possessed appropriate decision-making traits that had given their businesses the right direction. They have been all observed to be dominantly intuitive decision-makers. Despite being moderately rational thinkers, their innate intuitive skill could drive their businesses toward a growth path. The fast-changing business environment needs an intuitive mindset to act proactively as the recent pandemic has triggered businesses to respond at lightning speed and whoever could adapt seamlessly has not only survived the threat but also succeeded effortlessly.

This essay adds to the body of knowledge by suggesting an effective blend of intuition and cognition as evidence of successful entrepreneurship. Such studies may be used to influence pedagogy for entrepreneurship, whereby the training may bring about a balanced development of thinking out-of-the-box, idea generation based on "intuition" and opportunity evaluation, planning, launch and growth of a business based on "cognition". Independently, either of them may not drive the required positive outcome; the art of success will be in balancing the FI with NFC.

Appendix: Intuition cognition balance in the capacity building of entrepreneurship

Honest feedback is the only way to empower people to be the best they can be…

Dear Respondent,
In connection with the present research work on 'Intuition Cognition Balance in the Capacity Building of Entrepreneurship' being conducted by Dr. Ipsita C. Patranabis, Ms. Shrestha Chakrabarty and Prof. (Dr.) Sharmistha Banerjee, we seek your responses to a few questions. We assure you the responses gathered will be kept anonymous and strictly used for academic purposes only.

CONSENT: Checking the box "agree" below indicates that: You have read the above information. You voluntarily agree to participate in the research. You are at least 18 years of age.

Agree ☐

Signature (optional):	
Name (optional):	Type of Business: Production/Trade/ Service
	Mode of Business: Online/Offline/Both
Age:	Years in Business:

Sales (Rs) (optional) in the initial year of current business
Sales (Rs) (optional) in the current year
Asset (Rs) (optional) in the initial year of current business
Asset (Rs) (optional) in the current year
Loan (Rs) (optional) in the initial year of current business
Loan (Rs) (optional) in the current year
Scale (Micro/Small/Medium) in the initial year of current business
Scale (Rs) (optional) in the current year
Scope (Local/Regional/National) in the initial year of current business
Scope (Rs) (optional) in the current year
Employee Strength in the initial year of current business
Employee Strength (Rs) (optional) in the current year

Entrepreneurial self-assessment survey

Please rate the following statements if you **Strongly Agree as 5, Agree as 4, Somewhat Agree as 3, Disagree as 2 and Strongly Disagree as 1.**

1 I am willing to work 50 hours or more per week regularly.
2 My family will support my going into business.
3 I am willing to accept both financial and career risks when necessary.
4 I don't need all the fringe benefits provided by conventional employment.
5 I would like to take full responsibility for the successes and failures of my business.
6 I would experience more financial success by operating my own business.
7 I feel a great deal of pride when I complete a project successfully.
8 I have a high energy level that can be maintained over a long time.

9 I enjoy controlling my own work assignments & making all decisions affecting my work.
10 I believe that I am primarily responsible for my own successes and failures.
11 I have a strong desire to achieve positive results even when it requires a great deal of additional effort.
12 I have a good understanding of how to manage a business.
13 I can function in ambiguous situations.
14 One or both of my parents were entrepreneurs.
15 I believe that my abilities and skills are greater than those of most of my co-workers.
16 People trust me and consider me honest and reliable.
17 I always try to complete every project I start, regardless of obstacles and difficulties.
18 I am willing to do something even when other people laugh or belittle me for doing it.
19 I can make decisions quickly.
20 I have a good network of friends, professionals, and business acquaintances.

Self-reported measures of decision-making style

Please rate the following statements if you "Strongly disagree" was assigned 1 point, "Disagree" 2 points, "Neutral" 3 points, "Agree" 4 points, and "Strongly agree" 5 points.

- I trust my initial feelings about people.
- I believe in trusting my hunches.
- My initial impressions of people are almost always right.
- When it comes to trusting people, I can usually rely on my "gut feelings."
- I can usually feel when a person is right or wrong even if I can't explain how I know.
- I don't like to have to do a lot of thinking.
- I try to avoid situations that require thinking indepth about something.
- I prefer to do something that challenges my thinking abilities rather than something that requires little thought.
- I prefer complex to simple problems.
- Thinking hard and for a long time about something gives me little satisfaction.

-------------*Thank you for your precious time*---------

References

Bartol, K. M., & Martin, D. C. (1998). Performance appraisal: Maintaining system effectiveness. *Public Personnel Management*, *27*(2), 223–230.

Baum, J., & Wally, S. (2003). Strategic decision speed and firm performance. *Strategic Management Journal*, *24*(11), 1107–1129.

Bingham, C. B., & Eisenhardt, K. M. (2011). Rational heuristics: The 'simple rules' that strategists learn from process experience. *Strategic Management Journal*, *32*(13), 1437–1464.

Cacioppo, J. T., & Petty, R. E. (1982). The need for cognition. *Journal of Personality and Social Psychology*, *42*(1), 116–131. https://doi.org/10.1037/0022-3514.42.1.116

Casson, M. (1982). *The entrepreneur*. Totowa, NJ: Barnes & Noble Books.

Eisenhardt, K. M. (1989). Making fast strategic decisions in high-velocity environments. *Academy of Management Journal*, *32*(3), 543–576. https://doi.org/10.2307/256434

Eisenhardt, K. M., & Martin, J. A. (2000). Dynamic capabilities: What are they? *Strategic Management Journal*, *21*(10), 1105–1121.

Epstein, S., Pacini, R., Denes-Raj, V., & Heier, H. (1996). Individual differences in intuitive–experiential and analytical–rational thinking styles. *Journal of Personality and Social Psychology*, *71*(2), 390–405. https://doi.org/10.1037/0022-3514.71.2.390

Forbes, D. P. (2005). Are some entrepreneurs more overconfident than others? *Journal of Business Venturing*, *20*(5), 623–640.

Gustafsson, V. (2004). *Entrepreneurial decision-making: Individuals, tasks and cognitions*. Sweden: Jönköping International Business School.

Helfat, C. E., & Peteraf, M. A. (2003). The dynamic resource-based view: Capability lifecycles. *Strategic Management Journal*, *24*(10), 997–1010.

Judge, W. Q., & Miller, A. (1991). Antecedents and outcomes of decision speed in different environmental context. *Academy of Management Journal*, *34*(2), 449–463.

Miller, C. C., & Ireland, R. D. (2005). Intuition in strategic decision making: Friend or foe in the fast-paced 21st century? *The Academy of Management Executive*, *19*(1), 19–30.

Mintzberg, H., & Westley, F. (2001). Decision making: It's not what you think. *Sloan Management Review*, *42*(3), 89–93.

Pacini, R., & Epstein, S. (1999). The relation of rational and experiential information processing styles to personality, basic beliefs, and the ratio-bias phenomenon. *Journal of Personality and Social Psychology*, *76*(6), 972–987. https://doi.org/10.1037//0022-3514.76.6.972

Shane, S. & Venkataraman, S. (2000). The promise of entrepreneurship as a field of research. *Academy of Management Review*, *25*(1), 217–226.

Wally, S., & Baum, J.R. (1994). Personal and structural determinants of the pace of strategic decision making. *Academy of Management Journal*, *37*(4), 932–956.

Chapter 17

Cognitive insights on neuromarketing

Nudging intuitive marketing

Tanusree Dutta and Manas Kumar Mandal

Cognition and neuromarketing: Introduction

The brain and its function have often intrigued the human mind, especially researchers desirous of understanding the functions and generalizability of findings. Questions such as Are there differences in brain functioning? Does culture influence cognition? Does the same stimulus activate similar cognitive processes? Can we influence cognitive processes by external stimulation? How much information is too much for the brain to process? What are the underlying factors of cognitive fatigue and failure? Is some stimulus always processed erroneously? Answers to such and other questions are not only important to understanding the functioning of the brain but also have implications for researchers interested in cognitively challenging or influencing the functioning brain for enhanced decision-making. The functioning of the brain is best understood by measuring the activation of the brain. The answer to objective measurement of the brain lies in the use of neuroscientific techniques. Neuroscientific techniques have gained popularity over a period of time among researchers interested in understanding the consumer's brain.

Cognition and neuromarketing have become an emergent field in recent years, as marketers seek to understand how consumers make purchasing decisions and how they can use this information to improve customer satisfaction. Neuromarketing, in particular, has been a game-changer, providing marketers with new insights into how the human brain processes information and makes decisions.

Cognition involves acquiring any information, processing the acquired information further, and then storing and using the information. Understanding how these processes work can help marketers create more effective advertising and branding strategies, as well as design products and services that better meet consumers' needs and desires.

The field of Neuromarketing attempts to explore the response of the brain to marketing stimuli. This involves using neuroimaging tools such as fMRI, EEG, and eye-tracking to measure brain activity and eye movements and other neuroscientific tools. By analyzing these data, researchers can gain

DOI: 10.4324/9781003377757-20

insights into the cognitive and emotional processes involved in consumer decision-making and improving marketing strategies.

One of the key insights gained from neuromarketing research is the importance of emotions in decision-making. Studies have shown that emotions have a stronger impact on decision-making than previously thought, with many decisions being made on an emotional rather than rational basis. For example, a buyer may choose a particular brand of chocolate not because it is cheap or healthy, but because it evokes positive emotions and associations.

Another important finding from neuromarketing research is the importance of attention in making decisions. Attention is a limited resource, and marketers must compete for consumers' attention in a crowded marketplace. By understanding how the brain processes information and what stimuli are most likely to capture and hold attention, marketers can design more effective advertising and promotional campaigns.

Neuromarketing research has also highlighted the importance of context in decision-making. The perception of the same product or brand is influenced by the context. For example, a luxury watch may be perceived as a status symbol when presented in a high-end retail store, but as an unnecessary expense when presented in a discount store.

In addition to improving marketing strategies, neuromarketing research has the potential to enhance consumer happiness. By better understanding what consumers want and need, marketers can design products and services that more effectively meet their needs and provide greater satisfaction. For example, a company may use neuromarketing research to design a product that is more aesthetically pleasing or to create an advertising campaign that taps into consumers' emotional needs and desires.

Marketers, over a period, have realized the existence of a significant difference between customer happiness and customer satisfaction. The difference between satisfaction and happiness is affective. For this, understanding the consumer's thought process becomes meaningful and insightful. This marked the need to use neuroscientific techniques to understand cognitive processes, paving the way for Cognition and Neuromarketing.

The application of neuroscientific techniques in marketing is what defines neuromarketing. Neuromarketing has helped understand the consumer objectively and develop techniques and strategies to influence consumers successfully. It suggests techniques by which we can meaningfully engage a consumer and impress upon his mind both cognitively and emotionally. The objective of neuromarketing was not to replace the existing marketing techniques but to enhance them. Until now the major challenge that threatened the objective understanding of consumer behavior was that they meant not what they said. Probably, the consumers were failing to or not willing to communicate their true intentions. In such a situation ability to map brain function with neuroscientific techniques proved to be beneficial. The advantages of mapping brain function are, first, brain waves don't lie, it is difficult to influence brain functions, and second, with the advancement of neuroscientific techniques, researchers were able to understand the functions of not only the conscious brain but also those functions which were not available to the conscious brain.

The use of Neuromarketing tools in marketing has been prevalent since the 1960s. Pupil metering tools were used by Herbert Krugman to examine spontaneous pupil enlargement, indicating consumer interest in print packaging, and the use of Galvanic Skin Response (GSR) to examine customer emotional reactions to the advertisement (Sutherland, 2007). An advertising company, Bright House, used fMRI in marketing research (Fisher et al., 2010). In the late 1990s, Gerry Zaltman, Harvard University, reported the first use of fMRI as a technique in marketing research (Lewis & Bridger, 2005). However, Prof. Ale Smitds, Erasmus University, Rotterdam, first introduced the term Neuromarketing in 2002 (Mansor & Mohd Isa, 2020). Today Neuromarketing is a well-accepted technique that is gaining popularity as it helps researchers unravel the mysteries of the subconscious, decision-making, effectiveness of advertisements that are designed, product design, consumer branding, purchase behavior, understanding the consumer's emotion, attention and the list continues (Colaferro & Crescitelli, 2014; Genco et al., 2013; Sebastian, 2014).

The available neuromarketing tools popularly used can broadly be divided into central and peripheral measures. The central measures popularly used to measure the functioning of the brain include MRI (Magnetic Resonance Imaging), EEG (Electroencephalography), fMRI (functional Magnetic Resonance Imaging), PET (Positron Emission Tomography), ERP (Event Related Potential), QEEG (Qualitative Electroencephalography), TMS (Transcranial Magnetic Stimulation), MEG (Magnetoencephalography) and Steady State Topography. On the other hand, peripheral measures include techniques that help to infer about individuals by measuring activation other than the brain functions. The list of peripheral measures includes facial coding, popular among which is the FACS (Facial Action Coding System), IAT (Implicit Association Test), Eye tracking, GSR, Facial Electromyography, etc. The understanding of the behavior sought by the researcher determines the technique to be used. However, it is quite popular these days to use a combination of central and peripheral measures. For example, combining Eye tracking with EEG not only helps us to understand where the consumer is paying attention but also understand the brain activation pattern. Earlier the factor dampening the popularity of these instruments was inconvenient due to which real-time data could not be captured as most studies were conducted in the experimental setup. But with time, the portability of the instruments has been addressed successfully, which helps in collecting real-time data, thereby increasing the credibility and generalizability of the data collected.

Attention-retention-behavioral change: Role of cognition

Attention-retention-behavioral change is a concept that explains how our attention toward a particular stimulus or event can influence our ability to retain information and ultimately lead to behavioral change. This process is closely linked to cognition, which refers to the mental processes involved in perception, memory, and decision-making. When it comes to consumer happiness, understanding the role of attention, retention, and cognitive processes is crucial for creating effective marketing strategies and delivering positive customer experiences.

Attention is the initial cognitive process stage that occurs when we perceive a stimulus. In consumer behavior, attention can be drawn to various stimuli, such as advertising, product packaging, or in-store displays. Factors such as novelty, relevance, and emotional appeal can influence the attention given to a stimulus. For instance, a colorful and visually appealing advertisement is more likely to grab a consumer's attention than a dull and uninteresting one.

Retention refers to the process of encoding and storing information in memory. The level of attention given to a stimulus can influence the extent to which it is retained in memory. Factors such as repetition, relevance, and emotional appeal can also influence retention. For example, a catchy jingle or slogan repeated in an advertisement will likely be remembered by consumers.

Behavioral change is the final stage of the cognitive process, which occurs when the retained information leads to a change in behavior. In the context of consumer behavior, this could mean purchasing a product, switching brands, or adopting a new behavior. The effectiveness of marketing strategies can be measured by the extent to which they lead to behavioral change in consumers.

Cognition plays a crucial role in the process of attention-retention-behavioral change. The cognitive processes involved in attention, retention, and decision-making can influence consumer happiness. For instance, a positive experience with a product can lead to increased attention, retention, and, ultimately, behavioral change in favor of the brand. Likewise, a negative experience can lead to decreased attention, retention, and a shift in behavior away from the brand.

Today's market is consumer-driven. In such a situation understanding the consumer becomes pertinent and worthwhile. Consumers are usually rational in their thought process and emotional in their buying behavior. Behavioral economists believe that human decision-making is "predictably irrational" (Ariely, 2009) and systematically biased (Tversky & Kahneman, 1991; Bottom et al., 2004). Moreover, the plethora of options available to a consumer challenges their limited cognitive functioning process leading to decision paralysis. Thus, examining issues related to what catches the consumer's attention, how they decide, which information is processed, and what is overlooked, choice behavior, motivation, and attitude become meaningful variables to know and influence the consumer better. Broadly, this requires an understanding of the relationship between attention, retention, and behavioral change of the consumer. The intensity and impact of a stimulus to induce a particular behavior are dependent on information processing. Individual differences also play an important role. Change in opinion or attitude depends on the presentation of information and the perception of the information being presented, which triggers the tendency to react favorably or unfavorably. It is a constellation of events that happen at the cognitive level. Failure to match the consumer's cognitive expectation may eventually lead to cognitive dissonance. Leon Festinger (1957), who advocated the theory of cognitive dissonance, suggests that any inconsistency between belief and behavior is responsible for creating an aversive motivational state, something that costs marketers dearly.

Consumer cognition is also influenced by context and content. Consumer decision-making is influenced by experience, word-of-mouth, the capability of the product to fulfill the need of the consumer, advertisement, nature of association with the product, cognitive bias, and a host of other factors. In summary, customer satisfaction or happiness reflects attitude, customer retention, and behavior. As has been rightly pointed out, it is easier to retain an existing customer than to create a new one. Statistical analysis of data related to customer satisfaction and customer retention helps provide meaningful insight concerning identifying the areas of improvement.

In conclusion, attention-retention-behavioral change is a crucial concept in consumer behavior that highlights the importance of cognitive processes in shaping consumer happiness. By understanding the role of attention, retention, and cognition, marketers can create effective strategies that lead to positive customer experiences.

Consumption–happiness ratio

The consumption happiness ratio refers to the balance between how much an individual consumes and how happy they are as a result of their consumption. It is often used to measure the relationship between material possessions and happiness. Studies have shown that within limits there exists a positive correlation between income and happiness. Further, however, the correlation weakens. This is known as the Easterlin paradox, which suggests that while economic growth is important for improving living standards, it does not necessarily lead to greater happiness. Additionally, reducing consumption through sustainable practices can also lead to greater happiness. Studies suggest that individuals engaging in sustainable behaviors, such as reducing energy consumption or recycling, experience increased life satisfaction and happiness. Suggestively, the consumption–happiness ratio is a meaningful concept in trying to understand the relationship between consumption and happiness. By prioritizing non-material sources of happiness and engaging in sustainable behaviors, individuals can improve their consumption–happiness ratio and achieve greater well-being.

Ever since the interest in understanding the causes of happiness is increasing an increase in seeking information about life choices on happiness concerning consumption is also increasing. Economists, too, believe that an important parameter of satisfaction is consumption rather than income. Over time it has been noticed that the pursuit of happiness is universal (Veenhoven, 2010). We have considerable control over our happiness based on our choices (Lyubomirsky et al., 2005). In summary, it is the "informed pursuit of happiness" (Veenhoven, 2015). Extending this logic, it becomes interesting to understand whether or not daily spending choices influence consumer happiness. For example, are people spending large amounts of money for entertainment or on self-happier than people choosing to spend their money on charity or other social services? Does spending more generate happiness or the utility of the product? Answers to such questions are very meaningful for market researchers. It would help marketers design, advertise, and identify target groups for their products accordingly. This could, in due course of time, lead to happiness and well-being marketing strategies. But in reality, the situation is not that simple. Many times, consumers fail to predict their happiness with a particular product accurately (Frey & Stutzer, 2004). And as Kahneman et al., (1997) rightly point out, "expected utility" fails to align with "experienced utility".

Such positive views of consumption and happiness are not free from criticism. Religious traditions and moral philosophers have often suggested that beyond a specific limit, consumption has diverted people from noble goals that help them experience true happiness. According to Adam Smith, happiness is found more in tranquility than consumption (Busch, 2008). Enough evidence suggests that individuals seek happiness in wealth and possessions. But it is a futile attempt, wealth has never been proportional to happiness (Csikszentmihalyi, 2000; Myers, 2000; Van Boven, 2005). The cost–benefit relation has never shared a linear relationship.

After the 9/11 terrorist attacks, a spurt in buying behavior in record quantities was recorded in America. This was also in compliance with President Bush's slogan "go out shopping" (Arndt et al., 2004). In many countries, consumption is a patriotic behavior (Csikszentmihalyi, 2000). When U.S. citizens make a purchase, they attain short-term pleasure, substituting for meaningful experiences. However, when a purchase is meant for experiential or social consumption, the longer-term experience of happiness is achieved (Csikszentmihalyi, 1990; Russell, 1930; Van Boven, 2005). In Columbia, on the other hand, which also shares a history of countering terrorist attacks, people indulge more in family-binding or social experiences. And Columbians score higher than Americans in happiness ratings (Diener et al., 1995; Inglehart, 2007; NEF, 2007; Veenhoven & Kalmijn, 2005).

This difference between unhappy wealthy and happy poor countries can be ascribed to the individualist versus collectivist society. Empirical evidence suggests that collectivism has always been a successful survival mechanism for poor countries (Ahuvia, 2002). while individualism reduces happiness in wealthy countries.

Thoughts process: System I and System II

System I and System II thinking are two types of cognitive processes that can influence consumer happiness. System I is automatic and intuitive, while System II is deliberate and reflective. Both types of thinking can impact consumer behavior and ultimately, happiness.

System I thinking is fast, automatic, and effortless. This type of thinking occurs when we make snap judgments or react quickly to a situation. In the context of consumer behavior, System I thinking can lead to impulse buying or reliance on brand loyalty. While System I thinking can be convenient and efficient, it can also lead to irrational or suboptimal decision-making.

System II thinking, on the other hand, is slow, deliberate, and effortful. It involves reflection, analysis, and reasoning. In the context of consumer behavior, System II thinking can lead to more informed and rational decision-making. For example, taking the time to research a product before purchasing it or comparing prices across different brands.

Both types of thinking can influence consumer happiness. System I thinking can lead to immediate gratification and instant pleasure, but may not necessarily lead to long-term happiness. System II thinking, on the other hand, can lead to more deliberate choices that align with an individual's values and goals, which can ultimately lead to greater happiness and satisfaction. By understanding the role of System I and System II thinking in consumer behavior, individuals can make more informed decisions that align with their values and lead to greater happiness. Marketers can also use this knowledge to create strategies that appeal to both types of thinking, such as using emotional appeals to capture attention in System I thinking and providing factual information for System II thinking.

Understanding System I and System II thought processes of consumer behavior also helps ensure that both the subconscious and conscious thoughts and feelings are taken into account in understanding consumer decision-making.

Daniel Kahneman's book titled *Thinking, Fast and Slow*, published in 2011, discusses the phenomenon of System I and System II thinking. The book was greatly responsible for revolutionizing the understanding of the thought process. This book draws its conclusion from long years of research and debunks the idea that humans are capable of sound decision-making based on logical processing. The book replaces this understanding with thinking as a dual process; a function of System I and System II thinking. System I and System II have distinct characteristics and influence decision-making in different ways.

System I is fast, automatic, and intuitive. It is the default thinking that influences human judgment. Unlike System I System II is deliberative, effortful, and critical. It is majorly voluntary. Both System I and System II work to influence our thought process. Usually, thought processes are initiated by System I, and then an orderly thought process is exhibited by System II. System II either adopts System I thinking or tends to modify, examine, or correct System II thinking.

When brands want to influence customers and want them to choose their brands with minimal cognitive engagement, they have to devise ways by which they can trigger System I thinking. This can be achieved, for example, by advertising. Meaningful and engaging advertisements tend to influence the mind quickly. They get deep-seated in the brain and start influencing decision-making. System II may later get tagged with this System I thinking and impact decision-making meaningfully.

People believe that they are being objective in their decision-making when that is not. The objectivity is influenced by what Kahneman (2021) terms "noise". Noise comprises the influence of unseen factors. This also becomes difficult to counter as it is not explicit and unseen. This is very unlike the influence of bias, which, when noticed, can be rectified.

Role of heuristics and biases

Due to its quick-thinking nature, System I often uses heuristics and cognitive biases. Some examples of heuristics and cognitive biases are as below:

Affect heuristics: If a decision makes us feel good we tend to think that it is the right decision to take.

Availability heuristics: We tend to be influenced by information readily available to us.

Some examples of bias include the following.

Belief bias: Our beliefs regarding events, situations, and people tend to influence our decision-making.

Confirmation bias: We tend to believe in things that confirm our thought process and reject those that counter our existing thought process.

Helping consumers in decision-making: Emerging techniques

Since human thought processes are influenced by System I thinking, biases, and shortcuts, marketers are trying to adopt measures that would help consumers overcome these challenges and make meaningful decisions. Some of the techniques are listed below

Choice architecture

Choice architecture refers to the way in which choices are presented to consumers, which can influence their decision-making and ultimately impact their happiness. By designing the choice architecture to promote positive outcomes, marketers, and policymakers can improve consumer happiness.

One way in which choice architecture can impact consumer happiness is through default options. A default option is the option that is automatically chosen if a consumer does not make an active choice. For example, when enrolling in a retirement plan, the default option may be to contribute a certain percentage of income to the plan. Studies have shown that default options can significantly impact consumer behavior, making individuals more likely to choose the default option. By setting default options that align with positive outcomes, such as contributing to retirement savings or choosing healthy food options, choice architects can improve consumer happiness.

Another way in which choice architecture can impact consumer happiness is through the use of nudges. A nudge is a subtle change in the way choices are presented that can influence behavior without restricting options. For example, placing healthier food options at eye level in a cafeteria can nudge individuals toward making healthier choices. Nudges can be used to promote positive outcomes, such as encouraging individuals to save more or adopt sustainable behaviors, which can lead to greater happiness.

Choice architecture can also impact consumer happiness by reducing choice overload. When faced with too many options, individuals can become overwhelmed and stressed, leading to less satisfaction with their choices. By presenting choices in a clear and concise way, marketers and policymakers can help individuals make more informed decisions that align with their values and ultimately lead to greater happiness.

It is usually observed that consumer buying behavior is influenced by the way a product or information is presented. Choice architecture helps counter this situation by retaining consumer sovereignty. The origin of this concept may be traced to the book titled Nudge: Improving Decisions about Health, Wealth, and Happiness by Thaler and Sunstein (2008). It is based on liberal paternalism and influenced by research on behavioral economics. Liberal paternalism is a combination of freedom of choice while promoting or nudging certain actions. During purchase behavior, it has often been noticed that consumers tend to be influenced by "default options" and or "short-term benefits". Having understood this choice architecture would include presenting the desired response as the default option, reducing the number of alternatives presented, giving special offers so that consumers make the right choice, demeriting the goods so that consumers are not encouraged to buy, changing the packaging of the goods, etc. One best example of demeriting goods and packaging is the packaging of cigarettes. Across the globe, cigarette packets come with a warning as well as pics highlighting the consequences of smoking. Other examples include highlighting the consequences on health. For example, products showing that they have high sugar deter a consumer from buying them. At the same time, products displaying that they have low calorie, natural sweeteners, and or organic encourage the consumer to make the desirable decision. Unlike demerit goods, they are considered merit goods that are designed to encourage consumers to make better decisions.

Thus, different techniques can be used to design a choice of architecture. First, by reducing the number of alternatives available. The availability of too many choices causes choice overload, leading to decision paralysis. So, less is more when providing options to consumers. The same applies to product attributes. There is an inverse relationship between attributes and decision-making. Next is using the default option more carefully. Consumers prefer to continue with the default option. Further, between short-term and long-term benefits the human brain is capable of processing short-term benefits easily and quickly in comparison to long-term benefits

However, this technique has its limitations. Different consumers react differently to the same information. Some may not be willing to abide by the options presented and continue with their preferred choice.

Nudge

Nudge is very closely related to choice architecture. Nudge is based on Nudge theory, which suggests that positive reinforcement and implicit suggestion impact behavior (Thaler & Sunstein, 2008). Nudges are based on heuristics used by individuals for decision-making. Advocators of nudge theory suggest that successfully designed nudges help reduce market failure and encourage desirable actions. Nudges have been used across countries successfully by the government to promote desirable behavior such as organ donation, paying the electricity bill, wearing masks during COVID-19, etc. In fact, in the UK, a behavioral insight Unit has been initiated. Market researchers have identified a few nudges that help influence consumers. The first is simplifying support access to consumers. The lesser the amount of effort that a consumer has to exert and the quicker the problems are solved, the more likely they are to influence consumers positively. Nudges that help a consumer make a better choice tend to generate more positive feelings. One application of this is found in detailing default options. Predictive analysis and identifying the pattern of thinking of consumers help in choosing appropriate default options. At times, training the seller on concepts of alternative positioning of products also helps. However, skeptics of the use of nudges argue that this technique may be misused, resulting in the use of nudges as a social engineering technique to influence consumers to buy things that are not much needed.

However, some ways nudges can be used to generate consumer happiness are as follows. One way nudges can generate consumer happiness is by promoting healthy behaviors. For example, placing healthier food options at eye level in a cafeteria can nudge individuals toward making healthier choices, which can lead to greater well-being. Nudges can also encourage individuals to exercise more or adopt other healthy behaviors, leading to improved physical and mental health and greater happiness.

Another way in which nudges can generate consumer happiness is by promoting sustainable behaviors. For example, placing recycling bins in prominent locations can nudge individuals toward recycling more, leading to greater satisfaction with their environmental impact. Nudges can also be used to encourage individuals to reduce their energy consumption, which can lead to cost savings and a sense of satisfaction with their contributions to sustainability.

Nudges can also be used to promote financial well-being and happiness. For example, using default options to enroll individuals in retirement plans or savings accounts can nudge them toward saving more, leading to greater financial security and happiness. Nudges can also encourage individuals to make more informed financial decisions, such as by providing information on the long-term costs and benefits of different options.

Overall, nudges can be a powerful tool for promoting consumer happiness. By using nudges to encourage healthy, sustainable, and financially responsible behaviors, marketers and policymakers can help individuals make choices that align with their values and lead to greater well-being and satisfaction.

Subliminal cue

Until 1957, the use of subliminal messages was not known until marketing researchers proved their significance in influencing consumer behavior (Packard, 1957; Vicary, 1950; Verwijmeren et al., 2013). As the name suggests, subliminal cues include stimuli that are presented below the threshold of consciousness. These stimuli can be visual, auditory, olfactory, and or tactile. Since the conscious brain does not process these stimuli, they are difficult to resist or filter. The influence of subliminal messaging in marketing or consumer research is inconclusive (Karremans et al., 2006; Smeets & Dijksterhuis, 2014). Karremans et al. (2006) verified the study by James Vicary. Vicary used subliminal priming on two products, namely, Coca-Cola and popcorn. Flashing images were shown in a movie theatre, suggesting that people eat popcorn and drink Coca-Cola. Findings suggested that the sale of popcorn increased by 57.1% and Coca-Cola sales by 18.1%. The findings highlighted two major aspects. Firstly, subliminal priming impacts behavior, but it is most effective when the individual is in a deprivation state only (Vicary, 1955). Comparable results were also found in using subliminal messages in the media (Packard, 1957; Key, 1973, 1976; Thorne & Himelstein, 1984).

Critics argue that influencing the conscious brain with emotions is much more powerful than using subliminal messaging. Second, when the use of a subliminal message is made aware to the consumer, it loses its influence. Despite its shortcomings, this technique has been used effectively in psychological research and the field of marketing, advertising, and branding (Fennis & Pruyn, 2007; Fitzsimons et al., 2008; Johar et al., 2005) and other related areas. It has proved its effectiveness in influencing human thought and decision-making, but it requires systematic efforts to maximize its potential and effort.

Pattern thinking

The human brain seeks patterns. We seek a pattern in everything, such as predicting a person's behavior based on the pattern of behavior expressed in the past in similar or near similar situations. The strategy developed to solve a problem is an example of pattern thinking. Summarily, it may be conceptualized as a repetitive solution to a set of problems. Patterns give rise to narratives and to hypothesized solutions, establishing the importance of patterns.

Any marketing strategy's success depends on identifying the pattern behavior of consumers. Consumers usually have a default behavior and understanding that is the key to pattern behavior. For example, a consumer usually walks down a path in the morning, and on the way, he grabs a Starbucks coffee daily. This particular behavior is less conscious and more automatic, requiring less cognitive activation. But it reflects a pattern of behavior. Understanding the pattern behavior of consumers helps to understand the "why" and "how" of behavior helping marketers to strategize better. Buying behavior can broadly be classified into four categories. These include routine or regular purchases such as groceries, etc. The second includes limited decision-making purchases. Examples of this category include a recommendation from friends, trustworthy people, people we value, people with credibility, and our near and dear ones. The third includes extensive decision-making processes. Examples of such purchases include buying a house, car, etc. And the last includes impulse purchases that do not require much thinking. Examples include buying candy at the counter. Consumer behavior in making purchases under each of these categories reflects a particular pattern. When a pattern is established, the consumer does not have to decide on every level. He repeats his established preference. Market researchers try to understand the pattern exhibited by unfolding the consumer journey through stages of awareness, consideration, and decision.

Another way in which pattern thinking can be utilized to generate consumer happiness is through the use of personalized recommendations. By analyzing an individual's past behaviors and preferences, businesses can identify patterns in their decision-making and provide tailored recommendations for products or services that align with their interests. This can lead to greater satisfaction and happiness with their purchasing decisions.

Another use of pattern thinking is gamification. By designing products or services incorporating play and reward elements, businesses can tap into consumers' natural tendency to recognize and engage with patterns. This can create a sense of enjoyment and accomplishment, leading to greater happiness with the overall experience.

Pattern thinking can also be utilized to create intuitive and user-friendly designs. By identifying patterns in how individuals interact with products or services, businesses can design interfaces or experiences that align with their mental processes and make it easier to accomplish their goals. This can lead to greater satisfaction and happiness with the overall experience.

Overall, understanding how consumers engage in pattern thinking can be valuable for businesses looking to generate consumer happiness. By designing products and services that align with their mental processes and preferences, businesses can create more engaging and enjoyable experiences, leading to greater satisfaction and happiness.

Companies usually invest a lot to launch a product only to find that it fails to impress the consumer. The use of neuroscientific techniques, however, helps toward a better understanding. It helps toward a better understanding of consumers' cognitive and affective responses. It also helps in examining and testing beforehand the sensorimotor reaction of the consumer to a product even before it is launched. This allows market researchers the advantage of making meaningful changes so that they increase purchase behavior. Neuroscientific techniques help uncover not only the dynamics of the conscious brain but also the unconscious brain, which helps develop a better understanding of the consumer thought process.

Sensory engagement

Another interesting technique used to keep the consumer happy is sensory engagement. This technique, over the period, has developed into a powerful technique. Sensory engagement, as the name suggests, is engaging the senses, namely, visual, auditory, olfactory, taste, and tactile, to influence consumer behavior. The experience gained from these five senses usually triggers an emotional connection, creating a gateway for meaningful experiences. Brands and retail stores have used sensory engagement to influence customers for a long time. Right from the packages of the goods, the product's shape, the product, the positioning of the product on the shelf, the music to be played in retail stores, and the smell of the lighting to be used are all examples of initiatives marketers take to engage their customers sensorily. Brands attempt to provide multi-sensory engagement to provide them with a memorable experience and retain them. Sensory engagement has shown positive results both in the real setting and in virtual reality (Brengman et al., 2022).

One way in which sensory engagement can be utilized to promote consumer happiness is through the use of ambient scenting. By incorporating pleasant scents into the environment, businesses can create a more welcoming and relaxing atmosphere, leading to greater customer satisfaction and happiness.

Similarly, businesses can use soundscaping to create more immersive and engaging environments. By incorporating music or other sounds that align with the brand and the consumer experience, businesses can enhance the emotional connection with their customers, leading to greater happiness and loyalty.

Visual elements can also be utilized to promote sensory engagement and consumer happiness. By creating visually appealing displays or packaging, businesses can create a more attractive and enjoyable customer experience, leading to greater satisfaction and happiness.

In addition, businesses can incorporate tactile elements into the consumer experience, such as through the use of textured packaging or product designs. This can create a more engaging and memorable experience, leading to greater satisfaction and happiness.

Finally, businesses can utilize taste and culinary experiences to enhance the consumer experience. By incorporating unique and delicious flavors into their products or services, businesses can create a more enjoyable and satisfying customer experience, leading to greater happiness and loyalty.

Overall, sensory engagement can be a powerful tool for promoting consumer happiness. By engaging multiple senses, businesses can create more immersive and memorable experiences, leading to greater customer satisfaction and loyalty.

In fact, the Marketing Science Institute (2010) emphasizes the importance of non-transactional initiatives to create and nurture the customer-firm relationship.

Ethical concerns

The field of neuromarketing has often been targeted for ethical concerns. It has raised many eyebrows on ethical grounds. Concerns relate to the protection of participants and vulnerable groups from being manipulated, providing the public with misleading knowledge (Nyoni & Bonga, 2017; Lim, 2018), manipulating consumers into making purchases that they otherwise would not make, or infringing on their privacy by monitoring their brain activity without their knowledge or consent. These ethical concerns arise mainly from a lack of understanding and knowledge (Wilson et al., 2008).

Every consumer believes that their purchase decisions are personal and private. However, the application of neuroscience in marketing suggests that marketers are better able to understand, predict, and influence consumer decision-making.

Predictions of a large consumer base are done by extrapolation of data collected from a small sample size. This raises serious concerns about ethics.

Another major concern relates to subconscious activation to influence behavior. Since such content is designed for the subconscious consumers are unable to process it consciously. Thus many times consumers are influenced to behave in a particular way without being fully aware of it.

Way forward

In conclusion, cognition and neuromarketing are emergent fields with significant implications for marketing and consumer happiness. By understanding how the brain processes information and makes decisions, marketers can design more effective advertising and promotional campaigns, as well as create products and services that better meet consumers' needs and desires. However, it is important for researchers and marketers to approach these techniques with caution and to ensure that they are used ethically and transparently.

Happiness is a process and not a destination to be achieved. The nested relationship between variables subtly and explicitly influencing consumer happiness has been discussed in this chapter. This paves the way for future research and triggers thoughts about how we can foster consumer happiness. Emotions have always been an integral part of our lives, and we find meaning and expression in our behavior.

Marketing research has come a long way in understanding the importance of consumer happiness. Much has been done but much remains toward understanding consumer happiness's science. Identifying factors, processes, and initiatives that would lead to long-lasting happiness has to be made an integral part of product development and product communication. It is not about the art (practices) or science (use of neuroscientific techniques); it is all about integrating both (intuitive marketing) to get the best and most meaningful results. The key lies in fostering intuitive marketing. Intuitive marketing nurtures an understanding of consumer behavior strategies that find resonance at the emotional, psychological, or behavioral levels. Apple's product launches or Coca-Cola's "Share a Coke" campaign are some examples of successful intuitive marketing. Marketing has to be more customer-centric. Research has to think beyond consumer satisfaction and find answers to questions such as the following: Will the inclusion of design thinking help foster customer happiness? Does consumer happiness influence consumer loyalty? Is it the product or the service that influences consumer happiness? How will the replacement of human interaction with robots influence consumer happiness?

References

Ahuvia, A. C. (2002). Individualism/collectivism and cultures of happiness: A theoretical conjecture on the relationship between consumption, culture and subjective well-being at the national level. *Journal of Happiness Studies*, 3(1), 23–36

Ariely, D. (2009). *Predictably irrational: The hidden forces that shape our decisions.* Rev. and expanded ed. New York, NY: Harper Collins Publ.

Arndt, J., Solomon, S., Kasser, T., & Sheldon, K. M. (2004). The urge to splurge: A terror management account of materialism and consumer behavior. *Journal of Consumer Psychology*, 14(3), 198–212.

Bottom, W. P., Thomas, G., Dale, G., & Daniel, K. (2004). Heuristics and biases: The psychology of intuitive judgment. *Academy of Management Review*, 29, 695. https://doi.org/10.2307/2015908

Brengman, M., Willems, K., & De Gauquier, L. (2022). Customer engagement in multi-sensory virtual reality advertising: The effect of sound and scent congruence. *Frontiers in Psychology*, 13, 1064–1078. https://doi.org/10.3389/fpsyg.2022.747456

Busch, M. (2008). Adam Smith and consumerism's role in happiness: Modern society reexamined. *Major Themes in Economics*, 10, 65–77. Available at: https://scholarworks.uni.edu/mtie/vol10/iss1/6

Colaferro, C. A., & Crescitelli, E. (2014). The contribution of neuromarketing to the study of consumer behavior. *Brazilian Business Review*, 11(3), 123–143. https://doi.org/10.15728/bbr.2014.11.3.6

Csikszentmihalyi, M. (1990). *Flow: The psychology of optimal experience.* New York, NY: Harper.

Csikszentmihalyi, M. (2000). The costs and benefits of consuming. *Journal of Consumer Research*, 27(2), 267–272.

Diener, E., Diener, M., & Diener, C. (1995). Factors predicting the subjective well-being of nations. *Journal of Personality and Social Psychology*, 69(5), 851–864

Fennis, B. M., & Pruyn, A. T. H. (2007) You are what you wear: Brand personality influences on consumer impression formation. *Journal of Business Research*, 60, 634–639

Festinger, L. (1957). *A theory of cognitive dissonance.* Stanford, CA: Stanford University Press.

Fisher, C. E., Chin, L., & Klitzman, R. (2010). Defining neuromarketing: Practices and professional challenges. *Harvard Review of Psychiatry*, 18(4), 230–237. https://doi.org/10.3109/10673229.2010.496623

Fitzsimons, G. M., Chartrand, T. L., & Fitzsimons, G. J. (2008). Automatic effects of brand exposure on motivated behavior: How apple makes you "think different". *Journal of Consumer Research*, 35, 21–35.

Frey, B. S., & Stutzer, A. (2004). *Economic consequeneces of mis-predicting utility* [Working Paper]. Institute for Empirical Research in Economics.

Genco, S., Pohlmann, A., & Steidl, P. (2013). *Neuromarketing for dummies.* Mississauga: John Wiley & Sons, Inc.

Inglehart, R. (2007). *World values survey online data analysis.* World Values Survey. Retrieved December 10, 2007, from https://www.worldvaluessurvey.org/

Johar, G. V., Sengupta, J., & Aaker, J. L. (2005). Two roads to updating brand personality impressions: Trait versus evaluative inferencing. *Journal of Marketing Research*, 42, 458–469.

Kahneman, D., Sarin, R., & Wakker, P. (1997). Back to Bentham? Explorations of experienced utility. *Quarterly Journal of Economics*, 12, 375–405.

Kahneman, D., Sibony, O., & Sunstein, C. R. (2021). *Noise: A flaw in human judgement.* London: William Colins

Karremans, J., Stroebe, W., & Claus, J. (2006). Beyond vicary's fantasies: The impact of subliminal priming and brand choice. *Journal of Experimental Social Psychology*, 42, 792–798.

Key, B. W. (1973). *Subliminal seduction*, Englewood Cliffs, NJ, USA: Prentice-Hall.

Key, B. W. (1976). *Media sexploitation*; Englewood Cliffs, NJ, USA: Prentice-Hall.

Lewis, D., & Bridger, D. (2005). Market researchers make increasing use of brain imaging. *Advances in Clinical Neuroscience and Rehabilitation*, 5(3), 36–37

Lim, W. M. (2018). Demystifying neuromarketing. *Journal of Business Research*, 91, 205–220. https://doi.org/10.1016/j.jbusres.2018.05.036

Lyubomirsky, S., Schkade, D. A., & Sheldon, K. M. (2005). Pursuing happiness: The architecture of sustainable change. *Review of General Psychology*, 9, 111–113.

Mansor, A. A., & Mohd Isa, S. (2020). Fundamentals of neuromarketing: What is it all about? *Neuroscience Research Notes*, 3(4), 22–28. https://doi.org/10.31117/neuroscirn.v3i4.58

Marketing Science Institute [MSI]. (2010). *2010–2012 Research priorities*. Cambridge, MA: MSI.

Myers, D. G. (2000). Wanting more in an age of plenty. *Christianity Today*, 44(5), 94.

NEF. (2007). *The (un) happy planet index: An index of human well-being and environmental impact*. The Happy Planet Report. Retrieved July 15, 2007, from https://www.neweconomics.org/gen/z_sys_PublicationDetail.aspx?pid=225

Nyoni, T., & Bonga, W. G. (2017). Neuromarketing: No brain, no gain! *Journal of Economics and Finance (DRJ-JEF)*, 2(2), 17–29.

Packard, V. (1957). *The hidden persuaders*. New York, NY, USA: McKay.

Russell, B. A. W. (1930). *The conquest of happiness*. Oxford, England: Liveright.

Sebastian, V. (2014). Neuromarketing and evaluation of cognitive and emotional responses of consumers to marketing stimuli. *Procedia – Social and Behavioral Sciences*, 127, 753–757. https://doi.org/10.1016/j.sbspro.2014.03.349

Smeets, M., & Dijksterhuis, G. (2014). Smelly primes: When olfactory primes do or do not work. *Frontiers in Psychology*, 5, 96.

Sutherland, M. (2007, March 1). *Neuromarketing: What's it all about?* https://www.sutherlandsurvey.com

Thaler, R. H., & Sunstein, C. R. (2008). *Nudge: Improving decision about health, wealth and happiness*. New Haven & London: Yale University Press.

Thorne, S. B. & Himelstein, P. (1984). The role of suggestion in the perception of satanic messages on rock-and-roll recordings. *Journal of Psychology*, 116, 245–248

Tversky, A., & Kahneman, D. (1991). Loss aversion in riskless choice: A reference-dependent model. *The Quarterly Journal of Economics*, 106, 1039–1061. https://doi.org/10.2307/2937956

Van Boven, L. (2005). Experientialism, materialism, and the pursuit of happiness. *Review of General Psychology*, 9(2), 132–142.

Veenhoven, R. (2010). How universal is happiness? In Diener, E., Helliwell, J. F., & Kahneman, D. (Eds.), *International differences in well-being* (pp. 328–350). New York: Oxford University Press.

Veenhoven, R. (2015). Informed pursuit of happiness: What we should know, do know and can get to know. *Journal of Happiness Studies*, 16, 1035–1071.

Veenhoven, R., & Kalmijn, W. (2005). Inequality-adjusted happiness in nations: Egalitarianism and utilitarianism married in a new index of societal performance. *Journal of Happiness Studies*, 6(4), 421–455.

Verwijmeren, T., Karremans, J. C.., Bernritter, S. F., Stroebe, W., & Wigboldus, D. H. J. (2013). Warning: You are being primed! The effect of a warning on the impact of subliminal ads. *Journal of Experimental Social Psychology*, 49, 1124–1129

Vicary, J. M. (1950). How psychiatric methods can be applied to market research. *Printer's Ink*, 11, 39–40.

Vicary, J. M. (1955). The circular test of bias in personal interview surveys. *Public Opinion Quarterly*, 19, 215–218.

Wilson, R., Gaines, J., & Hill, R. P. (2008). Neuromarketing and consumer free will. *Journal of Consumer Affairs*, 42(3), 389–410. https://doi.org/10.1111/j.1745-6606.2008.00114.x

Chapter 18

At the crossroad

Intuition beyond artificial intelligence

Kaustav Manna and Swarup Poria

Introduction

Artificial Intelligence in recent times has seen a boom in its development as well as application in diverse areas ranging from chemistry, medicine, and public health to audit and accounting development (Kubassova et al., 2021). However, back in the early 1950s, Alan Turing put forth a question, "Can a machine think?" questioning the credibility of machines and its ability to compute complex decision proposition. There are several reasons to answer the question positively. However, there are two most important and earliest outcomes of computational theory—one being Church's notion of recursive computation and the other being the Turing machine.

Recursive computation means more specifically that there is a finite set of operations that can be applied to a given input, and then applied repeatedly to the successive results of such applications to yield the function's output in finite time (Deutsch, 1985). The theory put forth that computability stands for the ability to solve problems in an effective manner. Effective computation implies that there is a mechanical procedure for determining the output of the function for a given input in a limited time (Churchland & Churchland, 1990). Although Church's thesis does not provide formal proof, it does indicate what is meant by computation.

Alan M. Turing demonstrated that any recursively computable function can be computed in a limited time by a maximally simple sort of symbol-manipulating machine that is called a Turing machine (Blum, 2011). This machine operates based on a set of recursively applicable rules that respond to the identity, sequence, and arrangement of the elementary symbols it processes as input. These findings showed that a standard digital computer, with the right program, a large enough memory, and sufficient time, can compute any rule-governed input-output function (Burgin, 2006). In other words, it can exhibit any systematic pattern of responses to its environment. More specifically, these results imply that a suitably programmed symbol-manipulating machine should be able to pass the Turing test for conscious intelligence.

DOI: 10.4324/9781003377757-21

The only remaining problem is to identify the undoubtedly complex function that governs the human pattern of response to the environment and then write the program by which the machine will carry out complex problem-solving (Grossberg, 1987). Although initial results seemed positive and some of the symbol-manipulating machines were able to perform a variety of tasks mimicking complex cognitive computations such as responding to complex instructions, solving complex arithmetic, algebraic and tactical problems, playing checkers and chess, proving theorems, and engaging in simple dialogue (Hanson & Burr, 1990).

In spite of the fact that human beings are bombarded with a lot of information, the human brain is capable of adapting with limited working memory capacity and carrying out complex cognitive tasks (Lyon, 2005). In other words, the human mind is capable of selectively attenuating the situation with inappropriate information to carry out the task at hand. On the contrary, the symbol-manipulating machine solves problem algorithmically, this algorithm is constructed of finite set of operations with which it can execute limited set of functions in a limited amount of time.

Hubert L. Dreyfus (1972) was highly critical of the inadequacy of the simulation of cognition; he believed this could not be achieved solely by symbol manipulation at the hands of recursively applicable rules. Dreyfus (1972) suggested that the simulations lacked the vast store of inarticulate background knowledge every person possesses and the commonsense capacity for drawing on relevant aspects of that knowledge as changing demand of the circumstances (Dreyfus, 1994). For example, the simulation of object recognition in the visual system proved computationally intensive to an unexpected degree. Solutions to realistic problems require longer computing time, compared to the human visual system.Not only is the computer able to process signals at a much faster rate the clock frequency of a computer's central processor is much greater than the brain (Cox & Dean, 2014), and yet, on realistic problems, the brain outperforms the simulations.

Moreover, successful performance on realistic problems would require access to an exceptionally rich knowledge-base of the computer program. Constructing such a huge knowledge-base is a challenge in itself. On the other hand, the task of efficiently accessing only contextually relevant parts of that knowledge-base in real time takes excessive searching time. Any attempt to employ heuristics to search for relevant information has only resulted in uncorrelated findings (Dreyfus, 1994). This issue of excessive search time increases as the knowledge-base gets bigger.

Any system that manipulates physical symbols based solely on structure-sensitive rules is at best a superficial imitation of genuine conscious intelligence. This is because generating authentic semantics is an unattainable feat through the sole act of mechanical operation with "empty syntax" (Searle, 1980).Here, we should point out that Searle (1980) is imposing a non-behavioral test for consciousness: the elements of conscious intelligence must possess real semantic content. With these criticisms of Searle's argument in mind, we return to the question of whether the classical AI research program has a realistic chance of solving the problem of conscious intelligence and creating a machine that can truly think. The question remains—how does the brain achieve cognition and how does it address the issues of limited working space?

Cognition

Cognition is the ability to perceive, understand, retain information, and apply it to problem-solving. Hammond (2007) proposed a cognitive continuum—one, which is conscious, deliberate, and bound by the limits of working memory called analytic cognition (Patterson & Eggleston, 2017) and the other, is unconscious, fast, and not restricted by the limits of working memory called intuitive cognition. Daniel Kahneman (2003) further clarified the two styles of processing as two different systems—one system being slow based on logical analytic thoughts and facts and requires allocation of attention to solve complex problems. Deliberate or analytic cognition is voluntary and effortful in nature, but it is limited in capacity, and slow. The other system is fast, is involuntary, and is responsible for intuitive understanding. Intuitive cognition involves unconscious situational pattern synthesis and recognition; it is not bound by the limits of working memory.

Deliberate System operations need attention and effort, they are poorly executed when attention is missed or effort is low. Attention and effort are allocated voluntarily and have an upper limit. When this system has to deal with too many tasks, it gives priority to the most important piece of information, for example, just think about being the passenger during a road trip; the driver is able to have a conversation with you but during a tough road, probably, they stop talking. Some actions may be executed exactly as they come, others need to be modified or suppressed.

Any kind of input received in the intuitive system turns on an automatic mechanism of associations that links visual percepts to auditory, to somatosensory information, to concepts, and to memories. Associations are activated quickly and involuntarily, often resulting from a combination of inputs and the system's effort to make sense of the situation one is experiencing, enabling preparedness for what lies ahead. Activation of the nodes provokes a big activity without complete awareness. Then, memory can be conceptualized as a network where objects are connected to their characteristics, causes to effects, and facts to its habits.

Affect tends to influence this process. Positive affect increases accuracy, while negative affect leads to erroneous decisions. It implies that intuition works well while experiencing positive emotions (Isen & Labroo, 2003). This system tries to guess responses and solutions when it experiences problem situations. If the probable solution is easy and the prediction correct, the computation time is avoided, but an error-free solution is not guaranteed. The predictor then learns from the mistakes and gains experiences to ultimately make error-less decisions.

Humans are conceived to be rational decision-makers capable of making decisions to maximize utility (Simon, 1986). However, a lot of the decision-making takes place through heuristics which are often driven by an emotional process. Hammond (2010) calls this a quasi-rational decision-making process. It is suggested that effective decision-making requires functional interaction between analysis (conscious processes) and intuition (unconscious processes).

Intuition

Intuition is "the ability to understand something instinctively, without the need for conscious reasoning". It is quicker and more powerful compared to logical reasoning. Intuitive cognition can enrich the solution almost in zero time implying that it requires almost zero computation time. Herbert Simon (1986) defined intuition to be a "form of recognition". An intuition assists in reaching a solution, based on our past experiences, without the certainty for its correctness. Therefore, intuition is the ability to appreciate the resemblance betweenthe problem one is facing and problems one has faced, and re-applying the solutions from the past in a similar, but non-identical way.

Chess masters, doctors, and others are able to predict intuitively the best play or the disease, respectively, looking to the board or to the patient, most of the time. It is not a trick, during years of practice, they gain a lot of experience and when face a new problem they are able to recognize the situation and automatically get the answer (Kahneman & Klein, 2009). The situation provides a cue; this cue gives the expert access to information stored in memory, and the information provides the answer (Simon, 1986).

A significant hurdle in decision-making involves handling extensive, unstructured datasets rooted in partially unknown information, alongside the existence of multiple states that can be represented by intricate networks like dependency networks and Bayesian networks (Johnny et al., 2019). Most of these models are logic-driven and are time-dependent (Dundas & Chik, 2011). Moreover, there are potentially a large number of parameters, which increases the overall computational complexity in some scenarios (Trovati & Bessis, 2016).

Nevertheless, in critical and time-sensitive decision-making situations, such as emergency medical diagnoses, human beings rely on intuition to resolve problems (Payne, 2015; Graber et al., 2012). Human intuition is an "unconscious mental process aimed to solve problems without using a rational decision-making process" (Diaz-Hernandez & Gonzalez-Villela, 2017). In other words, intuition is the ability to see connections between concepts or properties that can be interpreted as valid with respect to some networks. A system can extract subsets from two networks and process them to identify relationships that allow for predicting future decisions, without requiring a deep understanding of the scenario or its associated parameters. Intuition is a tool that helps humans move forward in the realm of the unknown (Dörfler & Bas, 2020). It is human intuition that conjures up metaphors that capture the meaning of complex situations, and creates a narrative that allows one to move forward in the conditions of unknowable.

Mathematical models of intuition

The concept of intuition is difficult to capture and quantify using a mathematical model because it often involves subconscious processing and non-linear thinking. Mathematically, this integration can be described using weighted combinations or probabilistic models, where the weights reflect the relative contribution of each process to the overall intuitive judgment.

Kahneman's model (2003) suggests that intuition is the result of pattern recognition and associative thinking. Our brains are constantly exposed to a vast amount of information, and the adaptive unconscious processes this information to identify patterns and make quick judgments or decisions based on past experiences. These intuitive judgments are often accurate and efficient, but they can also be biased or prone to error.

Intuition is often considered a subjective and complex phenomenon, making it challenging to create a precise mathematical model. However, researchers have proposed various mathematical frameworks and models to capture certain aspects of intuition. Here are a few examples:

a **Dual-process theory**: As previously mentioned, the dual-process theory implies that intuition can be modeled as the outcome of rapid, non-conscious pattern recognition, and associations (Evans, 2010).
b **Bayesian inference**: The Bayesian model of intuition combines the principles of Bayesian probability theory with the concept of intuition. Bayesian probability is a mathematical framework that deals with uncertainty and updates beliefs based on new evidence. Intuition, on the other hand, refers to the ability to understand or know something without the need for conscious reasoning (Harbort, 2016).

In the context of decision-making and cognitive processes, the Bayesian model of intuition suggests that our intuitive judgments and decisions are influenced by our prior beliefs and the evidence available to us at a given moment. It posits that our intuitions are not purely random or irrational, but result of our brain's attempt to integrate and make sense of various sources of information.

Key components of the Bayesian model of intuition include the following.

i **Prior beliefs:** These are our initial beliefs or expectations about a situation or problem. These beliefs can be based on past experiences, cultural factors, personal biases, and more.
ii **Likelihood:** The likelihood represents the probability of observing a certain set of evidence or data given a particular hypothesis or belief. It quantifies how well the evidence supports or contradicts our initial beliefs.
iii **Posterior beliefs:** The posterior beliefs are updated versions of our prior beliefs based on new evidence. This update is performed using Bayes' theorem, which combines the prior beliefs and the likelihood to compute a revised probability distribution reflecting our updated understanding of the situation.
iv **Intuition:** In the context of this model, intuition arises as a result of our brain's rapid and automatic processing of information. Our brain combines prior beliefs and current evidence to generate an intuitive judgment or decision without conscious deliberation.

The Bayesian model of intuition can explain how people make quick decisions in situations where conscious reasoning would be too time-consuming or impractical. It also highlights how our intuitions can be adaptive when the prior beliefs and evidence align, but can lead to biases or errors when they do not.

It's important to note that while the Bayesian model of intuition provides a framework for understanding how intuition and probability reasoning interact, it is a theoretical model that has been proposed to explain certain cognitive phenomena. As with any model, it has limitations and may not capture all aspects of human intuition and decision-making.

c **Neural network models:** Some researchers have proposed neural network models to represent intuition. These models simulate how the brain processes information through interconnected nodes, with weights representing the strength of connections. Intuition is seen as the result of the network's ability to recognize patterns and generalize from past experiences (Davies et al., 2021).

Artificial neural networks, inspired by the structure of the brain, have been used to model and simulate intuitive processes. These models attempt to capture the pattern recognition and associative abilities often associated with intuition. Deep learning models, such as convolutional neural networks (CNNs) and recurrent neural networks (RNNs), have been successful in various intuitive tasks, such as image recognition and natural language processing.

Here's a simplified outline of how a neural network model of intuition might work:

i **Architecture selection:** Choose an appropriate neural network architecture, which can vary depending on the task. RNNs, CNNs, or even more advanced architectures like Transformers, could be used depending on the nature of the problem.
ii **Training data:** The model is trained on a dataset that contains examples of intuitive decisions or patterns. The dataset should ideally be diverse and representative of the situations where intuition is relevant.
iii **Feature extraction:** Intuitive thinking often relies on recognizing subtle patterns that might not be immediately apparent. The neural network extracts relevant features from the input data that capture these patterns.
iv **Learning:** The network learns the relationships between these features and the output decision. During training, the model adjusts its internal parameters through backpropagation to minimize the difference between predicted outputs and actual intuitive decisions present in the training data.
v **Inference:** Once trained, the model can be used to make intuitive decisions on new, unseen data. It processes the input data and generates an output that represents an intuitive response or decision.
vi **Feedback and fine-tuning:** Similar to human intuition, the model's performance might improve with experience. Feedback from the model's decisions can be used to fine-tune its parameters, making its intuitive responses more accurate over time.
vii **Interpretability:** A significant challenge in creating a neural network model of intuition is interpreting why the model makes a particular decision. This is particularly important to avoid biased outcomes. Techniques like attention mechanisms or feature visualization can help shed light on the model's decision-making process.
viii **Ethical considerations:** Just as with any AI model, ethical considerations are crucial. If the model is being used to make critical decisions, its biases and potential errors need to be carefully evaluated and managed.

It's important to note that while neural network models can emulate certain aspects of intuitive thinking, they might not fully capture the depth and complexity of human intuition. Human intuition is influenced by emotions, past experiences, and cultural factors that are difficult to replicate in a purely computational model.

Also, the term "intuition" can be used in various contexts and disciplines, so the exact model structure and process might differ based on the specific problem being addressed. The field of research regarding neural network models of intuition is still evolving, and the above outline provides a simplified perspective on the topic.

d **Neurocognitive models:** Intuition involves various brain regions and processes, such as the amygdala, hippocampus, and prefrontal cortex (McCrea, 2010). Neurocognitive models attempt to map these regions' interactions and functions to explain how intuition emerges. These models often combine neuroimaging data with cognitive theories to provide a more comprehensive understanding of intuitive processes (Reber et al., 2013).

e **Embodied cognition:** Embodied cognition suggests that cognition is influenced by the body's interactions with the environment. Intuition, from this perspective, is the result of our body's past experiences and sensory perceptions (Lipson Lawrence, 2012). Models within this framework might focus on how sensory inputs and bodily sensations contribute to intuitive judgments.

The Embodied Cognition model of intuition is a theoretical framework within the field of cognitive science that suggests that human intuition and decision-making are not solely driven by abstract reasoning and conscious thought processes, but are also influenced by the body, sensory experiences, and the environment (Antle et al., 2009).

Traditionally, cognition has been thought of as a process that occurs primarily within the brain that processes information and makes decisions based on logical reasoning. However, the Embodied Cognition perspective challenges this view by emphasizing the role of the body and sensory experiences in shaping our thoughts and behaviors.

According to this model, our interactions with the environment, our physical sensations, and even our bodily movements contribute to our cognitive processes, including intuition. This means that our bodily experiences and the way we perceive and interact with the world can have a profound impact on how we understand and respond to various situations. In other words, our intuition is not detached from our physical being; rather, it emerges from the dynamic interplay between our bodies, minds, and the context in which we find ourselves.

Key concepts in the Embodied Cognition model of intuition include the following.

i **Sensory-motor grounding:** This concept posits that cognitive processes, including intuitive judgments, are grounded in our sensory experiences and motor actions. For instance, the way we physically interact with objects and the environment can influence our understanding and decision-making.

ii **Body schema:** The body schema is a cognitive representation of our body's spatial characteristics and how it interacts with the world. It plays a role in shaping our intuitive responses, as our understanding of our body's capabilities and limitations affects how we approach various situations.

iii **Perceptual simulation:** This concept suggests that when we think about a particular situation or scenario, we simulate it mentally by recreating sensory and motor experiences associated with that situation. These simulations can contribute to our intuitive understanding of the situation.
iv **Embodied metaphors:** Metaphors that relate to the body or physical experiences are often used to describe abstract concepts. These metaphors can influence our intuitive thinking and understanding of complex ideas.
v **Contextual influence:** The environment in which we are situated can impact our intuitive judgments. Our surroundings, cultural background, and social context play a role in shaping how we perceive and respond to different situations.

In summary, the Embodied Cognition model of intuition challenges the notion that intuitive thinking is purely a product of abstract reasoning. Instead, it emphasizes the interconnectedness of our bodies, minds, and environment in shaping our intuitive responses and decision-making processes. This perspective has implications for various fields, including psychology, philosophy, and even artificial intelligence, as it highlights the need to consider the holistic nature of human cognition.

f **Dynamical systems theory:** The Dynamical Systems Theory (DST) offers a perspective on understanding various complex phenomena, including human cognition and behavior. When it comes to intuition, the DST model provides a framework to explain how intuitive thinking emerges and operates.

Intuition, in this context, refers to the ability to arrive at conclusions or make decisions without consciously analyzing every piece of information. It's often described as a "gut feeling" or a sudden realization that arises seemingly out of nowhere. The DST model of intuition suggests that this phenomenon can be understood through the interaction of various interconnected components within the cognitive system. Here's how the DST model might be applied to explain intuition.

i **Complex adaptive systems:** The DST views the mind as a complex adaptive system, with numerous elements (such as neurons, cognitive processes, and emotions) interacting in nonlinear ways. These elements self-organize and adapt based on feedback from the environment. Intuition is believed to arise from the complex interactions and patterns that emerge within this system.
ii **Nonlinear dynamics:** Intuitive insights are thought to emerge from the nonlinear dynamics of the cognitive system. Unlike linear systems, where cause and effect are directly proportional, nonlinear systems exhibit

unexpected and non-obvious behaviors. In the context of intuition, this means that a seemingly small input or piece of information could lead to a sudden and significant change in the cognitive state, resulting in an intuitive insight.

iii **Attractors and bifurcations:** DST describes attractors as stable states toward which a dynamic system tends to move. Bifurcations are sudden shifts that can lead a system from one attractor to another. Intuitive insights could emerge from the transition between attractors, where the system undergoes a rapid change in its cognitive state, leading to a new perspective or understanding.

iv **Self-organization and emergence:** Intuition can be seen as an emergent property of the cognitive system's self-organizing tendencies. As elements within the system interact and adapt, novel patterns and connections can emerge, leading to insights that aren't immediately apparent through conscious analysis.

v **Context and feedback:** The environment and context play a crucial role in shaping intuitive thinking. The cognitive system constantly receives feedback from the environment, which can influence the emergence of intuitive insights. Contextual cues, previous experiences, and implicit knowledge contribute to the formation of these insights.

vi **Fast and parallel processing:** Intuition is often characterized by its speed and parallel processing. This aligns with the DST view of cognition, where multiple cognitive processes operate simultaneously and interact to produce complex behaviors. Intuitive insights can arise when these processes converge on a solution or understanding.

In summary, the Dynamical Systems Theory model of intuition emphasizes the role of complex interactions, nonlinear dynamics, self-organization, and emergent properties within the cognitive system. Intuitive insights are seen as products of these interactions, emerging from rapid shifts in cognitive states, often triggered by subtle cues or feedback from the environment. This model provides a different perspective on understanding how intuition operates and complements traditional cognitive approaches to studying intuitive thinking.

g **Quantum mechanical model:** Quantum mechanics is a fundamental theory that describes the behavior of particles and systems at the microscopic scale. While it is primarily used in the realm of physics, some researchers have proposed applying quantum principles to cognitive processes, including intuition (Donald, 1990). The idea of a quantum mechanical model of intuition is based on the notion that certain aspects of human cognition, such as decision-making and information processing, exhibit characteristics similar to quantum phenomena (Pothos & Busemeyer, 2022). However, it is important to note that this approach is highly speculative and stills a subject of ongoing debate and research. Here are a few key concepts that have been proposed in quantum models of intuition:

i **Quantum superposition:** In quantum mechanics, particles can exist in a superposition of multiple states, meaning they can simultaneously be in different states until observed or measured, much like Schrödinger's equation. Some researchers suggest that intuitive decision-making involves a similar superposition of multiple possibilities or options. Instead of considering only one option at a time, the quantum model proposes that the brain can hold and process multiple potential choices simultaneously, allowing for a broader exploration of alternatives.

ii **Quantum entanglement:** Entanglement is a quantum phenomenon where the states of two or more particles become correlated, such that the measurement of one particle instantaneously affects the state of the other, regardless of the distance between them. In the context of intuition, it has been suggested that entanglement could occur between different cognitive processes or neural networks, enabling rapid and coordinated information transfer and integration across the brain. This interconnectedness may contribute to the emergence of intuitive insights.

iii **Quantum measurement and collapse:** In quantum mechanics, the act of measurement or observation causes the superposition of possibilities to collapse into a single definite outcome. Similarly, in the quantum model of intuition, the selection of a specific intuitive judgment or decision occurs through a collapse of the superposition of potential choices into a single coherent thought or action. This collapse could be influenced by various factors, including the context, emotional states, and personal biases.

iv **Quantum probability and uncertainty:** Quantum mechanics deals with probabilistic predictions rather than deterministic outcomes. Similarly, quantum models of intuition incorporate notions of probabilistic reasoning and uncertainty. These models suggest that intuitive judgments involve the evaluation of probabilities, with different options assigned certain weights based on their likelihood. However, unlike classical probability theory, the quantum approach allows for a more refined treatment of uncertainty, incorporating the idea that probabilities can interfere with each other, leading to more flexible decision-making.

The application of quantum ideas to the brain is still in its infancy because it is a complex organic system. Further research and empirical evidence are needed to determine the validity and utility of quantum models in understanding intuition or any other cognitive process. It's important to note that these mathematical models of intuition are theoretical constructs and are limited in their ability to fully capture the complexity and variability of human intuition. While they offer valuable insights into the cognitive processes underlying intuition, intuition itself remains a multifaceted and subjective phenomenon that is not fully understood or quantifiable.

The butterfly effect

Although artificial intelligence is still in its infancy, AI systems are being tested to recognize and comprehend human emotions and interact and make decisions accordingly utilizing the aforementioned models. AI has been effective in increasing efficiency and productivity by automating repetitive and mundane tasks by assisting in analyzing medical data and identifying patterns in patient records, by providing personalized learning experiences, improving customer service, forecasting business trends, and improving the lives of people with disabilities to name a few. However, AI brings about various challenges that have the potential to negatively impact the society. The major problem is the butterfly effect caused by the small biases and skewed input data resulting in significant but unfair outcomes (Ferrara, 2024). Since AI systems are dependent upon large data sets, algorithms and user interactions, biases in any of these components can lead to biased decision-making. The sources of bias in AI systems include already biased input data, algorithm, and feedback loops that magnify the biases (Ferrara, 2024). AI systems are fed huge data sets to introduce it to a new concept. If the data collection process is not careful it can result in biased training data set (Haibo & Garcia, 2009). The outcomes of such a system may not translate well for the underrepresented groups and result in biased decision making.

Buolamwini & Gebru (2018) examined several machine learning algorithms to analyze facial datasets and concluded that there are widespread biases in the existing classification systems. They found the algorithms to be discriminatory against race and gender. The study compared the algorithm error rates of facial classification and observed that all the classifiers performed better for male faces with a minimum of 8% error rate; compared to dark-skinned faces fair-skinned face classification error rate was 11.8%; dark-skinned female faces had the maximum error rate of 20.8%. These facial algorithms are applied to recognize and classify faces based on some predefined classifiers. However, the commercially available facial recognition systems failed to provide a detailed account of the training data set; neither did they report the true positive or false positive rates of the systems. Similarly, Obermeyer et al. (2019) analyzed commercial machine learning algorithms that are used to identify and provide patients with healthcare needs. They found that the algorithm is fed a large data set comprising of demographic details, insurance details, diagnosis, medication, and information regarding healthcare expenditure. The algorithm failed to take race into consideration. As a result, the outcome of such a system yielded prediction of health needs based on health care cost. The algorithm failed to account for economic disparities based on race, geography, availability of transport, and occupational demands.

Going forth, researchers have to be mindful of which features they include to train AI systems because the features determine future AI outcomes. The inclusion or exclusion of features from a training data set may ultimately result in a biased AI system. Algorithmic biases can be reflected in the choices of data modeling which may or may not be supported by the training data set. Feedback loops has the tendency to magnify the biases in an already skewed input data. Such a biased system can lead to erroneous prediction and amplify the pre-existing biases. It will ultimately create a system that reinforces the users' biased preferences by recommending biased content that lacks diversity and contributes to the social polarization. Thus, the initial input biases will eventually result in a self-perpetuating cycle of biased outcomes.

Conclusion

Although most beings use intuition in solving everyday problems,research has mostly focused on logical deliberate cognition. For the major part, research in the area of artificial intelligence has also focused on logic to understand higher cognitive functions. The whole fifth-generation computer project focused on this and the result did nothing to further our understanding of high human cognition or decision-making. However, the challenge that remains is coping with the large unstructured datasets based on partial, unknown knowledge that can be modeled by complex networks. Since, most of these models are logic-driven and are time-dependent (Dundas & Chik, 2011), a large number of parameters, may increase the overall computational complexity (Trovati & Bessis, 2016). In this context, the challenge is to develop a computational-based model of Artificial Intuition in decision-making that will be able to automatically process alternatives and reach useful responses in a short period of time without iterative search of solutions for a given problem (Diaz-Hernandez & Gonzalez-Villela, 2017). Turing (1950) best describes the current scenario: "We can only see a short distance ahead, but we can see plenty there that needs to done". However, researchers have to be mindful which features they include to train AI systems because the features determine the future AI outcomes. Algorithmic biases can lead to feedback loops that can result in erroneous prediction and amplify the pre-existing biases. Thus, the initial input biases will eventually result in a self-perpetuating cycle of biased outcomes.

References

Antle, A. N., Corness, G., & Droumeva, M. (2009). Human-computer-intuition? Exploring the cognitive basis for intuition in embodied interaction. *International Journal of Arts and Technology*, 2(3), 235. https://doi.org/10.1504/ijart.2009.028927

Blum, E. K. (2011). The heart of computer science. *Computer Science*, 17–52. https://doi.org/10.1007/978-1-4614-1168-0_3
Buolamwini, J., & Gebru, T. (2018). Gender Shades: Intersectional Accuracy Disparities in Commercial Gender Classification. *Proceedings of the1st Conference on Fairness, Accountability and Transparency, PMLR*, 77–91. New York, NY, USA.
Burgin, M. (2006). *Super-recursive algorithms* (Monographs in Computer Science). Springer.
Churchland, P. M., & Churchland, P. S. (1990). Could a machine think? *Scientific American*, *262*(1), 32–37.
Cox, D. D., & Dean, T. (2014). Neural networks and neuroscience-inspired computer vision. *Current Biology*, *24*(18). https://doi.org/10.1016/j.cub.2014.08.026
Davies, A., Veličković, P., Buesing, L., Blackwell, S., Zheng, D., Tomašev, N., Tanburn, R., Battaglia, P., Blundell, C., Juhász, A., Lackenby, M., Williamson, G., Hassabis, D., & Kohli, P. (2021). Advancing mathematics by guiding human intuition with AI. *Nature*, *600*(7887), 70–74. https://doi.org/10.1038/s41586-021-04086-x
Deutsch, D. (1985). Quantum theory, the Church–Turing principle and the Universal Quantum Computer. *Proceedings of the Royal Society of London. A. Mathematical and Physical Sciences*, *400*(1818), 97–117. https://doi.org/10.1098/rspa.1985.0070
Diaz-Hernandez, O., & Gonzalez-Villela, V. J. (2017). Analysis of human intuition towards artificial intuition synthesis for robotics. *SSRN Electronic Journal*. https://doi.org/10.2139/ssrn.3427647
Donald, M. J. (1990). Quantum theory and the brain. *Proceedings of the Royal Society of London. A. Mathematical and Physical Sciences*, *427*(1872), 43–93. https://doi.org/10.1098/rspa.1990.0004
Dörfler, V., & Bas, A. I. (2020). Intuition: Scientific, non-scientific or unscientific? In M. Sinclair (Ed.), *Handbook of intuition research as practice* (pp. 293–305). (Handbooks of research methods in management series). https://doi.org/10.4337/9781788979757.00033
Dreyfus, Hubert L. (1972). *What computers can't do: The limits of artificial intelligence*. Harper & Row.
Dreyfus, Hubert Lederer. (1994). *What computers still can't do: A critique of artificial reason*. MIT Press.
Dundas, J., & Chik, D. (2011). Implementing human-like intuition mechanism in artificial intelligence. *arXiv Preprint*.
Evans, J. S. (2010). Intuition and reasoning: A dual-process perspective. *Psychological Inquiry*, *21*(4), 313–326. https://doi.org/10.1080/1047840x.2010.521057
Ferrara, E. (2024). The butterfly effect in artificial intelligence systems: Implications for AI bias and fairness. *Machine Learning with Applications*, *15*, 100525. https://doi.org/10.1016/j.mlwa.2024.100525
Graber, M. L., Kissam, S., Payne, V. L., Meyer, A. N., Sorensen, A., Lenfestey, N., Tant, E., Henriksen, K., LaBresh, K., & Singh, H. (2012). Cognitive interventions to reduce diagnostic error: A narrative review. *BMJ Quality & Safety*, *21*(7), 535–557. https://doi.org/10.1136/bmjqs-2011-000149
Grossberg, S. (1987). Competitive learning: From interactive activation to adaptive resonance. *Cognitive Science*, *11*(1), 23–63. https://doi.org/10.1111/j.1551-6708.1987.tb00862.x

Haibo, H., & Garcia, E. A. (2009). Learning from imbalanced data. *IEEE Transactions on Knowledge and Data Engineering*, *21*(9), 1263–1284. https://doi.org/10.1109/tkde.2008.239

Hammond, K. R. (2007). *Beyond rationality: The search for wisdom in a troubled time*. Oxford University Press.

Hammond, K. R. (2010). Intuition, no! ...quasirationality, yes! *Psychological Inquiry*, *21*(4), 327–337. https://doi.org/10.1080/1047840x.2010.521483

Hanson, S. J., & Burr, D. J. (1990). What connectionist models learn: Learning and representation in connectionist networks. *Behavioral and Brain Sciences*, *13*(3), 471–489. https://doi.org/10.1017/s0140525x00079760

Harbort, B. (2016). Thought, action, and intuition in practice-oriented disciplines. In R. Davis-Floyd, & P. Sven Arvidson (Eds.), *Intuition: The inside story* (pp. 129–144). Routledge.

Isen, A. M., & Labroo, A. A. (2003). Some ways in which positive affect facilitates decision making and judgment. In *Emerging perspectives on judgment and decision research* (pp. 365–393). https://doi.org/10.1017/cbo9780511609978.013

Johnny, O., Trovati, M., & Ray, J. (2019). Towards a computational model of artificial intuition and decision making. In *Advances in intelligent networking and collaborative systems* (pp. 463–472). https://doi.org/10.1007/978-3-030-29035-1_45

Kahneman, D. (2003). A perspective on judgment and choice: Mapping bounded rationality. *American Psychologist*, *58*(9), 697–720. https://doi.org/10.1037/0003-066x.58.9.697

Kahneman, D., & Klein, G. (2009). Conditions for intuitive expertise: A failure to disagree. *American Psychologist*, *64*(6), 515–526. https://doi.org/10.1037/a0016755

Kubassova, O., Shaikh, F., Melus, C., & Mahler, M. (2021). History, current status, and future directions of Artificial Intelligence. In *Precision medicine and artificial intelligence* (pp. 1–38). https://doi.org/10.1016/b978-0-12-820239-5.00002-4

Lipson Lawrence, R. (2012). Intuitive knowing and embodied consciousness. *New Directions for Adult and Continuing Education*, *2012*(134), 5–13. https://doi.org/10.1002/ace.20011

Lyon, P. (2005). The biogenic approach to cognition. *Cognitive Processing*, *7*(1), 11–29. https://doi.org/10.1007/s10339-005-0016-8

McCrea, S. (2010). Intuition, insight, and the right hemisphere: Emergence of higher sociocognitive functions. *Psychology Research and Behavior Management*, *1*. https://doi.org/10.2147/prbm.s7935

Obermeyer, Z., Powers, B., Vogeli, C., & Mullainathan, S. (2019). Dissecting racial bias in an algorithm used to manage the health of populations. *Science*, *366*(6464), 447–453. https://doi.org/10.1126/science.aax2342

Patterson, R. E., & Eggleston, R. G. (2017). Intuitive cognition. *Journal of Cognitive Engineering and Decision Making*, *11*(1), 5–22. https://doi.org/10.1177/1555343416686476

Payne, L. K. (2015). Intuitive decision making as the culmination of continuing education: A theoretical framework. *The Journal of Continuing Education in Nursing*, *46*(7), 326–332. https://doi.org/10.3928/00220124-20150619-05

Pothos, E. M., & Busemeyer, J. R. (2022). Quantum cognition. *Annual Review of Psychology*, *73*(1), 749–778. https://doi.org/10.1146/annurev-psych-033020-123501

Reber, P. J., Beeman, M., & Paller, K. A. (2013). Human memory systems: A framework for understanding the neurocognitive foundations of intuition. In *Foundations of augmented cognition* (pp. 474–483). https://doi.org/10.1007/978-3-642-39454-6_51

Searle, J. R. (1980). Minds, brains, and programs. *Behavioral and Brain Sciences*, *3*(3), 417–424. https://doi.org/10.1017/s0140525x00005756

Simon, H. A. (1986). Rationality in psychology and economics. *The Journal of Business*, *59*(4), S209–S224.

Trovati, M., & Bessis, N. (2016). An influence assessment method based on co-occurrence for topologically reduced big data sets. *Soft Computing*, *20*(5), 2021–2030. https://doi.org/10.1007/s00500-015-1621-9

Turing, A. M. (1950). Computing machinery and intelligence. *Mind*, *LIX*(236), 433–460. https://doi.org/10.1093/mind/lix.236.433

Chapter 19

Intuitive cognition

Reconfiguring the path ahead

Pritha Mukhopadhyay, Sharmistha Banerjee and Ishita U. Bharadwaj

This edited volume delves into multifarious dimensions of intuition from a multidisciplinary perspective. It intends to unravel the enigma of intuition, through a comprehensive overview of the concept highlighting its unique roles in decision-making, learning, and creativity. The book is an endevour to explore the intuitive process from multiple angles. However, it is imperative to arrive at a common denominator underlying the intuitive process despite the multifaceted uniqueness and also lay down a pathway for further explorations on the interface of intuition with other branches of knowledge. An emerging multidisciplinary pattern of intuitive cognition also depicts the power of intuitive mind in creating a lasting, harmonious, and unified mosaic of patterns, images, and relationships.

Humans are perceived as rational decision-makers through deliberate, sequential, and rational thinking. However, much of decision-making occurs mostly through heuristics. While Hammond refers to this as a quasi-rational decision-making process, which we know is based on associative thinking. It functions more effectively on an ingrained database in the associative nodes. This in turn gets integrated with a greater possibility of augmentation of true components in the decision, endorsed by one's gut feeling. Rational thinking based on incorrect data is also prone to errors and falsification. However, it is proposed that effective decision-making necessitates the functional interaction between analytical and intuitive processes.

The collective theme of the chapters reveals the crucial role of the associative network of the mind in the intuitive process. Intuition is an experience-based perception of coherence, comprising immediacy, reasoning, and sensing relationships, which precedes insightful learning. This idea is supported across chapters, from biology to social cognition, education, psychotherapy, art and creativity, neuromarketing, and even artificial intelligence. Current ideas are validated by the course of evolution, where intuition is intertwined with survival at various stages. It is a natural endowment for us. In the ancient evolutionary phase, when humans were hunter-gatherers, they relied on this tool to protect themselves from external threats. The

DOI: 10.4324/9781003377757-22

immediacy in response and implicit analysis of cues helped them to sustain life. This ability to anticipate probable threats extends beyond humans and is present in other higher-order animals as a survival strategy.

The template has emerged across the chapters, demonstrating that, unlike the logical, sequential processing of deliberate thinking, the intuitive process implicitly utilizes knowledge stored in neural nodes through a parallel distributed processing system. This knowledge ignites with immediacy during the course of decision-making, bringing all related concepts into a coherent frame. This phenomenon is reflected across various fields, including social cognition, art, entrepreneurship, neuromarketing, and psychotherapy. It involves an implicit understanding of social cues, motherly instincts, a sense of knowing in social interactions, inner rejuvenation from the process of *biraha*, the automatic execution of pre-existing knowledge, nudges, and self-absorption. These elements emerge into the conscious mind without deliberate effort, forming connections and leading to decisive outcomes.

Ultimately, the outcome fosters the means-end relationship, enabling the achievement of adaptive or high-end goals. In the field of education, the volume emphasizes metacognition, highlighting how thoughtful engagement with knowledge strengthens intuitive affirmations. Interestingly, training to activate the intuitive process not only aids in intellectually grasping complex concepts but also later facilitates the integration of experiential learning through intuition with deliberate learning processes. As cultivating the intuitive process remains relatively unexplored, it holds pedagogical promise for the future. This approach could enhance the assimilation of learning, build a robust knowledge structure at the level of wisdom, and make learning or its application more enjoyable by offering an experience of self-discovery.

Any personalized experience is enjoyable. Furthermore, novelty, the nurturing of autonomy, and exposure to diverse experiences transform immature epistemic beliefs into mature intuition. Reflecting this idea, the book illustrates how the unique combination of expertise and experience refines intuitive decision-making.

The interconnectedness of body and mind, at the molecular and genetic levels of behavior, also sheds light on the mysterious activity of intuition. This interconnectedness of thoughts, which brings anticipation and prediction to life, resides within us that artificial intelligence attempts to mimic. However, the essence of interconnected thoughts does not lie in their frequency, as artificial intelligence might try to replicate, but in the quality and the emotions each thought carries. This is the intuitive beauty of the human mind, which remains beyond the reach of any artificial algorithm.

Index

Pages in *italics* refer to figures and pages in **bold** refer to tables.

FSC
www.fsc.org
MIX
Papier | Fördert gute Waldnutzung
FSC® C083411

Kolibri 360 GmbH
Ferdinand-Jühlke-Straße 7
99095 Erfurt, Deutschland
produktsicherheit@kolibri360.de